From Evidence to Action

The Story of Cash Transfers and Impact Evaluation in Sub-Saharan Africa

Edited by
BENJAMIN DAVIS, SUDHANSHU HANDA,
NICOLA HYPHER, NATALIA WINDER ROSSI,
PAUL WINTERS, AND JENNIFER YABLONSKI

Published by
The Food and Agriculture Organization of the United Nations
and
The United Nations Children's Fund
and
Oxford University Press

Food and Agriculture Organization of the United Nations

unicef

OXFORD
UNIVERSITY PRESS

The designations employed and the presentation of material in this information product do not imply the expression of any opinion whatsoever on the part of the Food and Agriculture Organization of the United Nations (FAO) or the United Nations Children's Fund (UNICEF) concerning the legal or development status of any country, territory, city, or area or of its authorities, or concerning the delimitation of its frontiers or boundaries. The mention of specific companies or products of manufacturers, whether or not these have been patented, does not imply that these have been endorsed or recommended by FAO or UNICEF in preference to others of a similar nature that are not mentioned. The views expressed in this information product are those of the FAO(s) and do not necessarily reflect the views or policies of FAO or UNICEF.

FAO encourages the use, reproduction, and dissemination of material in this information product. Except where otherwise indicated, material may be copied, downloaded, and printed for private study, research, and teaching purposes, or for use in non-commercial products or services, provided that appropriate acknowledgement of FAO as the source and copyright holder is given and that FAO's endorsement of users' views, products, or services is not implied in any way.

All requests for translation and adaptation rights, and for resale and other commercial use rights should be addressed to www.fao.org/contact-us/licence-request or to copyright@fao.org

FAO information products are available on the FAO website (www.fao.org/publications) and can be purchased through publications-sales@fao.org

© FAO 2016

The moral rights of the authors have been asserted

First Edition published in 2016

Impression: 1

OXFORD
UNIVERSITY PRESS

Great Clarendon Street, Oxford, OX2 6DP,
United Kingdom

Oxford University Press is a department of the University of Oxford.
It furthers the University's objective of excellence in research, scholarship,
and education by publishing worldwide. Oxford is a registered trade mark of
Oxford University Press in the UK and in certain other countries

Published in the United States of America by Oxford University Press
198 Madison Avenue, New York, NY 10016, United States of America

British Library Cataloguing in Publication Data

Data available

Library of Congress Control Number: 2015951220

ISBN 978-0-19-876944-6
ISBN 978-92-5-108981-1 (FAO)

Printed in Great Britain by
Clays Ltd, St Ives plc

Links to third party websites are provided by FAO, UNICEF, and Oxford in good faith and for information only. FAO, UNICEF, and Oxford disclaim any responsibility for the materials contained in any third party website referenced in this work.

Foreword

Today, virtually every country in sub-Saharan Africa has some kind of cash transfer programme. These programmes are increasingly recognized as key to fighting poverty and hunger. Designed to reflect regional characteristics, they emphasize strong community participation and focus on economically and socially marginalized populations—including children, the elderly, families without earning power and people living with disabilities.

By providing predictable, direct transfers, the programmes protect vulnerable individuals and households from the worst impacts of poverty and help them build resilience. In fact, the success of cash transfers has contributed to a regional trend towards wider adoption of social-protection policies. Across sub-Saharan Africa, cash transfer initiatives are moving from donor-funded pilots to domestically funded national programmes.

In each country, the expansion of cash transfers has followed a unique course through a process of interplay among governments, civil society and international development partners. The region can now showcase rigorous, timely evidence demonstrating the impact of these transfers on the well-being of children, families and communities. The evidence points to positive impacts in areas such as school enrolment, health, food security, and agricultural investment. It also shows that cash transfers can generate multiplier effects bolstering local economies.

Against this backdrop, *From Evidence to Action: The Story of Cash Transfers and Impact Evaluation in Sub-Saharan Africa* advances the regional discourse on social protection. It documents the evidence base on cash transfers in the region and reflects on the development of social protection policies in eight countries across sub-Saharan Africa. The book's contributors and editors present this analysis through the experience of the Transfer Project, a joint effort of FAO and UNICEF, along with Save the Children, the University of North Carolina at Chapel Hill, and national governments and research institutions in each country.

The Transfer Project has participated in national evaluations of social cash transfer programmes in Ethiopia, Ghana, Kenya, Lesotho, Malawi, South Africa, Zambia, and Zimbabwe. The project serves as an 'honest broker' for governments and development partners, providing them with technical support on the design and implementation of the evaluations. In the process, it helps to identify country-specific issues and priorities that inform national policy dialogues on social protection.

This book highlights two major research innovations characterizing the Transfer Project's impact evaluations, and both have clear policy implications at the country level. First, the evaluations generate critical evidence on the economic and productive impacts of cash transfers; and second, they assess the economic and social drivers of HIV (Human-Immunodeficiency Virus) risk among adolescents.

To measure economic and productive impacts, the Transfer Project drew upon the work of the From Protection to Production (PtoP) initiative. Through this partnership among FAO, UNICEF, and national governments, the project was able to explore links among social protection, agriculture, and rural development. PtoP's work helped evaluators assess the impact of cash transfers on household outcomes, individual livelihoods and local economies. The results spoke to the concerns of ministries of finance and planning about the relevance of social cash transfers for growth. Evidence generated through PtoP countered the argument that social cash transfers lead to dependency, and squarely positioned them as an important element of effective rural development strategy.

Another important initiative, led by the University of North Carolina at Chapel Hill and UNICEF, examined the role of cash transfers in the transition to adulthood for young people in beneficiary households. Evaluators followed this line of study in response to high levels of HIV prevalence in the countries of East and Southern Africa, where the incidence of new infections is typically highest among young people, particularly young women. The results strengthened the case for social cash transfers as a means of addressing extreme poverty and inequity, which act as economic drivers of behaviours that increase the risk if HIV infection for many adolescents and young adults.

These pages also document the ways in which the Transfer Project has influenced the policy debate in each of the eight countries at hand. The project did not gather knowledge only to produce final impact analyses. Instead, it provided policy makers with critical information at key points in time, serving as a resource for the creation of government-owned learning agendas on social cash transfers. This innovative approach transcended impact evaluation and influenced wider social protection policies in each country.

Social cash transfer programmes are usually run by ministries of social development. But it is clear from the work of the Transfer Project that the implications of giving cash to poor and vulnerable households in sub-Saharan Africa go far beyond social development objectives. Cash transfers affect many other aspects of the lives of beneficiary families, including their livelihoods and the economic dynamics of their communities. The conclusions of this book further strengthen the case for moving from fragmented programmes to a systems approach to social protection, with the ability to provide comprehensive and multi-sector responses to the poorest households.

Foreword

FAO and UNICEF have long recognized the critical importance of working as strategic partners to strengthen the case for social protection. The added value of the Transfer Project is reflected in the commitment of national partners to pursue evidence-based policy making in this area. If governments, civil society, and development agencies can sustain that commitment, it will lead to real and sustainable change for future generations. We hope this book will strengthen their resolve to stay the course.

José Graziano da Silva
Director-General, FAO

Anthony Lake
Executive Director, UNICEF

Table of Contents

List of Figures	xiii
List of Tables	xv
List of Acronyms	xvii
Notes on Editors and Lead Authors	xxxi

1. The Transfer Project, Cash Transfers, and Impact Evaluation in Sub-Saharan Africa   1
   Benjamin Davis, Sudhanshu Handa, Nicola Hypher, Natalia Winder Rossi, Paul Winters, and Jennifer Yablonski

PART I. DESIGNING THE CASH TRANSFER IMPACT EVALUATIONS

2. The Political Economy of Cash Transfer Evaluations in Sub-Saharan Africa   17
   Anna McCord, Natalia Winder Rossi, and Jennifer Yablonski

3. Implementing Rigorous Evaluations in the Real World: The Quantitative Approach to Evaluation Design in the Transfer Project   43
   Benjamin Davis and Sudhanshu Handa

4. Qualitative Methods in Impact Evaluations of Cash Transfer Programmes in the Transfer Project in Sub-Saharan Africa   71
   Pamela Pozarny and Clare Barrington

5. Local Economy-Wide Impact Evaluation of Social Cash Transfer Programmes   94
   J. Edward Taylor, Karen Thome, and Mateusz Filipski

PART II. ASSESSMENT OF CASH TRANSFER PROGRAMMES: COUNTRY CASE STUDIES

6. The Cash Transfer Programme for Orphans and Vulnerable Children: The Catalyst for Cash Transfers in Kenya   117
   Joanne Bosworth, Carlos Alviar, Luis Corral, Benjamin Davis, Daniel Musembi, Winnie Mwasiaji, Samuel Ochieng, Roger Pearson, Pamela Pozarny, Patrick Ward, and Will Wiseman

7. Social Protection and the Livelihood Empowerment Against Poverty (LEAP) Programme in Ghana: Generating Positive Change through the Power of Evidence 146
Luigi Peter Ragno, Sarah Hague, Sudhanshu Handa, Mawutor Ablo, Afua Twun-Danso, Lawrence Ofori-Addo, Carlos Alviar, Benjamin Davis, Pamela Pozarny, and Ramla Attah

8. The Role of the Tigray Pilot Social Cash Transfer Programme and its Evaluation in the Evolution of the Tigray Social Protection Policy 168
Roger Pearson, Solomon Afaw, Angela Baschieri, Beyene Birru, Guush Berhane, Ted Chaiban, Benjamin Davis, Stephen Devereux, John Hoddinott, J. Hoel, J. Kagin, Natasha Ledlie, Heshe Lemma, Djanabou Mahonde, Remy Pigois, Pamela Pozarny, Keetie Roelen, Benjamin Schwab, Peter Salama, Ibrahim Sessay, Fredu Nega Tegebu, Yalem Tsegay, and Douglas Webb

9. The Role of Impact Evaluation in the Evolution of Zambia's Cash Transfer Programme 197
Paul Quarles van Ufford, Charlotte Harland, Stanfield Michelo, Gelson Tembo, Kelley Toole, and Denis Wood

10. Zimbabwe: Using Evidence to Overcome Political and Economic Challenges to Starting a National Unconditional Cash Transfer Programme 226
David Seidenfeld, Lovemore Dumba, Sudhanshu Handa, Leon Muwoni, Hannah Reeves, and Elayn Sammon

11. Does Evidence Matter? Role of the Evaluation of the Child Grants Programme in the Consolidation of the Social Protection Sector in Lesotho 247
Luca Pellerano, Silvio Daidone, Benjamin Davis, Mohammad Farooq, Mariam Homayoun, Andrew Kardan, Malefetsane Masasa, Ousmane Niang, Bettina Ramirez, and Naquibullah Safi

12. The Social Cash Transfer Programme of Malawi: The Role of Evaluation from the Pilot to the Expansion 281
Gustavo Angeles, Sara Abdoulayi, Clare Barrington, Sudhanshu Handa, Esmie Kainja, Peter Mvula, Harry Mwamlima, Maxton Tsoka, and Tayllor Spadafora

13. The Impact of a Promise Realized: South Africa's Child Support Grant 306
Michael Samson, Carolyn J. Heinrich, John Hoddinott, George Laryea-Adjei, Thabani Buthelezi, Lucie Cluver, Selwyn Jehoma, Maureen Mogotsi, Thilde Stevens, Ingrid van Niekerk, and Evelyne Nyokangi

PART III. SYNTHESIS OF RESULTS

14. Conclusions and Policy Implications for Cash Transfer Programmes 335
Benjamin Davis, Sudhanshu Handa, Nicola Hypher, Natalia Winder Rossi, Paul Winters, and Jennifer Yablonski

Index 359

List of Figures

2.1.	Summary of Key Factors Conditioning Policy Influence	22
3.1.	Conceptual Framework for Impact Evaluation of Malawi SCTP	57
5.1.	Illustration of Possible Impacts of SCT in a Local Market	97
5.2.	Real and Nominal Income Multipliers with Confidence Bounds for SCT Programmes in Seven Countries	112
6.1.	Kenya CT-OVC Programme Expansion	122
7.1.	The Expansion of LEAP	154
8.1.	Evolution of Tigray Pilot Social Cash Transfer Programme	171
9.1.	Timeline with Main Policy and Evaluation Milestones Related to Zambia's Cash Transfer Programme	201
9.2.	Comparison of Impacts between CG and MCTG	213
9.3.	Overview of Factors Contributing to the Government's Decision to Scale Up Cash Transfers	215
10.1.	Timeline of Programme Milestones, Roll-out, and IE Activities	229
10.2.	Age Distribution of Household Members	237
10.3.	Beneficiary Poverty Rates for Selected Cash Transfer Programmes	238
11.1.	Child Grants Programme Timeline	250
12.1.	Key Events and SCT Programme Coverage by Year (2007–16)	292
13.1.	Food Poverty Gap as Percentage of National Income	307
13.2.	The Impact of Social Grants on Inequality	308
13.3.	The Evolution of the CSG (1998–2012)	311

List of Tables

1.1.	Cash Transfer Programmes Included in Transfer Project	5
1.2.	Methods Used by Transfer Project	8
3.1.	Core Evaluation Designs	46
3.2.	Estimation Features	55
3.3.	Example of Questionnaire: Topics from Malawi SCTP Evaluation	58
3.4.	Standard Productive Activity Questions Introduced as Part of PtoP Project	61
3.5.	Summary of Data Collection in Modules for Young People	63
4.1.	Overview of Transfer Project Impact Evaluations by Qualitative Approach	73
4.2.	Comparison of Qualitative Design Approaches	88
5.1.	Accounts in the SCT-LEWIEs	100
5.2.	ZOI Definitions and Evaluation Designs	101
5.3.	Market Closure Assumptions	102
5.4.	Data Sources and Timing	105
5.5.	Robustness Tests and Experiments	111
6.1.	Summarized Key Impacts of CT-OVC Impact Evaluation Round 1 and 2	130
7.1.	LEAP's Impacts Summary Table	157
8.1.	Survey Timing by Round	179
8.2.	Sample Sizes, by Location and Treatment Status	179
8.3.	Impact of SCT on Development Outcomes in the Tigray Pilot	183
8.4.	Self-Reports on Use of Last Transfer	184
A8.1.	Summary Impacts of SCT on Development Outcomes in the Tigray Pilot	196
9.1.	Statistically Significant Impact of the CG and the MCTG on Per-Capita Monthly Expenditures (in ZMW)	210
9.2.	Statistically Significant Impacts of the CG and the MCTG on Food Security	210
9.3.	Statistically Significant Impacts of the CG and the MCTG on Poverty Indicators	210
9.4.	Statistically Significant Impacts of the CG and the MCTG on Children	211
9.5.	Statistically Significant Impacts of the CG and the MCTG on Asset and Livestock Ownership	212
10.1.	Summarized Key Impacts of Zimbabwe HSCT	242

… List of Tables

11.1.	Statistically Significant Impacts of the CGP on Children, Education, and Enrolment	261
11.2.	Statistically Significant Impacts of the CGP on Birth Registration and Child Health	262
11.3.	Statistically Significant Impacts of the CGP on Food Security	263
11.4.	Statistically Significant Impacts of the CGP on Livelihoods	264
11.5.	Statistically Significant Impacts of the CGP on Risk-Coping Strategies	265
11.6.	Statistically Significant Impacts of the CGP on Community Networks	265
A11.1.	Main Characteristics of CGP Evaluation Components	276
12.1.	Transfer Amounts by Household Size and School Bonus	287
12.2.	Summarized Key Impacts of the SCTP Mid-line Impact Evaluation Results	299
13.1.	Dose-Response Estimates of CSGs' Impact on Child Outcomes	318
13.2.	Dose-Response Estimates of CSGs' Impact on Adolescents' Outcomes	320

List of Acronyms

3ie	International Initiative for Impact Evaluation
AIDS	Acquired Immune Deficiency Syndrome
AIR	American Institutes for Research
ANC	African National Congress
ASWO	Auxiliary Social Welfare Officer
BEAM	Basic Education Assistance Module
BoLSA	Bureau of Labour and Social Affairs
CBS	Capacity Building Strategy
CBT	Community-Based Targeting
CC	Community Committee
CCC	Community Care Coalitions
CCT	Conditional Cash Transfer
CG	Child Grant model
CGP	Child Grant Programme
CIHD	Center for International Health and Development
CPC	Child Protection Committee
CPF	Child Protection Fund
CSG	Child Support Grant
CSO	Civil Society Organization
CSP	Child Support Grant
CSR	Centre for Social Research
CSSC	Community Social Support Committee
CT	Cash Transfer
CTM	Common Targeting Mechanism
CT-OVC	Cash Transfer Programme for Orphans and Vulnerable Children
CT-PWSD	Cash Transfer-Persons with Severe Disability
CWAC	Community Welfare Assistance Committee
DA	District Assembly
DC	District Commissioner
DC	District Committee
DCS	Department for Children's Services
DCWPS	Department of Child Welfare and Probation Services

List of Acronyms

DFID	Department for International Development, UK
DHS	Demographic and Health Survey
DMA	Disaster Management Authority
DSB	Direct Support Beneficiaries
DSD	Department of Social Development
DSS	Department of Social Services
DSW	Department of Social Welfare
DSWO	District Social Welfare Officer
EC	European Commission
ECD	Early Childhood Development
ED	Electoral Division
EDF	European Development Fund
EFFORT	Endowment Fund for the Rehabilitation of Tigray
EPRI	Economic Policy Research Institute
ETB	Ethiopian Birr
EU	European Union
FAO	Food and Agriculture Organization of the United Nations
FCG	Foster Child Grant
FGD	Focus Group Discussion
FISP	Fertilizer Input Subsidy Programme
FNDP	Fifth National Development Plan
GDP	Gross Domestic Product
GHS	General Household Survey
GHS	Ghana Cedis
GLSS5	Ghana Living Standard Survey 5
GoL	Government of Lesotho
GoM	Government of Malawi
GRZ	Government of the Republic of Zambia
GTZ	German Agency for Technical Cooperation
HAZ	Height-for-age Z Scores
HDI	Human Development Index
HH	Household
HIPC	Highly Indebted Poor Countries
HIV	Human-Immunodeficiency Virus
HIV/AIDS	Human Immunodeficiency Virus/Acquired Immunodeficiency Syndrome
HSCT	Harmonized Social Cash Transfer

List of Acronyms

HSNP	Hunger Safety Net Programme
ICROP	Integrated Community Registration Outreach Programmes
IDI	In-depth interview
IDS	Institute for Development Studies
IE	Impact Evaluation
IFPRI	International Food Policy Research Institute
IHS2	Second Integrated Household Survey
IHS3	Third Integrated Household Survey
IMF	International Monetary Fund
ISSER	Institute for Statistical, Social, and Economic Research, University of Ghana
IYCF	Infant and Young Child Feeding
JAZ	Joint Assistance for Zambia
KfW	Kreditanstalt für Wiederaufbau (German Development Bank)
KIHBS	Kenya Integrated Household Budget Survey
KII	Key informant interview
LEAP	Ghanaian Livelihood Empowerment against Poverty programme
LEWIE	Local Economy-Wide Impact Evaluation
LIPW	Labour Intensive Public Works Programme
M&E	Monitoring and Evaluation
MCTG	Multiple Categorical Targeting Grant
MDG	Millennium Development Goal
MESW	Ministry of Employment and Social Welfare
MGDS	Malawi Growth and Development Strategy
MIS	Management Information System
MoA	Ministry of Agriculture
MoFEPD	Ministry of Finance, Economic Planning, and Development
MOF	Ministry of Finance
MoGCSP	Ministry of Gender, Children, and Social Protection
MoGCDSW	Ministry of Gender, Children, Disability, and Social Welfare
MOHSW	Ministry of Health and Social Welfare
MoLSA	Ministry of Labour and Social Affairs
MOSD	Ministry of Social Development
MPSLSW	Ministry of Public Service, Labour, and Social Welfare
MWK	Malawi Kwacha
NAC	National AIDS Commission

NAP	Zimbabwe National Action Plan for Orphans and Vulnerable Children
NHIS	National Health Insurance Scheme
NIDS	National Income Dynamics Survey
NIH	National Institutes for Health
NISSA	National Information System for Social Assistance
NPA for OVC	National Plan of Action for Orphans and Vulnerable Children
NSDP	National Social Development Policy
NSNP	National Safety Net Programme
NSPP	National Social Protection Policy
NSPS	National Social Protection Strategy
NSSP	National Social Support Policy
OAP	Old Age Pension
OIBM	Opportunity International Bank of Malawi
OPCT	Older Persons Cash Transfer
OPM	Oxford Policy Management
OVC	Orphans and Vulnerable Children
PA	Public Assistance
PATH	Jamaican Programme of Advancement Through Health and Education
PCK	Postal Corporation of Kenya
PF	Patriotic Front
PfR	Programme for Results
PMT	Proxy Means Test
PoS	Program of Support
PRSP	Poverty Reduction Strategy Paper
PSM	Propensity Score Matching
PSNP	Productive Safety Net Programme
PtoP	From Protection to Production
PWAS	Public Welfare Assistance Scheme
RDP	Reconstruction and Development Programme
SASSA	South African Social Security Agency
SCT	Social Cash Transfer
SCTP	Social Cash Transfer Programme
SCTPP	Social Cash Transfer Pilot Programme
SCTS	Social Cash Transfer Scheme

List of Acronyms

SIDA	Swedish International Development Agency
SIU	Special Investigating Unit
SMG	State Maintenance Grant
SNDP	Sixth National Development Plan
SOCPEN	Social Pension System
SP-SAG	Social Protection Sector Advisory Group
SPSC	Social Protection Steering Committee
SPTC	Social Protection Technical Committee
StatsSA	Statistics South Africa
TA	Traditional Authority
TB	Tuberculosis
TPLF	Tigray People's Liberation Front
UCT	Unconditional Cash Transfer
UNAIDS	Joint United Nations Programme on HIV/AIDS
UNC	The University of North Carolina at Chapel Hill
UNICEF	United Nations Children's Fund
USAID	United States Agency for International Development
USD	United States Dollar
VAC	Village Assistance Committee
VAT	Value Added Tax
VC	Village Cluster
VDC	Village Development Group
WFP	World Food Programme
WHZ	Weight-for-height Z Scores
WSCTS	Woreda Social Cash Transfer Secretariat
WVI	World Vision International
ZDHS	Zimbabwe Demographic and Health Survey
ZIMASSET	Zimbabwe Agenda for Sustainable Socio-Economic Transformation
ZIMSTATS	Zimbabwe National Statistics Agency
ZMW	Zambian Kwacha

ACRONYMS BY CHAPTER

Political Economy Acronyms

AIR	American Institutes for Research
CCC	Community Care Coalitions
CGP	Child Grant Programme
CSP	Child Support Grant
CT	Cash Transfer
CWAC	Community Welfare Area Committee
FAO	Food and Agriculture Organization of the United Nations
FGD	Focus group discussion
HSCT	Harmonized Social Cash Transfer
IE	Impact Evaluation
KII	Key informant interview
LEWIE	Local Economy-Wide Impact Evaluation
OPM	Oxford Policy Management
PtoP	From Protection to Production
SCT	Social Cash Transfer
SCTPP	Social Cash Transfer Pilot Programme
UNC	The University of North Carolina at Chapel Hill
UNICEF	United Nations Children's Fund

Kenya Acronyms

AIDS	Acquired Immune Deficiency Syndrome
CBS	Capacity Building Strategy
CCT	Conditional Cash Transfer
CTM	Common Targeting Mechanism
CT-OVC	Cash Transfer-Orphans and Vulnerable Children
CT-PWSD	Cash Transfer-Persons with Severe Disability
DCS	Department for Children's Services
DFID	Department for International Development, UK
FAO	Food and Agriculture Organization of the United Nations
HIV	Human-Immunodeficiency Virus
HSNP	Hunger Safety Net Programme
KIHBS	Kenya Integrated Household Budget Survey

List of Acronyms

LEWIE	Local Economy-Wide Impact Evaluation
M&E	Monitoring and Evaluation
MIS	Management Information System
NIH	National Institutes for Health
NSNP	National Safety Net Programme
OPCT	Older Persons Cash Transfer
OPM	Oxford Policy Management
OVC	Orphans and Vulnerable Children
PCK	Postal Corporation of Kenya
PfR	Programme for Results
PMT	Proxy Means Test
PtoP	From Protection to Production
SIDA	Swedish International Development Agency
TB	Tuberculosis
UCT	Unconditional Cash Transfer
UNAIDS	Joint United Nations Programme on HIV/AIDS
UNICEF	United Nations Children's Fund
VAT	Value Added Tax

Ghana Acronyms

CBT	Community-Based Targeting
CC	Community Committee
DC	District Committee
DFID	Department for International Development, UK
DSWO	District Social Welfare Officer
FAO	Food and Agriculture Organization of the United Nations
GHS	Ghana Cedis
GLSS5	Ghana Living Standard Survey 5
IMF	International Monetary Fund
ISSER	Institute for Statistical, Social, and Economic Research, University of Ghana
LEAP	Ghanaian Livelihood Empowerment Against Poverty programme
LEWIE	Local Economy-Wide Impact Evaluation
LIPW	Labour Intensive Public Works Programme
M&E	Monitoring and Evaluation

xxiv | *List of Acronyms*

MESW	Ministry of Employment and Social Welfare
MIS	Management Information System
MoGCSP	Ministry of Gender, Children, and Social Protection
NHIS	National Health Insurance Scheme
NSPS	National Social Protection Strategy
OPM	Oxford Policy Management
OVC	Orphans and Vulnerable Children
PMT	Proxy Means Test
PSM	Propensity Score Matching
UNICEF	United Nations Children's Fund

Ethiopia Acronyms

BoLSA	Bureau of Labour and Social Affairs
CCC	Community Care Coalitions
CSO	Civil Society Organization
DHS	Demographic and Health Survey
DSB	Direct Support Beneficiaries
EFFORT	Endowment Fund For The Rehabilitation of Tigray
ETB	Ethiopian Birr
FAO	Food and Agriculture Organization of the United Nations
GDP	Gross Domestic Product
HAZ	Height-for-age Z Scores
HIV/AIDS	Human Immunodeficiency Virus/Acquired Immunodeficiency Syndrome
HESPI	The Horn Economic and Social Policy Institute
LEWIE	Local Economy-Wide Impact Evaluation
MoA	Ministry of Agriculture
MoLSA	Ministry of Labour and Social Affairs
OPM	Oxford Policy Management
PSNP	Productive Safety Net Programme
SCT	Social Cash Transfer
SCTPP	Social Cash Transfer Pilot programme
TPLF	Tigray People's Liberation Front
UNICEF	United Nations Children's Fund
WSCTS	Woreda Social Cash Transfer Secretariat
WHZ	Weight-for-height Z Scores

List of Acronyms

Zambia Acronyms

CG	Child Grant
CWAC	Community Welfare Assistance Committee
DFID	Department for International Development, UK
GDP	Gross Domestic Product
GTZ	German Agency for Technical Cooperation
FISP	Farmer Input Support Programme
FNDP	Fifth National Development Plan
GRZ	Government of the Republic of Zambia
HIPC	Highly Indebted Poor Countries
IYCF	Infant and Young Child Feeding
JAZ	Joint Assistance for Zambia
MCTG	Multiple Categorical Targeting Grant
NSPP	National Social Protection Policy
NSPS	National Social Protection Strategy
PF	Patriotic Front
PRSP	Poverty Reduction Strategy Paper
PWAS	Public Welfare Assistance Scheme
SNDP	Sixth National Development Plan
SCT	Social Cash Transfer
SP-SAG	Social Protection Sector Advisory Group
ZMW	Zambian Kwacha

Zimbabwe Acronyms

AIR	American Institutes for Research
BEAM	Basic Education Assistance Module
CGP	Zambian Child Grant Programme
CPC	Child Protection Committees
CPF	Child Protection Fund
CT-OVC	Cash Transfer Programme for Orphans and Vulnerable Children
DCWPS	Department of Child Welfare and Probation Services
DfID	Department for International Development, UK
DSS	Department of Social Services
FGD	Focus Group Discussion
GDP	Gross Domestic Product

HSCT	Harmonized Social Cash Transfer
IDI	In-depth Interview
IE	Impact Evaluation
LEAP	Ghanaian Livelihood Empowerment Against Poverty programme
LEWIE	Local Economy-Wide Impact Evaluation
M&E	Monitoring and Evaluation
MIS	Management Information System
MPSLSW or MoPSLSW	Ministry of Public Service, Labour, and Social Welfare
NAP	Zimbabwe National Action Plan for Orphans and Vulnerable Children
PATH	Jamaican Programme of Advancement through Health and Education
PoS	Program of Support
PtoP	From Protection to Production
UNC	The University of North Carolina at Chapel Hill
UNICEF	United Nations Children's Fund
USD	United States Dollar
ZDHS	Zimbabwe Demographic and Health Survey
ZIMASSET	Zimbabwe Agenda for Sustainable Socio-Economic Transformation
ZIMSTATS	Zimbabwe National Statistics Agency

Lesotho Acronyms

AIDS	Acquired Immune Deficiency Syndrome
ASWO	Auxiliary Social Welfare Officer
CGP	Child Grants Programme
DMA	Disaster Management Authority
DSW	Department of Social Welfare
EC	European Commission
ED	Electoral Division
EDF	European Development Fund
EU	European Union
FGD	Focus Group Discussion
GDP	Gross Domestic Product
GoL	Government of Lesotho

List of Acronyms

HDI	Human Development Index
HH	Household
HIV	Human Immunodeficiency Virus
IMF	International Monetary Fund
KII	Key Informant Interview
LEWIE	Local Economy-Wide Impact Evaluation
MIS	Management Information System
MOF	Ministry of Finance
MOHSW	Ministry of Health and Social Welfare
MOSD	Ministry of Social Development
NISSA	National Information System for Social Assistance
NSDP	National Social Development Policy
NSPS	National Social Protection Strategy
OAP	Old Age Pension
OPM	Oxford Policy Management
OVC	Orphans and Vulnerable Children
PA	Public Assistance
PMT	Proxy Means-Testing
PtoP	From Protection to Production
UNICEF	United Nations Children's Fund
VAC	Village Assistance Committee
WFP	World Food Programme
WVI	World Vision International

Malawi Acronyms

3ie	International Initiative for Impact Evaluation
CIHD	Center for International Health and Development
CSPC	Community Social Protection Committee
CSR	Centre for Social Research
CSSC	Community Social Support Committee
CT	Cash Transfer
DA	District Assembly
DC	District Commissioner
DFID	Department for International Development, UK
DSWO	District Social Welfare Office

List of Acronyms

EU	European Union
FAO	Food and Agriculture Organization of the United Nations
FISP	Fertilizer Input Subsidy Programme
GoM	Government of Malawi
HIPC	Highly Indebted Poor Countries
IE	Impact Evaluation
IHS2	Second Integrated Household Survey
IHS3	Third Integrated Household Survey
IMF	International Monetary Fund
KfW	Kreditanstalt für Wiederaufbau (German Development Bank)
MGDS	Malawi Growth and Development Strategy
MIS	Management Information System
MoFEPD	Ministry of Finance, Economic Planning, and Development
MoGCDSW	Ministry of Gender, Children, Disability, and Social Welfare
MWK	Malawi Kwacha
NAC	National AIDS Commission
NPA for OVC	National Plan of Action for Orphans and Vulnerable Children
NSSP	National Social Support Policy
OIBM	Opportunity International Bank of Malawi
OPM	Oxford Policy Management
PMT	Proxy Means Testing
SCT	Social Cash Transfer
SCTP	Social Cash Transfer Programme
SCTS	Social Cash Transfer Scheme
SPSC	Social Protection Steering Committee
SPTC	Social Protection Technical Committee
TA	Traditional Authority
UNC	The University of North Carolina at Chapel Hill
UNICEF	United Nations Children's Fund
USAID	United States Agency for International Development
VC	Village Cluster
VDC	Village Development Group

South Africa Acronyms

ANC	African National Congress
CSG	Child Support Grant
DSD	Department of Social Development
ECD	Early Childhood Development
EPRI	Economic Policy Research Institute
FCG	Foster Child Grant
GHS	General Household Survey
HAZ	Height-for-age Z-score
HIV	Human Immunodeficiency Virus
ICROP	Integrated Community Registration Outreach Programmes
IDS	Institute for Development Studies
IFPRI	International Food Policy Research Institute
M&E	Monitoring and Evaluation
MDG	Millennium Development Goal
NIDS	National Income Dynamics Survey
OPM	Oxford Policy Management
RDP	Reconstruction and Development Programme
SASSA	South African Social Security Agency
SIU	Special Investigating Unit
SMG	State Maintenance Grant
SOCPEN	Social Pension System
StatsSA	Statistics South Africa
UNICEF	United Nations Children's Fund

Notes on Editors and Lead Authors

Gustavo Angeles is an economist and faculty member of the School of Public Health at the University of North Carolina at Chapel Hill. His research is on methodological and measurement problems for evaluating programme impact. He has extensive experience working on applied evaluations of social and health programmes in Latin America, Africa, and Asia.

Joanne Bosworth is Chief of Social Policy at the United Nations Children's Fund (UNICEF) in Kenya. Her work covers child poverty and inequality, social protection, and public finance for children in Kenya. She is particularly interested in urban poverty and inequality, local governance, and accountability for children's rights.

Benjamin Davis is Leader of the Strategic Programme on Reducing Rural Poverty at the Food and Agriculture Organization (FAO). He previously served as Deputy Director of the Agricultural Development Economics Division at FAO and team leader of the From Production to Protection (PtoP) project. He has also served as Social Policy Advisor for the UNICEF Regional Office in Eastern and Southern Africa and as a Research and Post-Doctoral Fellow at IFPRI. He holds a PhD in Agricultural Economics and a Master's in Public Policy from UC Berkeley.

Sudhanshu Handa is a development economist specializing in poverty, human resources, and public policy in developing countries. He is Professor of Public Policy at the University of North Carolina at Chapel Hill and at the time this book was published, serving as Chief of Social & Economic Policy at the UNICEF Office of Research-Innocenti in Florence, Italy. From 2010 he has led five large-scale evaluations of national cash transfer programmes in sub-Saharan Africa as part of the Transfer Project. He was previously a Lecturer at the University of the West Indies, Mona Campus, Jamaica, Professor of Agricultural Economics at the Eduardo Mondlane University, Maputo, Mozambique, Social Development Specialist at the Inter-American Development Bank in Washington DC, and Regional Social Policy Advisor, Eastern and Southern Africa Regional Office, UNICEF. He received his PhD in Economics from the University of Toronto in 1993.

Nicola Hypher is Senior Social Protection Adviser at Save the Children. Nicola holds an MSc in Development Studies from London School of Economics. She has also worked as a Research Analyst for the United Nations Research Institute for Social Development (UNRISD) and the UK Public Sector. Nicola's areas of expertise include child-sensitive social protection, social policy, and social housing.

Anna McCord is a sociologist with a PhD in economics, and over twenty-five years of experience working in international development. She is a research economist specializing in social protection programme design and evaluation, with a particular interest in programme impact at household level and also in labour markets and employment creation in Africa. Anna has experience throughout Africa, as well as Asia, having worked with a range of major donors, governments, and non-governmental agencies, and has published widely in a variety of media.

Roger Pearson works on social protection and evaluation for UNICEF, based in Kenya. Starting in refugee camps in Somalia in 1981, his work in Africa and Asia has focused on policy advocacy, strategy development, management, and evaluation of actions aiming to accelerate children's rights.

Luca Pellerano is a technical advisor on social security for the International Labour Organization (ILO) office for Zambia, Malawi and Mozambique. Previously he was team leader of the Poverty and Social Protection team in Oxford Policy Management (OPM) and Research Economist at the Centre for Evaluation of Development Policies (EDePo) at the Institute of Fiscal Studies (IFS). He has taken part in social protection reform projects in several African countries and has participated in the rigorous impact evaluation and the analysis of targeting effectiveness of social protection programmes in sub-Saharan Africa and Asia. He holds a PhD in Economics and Applied Quantitative Methods from the University of Genoa and an MSc in Economics from the University College London.

Pamela Pozarny, Rural Sociologist for the Africa Service in FAO's Investment Centre, holds a PhD in anthropology and has worked in and on Africa for thirty years focusing on sustainable livelihoods, inclusive rural development, and social protection. She has been leading the qualitative research in FAO's mixed method impact evaluations.

Luigi Peter Ragno is a social protection specialist with UNICEF and Research Fellow at the Brooks World Poverty Institute, the University of Manchester. He leads the social protection technical assistance to the Government of Ghana. His research interests and publications focus on social protection, behavioural economics, and poverty.

Michael Samson is Director of Research of the Economic Policy Research Institute (EPRI). He has twenty-nine years of experience working in social protection, and specializes in designing, implementing, monitoring, and evaluating social protection policies, systems, and programmes. He has worked on social protection policy design, implementation, evaluation, and capacity building projects in numerous countries. Michael co-ordinated and co-led the team implementing the first-ever integrated impact assessment of the Child Support Grant in South Africa. He is on the Economics faculty at the Williams College Center for Development Economics and holds a PhD in Economics from Stanford University.

David Seidenfeld is Principal Researcher at the American Institutes for Research (AIR) in their International Development, Research, and Evaluation programme. He works with government agencies, NGOs, and community organizations to help them learn what works and areas for improvement with their policies and programmes. He specializes in designing and implementing impact evaluations of economic, health, and education programmes in developing countries, including impact evaluations of cash transfer programmes in Zambia and Zimbabwe.

J. Edward Taylor is a Professor of Agricultural and Resource Economics at the University of California, Davis. He has written extensively on the microeconomics of development, the environment, and labour. He has co-authored *Beyond Experiments in Development Economics: Local Economy-Wide Impact Evaluation* (2014) and *Essentials of Development Economics* (2012). He is listed in Who's Who in Economics.

Paul Quarles van Ufford is Chief of Social Policy and Economic Analysis with UNICEF Zambia. His main fields of work include social protection, social cash transfers, and public policy evaluation. Before joining UNICEF Zambia, he worked with UNICEF in Vietnam and Senegal.

Natalia Winder Rossi is Senior Social Protection Officer and Social Protection team leader at FAO. She leads FAO's work in strengthening policy and programmatic linkages between social protection, productive inclusion, nutrition, and resilience. Prior to joining FAO, she was the Senior Programme Specialist (Social Protection) at UNICEF's Regional Office for Eastern and Southern Africa, where she led UNICEF support for social protection across twenty-one countries. Winder co-led and co-authored the development of UNICEF's first ever Social Protection Strategic Framework, which lays out the rationale for a systems approach for social protection. Prior to joining UNICEF, Winder worked at the Inter-American Development Bank in social protection in the design and implementation of indigenous people's development, and education programmes.

Paul Winters is the Director of Strategic Planning and Impact Assessment at the International Fund for Agricultural Development and Professor in the Department of Economics at American University in Washington, DC. He previously worked at the International Potato Center in Lima Peru, the University of New England in Australia, and the Inter-American Development Bank in Washington, DC. He has published numerous journal articles and working papers in the areas of impact evaluation, migration, cash transfer programmes, and smallholder agriculture.

Jennifer Yablonski works as a Social Protection Specialist for UNICEF in New York. Her experience includes technical support on social protection policy development and programme design and cash transfer impact evaluation, particularly in sub-Saharan Africa. Her previous work has focused on inequality, exclusion, and poverty analysis. She holds an MSc in Economics from the School for Oriental and African Studies, University of London.

1

The Transfer Project, Cash Transfers, and Impact Evaluation in Sub-Saharan Africa

Benjamin Davis (FAO), Sudhanshu Handa (University of North Carolina at Chapel Hill and UNICEF), Nicola Hypher (Save the Children), Natalia Winder Rossi (FAO), Paul Winters (IFAD and American University), and Jennifer Yablonski (UNICEF)

1.1 INTRODUCTION

For impact evaluations to be effective in influencing policy in a given context, they need to be embedded in the ongoing process of policy and programme design. Much of the policy impact lies in the credibility of the programme created by having an evaluation, as well as a learning environment where implementation and design issues are addressed. Programmes can be thus promoted and directed in a manner in which evidence is brought to bear as needed in the process of decision-making. This is the primary lesson found in this book, which is based on the evaluations of cash transfer programmes undertaken in eight sub-Saharan African (SSA) countries as part of the Transfer Project.

Cash transfer programmes have become a key means of social protection in developing countries and have expanded dramatically, at least in part due to the convincing evidence of their effectiveness. While cash transfers have been employed and evaluated in a number of countries, much of the known evidence of effectiveness of transfer programmes has been from conditional programmes implemented in Latin America. Evidence on the effectiveness of unconditional cash transfers provided through government programmes in SSA has not been substantially documented. This is changing partly as a result of the work of the Transfer Project. The body of evidence on the effectiveness of unconditional cash transfers in SSA now exceeds other regions both in its breadth of analysis across country and in its depth of analysis within countries. One key objective of this book is to provide an overview of this accumulated evidence—that is, the broad reaching impacts of cash transfer programmes in the region, focusing on evidence emerging from countries supported by the Transfer Project.

An equally important focus of this book is the documentation of *how* this evidence was generated and the systematic collaborative efforts undertaken by the respective governments, development and research partners, and the Transfer Project to collect consistent and comprehensive information about programme impact. While other evaluations of cash transfers in SSA exist, the Transfer Project sought to do this within one coherent framework and has made a concerted effort to integrate the evaluations into the process of programme implementation by the respective governments. Given this approach, the book goes much beyond the reporting of the impact of cash transfer programmes to analyse the relationship between the impact evaluations and the policy and programme implementation process occurring in each country and the role that evaluations played in that process. As such, another key objective of the book is to provide lessons on the political economy of cash transfer programme impact evaluations.

The book focuses on studies from eight SSA countries that were directly supported by the Transfer Project: Ethiopia, Ghana, Kenya, Lesotho, Malawi, South Africa, Zambia, and Zimbabwe. While the approaches and details of the impact evaluations and the level of interaction with the governments have necessarily varied to match the context of particular programmes and meet the needs of national governments, efforts have been made to ensure consistency across the studies. As such, the efforts undertaken by the Transfer Project represent a comprehensive analysis of cash transfer programmes in SSA.

This chapter provides background for the book, and the remainder of the chapter is organized as follows. Section 1.2 provides a brief overview of key literature on the evaluation of cash transfers in order to highlight how this book builds on this literature. Section 1.3 discusses the overall Transfer Project and the particular programmes analysed in this book. The approach to analysing the transfer programmes as well as the approach to presenting country case studies are discussed in Section 1.4. Finally, Section 1.5 presents the structure of the book and the underlying logic of the organization of the chapters.

1.2 BACKGROUND AND MOTIVATION

Part of the expansion of cash transfer programmes in developing counties has been due to the evidence base that has been built regarding their effectiveness in achieving social objectives. The evidence has been presented in a variety of reports, books, and journal articles, as well as in regional and international fora, reaching such a critical mass that a number of synthesis books and papers have been written.

Yet there is little literature that focuses on the evidence and experience from the numerous recent cash transfer programmes implemented by governments in SSA. There is a recent book on cash transfer programmes in SSA by Garcia and Moore (2012), but while it provides a useful overview of programmes prior to 2010 the insights provided are primarily anecdotal and not based on rigorous evaluation of government programmes. An edited volume on social protection published by Handa, Deveraux, and Webb (2011) provides some rigorous analysis of cash transfer programmes, but on a smaller scale and focusing on a narrower set of outcomes. Unlike this book it does not focus on the role of evaluation in the policy process. Davis et al. (2012) is the first and only published article to note and review the emerging "revolution" in cash transfer impact evaluation in SSA, but again touches only lightly on the political economy aspects of these evaluations.

Fizbein and Schady (2009) review the evidence on conditional cash transfer programmes (CCTs), mostly those in Latin America and focus on individual sets of indicators rather than country case studies; the book also discusses design options for CCTs but does not address the role of evaluation in the policy process. The authors conclude that CCTs have been an important tool for redistribution to the poor, reducing poverty, increasing consumption, and improving children's access to school and health facilities. However, their impacts on final human development outcomes (e.g., nutritional status or learning) are mixed. The book says little about SSA because in that region the vast majority of programmes are unconditional and at the time the book was written little evidence had emerged.

The most closely related book was published by Adato and Hoddinott (2010), which, like this book, covers qualitative and quantitative approaches to evaluating cash transfer programmes as well as the politics of the promotion of the programmes. That book also focuses on CCTs in Latin America and, while discussing some of the political economy of cash transfer programmes in key countries, it does not describe the role of evaluation in this process. The chapters of the book show that CCTs in Latin America have strong positive impacts on a wide range of education, health, and nutrition indicators. In concluding, the editors of the volume note that knowledge gaps in understanding remain (i) the pathways through which CCTs affect these indicators, (ii) the role conditionality plays, and (iii) the relative importance of cash versus service provision versus changes in knowledge and attitudes.

This book builds on these previous efforts by analysing cash transfers in SSA across a number of countries and goes beyond a focus solely on the evidence, to include the political and institutional processes which feed into, and are fed by, the programme impact evaluations. There are also research innovations incorporated into the Transfer Project, such as the systematic use of mixed methods approaches, data collection and analysis of adolescent behavioural risk and productive activities, and the assessment of local economy effects. The book moves beyond the existing literature in its geographic focus on a large selection of SSA countries, its emphasis on both impacts and the process of evaluation, and its research innovations.

1.3 THE TRANSFER PROJECT AND ASSOCIATED CASH TRANSFER PROGRAMMES

The Transfer Project is a joint initiative of United Nations Children Fund (UNICEF), the Food and Agriculture Organization of the United Nations (FAO), Save the Children, and the University of North Carolina at Chapel Hill, in partnership with national governments, and numerous national and international researchers. The project is a research and learning initiative which supports improved knowledge and practice on social cash transfers in Africa in several key areas including (i) support to national longitudinal quantitative and qualitative impact evaluations in the region to help understand not only what impacts cash transfers are achieving, but also how and why; (ii) cross-regional analysis to draw thematic and operational lessons based on the diversity of social transfer programmes in the region; (iii) creation of mechanisms for regional learning and exchange among regional policy makers, implementers, researchers, and civil society through workshops, web resources, public data availability, and publications.

The objective of cash transfer programmes is to protect individuals or households from the impacts of shocks and support the accumulation of human, financial, and productive assets (UNICEF, 2012). Given this objective, the Transfer Project supports assessment of programme impact on key social outcomes in conjunction with a broader range of indicators. A key initiative under the Transfer Project is the From Protection to Production (PtoP) project. Working in tandem with the Transfer Project, the PtoP project is a collaborative effort between the FAO, UNICEF, and national governments, which explores the linkages between social protection, agriculture, and rural development by assessing the impact of cash transfer programmes on productive outcomes and the local economy. The objective is to understand these potential linkages in order to strengthen coordination between social and productive policies. As such, the Transfer Project through the PtoP and other initiatives described in this book moves beyond the evaluations of cash transfer programmes conducted previously.

The programmes forming part of the project and included in this book are noted in Table 1.1. In most cases the programmes were initiated in some form prior to the evaluation. These were often basic pilots (or pre-pilots as described in Chapter 6) that were designed to test the concept and to work out administrative procedures. The evaluations themselves are then often linked

Table 1.1. Cash Transfer Programmes Included in Transfer Project

Country	Programme	Year programme began	Implementing ministry	Target group	Conditions	Approximate reach at writing
Ethiopia	Tigray Social Cash Transfer Programme Pilot (SCTPP)	2011	Tigray Bureau of Labour and Social Affairs	Labour constrained, ultra-poor female, elderly, or disabled	none	3,800 households
Ghana	Livelihood Empowerment Against Poverty (LEAP)	2008	Ministry of Gender, Children, and Social Protection	Extreme poor with elderly, disabled, or OVC member	expected but not monitored	150,000 households
Kenya	Cash Transfers for Orphans and Vulnerable Children (CT-OVC)	2004	Ministry of Home Affairs, Department of Children's Services	Poor households with OVC	none	250,000 households
Lesotho	Child Grants Programme (CGP)	2009	Ministry of Social Development	Poor households with OVC	none	25,000 households
Malawi	Social Cash Transfer Programme (SCTP)—Expansion	2006	Ministry of Gender, Children, and Social Welfare	Ultra-poor, labour constrained	none	100,000 households
Malawi	SCTP—Mchinji pilot	same	same	same	same	same
South Africa	Child Support Grant (CSG)	1998	Department of Social Development	Poor children	none	11 million children
Zambia	Child Grant (CG) model of SCT	2010	Ministry of Community Development, Mother and Child Health	Household with a child under five years old in three poor districts	none	145,000 households (overall SCT)
Zambia	Multiple Categorical Targeting Grant (MCTG) model of SCT	2011	same	Poor female- and elderly-headed households with OVC; households with disabled person	None	same
Zimbabwe	Harmonized Social Cash Transfer (HSCT)	2011	Ministry of Public Service, Labour, and Social Welfare	Food poor and labour constrained	none	55,000 households

to an expansionary phase where the programme is reaching a larger scale. Only one programme, the Child Support Grant (CSG) in South Africa, has reached national scale.

The cash transfer programmes themselves are generally part of broader national social protection strategies, although is some cases the launch of cash transfer programmes preceded formal social protection policies. Many of the programmes originated from a concern about vulnerable populations, often in the context of food insecurity and HIV/AIDS. This has driven the emergence of home-grown design models where objectives emphasize ultra-poor, labour-constrained households, and/or households caring for orphans and vulnerable children (OVC). Since the context in which these programmes have emerged is different from other parts of the world some of the details have also differed.

One key characteristic of the majority of the transfer programmes in SSA is that they are unconditional. This runs in contrast to many of those promoted elsewhere, particularly in Latin America, where conditions usually linked to child health and schooling behaviour are placed in order to maintain status in the programme. There has been some attempt at experimentation in using conditions (e.g., Kenya, although it could not be properly implemented) and some stated conditions (e.g., Ghana, for some groups) although these have not been enforced so at most might be referred to as soft conditions; currently the Productive Social Safety Net in Tanzania is one of the few government programmes that invokes punitive conditions in SSA. Thus, while the programmes have been designed to improve food security, health, nutritional, and educational status, particularly in children, since cash is provided unconditionally and not tied to specific behaviour, households are free to invest in any way they would like, opening up the possibility of a wider range of impacts across non-traditional domains. Recipients in conditional programmes also have some flexibility in how they spend money, but there are clear incentives to spend on health and education and basic foods since receipt of the transfer is conditional on health and education behaviour. As a result, impact evaluations of CCTs have tended to focus on outcomes in these narrow areas.

A second key characteristic is the incorporation of the concept of vulnerability, along with poverty, into the targeting criteria of a number of countries. The consequent emphasis on ultra-poor, labour-constrained households and/or households caring for OVC has led to a demographic profile very different from the younger households with small children of CCTs in Latin America. Beneficiary households tend to have older heads, older children, and relatively few working-age adults, reflecting the lost generation brought on by the HIV pandemic.

Moreover, the targeting process itself has a much stronger focus on community participation, often in combination with other targeting methods such as geographic targeting. This is in contrast with other parts of the world such as Latin America where proxy means tests (also often combined with geographic targeting) have been the more dominant form of targeting. While some form of proxy means tests are being introduced in SSA, there still remains a strong element of community targeting in most cases. The analysis presented here also provides an opportunity to assess the success of this type of targeting in reaching the intended population.

The Transfer Project then seeks to create a regional social protection learning agenda by using comparable, rigorous approaches to evaluating the impact of a set of cash transfer programmes in SSA that, while unique, have similar characteristics. Through this approach, the Transfer Project hopes to generate externalities and foment cross-country learning across SSA.

1.4 APPROACH TO THE ANALYSIS

The approach taken to analyse the cash transfer programmes presented in this book can be divided into two parts. First, there is the research methodology used by the Transfer Project to analyse the impact of the programmes. Second, there is the approach taken in this book to present the results of the analysis performed under the Transfer Project and the role the project played in the countries in which it operated. Each of these is discussed in this section.

1.4.1 Research Methodology

To answer critical policy and research questions, the evaluations in the eight countries falling under the umbrella of the Transfer Project employed mixed methods approaches, linking rigorous quantitative evaluation of impacts with qualitative field work, general equilibrium modelling, and specific studies on targeting, operations and cost, and fiscal sustainability. The evaluations incorporated widely accepted state-of-the-art approaches that were broadly consistent across countries, but were innovative in their application in specific countries. Of particular note is the utilization of village economy general equilibrium modelling, which has not been a standard part of the impact evaluation toolbox. The use of mixed method approaches responds to the need to answer a range of research and policy questions some of which are not easily answered with one particular method. The particular mix of methods varied from country to country as appropriate and is highlighted in Table 1.2.

The core approach, followed in all but one of the countries, had three components. First, a statistical or quantitative impact evaluation based on experimental or non-experimental design is employed to attribute, with statistical certainty, the observed impact of cash transfers on programme recipients. This impact evaluation design varied across countries, depending on the

Table 1.2. Methods Used by Transfer Project

Country	Quantitative (years)	Qualitative (years)	LEWIE	Other analysis
Ethiopia	Non-Experimental 2012, 2014	PtoP (OPM), IDS (Institute for Development Studies) 2012, 2014	Yes	targeting, payment process
Ghana	Non-Experimental 2010, 2012	PtoP (OPM) 2012	Yes	analysis of transfer payments
Kenya	Experimental 2007, 2009, 2011	PtoP (OPM) 2012	Yes	operational effectiveness, targeting
Lesotho	Experimental 2011, 2013	PtoP (OPM) 2013	Yes	rapid appraisal, targeting, costing, and fiscal sustainability
Malawi	Experimental 2013, 2014	PtoP (OPM), UNC/CSR 2013, 2014, 2015	Yes	targeting, analysis of transfer payments
Malawi (Mchinji pilot)	Experimental 2007, 2008	BU (Boston University)/CSR 2007	No	operational effectiveness, targeting
South Africa	Non-experimental 2010, 2011	IDS 2010	No	take-up rate, targeting
Zambia (CG model)	Experimental 2010, 2012, 2013, 2014	IDS 2013	Yes	impact comparisons across programme, targeting
Zambia (MCTG model)	Experimental 2011, 2013, 2014		No	impact comparisons across programme, targeting
Zimbabwe	Non-experimental 2013, 2014	PtoP, AIR 2012, 2013, 2014	Yes	institutional capacity assessment, rapid assessment, targeting, MIS (Management Information System) analysis, process evaluation

particular challenges of evaluating a real-life, government-run programme; It followed a continuum from gold standard experimental design to a variety of non-experimental approaches. The data collection in the quantitative component was primarily through questionnaires administered to treatment and control households, which were designed based on carefully considered theories of change. There were a number of innovative aspects of the data collection including countries where information is collected on productive outcomes, the transition to adulthood, and the psychology of poverty and decision-making. With the collected data, a careful analysis was conducted to ensure unbiased impact estimates. Details of the quantitative approach taken in each country are provided in Chapter 3.

Second, qualitative methods were incorporated in the evaluations and sought to understand in greater depth the causes and processes surrounding programme impact, contextual factors mediating outcomes, and people's perceptions and experiences. Three qualitative design approaches were used in the mixed-methods impact evaluations covered in this book: (1) comparative cross-country case; (2) longitudinal; and (3) thematic focus. Chapter 4 notes the design approach taken in each country and provides critical analysis of each approach.

Third, while poor households are the focus of cash transfer programmes, they are also a conduit through which cash enters local economies. As beneficiaries spend their transfers, local demand increases. If local production expands to meet this demand, cash transfer programmes can create income multipliers; each dollar transferred can increase local income by more than one dollar. For this reason, general equilibrium modelling was employed to look beyond the direct impact of transfers and to follow the cash distributed by the programmes as it flows through the local economy. The methodology, which is explained in Chapter 5, was consistent across countries—the LEWIE (Local Economy-Wide Impact Evaluation) model—but the data available and the nature of programme implementation and local space varied across countries.

There was no one method followed by each country, but instead each approach responded to the needs, to the programme context and to the budget considerations in each particular country (Table 1.2). Each country experience presented its own challenges in terms of coordinating the different components. Whether experimental or non-experimental the statistical approach is relatively fixed, with a minimum bound of flexibility—all countries have treatment and control households, to which a baseline household survey and one and sometimes two or three follow-up household and community surveys were applied.

Seven of the countries (all except South Africa) participated in the PtoP project, which had a specific focus on ascertaining the economic and productive impacts of cash transfer programmes. The PtoP project aimed to carry out a consistent approach, across countries, to analysing the impact of the programme on beneficiary household economic decision-making and risk management in both quantitative and qualitative terms, as well as simulating the impact of the programme on the local economy. This entailed ensuring that the household surveys collected adequate data on household livelihoods, social networks, and risk management, the inclusion of business enterprise surveys to estimate the LEWIE and qualitative data to understand in more detail the economic and social network impacts of the programmes. Moreover, data analysis and modelling were as consistent as possible across countries. The general equilibrium modelling was built off the data collected in the household surveys, as well as the additional business enterprise survey. Ideally LEWIE models should be constructed at baseline and recalibrated at follow-up, but due to budget and timing constraints it was constructed only once in each country, in some cases at baseline and others at follow-up. Ideally qualitative fieldwork should be done before, during, and after the household data collection although, as seen in the description of the qualitative work (Chapter 4), this was not always possible.

Taking advantage of the mixed method approach requires dealing with challenges in bringing the different approaches to bear on each other. The quantitative impact analysis is an important input into a follow-up, recalibrated, LEWIE model—in terms of analysing how the behavioural implications of the cash transfer programme affects the demand and supply of goods and services within the local economy. The qualitative fieldwork can corroborate some of the assumptions of the LEWIE model regarding market functioning, particularly in terms of labour elasticity and inflation. Ideally qualitative fieldwork should be done before, during, and after the household surveys and the LEWIE modelling, serving as both an input into hypothesis making and design of quantitative data collection instruments, interpretation of results from both the quantitative impact analysis and the general equilibrium modelling. This is often difficult to do, because of budget, logistics, and timing (of intervention budgeting and planning).

And in the final instance, the ideal is to bring together the results of all three to create a consistent story, though again this is often difficult in practice. There is a tendency for teams focusing on the particular approaches to work separately, and in practice they were often physically separated both in time and in space. In part then, this book is an attempt to bring the various teams together to provide a coherent narrative of the programme's impacts across different domains, and to reflect on the role of the evaluation in the implementation and policy process.

Beyond the core approach, additional studies were included in different countries, creating in some cases an ongoing learning agenda well beyond traditional programme impact evaluation. These included assessments of targeting systems, ex ante partial equilibrium simulations of programme impact, focused studies on the process of implementation or programme operations, and studies of costing and fiscal sustainability. As explored in Chapter 2, these related research products and broader learning agendas were important for national policy and programme debates/changes.

The book will offer insights into the innovative approaches used by the Transfer Project and PtoP project to assess the impact of these programmes as well as how to organize such an undertaking with partners within countries. In addition to a mixed methods approach, the innovations incorporated into the Transfer Project also include data collection and analysis of (i) adolescent behavioural risk, particularly related to HIV prevention, and the impact of programmes on this behaviour; (ii) programme impact on productive activities in both the agricultural and non-agricultural sectors; and (iii) the local economy effects of cash transfers. As such, the rationale for the book is both to provide policy and research insights as well as to offer guidance on the implementation of a multi-country, innovative impact evaluation approach.

1.4.2 Focus of Country Case Studies

The standard approach to conveying the result of impact evaluations is through reports provided, and often presented, to the government, including a baseline and subsequent reports on the impact of the programme on key sets of indicators as well as results of associated studies. If the evaluation team is research oriented some of the results of the evaluation may make their way to publication in journal article or book chapters and provide useful insight into the impact of certain programmes on particular sets of indicators. The methods used to evaluate the programmes have been sufficiently rigorous to merit publication and a number of articles and chapters have come out of this process focusing on particular issues related to cash transfers.

An issue with this approach is that it tends to only tell a portion of the story of a programme's impact and influence in a given country. Reports are presented when results are ready and there is often little follow-up on what happens with the information provided in those reports. Publications are necessarily narrowly focused to be sufficiently precise to meet the standards of academic journals. Neither gives a complete picture of the evaluation and its influence.

This book focuses on the story of programme impact and the role of impact evaluation in the policy process in each country. As such, the underlying concept is to avoid the standard practice of reporting the impact on individual sets of indicators, but to focus on the overall effect of the programme given the extensive analysis completed on a wide range of indicators—of course, with reference to the specific results for those interested. Further, the idea is to present the on-the-ground story of social protection and cash transfer programmes in the country, how the evaluation was initiated within the country, and the role of the evaluation in informing policy.

Obviously, this goes beyond reporting the evidence generated by the evaluations that form the Transfer Project and requires obtaining insights from stakeholders in each of the countries considered. The approach taken is to have those who have participated in this process in each country participate in the writing of the chapters presented in the book. These include the researchers involved in the evaluations, donors, development partners, and key government personnel. The input from these individuals allows for a more complete narrative of the story of the programme and the evaluation in each country. Where information is missing from the authors, other key stakeholders were asked to help complete the picture.

The approach taken in the country chapters is then to mix the results of the evaluation along with historical narratives and analysis of policy processes within the country. Through this combination, the country-specific story of how the political and institutional process fed into, and was fed by, the programme impact evaluation emerges.

1.5 STRUCTURE OF THE BOOK

The book is comprised of three parts. Part I focuses on the design of the impact evaluation highlighting both the political economy of conducting the impact evaluations as well as the methodological approach. Chapter 2, the political economy chapter, provides the detailed background of the Transfer Project and discusses broadly the relationship between the impact evaluation and the public policy and programme implementation process. The technical details of the methodology are presented in Chapters 3, 4, and 5 on the quantitative, qualitative, and LEWIE approaches, respectively. The objective of this part is twofold. First, it will lay the groundwork for the second part of the book where the impacts and lessons learned from each country are provided. This is done to avoid the country studies being bogged down in the details of the methodology. Second, it is of interest in itself in those seeking to implement impact evaluations since it provides insights into working with governments and across research teams as well as methodologies that can be employed in the context of real-world interventions.

Part II of the book focuses on providing a narrative for each country case study on the specific objectives and design of the programme, the impact of the programme, the relationship between evaluation research and social protection policy and programmes, and the lessons that can be learned from programme implementation and the evaluations. This includes a synthesis of the social and productive impacts garnered from the mixed methods approaches. While some of the outputs from the evaluations of the country programmes have been written up and even published, these have tended to focus on the use of one method (quantitative or qualitative) and not provided an integrated understanding of the programmes.

Part III of the book brings together the whole story. This includes a synthesis of the results, political economy, and policy implications in a comparative, cross-country perspective.

REFERENCES

Adato, M. and J. Hoddinott (2010). *Conditional Cash Transfers in Latin America*. Baltimore, MD: Johns Hopkins University Press.

Davis, B., M. Gaarder, S. Handa, and J. Yablonski (2012). 'Evaluating the impact of cash transfer programs in sub Saharan Africa: an introduction to the special issue'. Journal of Development Effectiveness, 4(1) (March): 1–8.

Fizbein, A. and N. Schady (2009). *Conditional Cash Transfers: Reducing Present and Future Poverty*. Washington, DC: The World Bank.

Garcia, M. and C. Moore (2012). *The Cash Dividend: The Rise of Cash Transfer Programmes in Sub-Saharan Africa*. Washington, DC: The World Bank.

Handa, S., S. Deveraux, and D. Webb (2011). *Social Protection for Africa's Children*. New York: Routledge.

UNICEF (2012). 'Integrated Social Protection Systems: Enhancing Equity for Children. UNICEF Social Protection Strategic Framework'. New York: UNICEF.

Part I

Designing the Cash Transfer Impact Evaluations

2

The Political Economy of Cash Transfer Evaluations in Sub-Saharan Africa

Anna McCord (ODI and University of Manchester), Natalia Winder Rossi (FAO), and Jennifer Yablonski (UNICEF)

2.1 INTRODUCTION

Since the mid-2000s, countries in sub-Saharan Africa have experienced an important rise in the number, scope, and reach of social protection programmes, particularly cash transfers. Earlier social protection programmes were characterized by a combination of long-standing programmes in middle-income countries in southern Africa, a few largely development partner-supported pilots, and in a small number of crisis-prone countries a transition from repeated donor-supported humanitarian crisis responses to predictable social protection programming. The most recent wave of programmes are a response to the limited progress on poverty reduction despite economic growth, the negative impact of HIV/AIDs on family structures and support networks, and repeated food-related crises linked in part to climate change. Governments and development partners have adopted social protection programmes in order to address the outstanding challenges of chronic poverty, human development deficits, and vulnerability.

Social protection is now widely recognized by national governments in the region as an effective strategy to strengthen families' capacity to cope with risks and stresses, promote access to essential services, and contribute to inclusive economic growth. Today, most countries in Eastern and Southern Africa have some form of cash transfer programme, and many countries in Western and Central Africa are moving in this direction. Many countries are now allocating domestic resources to finance scale-up and expansion plans. While the landscape is heterogeneous, there is overall a rising trend in terms of social protection provision.

What has motivated this critical momentum for social protection? What has influenced policy makers to adopt social protection as a key policy option for poverty alleviation? To what extent has the existing and emerging evidence coming from impact evaluations (IEs) at national level played a role in the region? Using the experience of the Transfer Project, this chapter aims to shed light on the relationship between the development and expansion of national cash transfer programmes and their corresponding evaluations. Specifically, the objectives of the chapter are to understand the relationships between the different actors that played a role in the implementation and evaluation of the programmes and highlight the factors that were critical in building these relationships; to explore how the evaluations and associated studies and communication were used to inform policy makers; and to assess the extent to which they influenced policy changes.

The chapter explores the question of evaluation and policy change from a number of different perspectives and provides a contextual analysis of the impacts presented in the country chapters, drawing out broader implications of the findings in a systematic way. In order to achieve this, the chapter builds on a review of the literature exploring the role of programme evaluation in informing policy change, as well as on an analysis of the experience of the Transfer Project. This discussion looks at how both the process and the results of national evaluations have influenced specific elements of programme design and key policy processes (such as scale-up, expansion, and allocation of resources). It assesses the extent to which design and implementation of an IE as part of a programme's strategy requires not only coordination with, but also political support from policy makers and programme administrators. The analysis is based on evidence derived from in-depth discussions and interviews with key informants in selected case study countries, as well as first-hand observation of the authors, in an effort to understand the relationships between the different actors involved in the evaluation of social cash transfers and the extent to which the model and approach of the Transfer Project contributed (or not) to critical changes.

The chapter is divided into six sections. The first presents a synthesis of the literature on the role of evidence, on policy and programming. The second discusses the specific model and approach of the Transfer Project, at different stages of design, implementation, and dissemination of findings. The third reviews the evidence relating to the influence of impact evaluation on policy and programming. The fourth section considers factors relating to the IE process itself which contribute to policy impact. The fifth explores external factors which are also key drivers of policy decision making, including consideration of national government perspectives, development partner practices and resource availability. In the sixth and final section key lessons learned from the experience of the Transfer Project-led evaluations are set out.

2.2 IMPACT OF RESEARCH ON SOCIAL POLICY: OVERVIEW OF LITERATURE

A large range of literature has explored the impact of research on social policy since the 1990s, associated with increasing interest in the concept of evidence-based policy making. However, the literature on the challenges and opportunities associated with assessing the impact of policy-oriented research remains limited (Pellini et al. 2011), and to date there has been little work examining the role of IEs in the social protection sector specifically, and their influence on policy development. The findings of the literature in relation to social policy and policy influencing however are consistent, and provide valuable insights into the research–policy nexus which underpin the findings in this book.

The key insight from the literature is the complexity of the policy influencing and development process and the somewhat limited role of evidence itself in comparison to advocacy processes, with key roles being ascribed to the medium through which policy messages are presented, the framing of debate, the credibility of the evidence provider, and the relationship between the evidence provider and the policy makers which underlies the whole (ODI 2014). Throughout the literature, the importance of ensuring that the research and the associated policy influencing strategy take into account the political economy context is highlighted.

The primary insight from the literature is that influencing policy is a non-linear process and that policy making itself is not linear but iterative, interactive, and based on trust, respect, and influence, with evidence playing a 'relatively modest role in policy making, which is dominated by political expediency' (Gadeberg and Victor 2011).

The research–policy relationship is not characterized by value-free supply and demand for objective information. Both researchers (evidence providers) and policy makers (evidence consumers) are seeking to promote particular visions and outcomes. Also, policy development is subject to multiple causality, with the policy making process being characterized by reactive decision making and by political expediency. This complex process is mediated by interpretations and different understandings, and is a participatory multi-actor process which is significantly influenced by personal interactions. In this way the 'evidence to policy' process is not one of objective information generation, sharing, and usage, but of multivariate processes and factors (Gadeberg and Victor 2011).

There is an argument that within this context of multi-causality evidence itself is only one of many inputs, and process may be at least as important as content in determining outcomes. For these reasons the literature counsels caution and recommends the avoidance of 'attribution' of impact, in preference advising that the link that should be made between research and policy development is one of 'contribution'.

In terms of policy influencing approaches, there is consensus that the *medium* may be as important as the message, and that factors such as accessible and appropriate language, presentation and packaging, and authorship by known and respected individuals play a key role in take-up (Beynon et al. 2012). Where research is to be effective a cooperative relationship based on trust and understanding between the evidence creator, advocate, and policy target is important. Similarly, how the findings are communicated is also key, and impact is associated with strategic and iterative engagement with key targets, using multiple channels over time, depending on the intended outcome. Examples include making use of a mix of research papers, policy briefs, books, traditional media appearances, and electronic media (twitter and youtube), together with programme exposure, for example through field trips, and making findings accessible through individual stories and anecdotes, as well as formal quantitative reporting, and channelling communication through existing respected networks and communities of interest. In this way visibility, credibility, and interest can also be promoted, and such approaches tend to enhance impact.

In terms of content perhaps the most important consideration is the *framing* of the findings, which entails the presentation of key ideas as solutions to topical policy challenges and existing political needs such that they can readily be adopted within the ongoing political discourse. Examples from the current study include 'cash transfers are effective at reducing poverty', 'cash transfers are affordable', and 'cash transfers stimulate local economic growth'. These simplified research summaries and messages seem to be highly effective in terms of influencing the policy debate, if given credibility through association with recognized and trusted processes and institutions.

The literature indicates that policy influencing can have a range of different dimensions, with Keck and Sikkink (1998) identifying five potential 'areas of influence':

- Framing debates and getting issues on the political agenda;
- Encouraging commitments from states and other policy actors;
- Securing procedural change at international and domestic level;
- Influencing policy and legislation (policy change and content); and
- Changing the behaviour of policy actors, civil society actors, and citizens (ownership and sustainability).

These can be grouped into two types of outcomes: those which are instrumental, informing policy change, practice, and behaviour; and those which are conceptual, changing knowledge, understanding, and attitudes (Davies, Nutley, and Walter 2005), with the behavioural aspects of the former being extensively explored in the Outcome Mapping literature (Earl, Carden, and Smutylo 2001). Depending on the desired outcome, an appropriately designed approach entailing evidence provision, debate framing, and advocacy is required.

Similarly, the requirements for success identified in the literature are linked to the effective integration of research findings, and even the research process itself, into the policy process, in order to ensure relevance. The key requirement is understanding and addressing the political economy context in order to ensure research addresses recognized policy challenges, and meets a demand for evidence and policy inputs. To this end engagement with policy makers, focusing on communication, engagement, and relationships, and critically, taking an opportunistic approach, responding flexibly to policy opportunities as they arise, are key criteria for success (Young 2008).

This engagement can, however, take various forms, depending on the nature of the political settlement and also the kind of policy change required. When attempting to bring issues onto the political agenda, as opposed to promoting policy design nuances, there may be merits to a more adversarial 'outsider' approach, as opposed to the trusted 'insider' perspective, for example working with civil society coalitions or opposition groups to politicize issues and bring them into the political debate (Start and Hovland 2004), although again credibility and sensitivity to the political economy context remains key.

The way research is introduced into the policy debate is also critical in terms of whether it is recognized as relevant and can input into the debate effectively. In this way, the major barriers to policy impact have been identified as: the failure of research to address issues perceived as politically important, research which is ill timed in terms of the scheduling of national debates and policy processes, and findings which are communicated poorly and fail to present clear, empirically based recommendations (Walt 1994). Ensuring that evaluation and advocacy are politically relevant in terms of their timing may be challenged by the external institutional factors which drive schedules of programme of evaluation, particularly among international agencies, a challenge compounded by uncertainties relating to the timing of political processes. This challenge is illustrated in several of the country case studies in the book, where evaluation findings only became available after major policy decisions had been taken, thereby limiting potential impact in terms of input into broad policy choice and design processes.

Hence the literature indicates that the role of research in influencing policy outcomes is dependent on a range of conditioning factors, which extend beyond the empirical findings of the research itself. These relate to *the nature of the research*, in terms of its perceived credibility and the extent of identification between the policy maker and evidence generation process, *the articulation and framing of the evidence*, and its linkage to existing policy challenges,

Research
- Credibility—author, institutional backing, process
- Ownership—engagement of policy makers

Evidence
- Framing of evidence
- Linkage to policy problem
- Clarity of messages

Process
- Linkage to policy processes
- Appropriate media (reports, briefings, events, etc.)
- Trusted actors
- Opportunism

Outcome
- Mediated by multiple external factors—fiscal context, political expediency, ideological preferences

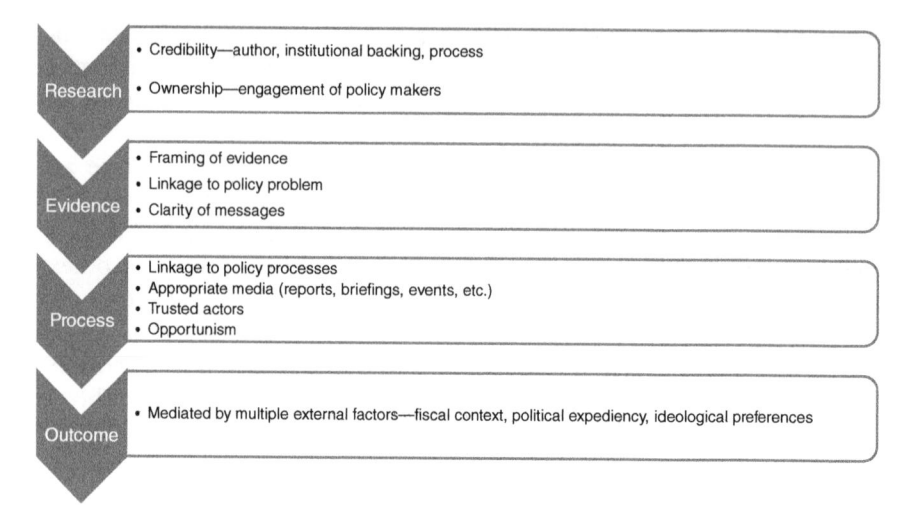

Figure 2.1. Summary of Key Factors Conditioning Policy Influence

the advocacy process by which it is introduced into the debate, and finally *the contextual factors*, which have a significant impact on mediating outcomes, notably fiscal and ideological preferences and political expediency. These factors are summarized in Figure 2.1.

2.3 THE TRANSFER PROJECT STORY

This section gives a brief overview of the history and approach of the Transfer Project, focusing on key relationships and processes that contributed to the way in which evidence was generated and used, which informs analysis in subsequent sections.

When the design phase of the Transfer Project began in 2008, there was increased momentum around social protection, but among sceptics and committed policy makers/implementers alike there remained a set of outstanding questions relating to starting or scaling up social transfer programmes, and the applicability of the existing evidence on cash transfers. As interest was beginning to grow in the potential for social protection to address challenges of chronic poverty, food insecurity, and HIV in the early 2000s, the existing evidence base was still limited in terms of its capacity to address decision-makers' needs in the African context. Much of the social protection evidence at this time was from programmes in Latin American countries, many of which had key design features which differed from those of African programmes, and which were implemented in very different contexts in terms of the supply and quality of services, administrative capacities, fiscal resources, and levels (and patterns) of poverty and inequality. The applicability of evidence from well-documented South African programmes was also questioned for similar reasons.

In an effort to respond to the evidence gap, and with the explicit intention of informing policy, design, and implementation choices in the region, a group of development partners began to examine the scope and feasibility of a multi-country research project and created the Transfer Project in 2009.

The Transfer Project is a partnership of international organizations, national governments, and international and national researchers with three objectives: 1) to provide evidence on the effectiveness of social cash transfer programmes in achieving impacts for children; 2) to inform the development and design of social cash transfer policy and programmes; and 3) to promote learning across the continent on the design and implementation of social cash transfer evaluations and research. In line with these objectives, the Transfer Project has three key pillars: 1) regional learning, information exchange, and network/community of practice; 2) technical assistance on design and implementation of IE and identification of research areas; and 3) synthesis of regional lessons on programme design.[1]

Initially, the partners leading the project were Save the Children UK, UNICEF (United Nations Children Fund), and DFID (Department for International Development, UK). They were subsequently joined in the consortium by FAO (Food and Agriculture Organization of the United Nations), driven by their institutional interest in the relationship between social protection and production, and the University of North Carolina at Chapel Hill (UNC), who joined after a competitive process to select an international research partner. An initial seven-month design phase focused on six countries where either impact studies or discussion of cash pilots/scale-up were already under way,[2] entailing country missions to scope ongoing monitoring and evaluation plans, and levels of interest among national governments, national and international research partners, and other development partners. The country missions and an initial design workshop were used to identify the research questions of most value to policy makers and programme implementers, resulting in an extension of the original research to cover not only the impacts of social transfers, but also how these effects were achieved and why they might be different across programmes. The consultation with government and other partners during the design phase reinforced the initiative's importance not just as a research project, but also as a learning project, focusing on an ongoing

---

[1] By close of edition, there are ten participating countries, some of which receive direct technical support on impact evaluation, others participating through sharing experience, findings, and data.

[2] Ethiopia, Kenya, Malawi, Mozambique, Rwanda, and Tanzania.

exchange of lessons on research, policy, implementation, and adaptation based on findings at national and regional levels.

Since its inception the Transfer Project has functioned as an 'umbrella' and network, building on, supporting, and connecting a number of national IE processes. The project has financed specific pieces of work which have helped to strengthen national IE surveys, national and regional analysis of key issues, and communications work. At its core are three overlapping relationships which are central to its success. The first is a grouping of international partners who act as convenors and facilitators, the second is the ongoing relationship between these international partners and national policy makers and programme implementers, and the third is a supportive (although sometimes challenging) network of national and international researchers.

2.3.1 Key Elements of Process at Three Stages

Although the timeline and process of the cash transfer IEs was different in each country, it is useful to look at key elements of the process at three different stages: design, implementation and analysis, and dissemination of findings.

In the design stage of the IEs, there was close collaboration between policy makers, programme implementers, development partners, and researchers at national level to identify priority questions relating to programme objectives and also to ensure the IEs dovetailed with programme roll-out plans, inasmuch as this was feasible. The role of UNICEF country offices, who were already engaged in ongoing dialogue on social protection with their government counterparts and other development partners, was a critical part of this process. The Transfer Project also played a role as an 'honest broker' in relation to national IEs, helping governments and development partners to better understand and make decisions relating to design, commissioning, and implementation of the evaluations. This role ranged from supporting government and UNICEF and other staff to develop Terms of Reference (TORs) and technically evaluate proposals for IEs, to reviewing draft survey modules and reports, and to working with various stakeholders in the interpretation of results. At regional level, a consultation took place with national governments and other stakeholders to identify key questions, including those common across countries.

Collaborative, consultative processes involving multiple partners and stages have also been a feature of the implementation of the IEs. The methods, timing of data collection, and discussion of findings at country level were jointly defined between researchers and national counterparts to respond to national processes and information needs. This joint process promoted participation and the inclusion of findings in critical debates and ongoing policy processes. The use of multiple methodologies, including quantitative, qualitative, and simulation-based approaches, helped to triangulate findings and unpack 'the story' of what is happening (or not) as a result of the programmes and possible reasons why—helping policy makers to identify key programme design and implementation issues.

The third stage, dissemination of the findings, included national policy events to present and discuss draft and final results with various stakeholders, the public release of reports as national evaluations with official endorsement, and the subsequent production of a range of materials including national policy briefs. This process included the presentation of findings to key stakeholders throughout the process, rather than only at the final results stage, including the presentation of baseline findings and discussion of their implications in terms of the results that might be expected from the final IE. In addition, stakeholders from participating countries and researchers came together at Transfer Project and From Protection to Production (PtoP) project technical annual workshops to discuss and learn about progress across countries. While the impacts on production and economic activities have entailed work on the popularization and communication of findings through diverse media, the dissemination stage of the process is the weakest in terms of joint strategic activities among the various Transfer Project partners.

In line with the importance of process in determining the impact highlighted in the international literature, the unique Transfer Project process described in this section has been an important factor in determining the level of influence that the evidence generated through the evaluations has had on social protection policy and programme processes in the countries discussed in this book. The following sections explore the extent to which the evidence generated did in fact influence social protection policies and programmes, and the nature of the relationship between this influence and factors internal and external to the evaluation process.

2.4 WHAT DOES THE EVIDENCE SAY? THE EXPERIENCE OF THE TRANSFER PROJECT-LED EVALUATIONS IN INFLUENCING POLICY/PROGRAMMES IN AFRICA

In this section the role of research, in the form of IE, in influencing social protection policy making and design is examined. A review of the experiences outlined in this book, together with interviews with key national and international UNICEF staff and national government counterparts working on social protection in each of the case study countries,[3] provides insights into the relationship between research and policy making. It is not only formal IEs, in the form of a single study, which are considered here, but the whole series of evaluative research and learning products that were carried out within the umbrella of the evaluation, including baseline reports containing analysis of targeting and transfer size, costing and affordability studies and the modelling of local multiplier effects. The findings confirm the argument in the literature review that the relationship between evaluation and policy processes is not linear or direct, but rather depends on a variety of factors which are discussed in Sections 2.5 and 2.6.

While there is considerable diversity across the case study countries, a number of broad themes emerge, and an analysis of the process across the various countries suggests that evidence coming from the national evaluations and related research contributed to:

- Building the overall *credibility* of an emerging social protection sector;
- Strengthening the case for social protection as an investment, not a cost and addressing public perceptions and misconceptions;
- Supporting learning around programme design and implementation to inform programme improvements in key areas such as targeting, access, transfer size, and the role of complementary activities; and
- Shaping policy discussions beyond the national context and informing regional social protection agendas.

2.4.1 Building Credibility of the Social Protection Sector

The evidence suggests that the evaluation process had the greatest impact on promoting the overall credibility of an emerging national social protection sector as a feasible, effective, and affordable approach to poverty reduction. Moreover, it contributed to addressing reported scepticism relating to cash transfers as 'welfarism'. Illustrating the impacts in terms of poverty reduction and economic and productive impacts across a variety of popular media enabled supporters within the government to challenge concerns about 'hand outs' and 'dependency' among the public and other sections of the government and win support for ongoing government expenditure in the

---

[3] This chapter was informed by an analysis of each of the national chapters included in this book, a review of presentations and the discussion of country experience at a regional workshop, and semi-structured interviews with both UNICEF staff working at country and regional levels, and national officials responsible for social protection policy and programme implementation in all but two of the countries discussed in the book (South Africa and Ethiopia), in order to triangulate the findings and explore differing perspectives.

sector. Across the studies it was reported that the evidence most valued by policy makers and other key targets comprised of the pieces which contributed to an understanding of social protection in terms of its effectiveness in reducing poverty, contribution to local economic growth, and affordability.

These evaluation findings were repeatedly used as a tool for advocacy, to promote the broad and, in some country contexts, emerging concept of social protection, and address the prevailing scepticism of many senior government officials and politicians, as well as the general public about its efficacy and desirability as a major policy instrument for addressing poverty. Examples of this are the impact ascribed to the '13% poverty reduction' message which emerged from the evaluation process in Kenya,[4] which was perceived as radically altering perceptions of the role of social protection in the development process among senior government officials, and the equally influential message that the cash transfer was 'affordable without undermining macro-economic stability' in Lesotho. Evidence from the evaluations was used to promote high level dialogue about the economic and social value of social protection, and in this way lent credibility to and strengthened the profile of the often relatively weak and capacity-constrained ministries responsible for social protection provision. This enabled them to strengthen their case with the stronger political actors controlling access to financial resources and political support, such as the Ministry of Finance and senior political institutions such as cabinet groupings. Such dominant political institutions which have *de jure* (or *de facto*) control over resource allocations were identified in all countries as key targets for policy advocacy. By influencing perceptions of the poverty reduction and economic benefits of social protection among senior policy makers, the evaluations had benefits which extended beyond the cash transfer programming which was their immediate subject.

However, while evaluation findings were found to be effective in promoting perceptions of impact and affordability and building political momentum for social protection generally, the evidence they provided was not in most cases perceived as the major driver of government decisions to scale up or increase financing, although they may in some instances have been major political *enablers* of such a scale-up, as in the case of Zambia. Scale-up, expansion, and domestic financing decisions were found to be primarily determined by political considerations which were independent of the evaluation process, and by considerations relating to the fiscal context, particularly in the wake of the financial crisis. This is illustrated by the case of Zimbabwe, where political decisions to scale up were not subsequently carried through as planned due to severe fiscal constraints and the reprioritization of the available resources. In Lesotho and Ethiopia-Tigray the decisions to expand provision and redesign

---

[4] See discussion in Chapter 6.

provision were taken independently of, and prior to, the completion of the evaluation process, but were influenced by intermediary evaluation products such as targeting analysis, and rapid assessment. The stance of other key actors, able to influence programme design through financing and other geopolitical incentives, such as the International Monetary Fund (IMF) and other development institutions, also played a significant role in influencing national policy choices, independently of evaluation findings.

2.4.2 Changing the Narrative: Social Protection as an Investment, Not a Cost

Research findings, both IE results and also accompanying costing analyses, were found to be influential in terms of promoting perceptions of 'affordability'—which are informed by not only an understanding of costs, but also perceptions of whether social protection is a worthwhile investment. In several countries, the translation of impact evidence and costing analysis into a clear and accessible message that cash transfers are 'affordable' and represent an investment with economically beneficial outcomes, rather than just a cost, played a key role in promoting the perception of affordability and hence political support from those concerned with the fiscal implications of provision. This has been particularly relevant in the wake of the financial crisis of 2008–9 (Ortiz and Cummins 2013), a situation exacerbated in some contexts by donor aid freezes due to political impropriety (as, for example, in the case of Malawi), which has resulted in many governments in the region experiencing significant fiscal contraction, representing a potential barrier to increased expenditure in the social protection sector.

In addition to identifying positive impacts in terms of social indicators, evidence from productive and economic indicators, including the Local Economy-wide Impact Evaluation (LEWIE) model (see Chapter 5), highlighted the potential of social protection to generate economic multiplier effects, and set out the potential impact of cash transfers on local economic development. This evidence appealed to key policy actors concerned with the need to stimulate economic growth, who may otherwise not have supported ongoing funding allocations to the sector. The LEWIE findings were well received at highest levels of government in Lesotho, Zambia, and Ghana. While the LEWIE indicators are based on models and provide simulated, rather than actual, impacts, effective framing of the findings helped to generate support for the sector, by reinforcing the argument that a cash transfer intervention could have benefits beyond the immediate beneficiaries and was therefore an appropriate policy choice in contexts where discourses around productivity, growth, and household graduation out of poverty were of primary importance.

2.4.3 Programme Design and Operational Modalities

The evaluations provided a range of programme design and operational recommendations, relating to targeting, access, the regularity and frequency of transfers, transfer size, delivery mechanisms, and the role of complementary activities. Some design elements which adversely affected performance were identified in the baseline studies, most notably insufficient transfer values and high exclusion rates. Insights relating to poverty targeting (with programmes being found to be well or poorly targeted) were also identified, with the presentation of the findings creating an opportunity for reflection on programme design. Operational evaluations also highlighted implementation issues and provided insights into ways to improve programme performance which resulted in some operational adjustments.

Specific design and operational changes were made to programmes in Kenya, South Africa, Lesotho, and Ghana following presentation of the evaluation findings. Evidence relating to the performance of the Proxy Means Test (PMT) in Kenya resulted in the adjustment of the formula adopted in order to better accommodate regional and livelihood diversity and hence reduce the exclusion errors identified in the evaluations. In South Africa, the review of targeting and effective reach of the programme led to increased awareness of the administrative barriers that prevent access to services by eligible families, and a thorough revision was carried out to address these barriers. In Ghana, the operational evaluation revealed that payment irregularity prevented families from smoothing consumption, and as a result a concerted effort was made for the LEAP (Ghanaian Livelihood Empowerment Against Poverty Program) programme to receive regular funding to prevent irregularities in future payments. In Lesotho, the recommendations of the rapid assessment led to a revision of the transfer size, changing from a flat rate to one that varied in line with household size, the creation of a complaint and case management structure to ensure effective implementation of the programmes, and a comprehensive review of the targeting system.

However, findings were not always automatically translated into design changes, in many instances due to competing priorities. For example, despite evaluation recommendations indicating the need to increase transfer values in order to enhance programme impact in Kenya and Malawi, resources were used to extend coverage rather than significantly increase transfer values or link them to inflation. In the case of Kenya, the decision was taken not to address the challenge represented by the use of a uniform family transfer value irrespective of family size, identified in the evaluation as inequitable and problematic, as this would have diverted resources from programme expansion. Likewise findings endorsing the effectiveness of the targeting mechanisms adopted in the cash transfer programmes in Zambia and Kenya failed to prevent ongoing criticism regarding the 'fairness of targeting' and subsequent programme redesign which was inconsistent with the evaluation recommendations (in terms of targeting criteria and processes), a decision informed by political, rather than evidential considerations.

2.4.4 Influence Beyond National Processes: Contribution to Regional Agendas

The examples in Sections 2.4.1 to 2.4.3 demonstrate ways in which the learning and research products developed under the IE framework, influenced and/or contributed to shape key national policy and operational processes. There are also indications that the body of evidence in aggregate has contributed to shape regional processes and sectoral debates.

The critical mass of evidence from multiple programmes has contributed to shape the discourse on social protection at regional level. For instance, the Government of South Africa and the African Union Commission, in collaboration with UNICEF, led the *African Union Expert Consultation on Children and Social Protection Systems*, which took place in Cape Town in April 2014. The consultation gathered government delegates from over forty countries across the continent. Evidence on impacts as well as lessons learned from programme implementation and financing were presented by and discussed among government delegates, including representatives from social development and welfare ministries, as well as finance, planning, and other related ministries.

A key result of this gathering was a set of recommendations which fed into the Ministerial Declaration of the 2014 Fourth Session of the African Union Ministers of Social Development (CAMDS4), and of the 2015 First Session of the Specialized Technical Committee on Social Development, Labour and Employment (STC-SDLE-1). The African Union has recognized social protection as an important component for the continent's social development, as reflected in the 2008 Africa Union (AU) Social Policy Framework as well as in other declarations.[5] However, raising the profile and ownership of this evidence, coupled with strong political will and championship of key leaders, such as the Government of South Africa, contributed to further specific commitments around expansion of coverage, a minimum package of social protection for all, as well as financing (and ring fencing) national allocations to

---

[5] For example, the 2004 Ouagadougou Declaration and Plan of Action on Employment and Poverty Alleviation in Africa acknowledged the need for increased coverage and enhanced effectiveness of social protection as a response to chronic poverty; the 2006 Livingstone Accords further recognized social protection as a human right, and also included specific government commitments to social protection.

social protection. The strategic combination of strong evidence, a growing momentum around social protection, strong political will from key actors, and taking advantage of critical regional entry points has progressively contributed to prioritize social protection in AU discussions.

Another example relates to the impact of evidence coming from Kenya and South Africa on adolescent well-being and HIV risk. As stated earlier, many cash transfer programmes in Eastern and Southern Africa—Zimbabwe, Malawi, Kenya, and Lesotho for example—were initiated with donor support as responses to the negative impacts of the HIV and AIDS pandemic on orphan and vulnerable children, drawing on new HIV-related funding sources in the early 1990s. New evidence from the IEs of the Child Support Grant in South Africa and the Kenya CT-OVC (Cash Transfer Programme for Orphans and Vulnerable Children) programme, showed that in addition to mitigation, social cash transfers contributed to addressing the economic drivers of HIV risk among adolescents—yielding results in terms of delayed sexual debut, pregnancy, inter-generational sex, and other related risky behaviours.[6] The evidence on mitigation has been strengthened by the emerging evidence around impacts on HIV prevention and thus contributed to enhance the case for social protection as a critical component of an integrated HIV/AIDS response. For example, the recently launched DREAMS (Determined, Resilient, AIDS-free, Mentored, and Safe) initiative (part of the United States President's Emergency Plan for AIDS Relief, or PEPFAR), which supports evidence-based and scalable interventions to reduce new infections among adolescent girls, includes social protection as a component of the core package of interventions. The emerging evidence on social protection and adolescent well-being has also been presented and discussed in key global and regional HIV/AIDS forums.[7]

Similarly, there has been a growing discussion of the role of social protection as a key component of productive inclusion and sustainable rural development. For example, the evidence generated by the PtoP project has been discussed at the 2014 consultative workshop on *Strengthening Coherence Between Agriculture and Social Protection*, which took place in Cape Town, gathering government delegates from Ministries of Agriculture of over ten countries, as well as experts from social protection and agriculture. The

---

[6] UNICEF and EPRI. (2015) Social Protection Programmes Contribute to HIV Prevention. Available at: <https://transfer.cpc.unc.edu/wp-content/uploads/2015/09/SocialProtectionHIVBrief_Jan2015.pdf> (accessed on 20 November 2015).

[7] For example, including the Thematic Segment on Addressing social and economic drivers of HIV through social protection at the thirty-fourth Meeting of the UNAIDS Programme Coordinating Board (PCB), July 2014, as well as the Inter-Agency Task Team on Social Protection Care and Support Research Meeting on Social Drivers and Structural Interventions, January 2015. A key outcome is the agreement of action points from the PCB, which will be a critical input to the ongoing revision of the UNAIDS (Joint United Nations Programme on HIV/AIDS) strategy.

participants discussed the linkages between social protection and agriculture and the role a combined and comprehensive approach can play in promoting a sustainable move out of poverty for poorest rural populations. Moreover, the evidence on the linkages between social protection and agriculture was discussed during a series of technical meetings on food security, nutrition, and rural development.[8]

The results from the PtoP project as well as the broader outcomes were presented on numerous occasions to the Africa Community of Practice on cash transfer programmes, which is facilitated by the World Bank and UNICEF. This Community of Practice brings together on a regular basis the implementers of government-run cash transfer programmes from thirty-two countries in the region. The economic and productive results have been critical in addressing key concerns regarding the importance of supporting the livelihoods of cash transfer beneficiaries, and thus have been helpful in facilitating discussions on how to improve implementation of cash transfer programmes to foster productive inclusion, including the design of potential complementary interventions.

2.5 FACTORS THAT SHAPE THE EXTENT AND NATURE OF THE INFLUENCE OF IES

Drawing on interviews and the country chapters, this section explores the key factors which shaped the role and relevance of evaluative research in influencing policy and programme changes. A number of factors were identified as having a positive effect on the influence of the evidence: (i) evaluations being embedded in national policy processes; (ii) relationship-building and multi-disciplinary research teams;(iii) messaging and packaging of evidence; (iv) the relationship between demand and supply of evidence; and (v) the creation of a regional learning agenda, including the establishment of a regional community of practice.

2.5.1 Evaluations as Part of National Policy Processes

As described in Sections 2.3 and 2.4, the evaluative research developed in each country under the umbrella of an IE framework was not envisioned or implemented as a stand-alone process. It was one component of ongoing

---

[8] For example, including the Renewed Partnership for Ending Hunger in Africa, which influenced the final recommendations approved by the High Level Forum and included in the 2014 Malabo Declaration.

national processes, with the potential to contribute to policy decisions. Although the initial motivation to develop a rigorous IE process often came from development partners and donors, responding to their specific organizational requirements,[9] these were adopted by government partners and used as strategic tools to promote sector credibility, build political momentum, and address specific questions and concerns around different aspects of the programme. The IEs were embedded in national policy processes, involving international experts and researchers, government counterparts, and national research institutions to ensure policy-relevant evaluation design and promote the use of results to inform policy and programme development. In this way close interaction between different stakeholders promoted the development of strong trust relationships and, most importantly, national ownership of the process and end-results.

In addition to addressing programme-specific objectives, the active involvement of policy makers in evaluation design allowed for the inclusion of particular questions that were critical to shed light on potential cash transfer impacts (such as the potential role of cash transfers to reduce violence in Zimbabwe) or to enable specific pieces of analysis at key moments. One example is the use of baseline data in Ghana to provide insights into programme performance in terms of exclusion errors and the value of the transfer at a key moment in the programme redesign process. One of the challenges associated with IEs—the long-term nature of the evaluation process versus the need for timely evidence to contribute to particular political processes—was addressed by producing timely analytical pieces of work based on rapid assessments and qualitative fieldwork, the simulation of local economy impacts, targeting analyses, and costing and affordability assessments using baseline data, which were deployed at critical points in time prior to the completion of the full evaluation, as discussed in the Lesotho case in Chapter 11. In Zimbabwe, the targeting analysis using baseline evaluation data combined with data from the Management Information System (MIS), was crucial in building confidence among the development partners that leakage rates were acceptable and that the programme's targeting was robust. This study also fed into an immediate decision to improve the targeting performance by adjusting the poverty cut-off score.

As much as these intermediate pieces were instrumental for policy makers, they were also useful for donors and partners in instances where they needed evidence to support the case for key changes in programme design. One example is the question of the transfer size in Malawi, where UNICEF and partners modelled different transfer sizes in terms of their impact, and used the results to make the case for an increase in transfer values in the context of a

---

[9] See, for example, the case of Kenya, Lesotho, and Ethiopia-Tigray, among others.

planned programme expansion. Another is the use of the LEWIE simulations on programme impact on the local economy in Zimbabwe, to make a case to the Ministry of Finance regarding the potential impact of the Harmonized Social Cash Transfer Programme (HSCT) and the need to ring-fence programme investments in a context of severe budget constraints. The availability and effective use of this analysis contributed to the Ministry of Finance's decision to double the allocation to the HSCT in the subsequent fiscal year, although the full allocation was not subsequently realized.

2.5.2 Relationship Building

Some elements of the process are implicit and not always formally reported in evaluation reports, including trust and relationship-building between the researchers and government counterparts. Embedding the learning and research agenda into national processes, as well as including both international and national members in the research teams, contributed to developing a strong sense of trust. In this way the evaluations were not stand-alone academic exercises, but an integral component of ongoing national policy processes which addressed national demands for evidence, as well as contributing to an evidence-based policy making culture at national and regional levels. This commitment to rigour was strengthened by the fact that the evaluations were used not only as 'proofs of concept', but also to provide evidence with the potential to shape national programmes reaching poor and vulnerable families.

Governmental research questions tended to take priority over more academic or global public good research questions. For this reason, research questions which were innovative from an academic standpoint were not always included where they were not perceived as central to governmental partners. This approach offered benefits in terms of national ownership, credibility, operational relevance, and quick wins in terms of gains in programmes' operational effectiveness. It also contributed to building momentum around scale-up, expansion, and fiscal commitment to social protection. In part because the evaluations were embedded in national processes, rather than stand-alone research pieces, they stimulated and became part of broader national learning agendas around social protection and cash transfers. These learning agendas encompassed not only the rigorous design and execution of quantitative and qualitative IEs, but also a series of other evaluative pieces of work, including targeting assessments, operational/process evaluations, LEWIE simulations, rapid assessments, and costing studies. Moreover, the IEs were used not simply to provide results at the end of the evaluation, but as processes for ongoing engagement, with analysis done using baseline data playing an important role in a number of countries in terms of leading to revisions in programme design and implementation. In this way the series of evaluative research and learning products which formed the Transfer Project agenda generated momentum for political and popular support and credibility for the sector as a whole, defended against possible fiscal challenges, and in some cases promoted specific evidence-based policy and design changes.

The ability to link the various evaluative studies to national learning agendas and policy processes was facilitated by the flexibility of the IE research teams, and their accessibility throughout the evaluation process. While some countries had a clear overall research plan from the outset, in most the research agenda evolved over time. The existence of research teams which included national and international quantitative and qualitative researchers from different disciplines alongside more operational and policy-oriented researchers in ongoing dialogue with national stakeholders meant that as the research agenda evolved, the teams could produce responsive research and analysis on specific issues arising. In some cases, these were stand-alone pieces, but often they drew upon other ongoing research, making use of baseline quantitative and qualitative data. Together, the responsiveness of multidisciplinary teams and prioritization of national government needs contributed to the strong sense of trust.

2.5.3 Messaging and Packaging of Evidence

Another factor which contributed to the extent to which evaluation evidence influenced policy and design was the way in which it was used. There were several dimensions to this related to the way messages were framed and presented, and the media through which they were communicated. Packaging of the evidence into products that were easily accessible to policy makers and programme implementers, such as policy briefs, direct presentations, and fact sheets using simple graphs and key messages, was central to this. For example, the impacts of the LEAP programme in Ghana were presented in a series of policy briefs produced by the Government of Ghana, with UNICEF support, and released under the government brand. The economic and productive impacts were illustrated in a series of accompanying briefs, as well as an advocacy video which was disseminated in national as well as regional forums, including the African Union Expert Consultation on children and social protection systems.

Timing was also important, and having information in the appropriate format, ready to feed into the debate at key policy moments, described as 'policy windows' (Kingdon 1984)—the right information at the right time—was central to participating opportunistically in the policy process. Also important was the ability to feed relevant evidence into the hands of social protection and cash transfer programme champions and others with access to decisions-makers at strategic moments in the process. For instance, in Zambia a strong emphasis on the poverty impact of cash transfers was placed at the centre of the official discourse that accompanied a highly political decision around the removal of fuel and maize subsidies and the subsequent scale-up of the national cash transfer programme. The timely use of information and the development of specific briefs and messages helped to address general concerns about dependency and inefficiency of welfare investments. The availability of the Child Grant evaluation findings and its multi-dimensional scope—looking at poverty, social, as well as economic impacts—helped to develop a specific policy brief on poverty impacts with a clear advocacy message on the effectiveness of the Social Cash Transfer programme for poverty reduction. As discussed in detail in Chapter 9, this message resonated due to relevant timing: providing insights at a moment in time where political will, political decisions, and a newly created policy framework on social protection created an environment where cash transfers had become a plausible policy option and investment.

As the Zambia example illustrates, the timing of major policy decisions was driven in many cases by political expediency linked to a range of political considerations, and the relevance and influence of evaluation findings is to a large extent determined by the point in the policy cycle at which they are delivered. This is hard to predict and accommodate within the funding and operational cycles of large donor institutions financing evaluation activities. Use of modelling approaches and analysis of baseline studies prior to the completion of the formal evaluation enabled some flexibility to produce timely inputs, as in the case of the Ghana process. Notwithstanding this flexibility, the potential impacts of the evaluation in Tigray, Lesotho, and Zimbabwe, for example, were significantly reduced due to the fact that major policy decisions were taken prior to the research findings being made available.

2.5.4 Relationship Between Demand and Supply of Evidence

A common theme across the case studies is the relationship between the political appetite for research-based inputs, and the level of influence that evaluations can yield, confirming that research impact is a matter of both supply *and* demand. The demand was primarily for domestic rather than regional or international evidence, and external evidence was not identified as an adequate substitute for domestically derived evidence in terms of effective policy influencing.

The types of evidence which generated most interest among policy makers were those that met their own needs by addressing concerns about the cost, impact, and feasibility of provision. The most influential findings were reported to be those linked to the growth agenda which indicated the economic and productive impacts of social protection, and which modelled potential economic multipliers. Cost modelling was also perceived to be highly influential, particularly with Ministries of Finance. These types of evidence directly addressed real political concerns which were potential barriers to ongoing political support, and were used by policy champions to build support for the broader social protection agenda.

2.5.5 Regional Learning Agenda: The Value Added of the Transfer Project

One further factor that shaped the contribution of the IE processes was the regional agenda and community of practice which evolved around national-level processes. Although in each country there were different contextual realities and elements that shaped the emergence and implementation of the evaluation process, there was a common thread in terms of the multi-disciplinary and multi-sector composition of the research teams under the umbrella of the Transfer Project. UNICEF, FAO, UNC, and Save the Children UK were common actors in almost all of the national processes described in this book, and this commonality contributed to the development of a regional learning culture, together with informal and formal mechanisms that promoted information exchange. Annual Transfer Project-supported workshops—where the design and findings of IEs (and other related research) were discussed among a range of researchers, programme implementers, and policy makers—provided the space for information and experience exchange as well as opportunities to raise awareness among policy makers and donors of the role of social protection in relation to a broad range of impacts and benefits.

2.6 EXTERNAL FACTORS INFLUENCING THE DEVELOPMENT OF THE SOCIAL PROTECTION SECTOR AND THE ROLE OF EVALUATION FINDINGS

While the factors outlined in Sections 2.5.1 to 2.5.5 have contributed to the influence of the evaluation process on policy and programming, a number of factors external to the evaluation process also play a strong role in influencing policy and programmatic change or condition the role that evidence plays in policy discussions. The relationship between the evidence and policy/programme change was not found to be linear, and there were a number of critical external factors which determined changes. These included trade-offs between evaluation recommendations and policy agendas, particularly in relation to programme design or scale-up choices, the influence of external actors, and financial or other capacity constraints.

2.6.1 National Political Drivers and Trade-Offs

National political considerations are critical to policy selection and design choices. Detailed evidence relating to policy design choices may be less effective when it is not readily compatible with broader political incentives, resulting in potential trade-offs between evaluation recommendations and policy preferences. This issue may be illustrated in terms of recommendations emerging from IEs in several countries to increase the transfer level substantially and link the transfer value to household size in order to ensure the significance of impacts at household level, and recommendations to extend coverage either geographically or in terms of the proportion of the population covered in any one area. These options all require additional financial resources and in a context of limited resources, the trade-offs between these options were found in some cases to be driven by financial and political rather than technical considerations. In Kenya, Ghana, and Malawi for example, decisions were made to prioritize the expansion of geographic coverage at the expense of evaluation recommendations to increase the transfer value significantly. In Kenya the choice to prioritize increased coverage over transfer value was driven by considerations related to a combination of equity concerns and the political requirement to maintain strategic parliamentary, geopolitical, and community support bases, and similarly in Ghana and Malawi the decision to extend provision across the country was driven by a political imperative to distribute resources evenly between administrative units, rather than the geographical distribution of poverty. The risk of a politicization of the transfer if it were not extended nationally was considered to outweigh the risk of inadequate transfer levels in terms of anticipated social and economic benefits at household level. In this way evidence relating to performance was not always sufficient to counter broader political concerns.

The fact that coverage was becoming an electorally relevant issue was identified as a key driver of policy development in Kenya, Lesotho, and South Africa. Whether such political relevance results in effective programming outcomes was found to be dependent on the extent to which the political process ensured accountability to popular manifesto promises (for example in Zambia), and the degree to which political stability could be ensured (a significant challenge in Malawi).

2.6.2 Influence of Development Partners

Analysis of evaluation impacts also indicated that evidence on design choices may in some cases be secondary to the policy preferences of not only national governmental actors, but also international development institutions (IDIs).

Political incentives to respond to the preferences of such institutions with significant fiscal or geopolitical power were found to dominate evidence findings in terms of programme design choices. In this way the orientation of key donors can either enhance or reduce the likelihood of evidence and recommendations being taken up.

In several countries including Ghana and Lesotho, the support of the IMF was noted as a key factor in promoting high level government endorsement for social protection financing, with ring-fencing of government expenditure in the sector being a condition of ongoing support. In some instances this process was reportedly driven in part by a concern to promote targeted social protection as a form of compensation or stabilizer in the context of subsidy reductions and tax increases as part of overall deficit reduction packages, examples being Kenya, Zambia, and Ghana. This endorsement of spending in the sector overall was associated with the promotion of particular design options (notably stricter targeting criteria in the case of Malawi) which were in tension with the evaluation recommendations, and ultimately determined government policy design decisions. This example illustrates how the stance of key institutions with the ability to influence programme design, through a range of financial or other geopolitical incentives, can also play a role in influencing national policy choices, independently of evaluation findings. Likewise World Bank- and International Labour Organization- (ILO)-supported initiatives promoting the harmonization and rationalization of cash transfer provision were perceived as key drivers of national policy change in Zambia and Ghana.

2.6.3 Capacity and Resource Constraints

Overall, fiscal constraints were found to be one of the major factors inhibiting the take-up of design revision recommendations relating to expanded provision or increased transfer values.

In Ghana, for example, the evaluation highlighted the need to increase the transfer value and extend provision beyond the poorest 10 per cent, highlighting the way that design shortcomings were limiting impact, but no commensurate additional resources were available to enable these insights to be addressed adequately through policy change, with the government preferring to continue geographical expansion of coverage, at the expense of increased transfer values. Similarly in Zimbabwe, fiscal constraints meant that the government was unable to contribute its intended share of the cash transfer budget for several years, and as such making programming improvements with increased budget implications based on evaluation findings would represent a significant fiscal challenge.

Insufficient human and administrative capacity to implement recommendations was also identified as a constraint. While recommendations were recognized as relevant, in the context of the significant challenges of ongoing programme delivery, not all were seen as being feasible without major investment in staffing and capacity building, as in the case of Malawi.

2.7 CONCLUSION

This chapter has reflected upon the influence of evaluation evidence on decision making processes on country (and to some extent also regional) policy agendas. The review of the country chapters presented in the book and a series of consultation of key actors of evaluation processes has shed some light on this. The findings of the analysis are consistent with the literature review: evidence is one component within a wider set of factors, and its influence on policy, design, and implementation outcomes is subject to a range of conditioning factors, rather than just the empirical findings of the research itself. These relate to the nature of the research, in terms of its perceived credibility, and the extent of identification between the policy maker and evidence generation process, the articulation and framing of the evidence, and its linkage to existing policy challenges, the advocacy process by which it is introduced into the debate, and finally the contextual factors, which have a significant impact on mediating outcomes, notably fiscal and ideological preferences and political expediency.

The review of the experience of the eight countries discussed in this book has shown that the evaluation process has had a clear influence over a number of dimensions of the policy process. Most importantly, the evaluation processes and their rigour have helped build the overall credibility of an emerging social protection sector. They have strengthened the case for social protection as an *investment*, not just a cost, and have addressed public perceptions and misconceptions. The evaluations supported learning around programme design and implementation which led to concrete programme improvements in key areas such as targeting, access, transfer size, and the role of complementary activities. Finally, the evaluations have shaped policy discussions beyond the national context, informing regional social protection agendas.

The recognition of the role of social protection has increased across the region. This has corresponded at country level with expansion in the coverage of programmes, promotion of harmonization to enhance impact and efficiency of programmes, as well as a growing trend of increased allocation of national resources to social protection. This momentum is not a direct result of evidence, but credible, timely, well-communicated and nationally embraced evidence has been a critical piece of the puzzle, which together with political decision and national champions has contributed to shape and strengthen this prioritization.

Four key lessons learned have emerged from this analysis and process. First, different methodologies and approaches should be combined in the development of a learning agenda. While the rigour of the evaluations provided impact evidence which promoted sectoral credibility, the case studies suggest that quantitative survey-based impact findings are not always necessary to inform policy and design debates, with modelling and rapid qualitative and quantitative baseline studies playing a key role and being amenable to timing and effective framing and clear policy messages. Second, approaches such as the LEWIE model have the appeal of being easy to understand. However, it is important to recognize that simulation techniques have limitations like other evaluation methodologies. Third, different types of evaluation techniques and approaches generate evidence which has different purposes and targets, and can be best used at different points in the policy cycle. Fourth, it is important to examine and understand in more depth the ways in which data is produced and used, and for what. This may allow a better understanding of which evaluation techniques are best suited to particular contexts and needs.

REFERENCES

Beynon, P., Chapoy, C., Gaarder, M., and Masset, E. (2012). 'What Difference Does a Policy Brief Make?' Full report of an IDS, 3ie, NORAD study. Brighton: Institute of Development Studies and the International Initiative for Impact Evaluation (3ie).

Davies, H., Nutley, S. M., and Walter, I. (2005). 'Approaches to Assessing Research Impact'. Report of the ESRC symposium on assessing the non-academic impacts of research, 12–13 May 2005. University of St Andrews: Research Unit for Research Utilisation.

Earl, S, Carden, F., and Smutylo, T. (2001). 'Outcome Mapping. Building learning and reflection into development programs'. Ottawa: International Development Research Centre (IDDRC).

Gadeberg, M. and Victor, M. (2011). 'Can Research Influence Policy?' CGIAR Challenge Program on Water and Food. Presented at the Mekong Forum on Water, Food and Energy, Phnom Penh, Cambodia, 7–9 December. Available online at: <http://www.slideshare.net/CPWFMekong/can-research-influence-policy> (accessed July 2014).

Keck, M. E. and Sikkink, K. (1998). *Activists Beyond Borders: Advocacy Networks in International Politics*. Ithaca, NY: Cornell University Press.

Kingdon, J. W. (1984). *Agendas, Alternatives, and Public Policies*. New York: Harpers Collins.

Ortiz, I. and Cummins, M. (2013). 'The Age of Austerity—A Review of Public Expenditures and Adjustment Measures in 181 Countries'. Initiative for Policy Dialogue and the South Centre, Working Paper, March. New York: Initiative for Policy Dialogue. Available at: <http://policydialogue.org/files/publications/Age_of_Austerity_Ortiz_and_Cummins.pdf> (accessed July 2014).

Overseas Development Institute (ODI) (2014). *ROMA (Rapid Outcome Mapping Approach): A Guide to Policy Engagement and Influence*. Available online at: <http://www.roma.odi.org/introduction.html> (accessed June 2014).

Pellini, A., Thao, V. P., and Hoang, N. L. (2011). 'Assessment of the Delivery of the Vietnam Development Report 2010—Modern Institutions and Its Impact on Policy Debates around Institutional Reforms in Vietnam'. London: Overseas Development Institute. Available online at: <http://documents.worldbank.org/curated/en/2011/07/16280472/assessment-delivery-vietnam-development-report-2010-modernbrinstitutions-impact-policy-debates-around-institutional-reforms-vietnam-final-report> (accessed July 2014).

Start, D. and Hovland, I. (2004). *Tools for Policy Impact. A Handbook for Researchers*. London: Overseas Development Institute.

Walt, G. (1994). 'How far does research influence policy?' *European Journal of Public Health*, 4: 233–5.

Young, J. (2008). 'Working with complexity: Impact of research on policy and practice'. *Capacity.org*, Issue 35 (December). Available online at: <http://r4d.dfid.gov.uk/PDF/Articles/YoungImpactofResearch.pdf> (accessed 23 October 2015).

3

Implementing Rigorous Evaluations in the Real World

The Quantitative Approach to Evaluation Design in the Transfer Project

Benjamin Davis (FAO) and Sudhanshu Handa (University of North Carolina at Chapel Hill and UNICEF)

3.1 INTRODUCTION

A key feature of the Transfer Project/From Protection to Production (PtoP) project is the focus on evaluating government programmes that are fully integrated into national ministries and associated budget and administrative systems. This has two crucial implications for the design and implementation of impact evaluations (IEs). First, the design of the IE has to fit into the operational procedures and roll-out plan of the programme, and second, not all evaluation design parameters are fully under the control of the researchers. In many cases this implies threats to internal validity in evaluation design. On the other hand, some operational issues such as payment delays are part of the 'real world' of programme implementation and so arguably give a better, more realistic picture of the actual impact of a national programme. In some other cases, design features such as the level of transfer or the target group are the outcomes of a delicate political process. These parameters may not be the ones chosen by the researcher in full control of a pure field experiment, but impacts stemming from such designs have a degree of external validity that is typically the Achilles heel of pure experiments.

In this chapter we provide an overview of quantitative designs implemented in the case studies contained in the book, focusing on the inter-play between quantitative rigour on the one hand and political and operational constraints on the other. Beyond design, we also highlight some of the key approaches and innovations that have been implemented across the quantitative evaluations in terms of questionnaire design and research topics, particularly the comprehensive approach of integrating both productive and social dimensions of household activity and behaviour into the studies.

3.2 THE EVALUATION PROBLEM

The objective of an IE is to attribute an observed impact to the programme intervention. Identifying the counterfactual is the organizing principle of an IE—that is, it tells us what would have happened to the beneficiaries if they had not received the intervention. Since one cannot observe the outcome of a household had they not been a beneficiary, an IE is essentially a missing data problem, and entails identifying the best possible counterfactual, a group of non-beneficiaries who are representative of the group of participants with one key difference: the control households did not receive the intervention. If the two groups are dissimilar in other dimensions, the outcomes of non-beneficiaries may differ systematically from what the outcomes of participants would have been without the programme, resulting in bias in the estimated impacts. This bias may derive from differences in observable characteristics between beneficiaries and non-beneficiaries (e.g., location, demographic composition, access to infrastructure, wealth, etc.) or unobservable characteristics (e.g., natural ability, willingness to work, etc.). Some observable and unobservable characteristics do not vary with time (such as natural ability), while others may vary (such as skills). Furthermore, the existence of unobservable characteristics correlated with both the outcome of interest and the programme intervention can result in additional bias (i.e., omitted variables).

The most direct way of ensuring a comparable control group is via an experimental design (a randomized control trial—RCT—or social experiment), in which eligible households are randomly assigned to control and treatment groups. This guarantees that receiving treatment is uncorrelated with other (observable and unobservable) variables, and as a result the potential outcomes will be statistically independent of treatment status.[1] On average the groups will be identical, except that only one of them receives the cash transfers. In other words, we can be certain that the observed impacts are indeed the result of participating in the programme, and not some other factor. See Annex 3.1 for a formal treatment of the counterfactual problem.

Experimental designs are often difficult to implement in practice, however, for political, ethical, institutional and/or logistical reasons, particularly when programmes are owned by national governments (as opposed to researchers). Non-experimental design methods are often used when a randomized experiment is not possible or when the experimental design fails to achieve a good balance among treatment and control groups, which can occur due to chance or when, for example, the number of units of randomization is relatively small.

---

[1] The validity of experimental estimators relies on the assumption that the control group units are not affected by the programme. However, control households may be affected through market interactions, and informal transactions and risk-sharing (also known as non-market interactions).

In non-experimental studies one has to invoke some identifying assumptions to solve the selection problem. The same is also true when differences between treatment and control groups at baseline emerge despite randomization. More systematic differences at baseline between treatment and control groups require econometric techniques to create a better counterfactual by removing pre-existing significant differences in key variables. A wide variety of non-experimental approaches exist in the literature, the most common of which are propensity score matching (PSM) methods. The non-experimental studies employ a variety of PSM methods in order to simulate the conditions of an experiment in which recipients and non-recipients are randomly assigned, allowing for the identification of a causal link between treatment and outcome variables.[2]

All studies except South Africa involved longitudinal data with a baseline and at least one follow-up. In an experimental setting simple mean comparisons can cleanly identify treatment impacts, but in a social experiment, when moving from outside the laboratory to the real world, impact estimates can be improved significantly by covariate adjustment in a multivariate regression framework to increase power (Bruhn and McKenzie 2009), and by employing a difference-in-differences (DD) approach to account for any baseline differences that occur due to sampling error, or chance (Wooldridge 2002). When there are differences between treatment and control groups at the baseline, the DD estimator with conditioning variables has the advantage of minimizing the standard errors as long as the effects are unrelated to the treatment and are constant over time (Wooldridge 2002).

Indeed all the studies in this volume use multivariate regression to account for observed differences and other important predictors of outcomes, and all studies (except in South Africa) use the DD methodology to wipe away any baseline differences. South Africa uses retrospective questions and variation in the duration of treatment to 'recover' DD estimators. Baseline differences turn out to be particularly important in the non-experimental studies in Ghana and Ethiopia, as well as for some individual indicators in the social experiments in Zambia, Kenya, and Malawi. In Ghana, given the non-experimental nature of the design, internal validity was strengthened by using household fixed effects models to estimate impact. Both the DD (which compares group level means) and the DD with fixed effects assume 'parallel trends', that is, that other factors at the community or regional level behave the same way across the two study arms. The parallel trends assumption is potentially most problematic in Zimbabwe and Ghana, where comparison households come from different districts than that of treatment households. No systematic attempt has been made in the project to test the parallel trends assumption; this is theoretically

---

[2] Please see Asfaw et al. (2012) for a formal treatment of propensity score matching methods in the context of these evaluations.

Table 3.1. Core Evaluation Designs

Country	Design	Level of randomization or matching	N	Ineligibles sampled?
Ethiopia	Propensity Score Matching (PSM and IPW)	Household level within a village	3351	Yes
Ghana	Propensity Score Matching (IPW)	Household and Region	1504	No
Kenya	Social experiment with PSM and IPW	Location	1811	No
Lesotho	Social experiment	Electoral District	2150	Yes
Malawi	Social experiment	Village Cluster	3369	Baseline only
Malawi (Mchinji pilot)	Social experiment	Village Cluster	766	No
South Africa	Propensity Score Matching	Households	2964	No
Zambia (CG model)	Social experiment	Community Welfare Assistance Committee	2519	No
Zambia (MCTG model)	Social experiment	Community Welfare Assistance Committee	3077	No
Zimbabwe	Matched case-control	District and wards	2630	Baseline only

All studies are longitudinal with a baseline and at least one post-intervention follow-up except for South Africa. N refers to households sampled at follow-up.

possible in studies that have more than two waves of data (Kenya, Zambia, Malawi, and Zimbabwe).

Table 3.1 shows the range of study designs implemented in the evaluations reported in this book. Given the challenges facing 'real-world' programmes in implementing rigorous IEs, the approach in the Transfer Project has been to sensitize governments and development partners to the key requirements of a rigorous evaluation, and the potential benefit of a credible design that can attribute impacts to the programme and not be questioned by other stakeholders and the general public. Raising awareness and building capacity around evaluation science (the need for a comparison group), coupled with the sensitivity of the evaluation team to not infringe heavily on programme operating structures, generated a trust that ultimately led to a set of extremely high quality IEs. Table 3.1 shows that four of the seven evaluations were actual social experiments and highlights other features of the design that also enhanced rigour. In all cases a serious attempt was made to construct a credible comparison group—in no evaluation was the design a purely reflexive one (before and after with no comparison group) which can lead to biased estimates as factors beyond the programmes can cause changes in impact indicators over time. The level of rigour achieved by the IEs was not the same in all cases since in some cases non-experimental designs had to be implemented. In the next section we provide additional detail on the study design in each country, focusing on the key features of the programme and roll-out which ultimately influenced the final evaluation approach.

3.3 THE SOCIAL EXPERIMENTS: ZAMBIA, MALAWI, LESOTHO, AND KENYA

In 2010, Zambia's Ministry of Community Development and Social Services (MCDSS) began implementing the Child Grant (CG) model of the Social Cash Transfer programme (SCTP) in the three districts—Kalabo, Kaputa, and Shongombo—with the highest rates of mortality, morbidity, stunting, and wasting among children under five years of age.[3] All households in these three districts with a child under five years of age were eligible to receive benefits. The baseline was carried out in September–October 2010, with follow-ups in 2012 and 2013; the study was later extended for another year and an additional round of data was collected in 2014. A seminar on IE 'essentials' followed by that on evaluation design options were presented to district officers and their provincial and national counterparts in Lusaka in June 2010. A key point of discussion was both the necessity of a control group and how to identify a credible control group given the roll-out of the CG model. Given budget constraints, it was not possible to scale up the programme immediately in the three districts, allowing for the possibility that otherwise eligible households could serve as controls for the evaluation. Since scale-up could only occur over a three–four-year period, ministry officials agreed that the fairest way to decide who would receive the programme first was by lottery, opening up the door for an experimental design. Subsequently, the names of each community welfare assistance committee (CWAC) in the three programme districts were placed into an urn, and ministry officials took turns pulling names out of the urn—the first thirty in each district would enter the study and half would be randomly assigned to control status after the baseline data collection. The random assignment was done via a coin flip by the permanent secretary of the ministry in December 2010, and treatment households entered the programme in January 2011.

The second model of the SCT programme in Zambia—the Multiple Categorical Targeting Grant (MCTG) model—was implemented in the Luwingu district in Northern Province and Serenje district in Central Province, beginning in late 2011. This model targets poor female- and elderly-headed households with Orphans and Vulnerable Children (OVC) and households

---

[3] AIR (2013) provides a detailed description of the evaluation design.

with persons with a disability. For the evaluation of the MCTG model, an experimental design was utilized, similar to the process followed in the case of the CG model. Baseline data were collected in November–December, 2011, with the twenty-four-month and thirty-six-month follow-ups taking place in the same time period in 2013 and 2014.[4]

In Malawi, the discussion around the evaluation design of the SCTP was quite similar to that of Zambia.[5] In the Malawi case the programme was not new, but rather was entering a new phase of rapid expansion which allowed the possibility of using late entrants as controls for early entrants. The discussion with government officials, much like in Zambia, hinged around the key idea that the programme could not scale up immediately in the districts of Salima and Mangochi; indeed in Malawi a few districts had only partial coverage of the programme for several years. A key issue in Malawi, unlike in Zambia, was that the targeting process was very heavy, involving extensive community meetings and participation of the District Commissioner's Office. This made it potentially problematic (costly) to undertake beneficiary selection in areas that might later end up as control villages. Ultimately the discussion with government and development partners centred around the political costs of undertaking the targeting in villages that might end up as controls versus the benefit of a rigorous design that could provide unquestioned results to help scale up the programme. This led to an agreement on a social experiment for one year in the first instance, followed by a review to see if it was politically feasible to continue to hold controls out of the programme. Immediately following this decision, two traditional authorities (TAs) in each of the two districts were randomly selected to enter the study. The random selection was done by district and national officials in front of development partners and the evaluation team and documented. Within each TA, village clusters were also randomly sorted and a coin flip conducted at the District Commissioner's Office in each district determined whether the top or bottom half of the list would enter into the programme. In both Zambia and Malawi, all lotteries were conducted in a public setting by government staff and fully documented, after extensive consultation and agreement; final assignment to intervention or control status was done after baseline data collection.

An earlier IE of the SCTP was implemented in the pilot district of Mchinji.[6] While the IE predates the Transfer Project, the results from the study were influential in the early years of the Project. The evaluation was administered in eight Village Development Groups covering twenty-three villages, four of which were randomly selected to be part of the treatment group, and four to the control group. The evaluation had three rounds of data collection, with the baseline

---

[4] See AIR (2014) for a more detailed description of the evaluation design.
[5] See Handa et al. (2014a) for a detailed description of the evaluation design.
[6] See Miller, Tsoka, and Reichert (2008) for a more detailed description of the sample design.

survey in March 2007 just prior to the commencement of treatment, the midline survey in September 2007, and the endline survey in April 2008, after which the control group began receiving transfers. Total sample size at follow-up was 766 households. The relatively small sample size and few units of randomization, compared to the other evaluations that formed part of the Transfer Project, required particular attention at the moment of estimating impacts.[7]

The strategic decision-making around the social experiments in Lesotho and Kenya were similar to those in Zambia and Malawi. In each case, a sensitization was held to explain the importance of obtaining a credible control group for the evaluation's success. In each case, the programmes were new and just beginning to expand, and given both capacity and financial constraints, many otherwise eligible households in the first few years would simply not receive the programme. Randomization via lottery thus provided a transparent way for the government to choose where to initiate the programme, while at the same time allowing for a rigorous evaluation design.

The IE of the Lesotho Child Grant Programme (CGP) took place during the Phase 1-Round 2 expansion of the programme. Randomization occurred at the level of the electoral district (ED);[8] randomization was possible as a consequence of the programme not having enough resources to cover the total eligible population in the ten community councils spread across five districts (Qacha's Nek, Maseru, Leribe, Berea, and Mafeteng) included in the expansion. First, all ninety-six EDs in the ten community councils were paired based on a range of characteristics. Once these forty-eight pairs were constructed, forty pairs were randomly selected to be included in the evaluation survey. Within each selected ED, two villages (or clusters of villages) were randomly selected, and in every cluster a random sample of twenty households (ten potentially called to enrolment and ten potentially non-called to enrolment) were selected from the lists prepared during the targeting exercise. In treatment EDs the CGP implemented the same targeting process, selected recipients, and proceeded to enrolment. In control EDs the CGP implemented the targeting process and selected recipients who should receive the transfer, but enrolment was delayed until after the follow-up data collection was completed. After the baseline survey data were collected in all evaluation EDs in mid-2011, public meetings were organized where a lottery was held to assign each ED in each of the pairs (both sampled and non-sampled) to either treatment or control groups. Follow-up data were collected in mid-2013. A second, mini follow-up survey was carried out in mid-2014 to evaluate a kitchen garden intervention linked to the CGP in two community councils.[9]

---

[7] See Boone et al. (2013) for a discussion of the challenges with the sample design.
[8] See Pellerano et al. (2014) for a detailed description of the IE design.
[9] See Dewbre et al. (2015) for a description of this mini impact evaluation based on the original panel sample.

In Kenya, the CT-OVC (Cash Transfer for Orphans and Vulnerable Children) programme was scheduled to be expanded to seven new districts in 2007 but not all Locations within each district would be covered.[10] Given budget and capacity constraints, it was estimated that two Locations within each district could enter the programme. Within each district, four Locations were 'paired' to potentially enter the programme, and two were randomly selected to enter the programme immediately (and thus served as intervention sites) for a total of fourteen control and fourteen intervention Locations. A nuance in the Kenya evaluation was that the targeting of households was not fully conducted in control Locations due to resource constraints. First stage (community level) targeting was done in each Location, but the final priority list, based on the age of the household head, was only drawn up in treatment Locations, because budget constraints limited the number of households that could ultimately enter the programme. An analogous priority list was not created in control Locations, so that the final study sample was drawn from a slightly expanded list in control Locations, resulting in minor differences in characteristics, notably the age of the head, across the two study arms (Ward et al. 2010; Kenya CT-OVC Evaluation Team 2012). As the Kenya evaluation was the first Transfer Project study, this was an important lesson learned for future evaluations.

The original IE was designed as a twenty-four-month study, with baseline data collected in mid-2007 and follow-up data in mid-2009. The Carolina Population Center at the University of North Carolina at Chapel Hill conducted a second follow-up survey in 2011, with a special focus on understanding the impact of the programme on the successful transition of OVC into young adulthood. The 2011 survey included a special module on sexual activity, mental health, and peers, for young people aged 15–25, administered face-to-face. The main household survey was expanded to include more detailed information on economic activities, the who and where of cash transactions, fertility, and time preferences.

3.4 THE NON-EXPERIMENTS: ETHIOPIA, GHANA, SOUTH AFRICA, AND ZIMBABWE

In Zimbabwe, Ghana, South Africa, and Ethiopia evaluation designs were non-experimental rather than experimental. We describe these designs with

---

[10] See Ward et al. (2010) and Handa (2012) for detailed descriptions of different phases of the evaluation design.

a focus on the context that guided the strategic decisions around the evaluation approach and the most important threats to internal validity.

In Zimbabwe the evaluation of the Harmonized Social Cash Transfer Programme (HSCT) is a two-year, 2630-household longitudinal design, comparing cash transfer recipient households from sixty wards in three Phase 2 districts (Binga, Mwenzi, and Mudzi) to eligible households in thirty wards in three Phase 4 districts (Uzumba-Maramba-Pfungwe—UMP), Chiredzi, and Hwange) that are not scheduled to enter the programme until 2016.[11] The design is a district level matched case-control. The three treatment districts from Phase 2 were paired or matched with three comparison districts from Phase 4 based on agro-ecological conditions, level of development, and culture; in fact the comparison Phase 4 districts are adjacent to the intervention districts. The Ministry of Public Service, Labour, and Social Welfare (MPSLSW), with support and oversight from United Nations Children Fund (UNICEF) and the evaluation team, randomly selected sixty wards from the three treatment districts to enter the study. The evaluation team then worked with the Ministry to select thirty wards from the comparison districts that were similar to the selected wards from the treatment districts. Wards were selected by similarity of geography, climate, overall development level, availability of services, access to other development programmes, and culture, with an emphasis on making sure that the agro-ecological environment of the treatment wards were similar to that of the comparison wards. Subsequently, the Ministry conducted targeting in the Phase 2 districts and the forty-five wards only in the Phase 4 districts to identify eligible households. Targeting was conducted in exactly the same way in both the treatment and the comparison wards to create equivalent and comparable groups. In this sense, households in the comparison group were precisely those that are eligible for the programme and that will enter the programme at a future date—they are thus a genuine 'delayed entry' comparison group.

The major factor in the choice of a non-experimental design was the stated policy of the Ministry that all eligible households will be enrolled in the programme once a district enters the programme. In other words, the programme would immediately be scaled up within each district. The Ministry determined that it would be ethically and politically unfeasible to provide the programme to some households while delaying others within the same district to serve as a control group because it would conflict with this stated policy. The second strategic decision was the 60:30 split between intervention and comparison wards. Here the key driver was the cost of targeting; the HSCT targeting approach involves a census of all households followed by the application of a proxy means test and a demographic eligibility criteria. Due to the

---

[11] See AIR (2014) for a detailed description of the impact evaluation design.

census approach, targeting is costly, and there was limited budget in Phase 2 to devote to Phase 4 targeting. In essence some of the budget for Phase 4 targeting was anticipated in order to target thirty wards for the purposes of the study. The 60:30 split meant that more households per ward were required to generate a large enough sample to achieve statistical power. As mentioned earlier in this section, in comparison districts households are truly 'delayed entry' since the exact targeting and selection process was conducted in these districts. The threat to internal validity is differences in the environment-agro-ecological conditions and access to services and other programmes across districts though this threat was mitigated by purposely selecting the forty-five comparison wards. The other key threat stems from the 'parallel trends' assumption if comparison districts have different economic growth rates or suffer from localized shocks such as flooding, crop disease, or drought.

In Ghana, political and ethical considerations were the main concern in discussions around a feasible evaluation design of the LEAP (Ghanaian Livelihood Empowerment Against Poverty Program) programme.[12] Though the programme was still quite small in 2009 when the evaluation was being set up, and the possibility of a delayed-entry control group was thus feasible, the Ministry of Employment and Social Welfare (MESW) was hesitant to pursue a social experiment by randomly selecting some areas to enter the programme early and others later. Such an approach would require the ministry to abandon its already established roll-out plan, and to target and identify households in control areas without then enrolling them in the programme. Both these factors were important in determining that the evaluation would be a reflexive (before and after) study that would sample a group of new LEAP households that were scheduled to enter the programme in 2010 as part of the Ministry's roll-out plan and apply a baseline and twenty-four-month follow-up. Somewhat fortuitously, during this period the Institute for Statistical, Social and Economic Studies (ISSER) of the University of Ghana in collaboration with Yale University was about to conduct a national panel survey. ISSER and Yale agreed to include the sample of future LEAP households in their survey to serve as the baseline. Funding was obtained by the University of North Carolina at Chapel Hill (UNC) (the evaluation implementer) from 3IE through an Open Window Call for Proposals (OW3.1075) to enable the Ministry to include a matched group of households from the ISSER/Yale sample in the twenty-four-month follow-up survey of LEAP beneficiaries. The final evaluation thus evolved into a longitudinal PSM design.

The conditions surrounding the LEAP study were virtually ideal for PSM to approximate the benchmark experimental estimator as indicated by Diaz and Handa (2006) and Heckman, Ichimura, and Todd (1997: 1) A rich set of

---

[12] See Handa et al. (2013) for a detailed description of the impact evaluation design.

pre-programme information was available from both groups of households; 2) information was collected in the same manner, in this case using the exact same instruments, survey protocols, and field teams; 3) longitudinal data were available to account for potential unobserved community differences across comparison and intervention sites over time. The main challenge, on the other hand, was the ability to generate enough observations from the national survey that were on the 'thick' region of common support given LEAP's unique eligibility criteria. This proved difficult and was ultimately addressed by applying inverse probability weights to the resulting samples. The potential threat stemming from the fact that comparison households were drawn from different districts of the country was addressed by the use of household fixed effects.

The most challenging evaluation problem was faced in South Africa, where the Child Support Grant (CSG) was already scaled up and there was no possibility of constructing an experimental control group from late entrants.[13] Moreover, since the CSG is a constitutional right, any eligible household that was found to not be in the programme would have to be immediately referred to the Department of Social Development for enrolment and could not be used as a comparison. Given these circumstances, the evaluation team worked with the South Africa Social Security Administration (SASSA) databases to identify a group of early and late entrants to the CSG and to match them using statistical matching techniques. The evaluation was thus a generalized PSM dosage design, where early entrants to the programme were 'matched' to similar looking late entrants based on factors that were believed to affect the timing and length of CSG receipt.

The South African case is a clear example of how programme scale and context (the rights-based nature of the grants system) limited the design options. On the other hand, changes in eligibility over the years (the age cut-off) and uneven implementation of the CSG lead to plausibly exogenous variation in the timing of age of entry into the programme which provided an avenue for generating a comparison group. Since all study participants were also already programme beneficiaries, there was no possibility of a baseline and so the South African IE is the only study in this volume which is not longitudinal. However, since many of the outcomes can be interpreted as cumulative changes since birth, the evaluators 'recovered' a DD estimator for some outcomes. The CSG IE was the most challenging to design and as a result there are several important threats to internal validity. The two main threats are the ability to find good matches between early and late entrants and the potential for unobserved heterogeneity to drive the timing of enrolment into the programme.

---

[13] See DSD, SASSA, and UNICEF (2012) for a detailed description of the evaluation design.

Finally, the Tigray Social Cash Transfer Programme IE also faced significant constraints that conditioned the design of the IE, reducing the robustness of the analytical outcomes.[14] First, randomization was not possible, given the roll-out of the pilot. One urban and one rural *woreda* (district) were purposefully selected for the pilot: Abi Adi town and Hintalo-Wajirat *woreda*, respectively. All residents of Abi Adi that met selection criteria were eligible for the programme, while in Hintalo-Wajirat only eight of twenty-two purposefully selected *tabias* (wards/neighbourhoods) were included. Second, the evaluators from IPFRI (International Food Policy Research Institute) argued that it was not possible to find comparable comparison communities (or *tabias*), thus comparison households were taken from the treatment *tabias*. It was not feasible in Abi Adi because all *tabias* in that locality were included, while in Hintalo-Wajirat, the excluded *tabias* are considerably closer to the regional capital of Mekelle. These *tabias* thus may differ in ways (such as access to markets) from households in the SCTP *tabias*.

Third, the evaluators originally planned to take advantage of the ranking system used in the targeting process to employ a Regression Discontinuity Design (RDD) to identify a comparison group. The programme is targeted via local community care coalitions (CCCs) at the *tabia* level, which act as an entry point and support mechanism for especially vulnerable households in the community. The CCCs first identify households that meet the criteria of extreme poverty and labour constrained and then rank these households by neediness. Beneficiaries are then selected from this ranked list. Given the level of resources available for the SCTP within this list there is a cut-off point; households ranked below this cut-off point are to receive payments, while households above the cut-off do not. Evaluators were not able to obtain detailed information on how the cut-off was constructed, however, and thus were not able to use a RDD. Instead, they used difference in difference with inverse probability score weights.

Fourth, transfers began in September 2011, nine months prior to the implementation of the baseline, in June 2012. Where possible, this was addressed by the inclusion of retrospective questions in the baseline survey. The exception was the *tabia* of Bahr Tseba in Hintalo-Wajirat *woreda*, which was brought in late to the pilot due to the availability of additional funds; the baseline in Bahr Tseba took place before the initial distribution of the cash transfer. The final household survey took place two years later in June 2014, while a series of five shorter monitoring series were fielded during the intervening period. Treatment households were drawn from lists of beneficiary households, while comparison households were drawn from those eligible households not selected for the programme. A random sample of non-eligible

[14] See detailed descriptions of the impact evaluation design in Berhane et al. (2012a), Berhane et al. (2012b), and Berhane et al. (2015).

households was also selected from *tabia* lists. For both treatment and comparison groups, elderly-, child- and female-headed households, as well as households with a disabled member, were oversampled.

3.5 OTHER ESTIMATION ISSUES

All of the IEs under the Transfer Project followed standard approaches to estimation—with some variation across countries (Table 3.2). Most of the IEs estimated OLS (ordinary least squares) models within the DD multivariate framework, with the exception of Ghana (GLM—generalized linear model) and South Africa (dose response models). All of the IEs used clustered standard errors, while the Malawi SCTP evaluation employed a finite population correction as well. Attrition was not a serious issue in most countries, with rates below 10 per cent, though rates reached 21 per cent in Kenya (severe

Table 3.2. Estimation Features

Country	IE models	Treatment of standard errors	Weighting	Household attrition (%), overall and by treatment and control
Ethiopia	OLS	Clustered	Matching (full baseline sample)	8.7 (overall) 10 (T)–6.8 (C)
Kenya	OLS	Clustered	Matching (panel sample)	21 (overall) 16.9 (T)–29.7 (C)
Ghana	OLS and GLM	Clustered	Matching (full baseline sample)	6.7 (overall) 7.5 (T)–6.1 (C)
Malawi	OLS	Clustered plus finite population correction	Sample	4.5 (overall) 4.1 (T)–4.9 (C)
Malawi (Mchinji pilot)	OLS	Clustered	Matching (full baseline sample)	6.5 (overall) 8.3 (T)–4.6 (C)
Lesotho	OLS	Clustered	Sample and attrition	8.8 (overall) 5.4 (T)–12.3 (C)
South Africa	Dose response functions	Clustered	Matching	N/A
Zambia (CG model)	OLS	Clustered	Attrition	8.7 (overall) 8.4 (T)–9 (C)
Zambia (MCTG model)	OLS	Clustered	Attrition	2.1 (overall) 1.8 (T)–2.5 (C)
Zimbabwe	OLS	Clustered	Attrition	14 (overall) 13.8 (T)–14.7 (C)

election-related violence took place between baseline and follow-up) and 14 per cent in Zimbabwe. All countries analysed for possible bias due to attrition and three (Zambia-CG, Zimbabwe, and Lesotho) used weights to correct for any potential bias. While the rate of attrition was relatively high, analysis in Kenya suggested that attrition was not systematic over the life of the panel (Handa 2012).

More variation among IEs was evident in the use of weights. The non-experimental IEs all employed PSM and/or IPW (inverse probability weighting), in Ethiopia and Ghana using the full baseline sample, and in Kenya the panel sample. Among the social experiment IEs, Zambia and Zimbabwe employed weights to correct for attrition, while Lesotho applied sample and attrition weights. In Malawi, only sample weights were applied, while the Malawi-Mchinji pilot used PSM to compensate for the relatively small number of units of randomization.

3.6 RESEARCH HYPOTHESES AND QUESTIONNAIRE DESIGN

A key innovation in the Transfer Project has been to extend the research questions around the impact of cash transfers thus contributing enormously to our understanding of the range of potential ways that cash can affect behaviour. This is motivated in large part by the fact that national programmes in Africa tend to be unconditional, so that impacts are not necessarily tied to specific indicators linked to conditionality as they were in Mexico, Nicaragua, and Colombia, for example. In other words, the nature of the intervention being studied allowed for a much wider conceptualization of the causal pathways and possible impact indicators than simply food security, consumption, and children's human capital. Indeed, this broad conceptualization is the key motivation for the FAO (Food and Agriculture Organization of the United Nations)-led Protection to Production component of the Transfer Project, whose explicit focus was to identify the productive and economic impacts of these programmes.

An example of a conceptual framework used to guide the questionnaire design is shown in Figure 3.1 taken from the Malawi SCTP IE. The figure is read from left to right, and shows that the cash first enters the households and generates a series of changes which ultimately filter down to certain individuals such as young children, adolescents, and caregivers. Within the household sphere, responses can include economic and productive decisions, not just about work but also use of inputs which can lead to changes in future income—these dynamic effects are not shown in this diagram but are an important part of the evaluation story. The figure also highlights the potential

Quantitative Approach to Evaluation Design

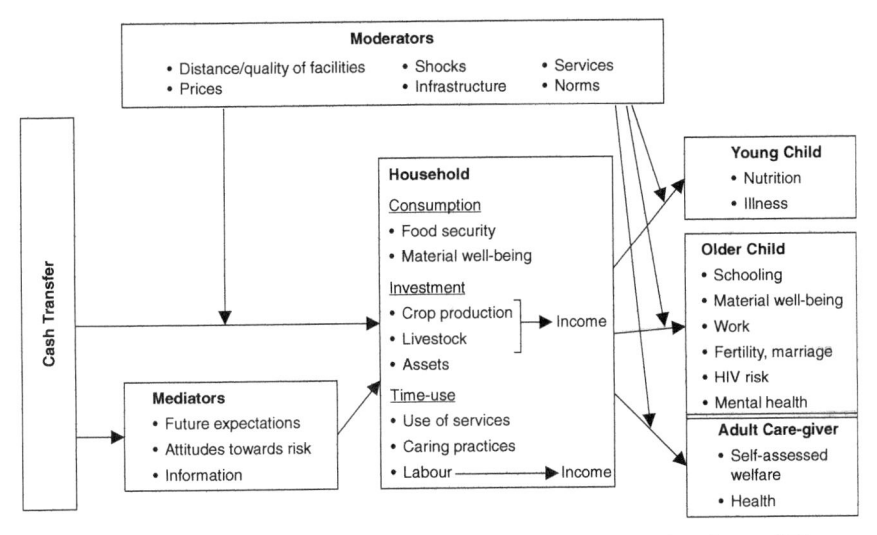

Figure 3.1. Conceptual Framework for Impact Evaluation of Malawi SCTP

importance of moderators, primarily contextual features of the local economy such as access to services and exogenous shocks, which can affect programme impacts. Key mediators, channels through which the cash affects behaviour, come from behavioural psychology and economics and include risk and time preference and expectations about the future.

Motivated by such a framework, the challenge has been to design a questionnaire which touches the range of domains implied by the framework (social, psychological, economic; adults, adolescents, children) while still being manageable; in practice, evaluations have sought to limit the household questionnaire to no more than two hours in length. All surveys except South Africa were also accompanied by a linked community questionnaire to gather information on the potential moderators, including prices. Table 3.3, again for Malawi, gives an example of the range of topics covered in the household and community questionnaires. As can be seen, the range is quite large, and the household instrument is indeed heavy. In Malawi and several other countries, a stand-alone adolescent questionnaire is also administered to understand the impacts of economic support to young people who are transitioning to adulthood—the topics covered in this questionnaire are listed at the top of column 2 and the adolescent surveys are discussed in more detail later in the chapter.

Since one objective of the Transfer Project has been to create regional learning on the impact of cash transfers, a strategic decision surrounded the extent to which survey instruments should be made consistent across countries or whether they should be based on, for example, existing national

Table 3.3. Example of Questionnaire: Topics from Malawi SCTP Evaluation

Household Survey	Young Person's Module—ages 13–19
Roster and Orphan Status	Future Aspirations
Education—3+ years	Expectations for Future Quality of Life and Health
Health—All	
Disability	Raven's Test for Logical Reasoning
Child Health and Anthropometry—0–5 Years	Mental Health
Access to Educational and Health Services	Sexual Activity
Fertility—women aged 12–49	Time Preference
Time-Use (Chores, Agriculture, Other)—Age 6+	
Labour (Wage/Ganyu)—Age 10+	Community Survey
Household Enterprises	Access to Basic Services
Transfers Received and Made	Access to Educational and Health Facilities
Other Income	
Credit	Educational Costs
Expectations for the Future	Agricultural Resources
Self-Assessed Poverty and Food Security	Agricultural Prices
Social Safety Nets	Ganyu Wage Rates
Shocks and Coping Strategies	Community Natural Resource Management External Shocks
Expenditure	
Land-Use	Community Norms and Culture
Crop Production and Sales	Prices of Food and Common Non-Food Items
Agriculture and Livestock	
Fishing	Businesses Activities
Hired Labour	
Sustainable Land Management	Enterprise Module
Housing Conditions and Household Assets	Revenue, Sales, Profits
Mortality and Changes in Household Membership	Source of Inputs or Raw Materials

household survey instruments such as MICS (Multiple Indicator Cluster Surveys), Demographic and Health Survey (DHS), and Living Standards Surveys. The first priority has been to standardize with existing national instruments as these have been field tested and subject to a national approval process. However, when no standard module was available nationally, or when new topics were introduced such as credit and loans, time preference, or intra household decision-making, the project tried to ensure these were standardized across countries to allow for comparisons.

Perhaps the most critical decision in the surveys in Zimbabwe, Lesotho, Zambia, and Malawi was to include the full consumption module from the Living Standards Survey of the respective country in the evaluation survey. This is very time-consuming, often entailing over 250 questions on specific food and non-food items. The logic behind this decision was to allow for a strict apples-to-apples comparison of poverty and consumption levels between programme beneficiaries and national populations, important to demonstrate to critics that programmes are well targeted and reach the poorest. From the impact perspective, since the primary objective of all programmes is consumption, and since almost all the transfer was likely to be consumed by these extremely poor households, investing in an accurate measure of consumption was thought to be crucial to understanding the behavioural response of households. Moreover, detailed consumption and spending allowed impact results in other domains such as health and schooling to be traced back to expenditures in these areas to understand the causal pathway of impacts in other domains. In the Zambia CG model for example, the large impacts on secondary school transition at age 11–14 could be traced back to large increases in spending on uniforms and shoes, which are known to be barriers to school enrolment for poor households. The example of Zambia is illustrative of the larger, strategic initiative to measure as much as possible all factors along the causal pathway as depicted in Figure 3.1, in order to understand not just what was impacted but why or how the cash transfer achieved that result.

3.7 RESEARCH INNOVATION: FROM PROTECTION TO PRODUCTION

The unconditional nature of the African cash transfer programmes allow for transfers to be spent as households most see fit, whether that be short-term consumption or productive activities. The key motivation behind the PtoP project is that poor rural households in Africa—most of whom rely on subsistence agriculture for their livelihoods and food security needs—face a series of market failures in credit and insurance that trap them into risk-averse production decisions. Moreover, agricultural households will often sell more than the optimal amount of labour off farm to obtain cash.[15] Small, predictable injections of 'unconditional' cash can ease liquidity constraints and help overcome the lack of access to insurance, allowing households to make productive investments or diversify income sources and thus serving an important potential pathway out of poverty. Also, over the course of the implementation of the IEs the issue of resilience became more prominent, a concept which relies in part on household economic potential. Taken together, this led to large investments in questions around productive and economic activity. Early results led to shifting emphasis in later countries and surveys,

---

[15] From a theoretical perspective, in the face of multiple market failures, the production and consumption decisions of agricultural households can be viewed as 'non-separable', in the sense that they are jointly determined (Singh, Squire, and Strauss et al. 1986). In this model, when markets function perfectly, production and consumption decisions can be viewed as 'separable'—profit maximization and utility maximization are solved recursively. First, the agricultural household maximizes profit from agricultural production based on standard economic theory. Second, given that profit, they seek to maximize utility. If markets are perfect, spending in agriculture is optimal, and the effect of the transfer should only be on consumption.

including an increased focus on household labour allocation and time use as well as social networks, which play an important part in survival strategies of the poor and which are often motivated by economic concerns. The PtoP project also introduced the idea of simulating the income multiplier generated by cash transfers in the local economies where programmes were implemented. As described in Chapter 5, in order to build the LEWIE (Local Economy-wide Impact Evaluation) general equilibrium models, additional questions were necessary in the household survey providing details on the where and who of cash exchanges, as well as sufficient information to estimate production functions on main household economic activities.

Given this recognition of the relevance of household livelihood activities, one challenge has been to convince managers of the IE process to collect more detailed information on productive activities in the context of an already overcrowded survey instrument. And since programmes are located in ministries of social welfare there is a natural tendency to only look at the poverty and social dimensions of programme impacts. However, increasingly, through the efforts of the PtoP project, both social welfare ministries and development partners have realized that capturing the productive impacts and income multipliers of these social programmes can be a powerful advocacy tool in Cabinet and with Ministries of Finance. These domains are now considered almost automatic when considering the full potential of cash transfer programmes in sub-Saharan Africa.

The deepening of survey instruments to capture productive and economic activity through the PtoP represents a very important innovation in the Transfer Project. Table 3.4 lists the standard information collected in each country on productive activities, though the depth and breadth of the information varied across countries. One relevant aspect of household productive activities that was not systematically collected was individual decision-making and ownership in household economic activities (such as farming and non-farming enterprises), which has limited the ability to distinguish by gender the economic and productive impact of these programmes.

Finally, risk management and coping strategies are ascertained in part through different modules of the survey, including the diversification of income-generating activities, decisions on food security and child schooling, the sales of assets, and specific questions on negative risk coping strategies, such as begging. Most surveys also collect basic information on receipt and provision of intra-household transfers, which provide an indication of social networks and informal safety nets. However, the importance of these networks of reciprocity in the African context, and the important role that the community plays in targeting and monitoring cash transfer programmes, calls for more innovative methods in detailing these social networks—which were attempted in only one country of the eight, Lesotho.

The results from these new modules show an impressive impact of unconditional transfers on economic activities, though the nature and magnitude of

Table 3.4. Standard Productive Activity Questions Introduced as Part of PtoP Project

Questionnaire Topic	Notes
Household roster and labour market participation at the level of a typical LSMS (living standards measurement survey)	
Adult and child time use in terms of household chores and own farm/business activities	Extra detail in Malawi and Zimbabwe
Access to land, land tenure, land use, and land quality	
Crop-level information on planting, harvest, and sales/barter and other uses of production (own consumption, storage, gifts, etc)	Plot level information in Malawi and Zimbabwe. Extra information on homestead gardening in Lesotho
Flow of livestock stocks (including births, deaths, consumption, sales/barter, etc) by animal	
Livestock by-product production and sales/barter	
Crop and animal input use, intensity of use and cost (seeds, fertilizer, chemicals, veterinary services, feed, etc), including hired and family labour	Extra detail in Malawi and Zimbabwe
Use and ownership of agricultural implements Non-agricultural business, including monthly costs and income, and use of hired and family labour	
Access to and use of credit, insurance, and savings	Extra detail on credit in Malawi and Zimbabwe
Social networks, including receipt and provision of cash and in-kind support	Extra detail in Lesotho
Intra-household decision-making	Available for Ghana, Malawi, and Zimbabwe
Sustainable land management	Available for Malawi
For all cash transaction, who purchased from and where purchased	Baseline only to construct LEWIE

impacts varied across programmes and countries, as is detailed elsewhere in this book. In the Zambia CG model, for example, households purchased more livestock and agricultural inputs, crop production increased significantly, and non-farm enterprise also increased. In Ghana, LEAP households paid off debt, reduced new debt, and showed increased integration into social networks through an increase in both receiving and giving gifts. In terms of productive time-use, results across counties (Kenya, Zambia, Malawi) show greater time allocation towards own farm activity and a reduction in casual labour, typically considered the labour of 'last resort' in rural Africa.

3.8 RESEARCH INNOVATION: THE TRANSITION TO ADULTHOOD

The second major research innovation in the project has been to assess the successful transition to adulthood of young people living in beneficiary households. The motivation for this area of study comes from the high prevalence of HIV in the Eastern and Southern African study countries where the incidence of new infections is typically highest among young people aged 18–24, particularly young women (e.g., Kenya, Malawi, Zimbabwe). Poverty is often cited as a structural determinant of HIV risk in Southern Africa (McCoy, Watts, and Padian 2010) and programmes in these countries target either labour-constrained households or those with OVC, meaning most target households have a large proportion of adolescents and orphans, precisely the group who are most at risk of HIV.

In five project countries—Kenya, Malawi, South Africa, Zimbabwe and Zambia—evaluation teams added a special module on adolescent development to the set of survey instruments. These questionnaires are administered face-to-face to up to three young people in the household in a private location by an enumerator of the same sex; survey protocols are similar to those used by DHS, who field similar types of questions, and full ethics board reviews have been conducted in each.[16] The length of the questionnaire is usually thirty minutes and the topics have varied from country to country depending on local circumstances and interests. As can be seen in Table 3.5, which lists the full set of topics covered in the five studies, questions around sexual debut, forced sex, and partner characteristics form the core of these modules and have been fielded in all surveys—this is because the age of first sex is a key risk factor for later HIV, as are partner characteristics (Stöckl et al. 2013). The Center for Epidemiological Studies Depression Index is a widely validated scale that has also been used in all four studies. Other modules that have been fielded in the youth surveys include peer networks and perceptions (Kenya), social support (Malawi, Zambia), and violence (Zimbabwe). Note that this information can be linked back to the main household questionnaire to obtain information on schooling, labour force participation, health, and fertility.

Results from the adolescent modules are just emerging and show that indeed cash transfers are protective of adolescent transitions to adulthood, though results vary by country. One somewhat robust result is the impact on delayed sexual debut ranging from 6 and 8 percentage points in Malawi (University of North Carolina, 2015) and Kenya (Handa et al. 2014c), respectively, to 11 and 13 percentage points in South Africa (Heinrich, Hoddinott,

---

[16] Readers should note that subjects under age eighteen are considered minors, and ethics review committees typically require approval from both the caregiver/parent of the child and the child herself.

Table 3.5. Summary of Data Collection in Modules for Young People

Questionnaire item	Zambia MCTG (n=2098; age 15–23)	Zimbabwe HSCT (n=1170; age 13–21)	Malawi SCTP (n=2109; age 13–19)	Kenya CT-OVC (n=2223; ages 15–25)	South Africa CSG (N=1726; age 15–17)
Depression (CES-D short form)	X	X	X	X	
Hope scale		X		X	
Cognitive test	X		X		
Time preference/patience	X		X	X	
Sexual debut and behaviours	X	X	X	X	X
Ever taken an HIV test (results not asked)		X	X	X	
Perceived HIV risk		X	X	X	
Educational attainment	X		X		X
Educational aspirations and expectations	X		X		
Future occupation/earnings aspirations	X		X		
Marriage aspirations and expectations	X		X		
Ideal number of children	X		X		
Social networks/social support	X		X	X	
Risk-taking	X		X		X
Self-rated health	X				
Alcohol and tobacco use		X	X		X
Sexual violence	X	X	X	X	X
Experienced forced sex or sexual acts	X	X	X	X	X
Transactional sex	X	X	X	X	X
Perpetration of forced sex/sexual acts	X				
Physical violence					
Experienced physical violence		X			
Sought help for violence		X			
Criminal activity and gangs					X
Survey year	2011, 2013, 2014	2013, 2014, 2016	2013, 2014, 2015	2011	2011

Zambia: MCTG=Multiple Categorical Targeting Grant; Zimbabwe: HSCT=Harmonized Social Cash Transfer; Malawi: SCTP=Social Cash Transfer Programme; Kenya CT-OVC=Cash Transfer for Orphans and Vulnerable Children.

and Samson 2015) and Zimbabwe (AIR, unpublished)—although the result for South Africa is only significant among females. In addition, impacts on first or any pregnancy range from 5 percentage points in Kenya to 10.5 percentage points in South Africa (Handa et al. 2015; Heinrich, Hoddinott, and Samson 2015). Impacts on mental health are less consistent, with positive impacts emerging in Kenya (Kilburn et al. 2015), particularly for males, but no impacts in Malawi or Zambia.

3.9 RESEARCH INNOVATION: BEHAVIOURAL PSYCHOLOGY AND ECONOMICS

Transfer Project evaluations have also consistently sought to include questions on behavioural psychology and economics to understand the 'psychology of poverty and decision-making' and the extent to which a predictable source of income changes the underlying decision-making calculus of beneficiaries. Time and risk preference are considered to be key behavioural parameters that affect decision-making in virtually all domains including human capital investment, productive activity, savings, and entrepreneurship (Frederick, Lowenstein, and O'Donahue 2002). For example, a cash transfer may make households less myopic and more willing to delay present for future consumption. Similarly, a household's predisposition towards risk will influence investment behaviour: risk-averse households may avoid investments which are perceived to be more risky even though the average return may be higher. Other psychological measures such as subjective risk assessments of life expectancy and future quality of life may also influence the planning horizon and thus affect inter-temporal decisions.

Household questionnaires in five of the eight evaluations have included hypothetical questions on risk and time preference, which are rarely included in multi-topic surveys. A review of the internal consistency of these questions by Handa et al. (2014b) shows rates of 'error' that are on the lower end of those reported from laboratory experiments among literate populations in rich countries (Bradford, Dolan, and Galizzi 2014), which provides a degree of confidence in their application in this context. The evidence does suggest that cash transfers affect inter-temporal choice. In Kenya recipients of the CT-OVC who were not credit constrained or who were in the bottom half of the consumption distribution were more likely to wait for future money (Handa et al. 2015) while in Zambia beneficiaries of the MCTG model of the Social Cash Transfer (SCT) were also more likely to wait for future money (Handa et al. 2013, unpublished). The implication of these results is that cash transfers may make households less myopic, and thus more likely to trade present for future consumption, a necessary condition to trigger investment. This may be a key mediator generating additional economic and productive impacts of unconditional cash transfer programmes.

3.10 CONCLUSION

The defining characteristic of the IEs supported by the Transfer Project is that they involve government-owned, 'real-world' programmes, fully integrated into national ministries and associated budget and administrative systems. Social experiments are not always possible (or even desirable) for political, logistical, or ethical reasons, and even when they are, any number of evaluation design parameters may not be under full control of the researchers. While these limitations may threaten the internal validity of the evaluation design, they strengthen its external validity—the relevance of the IE to the scale-up of the programme in a given country.

The story of the Transfer Project is one of balancing statistical rigour with political and operational constraints that govern the implementation of the programmes. The result is a continuum of IE approaches in terms of the rigour achieved in the design and implementation of the IEs. Four of the eight IEs are social experiments, for the most part successfully implemented, often under difficult circumstances. The other four are non-experimental approaches, with varying degrees of success in terms of rigour and robustness of results obtained. Together they build a solid body of evidence on similar government programmes across eight countries of sub-Saharan Africa—a remarkable, and perhaps unprecedented, achievement.

Based on this experience it is worth highlighting a few key lessons learned in terms of building rigorous IEs that feed directly into the decision-making process in complex institutional environments. First and foremost is what we consider the 'mirage' of an independent evaluation. The success of an evaluation requires close partnership and mutual trust between implementers and evaluators. Implementers must understand and trust that the evaluation will assist them in improving the programme and that the evaluators are there to help them strengthen the programme. This requires a close working relationship which is often thought to violate the impartiality and independence of an evaluation. In fact, the more 'arm's-length' the evaluation team the less likely they are to get crucial information on implementation and other parameters to help them truly interpret subsequent results. The more distant the evaluator, the more they are likely to be distrusted and the evaluation viewed as an attack on the programme. Our experience in the Transfer Project is that once mutual trust is built, implementers welcome 'bad news' and act upon it, understanding that such evidence provides important opportunities for learning and improving the programme rather than an excuse to shut down the programme. They recognize that improvements ultimately strengthen and protect the programme in both political and public discourse.

A second important lesson is the necessity to adopt a flexible approach to the evaluation design in order to minimize the burden of the study on programme implementation—this is part of building trust between the evaluator and programme managers. A key part of the design discourse is explaining the requirements of a rigorous evaluation, and the different threats to internal validity associated with different design options. Once these trade-offs are made clear, national governments are very quickly able to decide how much they value an airtight design and how much they will 'pay' in terms of altering roll-out or other implementation plans to obtain the gold standard. In Zambia, for example, given the history with previous evaluations which could not be used to unambiguously demonstrate impacts, achieving the gold standard was of utmost importance resulting in a large multi-site social experiment. In Ghana, on the other hand, programme managers were reluctant to fast-track targeting in districts slotted for later expansion in order to build a delayed entry control group, due to reputational and other concerns. The resulting evaluation design is one of the weaker ones in the portfolio, yet the evaluation led to significant changes in programme design to improve impacts on beneficiaries. Indeed the 'impact' of the evaluation in Ghana is probably just as big or bigger than in countries with much more rigorous designs such as Zambia or Lesotho.

ANNEX 3.1

The Counterfactual

To formalize the missing counterfactual problem, let D_i denote a dummy variable equal to 1 if a household receives a cash transfer and equal to 0 if a household does not receive a cash transfer. Similarly, let Y_i denote an outcome of interest such that potential outcomes are defined as $Y_i(D_i)$ for every household. The treatment effect of the programme for household i, T_i, is then given by (1):

$$T_i = Y_i(1) - Y_i(0) \qquad (1)$$

As mentioned, only one outcome is observable—either the household receives the transfer or it does not—leaving the counterfactual component $Y_i(0)$ in equation 1 unknown. The implications are twofold. First, the success of any IE relies on identifying a suitable counterfactual sample. And second, it is not possible to measure unit-specific treatment effects, but rather average treatment effects (ATEs) incorporating information from the counterfactual. In an RCT, the ATE of the cash transfer can be identified simply as the mean difference in outcomes between the two groups:

Quantitative Approach to Evaluation Design

$$E(T) = ATE = E[Y(1)] - E[Y(0)] \quad (2)$$

A large number of ATEs can be estimated, perhaps the most commonly reported being the average treatment effect on the treated (ATT), which measures the average impact of the cash transfer programme on those who actually receive the transfer. This is defined as:

$$ATT = E[T|D=1] = E[(Y(1)|D=1] - E[Y(0)|D=1] \quad (3)$$

Again, the counterfactual for those being treated (the last term in equation (3) is not observed, rendering crucial the choice of a proper substitute to estimate the ATT. In an experimental setting the counterfactual is observed (on average) because eligible units are randomly assigned to treatment or control status. However, in a non-experimental setting the key empirical issue is identifying non-treated units who are otherwise identical to those in the programme.

The DD Estimator

In a longitudinal context, the estimator in Equation (3) can be improved by subtracting off the difference in pre-programme outcomes between participants and non-participants, as in Equation (4):

$$ATT = E[\tau_t - \tau_{t-1}|D=1] = E[(Y(1))_t - Y(0)_t) - (Y(1)_{t-1} - Y(0)_{t-1})|D=1]$$

$$= E[(Y(1)_t - Y(1)_{t-1})|D=1] - E[(Y(0)_t - Y(0)_{t-1})|D=1] \quad (4)$$

where $t-1$ and t represent time periods before and after the introduction of the cash transfer programme.

By taking the difference in outcomes for the treatment group before and after receiving the cash transfer, and subtracting the difference in outcomes for the control group before and after the cash transfer is disbursed, the DD estimator controls for unobserved heterogeneity that may lead to selection bias (Wooldridge 2002). DD controls for pre-treatment differences between the two groups and, in particular, the time-invariant unobservable factors that cannot be accounted for otherwise. The key assumption is that differences between treated and control households remain constant through the duration of the project. If prior outcomes incorporate transitory shocks that differ for treatment and comparison households, the DD estimate will interpret these shocks as representing a stable difference, and thus contain a transitory component that does not represent the true programme impact.

Control variables are most easily introduced by turning to a regression framework which is convenient for the DD and is the most common approach in the IEs covered in this book. Equation (5) presents the regression equivalent of DD with covariates:

$$Y_{it} = \beta_0 + \beta_1 D_{it} + \beta_2 R_t + \beta_3(R_t{}^*D_{it}) + \sum \beta_i Z_i + \mu_{it} \quad (5)$$

where Y_{it} is the outcome indicator of interest; D_{it} is a dummy equal to 1 if household i received the treatment; R_t is a time dummy equal to 0 for the baseline and to 1 for the follow-up round; $R_t{}^*D_{it}$ is the interaction between the intervention and time dummies, and μ_{it} is an error term. To control for household and community characteristics that may influence the outcome of interest beyond the treatment effect alone, a vector of household and community characteristics, Z_i, is added to control for observable differences across households at the baseline which could have an effect on Y_{it}. These factors are not only those for which some differences may be observed across treatment and control at the baseline, but also ones which could have some explanatory role in the estimation of Y_{it}. In terms of coefficients, β_0 is a constant term; β_1 controls for the time-invariant differences between the treatment and control; β_2 represents the effect of going from the baseline to the follow-up period; and β_3 is the double difference estimator, which captures the treatment effect.

REFERENCES

AIR (American Institutes for Research) (2013). *Zambia's Child Grant Program: 24-Month Impact Report*, Washington, DC. Available at: <https://transfer.cpc.unc.edu/?page_id=1262> (accessed 20 November 2015).

AIR (American Institutes for Research) (2014). *12-Month Impact Report for Zimbabwe's Harmonised Social Cash Transfer Programmes*. Washington, DC: Author.

Asfaw, S., Covarrubias, K., Daidone, S., Davis, B., Dewbre, J., Djebbari, H., Romeo, A., and Winters, P. (2012). 'Methodological Guidelines: Analytical Framework for Evaluating the Productive Impact of Cash Transfer Programmes on Household Behaviour'. From Protection to Production Report, FAO.

Berhane, G., Devereux, S., Hoddinott, J., Nega Tegebu, F., Roelen, K., and Schwab, B. (2012a). 'Evaluation of the Social Cash Transfers Pilot Programme Tigray Region, Ethiopia'. Inception Report, IFPRI, Washington, DC.

Berhane, G., Devereux, S., Hoddinott, J., Nega Tegebu, F., Roelen, K., and Schwab, B. (2012b). 'Evaluation of the Social Cash Transfers Pilot Programme Tigray Region, Ethiopia'. Baseline Report, IFPRI, Washington, DC, December.

Berhane, G., Devereux, S., Hoddinott, J., Nega Tegebu, F., Roelen, K., and Schwab, B. (2015). 'Evaluation of the Social Cash Transfers Pilot Programme Tigray Region, Ethiopia'. Endline Report, IFPRI, Washington DC.

Boone, R., Covarrubias, K., Davis, B., and Winters, P. (2013). 'Cash transfer programs and agricultural production: the case of Malawi'. *Agricultural Economics*, 44(3): 365–378.

Bradford, W. D., Dolan, P., and M. M. Galizzi (2014). 'Looking Ahead: Subjective Time Perception and Individual Time Discounting'. Centre for Economic Performance, LSE (No. dp1255).

Bruhn, M. and McKenzie, D. (2009). 'In pursuit of balance: randomization in practice in development field experiments'. *American Economic Journal: Applied Economics*, 1(4): 200–232.

Diaz, J. J. and Handa, S. (2006). 'An assessment of propensity score matching as a non experimental impact estimator: evidence from Mexico's progresa program'. *Journal of Human Resources*, 41(2): 319–45.

Dewbre, J., Daidone, S., Davis, B., Miguelez, B., Niang, O., and Pellerano, L. (2015). 'Lesotho Child Grant Programme and Linking Food Security to Social Protection Programme'. From Protection to Production Report, FAO.

DSD, SASSA, and UNICEF (2012). 'The South African Child Support Grant Impact Assessment: Evidence from a Survey of children, Adolescents and Their Households'. Pretoria: UNICEF South Africa.

Frederick, S., Lowenstein, G., and O'Donoghue, T. (2002). 'Time discounting and time preference: a critical review'. *Journal of Economic Literature.* 40 (June): 351–401.

Handa, S. (2012). 'Kenya Cash Transfer for Orphans and Vulnerable Children Evaluation: Sample Design and Description'. UNICEF, UNC, and FAO. Available at: <http://www.fao.org/fileadmin/user_upload/p2p/Publications/Kenya_CT-OVC_Sample_Design_and_Description_2012.pdf> (accessed 8 November 2015).

Handa, S., Angeles, G., Abdoulayi, S., Mvula, P., and Tsoka, M. (2014a). 'Malawi Social Cash Transfer Program Baseline Evaluation Report'. Carolina Population Center, UNC.

Handa, S., Martorano, B., Halpern, C., Pettifor, A., and Thirumurthy, H. (2014b). 'Subjective Well-Being, Risk Perceptions and Time Discounting: Evidence from a Large Scale Cash Transfer'. Innocenti Working Paper 2014-2. Available at: <http://www.unicef-irc.org/publications/717> (accessed 8 November 2015).

Handa, S., Halpern C., Pettifor, A., Thirumurthy, H. (2014c). 'The government of Kenya's cash transfer program reduces the risk of sexual debut among young people age 15–25'. *PLOS One*, 9: 1–9.

Handa, S., Martorano, B., Thirumurthy, H., Halpern, C., and Pettifor, A. (2015). 'Time Discounting and Credit Market Access in a Large Scale Cash Transfer Program'. Journal of African Economies doi: 10.1093/jae/ejv031.

Handa, S., Park, M., Darko, R., Osei-Akoto, I., Davis, B., and Daidone, S. (2013). 'Livelihood Empowerment against Poverty Impact Evaluation'. Carolina Population Center, UNC.

Handa, S., Peterman, A., Huang, C., Halpern, C., Pettifor, A., and Thirumurthy, H. (2015). 'Impact of the Kenya Cash Transfer for Orphans and Vulnerable Children on early pregnancy and marriage of adolescent girls'. *Social Science & Medicine* 141: 36-45. UNC.

Handa, S., Seidenfeld, D., and Tembo, G. (2013). 'The Impact of a Large Scale Poverty Targeted Cash Transfer Program on Inter-Temporal Choice'. Carolina Population Center, UNC.

Heckman, J., Ichimura, H., and Todd, P. (1997). 'Matching as an econometric evaluation estimator: evidence from evaluating a job training program'. *Review of Economic Studies*, 64: 605–54.

Heinrich, C., Hoddinott, J., and Samson, M. (2015). 'Reducing Adolescent Risky Behaviors in a High-Risk Context: The Effects of Unconditional Cash Transfers in South Africa'. Working Paper, University of Texas at Austin.

Kenya CT-OVC Evaluation Team (Palermo, T., Alviar, C., Davis, B., Handa, S., Hurrell, A., Hussein, A., Musembi, D., Ochieng, S., Pearson, R., Pellerano, L., Visram, A., and Ward, P). (2012). 'The impact of the Kenya Cash Transfer Program for Orphans and Vulnerable Children on household spending'. *Journal of Development Effectiveness*, 4(1) (March): 9–37.

Kilburn, K., Thirumurthy, H., Halpern, C., Pettifor, A., and Handa, S. (2015). 'Effects of a Large-Scale Unconditional Cash Transfer Program on Mental Health Outcomes of Young People in Kenya: A Cluster Randomized Trial'. *Journal of Adolescent Health*, in press.

McCoy, S., Watts, C. H., Padian, N. (2010). 'Preventing HIV infection: turning the tide for young women'. *Lancet*, 376: 1281–2.

Miller, C., Tsoka, M., and Reichert, K. (2008). 'Impact Evaluation Report: External Evaluation of the Mchinji Social Cash Transfer Pilot'. Center for International Health and Development, Boston University, Boston, and Centre for Social Research, University of Malawi, Zomba.

Pellerano, L., Moratti, M., Jakobsen, M., Bajgar, M., and Barca, V. (2014). 'Child Grants Programme Impact Evaluation'. Follow-Up Report, Oxford Policy Management, Oxford.

Singh, I., Squire L., and Strauss, J. (eds) (1986). *Agricultural Household Models: Extension, Application and Policy*. Baltimore, MD: Johns Hopkins University Press.

Stöckl, H., Kalra, N., Jacobi, J., and Watts, C. (2013). 'Is early sexual debut a risk factor for HIV infection among women in sub-Saharan Africa? A systematic review'. *American Journal of Reproductive Immunology*, 69 (Suppl. 1): 27–40.

University of North Carolina (2015). *Malawi Social Cash Transfer Program Midline Impact Evaluation Report*. Chapel Hill, NC: Author.

Ward, P., Hurrell, A., Visram, A., Riemenschneider, N., Pellerano, L., O' Brien, C., MacAuslan, I., and Willils, J. (2010). 'Cash Transfer Programme for Orphans and Vulnerable Children (CT-OVC), Kenya—Operational and Impact Evaluation, 2007–2009'. Oxford Policy Management Report.

Wooldridge, J. M. (2002). *Econometric Analysis of Cross-Section and Panel Data*. Cambridge, MA: MIT Press.

4

Qualitative Methods in Impact Evaluations of Cash Transfer Programmes in the Transfer Project in Sub-Saharan Africa

Pamela Pozarny (FAO) and Clare Barrington (University of North Carolina at Chapel Hill)

4.1 INTRODUCTION

In this chapter, we describe the use of qualitative methods in mixed-method impact evaluations (IEs) of cash transfer (CT) programmes in sub-Saharan Africa conducted under the Transfer Project. Qualitative methods are used in varying ways in IE: to inform development of the methods and measures used in quantitative surveys; to triangulate and provide context to quantitative findings; to obtain opinions and recommendations directly from beneficiaries, programmers, and stakeholders; to make IE more participatory; and to provide greater depth and nuanced understanding of the pathways and mechanisms through which CT programmes impact health and development outcomes (World Bank 2011; Garabarino and Holland 2009). Viewed this way, qualitative methods complement quantitative methods by functioning as critical sources of information that shed light on both the context in which CT programmes occur as well as experience lived and people's responses to programmes (Garabino and Holland 2009). Through this combination of breadth and depth, qualitative methods can further understanding of the 'how' and the 'why' behind programme impact. Qualitative data can also reveal unanticipated outcomes and disclose impacts not captured in close-ended questionnaires by using iterative approaches, open-ended questions, and probing topics brought up by participants. Qualitative findings can also become powerful tools for communication and policy development by highlighting compelling narratives that document the impact of CT programmes on the target populations.

While most IE are guided by a priori hypotheses derived from theories of change and assessed through quantitative analysis, qualitative methods in the context of IE can be informed by both deductive (hypothesis or theory testing using predetermined question sets) and inductive (hypothesis or theory generating—which is more open-ended query seeking) approaches. The use of qualitative methods to inform intervention or evaluation design or to explore participants' experiences usually reflects an inductive approach, whereby data collection is not driven by a limited a priori hypothesis, and analysis is developed in response to narratives and observations obtained through fieldwork (Patton 2002). Alternatively, qualitative methods can also be used to assess specific theoretical constructs and confirm hypotheses (Bernard 2011).

There are several characteristics of qualitative methods that guide their use in IE. Principally, the contribution of qualitative insights is maximized when data collection and analysis occur simultaneously. This facilitates identification of emergent themes which can be explored further while information is still being collected. Related to this, optimizing the contribution of qualitative data requires flexibility and iteration with regard to design, data collection, sampling, and informants. The degree of flexibility may be constrained by the evaluation team's technical capacity, timelines, resources, and/or ethical review board permissions. The approach to sampling participants in qualitative evaluations is usually purposive, which means that informants who can contribute information related to the evaluation questions are intentionally sought out, rather than randomly selected from the population (Patton 2002). Purposive sampling is critical to making sure that participants have experiences, perceptions, and opinions to share which can provide contextual insights and/or greater depth of understanding about CT programmes.

Commonly used qualitative methods include: individual interviews with CT beneficiaries, programmers, stakeholders, community leaders, and others with knowledge about communities or CT programmes; focus group discussions (FGDs) with these same groups; household case studies; participatory tools; and observations. Individual interviews are used to obtain lived experiences with CT programmes and opinions and perceptions about the programmes and their impacts. FGDs are used to assess community-level norms and collective narratives related to CT programmes (Warr 2005). Focus groups are useful in bringing out differences in people's views and experiences of the programme and, through group interactions and probing, can reveal and stimulate critical reflection on programme impact. Observations can be used to better understand community context, social dynamics, and programme implementation (Patton 2002). Any of these methods may be used along a spectrum of participation, ranging from a sole focus on obtaining information related to IE questions to an interest in mutually generating ideas and understanding the topic of study together with CT programme beneficiaries and/or staff. Methods explicitly aimed to make evaluations more participatory and allow for triangulating of qualitative methods include community mapping, visual methods such as institutional analysis, decision-making matrices, and wealth ranking, among others.

Table 4.1. Overview of Transfer Project Impact Evaluations by Qualitative Approach

Country	Cash Transfer Programme	Qualitative Design Approach	Year of Fieldwork
Ethiopia	Social Cash Transfer Pilot Programme	Comparative cross-country; Thematic	2014; 2012 and 2014
Ghana	Livelihood Empowerment Against Poverty	Comparative cross-country	2012
Kenya	Cash Transfer to Orphans and Vulnerable Children	Comparative cross-country	2012
Lesotho	Child Grant Programme	Comparative cross-country	2013
Malawi	Social Cash Transfer	Comparative cross-country; Longitudinal	2014; 2013 and 2015
South Africa	Child Support Grant	Thematic	2010
Zambia	Child Grant Programme (Social Cash Transfer Scheme)	Thematic	2013 (two rounds)
Zimbabwe	Harmonized Social Cash Transfer Programme	Comparative cross-country; Longitudinal	2012; 2012, 2013, and 2014 (three rounds)

4.2 COMPARATIVE OVERVIEW OF QUALITATIVE DESIGN APPROACHES IN CT IMPACT EVALUATIONS

This chapter is organized around three qualitative design approaches used in mixed-methods IE applied in the country case studies included this book: (i) comparative cross-country case studies; (ii) longitudinal studies; and (iii) thematic focus studies. In Table 4.1, we provide an overview of the approaches by country and then discuss each approach, its key conceptual framework, design features, research questions, methods and implementation strategies, approaches to analysis, reporting, and dissemination.

4.2.1 Comparative Cross-Country Case Studies

4.2.1.1 Overview

The comparative cross-country approach, designed and applied by the From Protection to Production (PtoP) team at FAO (Food and Agriculture Organization), is based on a systematically applied common protocol—or roadmap—implemented in six countries including Ghana, Kenya, Lesotho, Zimbabwe, Malawi, and Ethiopia (OPM 2013a, 2013b, 2013c; OPM 2014a,

2014b, 2014c, 2014d).[1] In this design, consistency is emphasized in order to identify and compare patterns and trends across CT programmes. Likewise, the comparative design enables identification of variations and discrete characteristics that define particular impacts of different CT programmes, capturing issues of operations and implementation, country contexts, and community and cultural dynamics. One important intention of this approach is to allow for assessment of 'mediating' contexts and causal factors that shape particular outcomes. The qualitative component of the PtoP project was led by a team from Oxford Policy Management (OPM), in partnership with a national research team in each country, with overall technical oversight and coordination from the FAO specialist who participated in the methodological design and fieldwork in all of the countries.

4.2.1.2 Conceptual Framework and Research Questions

The cross-country protocol was based on a set of 'theories of change' corresponding to five areas of inquiry which covered five broad hypotheses regarding CT impacts on household economy, local economy, risk-sharing mechanisms, social networks and inclusion, and programme operation impacts. These hypotheses posed that under certain conditions CTs have the ability to foster: (i) broader economic development at household level (e.g., changes in labour supply; investment in productive activities; and reduction of detrimental risk-coping strategies); (ii) impacts on the wider economy (e.g., creditworthiness, local labour markets, and multiplier effects); (iii) an increase in risk-sharing and household resilience through expansion of social network engagement (e.g., social cohesion, increasing social capital, and mechanisms of reciprocity and self-confidence); and, more specifically, (iv) inclusion and more involvement in community decision-making and increasing people's entitlement sets and livelihood choices. In addition, a final hypothesis focused on operational arrangements of a CT programme (e.g., targeting, enrolment and payment processes, support services, and monitoring), assessing how these mediate impacts resulting in varying outcomes and effects on household and local economy and community dynamics.

The qualitative component of the PtoP mixed-method design was developed jointly by the FAO team and OPM. A detailed field guide comprising a fieldwork 'roadmap' was applied across all countries and includes: theory and rationale of the PtoP design; hypotheses and methods for sampling and data collection, including use of participatory tools; a semi-structured set of questions used to guide interviews in both intervention and comparison

---

[1] Additional information available at: <www.fao.org/economic/ptop/publications/reports> (accessed 25 October 2015).

communities; activities including daily debriefings, analysis, final community feedback, and national debriefing; and write-up processes and peer review. The guide also outlines the one-week pre-fieldwork training.[2]

4.2.1.3 Methods, Timing, and Sequencing

The comparative, cross-country approach included FGDs using participatory tools, key informant interviews (KIIs), and in-depth household case studies. While FGDs were conducted with a pre-established core set of groups (male and female beneficiaries and non-beneficiaries), iterative FGDs and key informant interviews were also conducted in response to emerging themes. While the comparative approach hinged on being replicable across the PtoP IE countries, this did not limit flexibility and adaptation in the line of questioning, thus retaining an appropriate degree of inductive openness. The context of each CT programme and country was examined, and new or unexpected responses were explored further during data collection. Emphasis was placed on 'responsiveness', seeking to capture the robust range of CT impacts in different contexts on various categories of the population (e.g., women, men, youth, and vulnerable households).

The first level of sampling was based on the selection of two different provinces in each country which reflect diverse agro-ecological, socioeconomic, and cultural settings (e.g., northern and southern Ghana). This strategy was designed to optimize insights into the range of CT impacts across different settings while also seeking the 'common' situation. Within the regions, a typical district in the programme was identified, and therein, two communities—one remote and the other closer to the main road and trade centres. At least one district in the qualitative sample was to overlap with where the quantitative study was to be conducted. A close-by community with a similar profile was also included, as 'comparison' to probe for differences that may have been caused by the CT and people's insights of the CT in neighbouring communities.

The qualitative data collection was supposed to be sequenced between baseline and follow-up surveys and following receipt of at least four transfers. The aim of this sequencing was to position the qualitative research so that it would validate findings of the quantitative econometrics analysis and the local economy-wide impact evaluation (LEWIE) to deepen understanding and help explain causal pathways of quantitative findings. One limitation in this approach was that qualitative data collection did not always occur after baseline, limiting the ability to elucidate surprising or uncertain results.

---

[2] The guide was developed iteratively, notably during the first 'pilot' case study in Ghana.

However, when ideal sequencing was possible in practice, and quantitative analysis was available, specific areas for probing were shared with the qualitative team (e.g., in Kenya, examining dynamics of shifts from agricultural wage labour (*maricho*) to on-farm labour).

4.2.1.4 Analysis and Reporting

The first and most critical step in analysing data was daily debriefings. These were used to bring out the main stories and information of the day, probe the meaning and significance of results, identify trends, and reveal gaps which should be addressed in the following day of fieldwork. The team reflected upon how daily findings added to overall understanding of each hypothesis. Debriefing at the end of fieldwork served to synthesize all collected information and develop cohesive narratives and analyses around each hypothesis. This process was facilitated by the team leader, who then consolidated all information, conclusions, and a set of programme recommendations for the country case report.

Debriefing also occurred at community, district, and national levels. At the completion of the fieldwork, a feedback session was conducted in each community to report back preliminary findings. This feedback is a critical part of an ethical approach to research, and also used to validate findings and preliminary conclusions, offering community members an opportunity to add points. This promoted community ownership and reduced the 'extractive' nature of the research. Key findings and preliminary conclusions and recommendations were shared with district officials, and at national level, debriefings with governments and development partners allowed for sharing results, discussing recommendations, and obtaining government and partners' views and 'buy in'. Finally, a joint FAO/OPM brainstorming to synthesize qualitative findings across all countries into a final report provided important insights, explanations, conclusions, and recommendations pertinent to qualitative design in IE and CT programme design in sub-Saharan Africa (Barca et al. 2015).

Final report writing was iterative and participatory, led by the team leader, with inputs from the national research team, and the FAO/PtoP qualitative research expert. Quality enhancement was provided through OPM, FAO, and an external peer reviewer and, once agreed, forwarded to the government and the UNICEF country office for approval. All country reports and 'briefs' were disseminated through the PtoP website and other global platforms for public access.

4.2.1.5 Critical Analysis

The comparative cross-country case study's main strength is that of bringing together a tremendous breadth of data through a systematic and coherent qualitative design. Findings resulting from this qualitative work informed, explained, and deepened understanding of the diverse impacts of CT programmes across different countries and contexts. The integration of quantitative and qualitative findings, however, was not fully maximized due to inconsistency and limited coordination and interaction between the quantitative and qualitative evaluation teams. This weakened the potential for qualitative findings to explain quantitative findings. Optimal sequencing was compromised due to limited control over timing of fieldwork for both quantitative and qualitative components largely as a result of required coordination with others' research programmes, in-country processes, logistical and administrative 'readiness', and research team availability. Also, a follow-up study would have strengthened the validity of the findings and their power to deepen understanding of the 'causal pathways' of impacts.

An important feature of the cross-country comparison design that contributed to its success was the use of the inductive, flexible approach. This flexibility was integrated into the fieldwork and analysis through intensive probing techniques and triangulation with multiple sources to examine unintentional outcomes, perceptions, and experiences of impacts of the CT programmes. This generated findings which were not necessarily obvious, expected, or easily forthcoming. Intense training emphasized 'thinking through' potential CT change processes and causal pathways before knowing actual hypotheses, a planned pilot exercise to become comfortable with the research guide, and the intensity of fieldwork and rigorous structured daily debriefing. The presence of the OPM team leader throughout the research, as well as the FAO qualitative specialist participating and contributing to fieldwork across all countries, added to the quality of the fieldwork process, depth of analysis, and presentation of results. The in-country validation process and discussions around findings, particularly at national level, strengthened their validity, promoted 'buy in' and consensus by government around results and, more specifically, recommendations, and provided strong entry points and a solid ground for influencing future programme and policy design. This is potentially catalytic in influencing future programmes, policy, and support. Governments and partners expressed appreciation for the depth of findings and understanding of the contexts. It was often remarked they had 'indicative' information on some findings, but no systematic validation or analysis, and lacked the 'objective' external evaluation conclusions. It was often the case that governments welcomed even the more contentious findings or those revealing programme gaps, as these provided them evidence to adjust CT programme design to further support and improve the programme, and contribute to policy development.

4.2.2 Longitudinal Approach

4.2.2.1 Overview

The longitudinal design was used in the evaluation by University of North Carolina at Chapel Hill (UNC) of the Malawi CT programme, in collaboration with the Centre for Social Research at the University of Malawi (UNC/Malawi), and by the American Institutes for Research (AIR) evaluation of Zimbabwe's Harmonised Social Cash Transfer (HSCT). The longitudinal approach entailed establishing a cohort of individuals and/or households to participate in qualitative interviews at multiple times during the implementation and evaluation of the CT programme (American Institutes for Research 2013; Handa et al. 2013a, 2013b; Handa et al. 2014; Matondi et al. 2012). These cohorts were 'embedded', meaning they were selected from the larger cohorts of participants in the quantitative evaluation. This sampling approach facilitated obtaining quantitative and qualitative data from the same individuals, allowing greater integration of findings and interplay between methods. The design in both countries was sequential; at both baseline and follow-up, participants first completed the quantitative survey and then (weeks or months) later, the qualitative in-depth interviews. In addition to the longitudinal qualitative cohorts, in both countries other qualitative methods were used at specific periods in the evaluations.

4.2.2.2 Conceptual Frameworks and Research Questions

The evaluation and research questions posed through the longitudinal design focused on improving depth of understanding beyond what could be obtained through the structured quantitative survey, as well as identifying mechanisms and processes of change at the individual and community levels between baseline and twelve-month follow-up.

The overall UNC/Malawi IE was organized within a conceptual framework with hypotheses about mediating and moderating factors of change. While there were several topics of a priori interest (i.e., social networks, food security, family support systems, and Human-Immunodeficiency Virus (HIV)), the evaluators were also interested in and receptive to topics and concepts identified in baseline interviews including mental health, gender dynamics, and social participation, which were explored in the follow-up data collection. The longitudinal qualitative component was intended to provide in-depth understanding of the outcomes and their mediators (mechanisms of change) and moderators (factors that enhance CT impacts). The qualitative evaluation questions focused on 'how' the CT affected vulnerable children and families, particularly family support systems, stability, the protective environment, and peer networks. The qualitative evaluation also examined the implementation experience, including the targeting process, complementary services, and community dynamics, in particular social cohesion and any tensions that emerged in response to the CT programme.

A similar approach was used by AIR in Zimbabwe, where a socio-economic conceptual model informed the development of hypotheses which were related to the pathways through which the CT would impact intended outcomes of the programme. However, in contrast to Malawi, where separate evaluation questions were elaborated to guide the qualitative work, both the qualitative and quantitative components of the Zimbabwe evaluation were guided by three overarching evaluation questions: (i) do CTs reduce food insecurity considering both the amount of food and diet diversity?; (ii) do CTs improve human development of children and adolescents, including improved access to health and education, reduced abuse, and HIV risk?; and (iii) do CTs improve the productive capacity of the household?

4.2.2.3 Methods, Timing, and Sequencing

The UNC/Malawi evaluation included four qualitative components: (i) longitudinal in-depth interviews with sixteen beneficiary households (both youth and caretakers) at baseline and again at twelve-month follow-up; (ii) focus groups at baseline using the 'stages of progress' methodology;[3] (iii) focus groups with beneficiaries and non-beneficiaries at twelve-month follow-up that focused on beneficiary selection processes, implementation, and perceptions of programme impact; and (iv) KIIs with community leaders and chiefs, teachers, and health workers at twelve-month follow-up about the overall CT programme and community dynamics. Sixteen households were recruited across two districts and four traditional authorities. A stratified, purposeful sampling approach was used, focused on characteristics of youth (e.g., gender and orphan status). Reflecting a robust mixed-methods design, the focus groups and KIIs at baseline and follow-up were used to provide contextual understanding and incorporate multiple different perspectives of processes of change that occurred at different stages of implementation. The baseline and follow-up in-depth interviews were conducted following implementation of the baseline and follow-up quantitative surveys.

Interviewing the same individuals provided the opportunity to establish rapport and follow-up on information shared in the first interviews. In the initial interview, participants were asked to describe the context of their lives, with emphasis on social networks and social capital. They were also asked about how their families function and manage in difficult times. Youth were

---

[3] This methodology aims to understand whether programme eligibility criteria are consistent with indigenous concepts of vulnerability, and what the community believes is necessary to move people out of extreme poverty (Krishna 2004).

asked about sexual behaviours and norms. In the follow-up interview, youth and caretakers were asked about the same topics covered previously as well as the impact of the programme on household coping and family and social network relationships, among other topics. One main advantage of the longitudinal follow-up interviews was that in addition to asking about some of the same topics again, new topics that had not been considered at baseline or that would not have made sense at baseline were added. Retention in the qualitative sample was high; of the sixteen households, nearly all caregivers and youth were located for follow-up interviews and those who were not either had passed away or had complicating circumstances. Interviews were conducted by Malawian researchers with prior qualitative experience who received specific training and contributed to revising the interview guides.

The approach used by AIR in Zimbabwe also included multiple qualitative methods to achieve triangulation and longitudinal in-depth interviews. There was an extensive formative component conducted as part of the aforementioned PtoP study in 2012, to obtain early insights about the programme and inform the design of the AIR qualitative study. Longitudinal in-depth interviews were conducted at baseline and twelve months later with twelve households (youth and caregivers), using a sampling approach similar to that of UNC/Malawi to facilitate comparative analysis around key strata. In contrast to UNC/Malawi, retention was more challenging in the AIR Zimbabwe study. Only nine households were interviewed at follow-up and not all of them were the same as baseline. If the youth or caregiver from baseline could not be reached at follow-up, the team identified a different caregiver or youth from the same household interviewed at baseline, or approached the nearest beneficiary household that was part of the quantitative study if the first option was not possible. Focus groups were also conducted, at one-year follow-up only. Semi-structured interviews with a few key informants were also planned at twelve months.

4.2.2.4 Analysis and Reporting

In Malawi, longitudinal data were analysed in two phases. During the fieldwork, interviewers completed detailed fieldwork summary forms on a daily basis. These forms were designed to document information regarding key topics of interest among youth and caregivers (e.g., social network composition, sources of social capital, educational experience, sexual behaviour, household concerns, and coping strategies), guide discussion of emerging themes during the fieldwork, and facilitate rapid analysis of key themes for baseline and follow-up reports. All interviews were audio-recorded, transcribed, and translated into English to enable more extensive analysis. Following completion of the baseline fieldwork, the UNC team wrote an analytical summary for each household using the summary forms and transcripts; these were then expanded with the follow-up data to document the CT programme 'story' over time. They were also used to develop a codebook including inductive and deductive codes that were systematically applied to all transcripts. Insights from the in-depth interviews and other qualitative methods were integrated into the IE baseline and follow-up reports. Research briefs with integrated findings will be disseminated.

In Zimbabwe, field notes, including documentation of quotes when possible, were taken during interviews and FGDs; some interviews and FGDs were audio-recorded and transcribed. Daily debriefing was used to monitor quality and content of information gathered through in-depth interviews, semi-structured interviews, and focus groups. Field notes and transcriptions were used to inform the development of a coding scheme including larger, overarching codes to chunk the data into broad categories as well as codes for sub-topics. Data were systematically coded and codes were reviewed for the frequency with which they were applied as well as their meaning for specific sub-groups of participants. Qualitative and quantitative findings were presented in an integrated manner for baseline and twelve-month reports, with qualitative quotes helping to illustrate key quantitative findings.

4.2.2.5 Critical Analysis

The longitudinal design provides in-depth information that is valuable as a stand-alone source of information as well as a complement to quantitative data and other forms of qualitative data. This approach prioritizes depth over breadth by focusing on obtaining large amounts of data from a small group of people and focusing on their unique experiences and change over time. The strength of this approach is that the evaluation team can obtain rich narratives that exemplify the processes hypothesized about in the theories of change and provide illustrative examples that can be highlighted as case studies. One potential pitfall is that the data obtained can be so in-depth and specific that it is hard to apply findings to other settings. It is critical to integrate discussion of the communities and contexts in which individuals live through interviews with other community members and observations to ensure information is transferable to other settings. This was a challenge in the baseline component in Malawi, where there was not much data obtained beyond the sixteen households. In the follow-up, the inclusion of key informants and focus groups with both beneficiaries and non-beneficiaries greatly improved the breadth of the data and facilitated triangulation. In Zimbabwe, even though participants were not all the same in the end, the in-depth interviews provided a rich picture of the life of families prior to the programme, as well as of how the programme changed beneficiaries' social and economic situation. Prior qualitative research (with

FGDs, KIIs, and participatory approaches) established a qualitative baseline upon which follow-up interviews, even if not with the same people, could build.

The longitudinal approach is also quite labour-intensive and time-consuming with regard to data management and analysis. In order to fully take advantage of the richness of the data, it was extremely helpful to audio-record, transcribe, and translate the interviews in Malawi. Without these transcripts it would have been difficult to explore processes of change over time between baseline and twelve months, and preserve the original words of the participants. Transcription allows for going back to the previous interviews to explore changes over time easily. In addition, transcription was an invaluable tool for conducting joint analysis of data when all team members were not actually present during the fieldwork. Transcription and translation are time-consuming and expensive, requiring resources and planning. Additionally, in both countries, in order to facilitate iterative analysis during data collection and to meet deadlines for initial reporting, it was important to use fieldwork analysis forms that allowed for systematic and rapid documentation and extraction of key themes while waiting for transcriptions to be ready for analysis. With the transcribed data, the UNC/Malawi team was able to engage in more extensive analysis that contributed to and even went beyond the original evaluation questions and hypotheses. In the case of Zimbabwe, where only some of the data was recorded and transcribed, the longitudinal interviews still provided critical inputs not available from other sources of data.

A final consideration to flag concerning the longitudinal approach is the potential to lose original participants during follow-up due to mobility, death, or refusal to participate. In Zimbabwe, the original sample included twelve youth and twelve caregivers, but at follow-up not all original twenty-four informants from baseline were interviewed. In Malawi, retention was much higher and the qualitative and quantitative components served to reinforce each other by extending the time and intensity of engagement with the target communities Nevertheless, loss to follow-up is always a consideration and, given the fairly small sample sizes used in in-depth studies, it is important to consider oversampling by a few participants at baseline and also assessing any major threats to retention (sickness, mobility, family conflict, etc).

4.2.3 Thematic Focus Studies

4.2.3.1 Overview

The thematic design approach was used for formative evaluation in South Africa to obtain targeted and/or operational information for programme and evaluation design (Department of Social Development, South African Social

Security Agency, and UNICEF 2011) and in Zambia and Ethiopia, to assess and inform implementation processes, all implemented by the Institute of Development Studies (IDS) (Berhane et al. 2012a, 2012b, 2012c; Devereux and Roelen 2012, Devereux et al. 2012; Institute of Development Studies 2012, 2014a, 2014b; Roelen and Devereux 2014).

4.2.3.2 Conceptual Frameworks and Research Questions

The IE of the Child Support Grant (CSG) in South Africa was guided by five hypotheses related to mechanisms through which the cash grants would impact children and poor households. Qualitative methods were used at the beginning of the process to inform the quantitative survey and explore five topics of particular interest to UNICEF: (i) the CSG application process; (ii) experiences receiving the grants; (iii) how the grant was spent and influenced access to education and health services; (iv) life circumstances and risk behaviours among adolescent girls and boys, and the influence of the grant on these practices; and (v) child protection and early childhood development. The need for such a formative approach was identified during an IE inception meeting attended by the South African Department of Social Development, Social Security Agency, and UNICEF.

The design of the evaluation of the Child Grant (CG) in Zambia included simultaneous implementation of quantitative and qualitative data collection activities at baseline and four months later. These activities were guided by the same evaluation questions, reflecting the highly integrated mixed-methods approach used in this evaluation. The evaluation design used the 3D Wellbeing Framework, a tool that defines three dimensions of wellbeing: material (the extent to which material needs are being met); relational (whether the person is able to do things (in relation to others) that are important to them); and subjective (whether people perceive themselves as experiencing a good quality of life). Guided by this tool, the evaluation assessed: (i) people's direct and indirect experiences of the CT programme processes; (ii) impacts and outcomes at the individual and household levels; and (iii) broader outcomes and impacts in the community. The use of the 3D Wellbeing Framework reflects a pragmatic and deductive approach. The evaluators went into the evaluation with a priori concepts and constructs that they were interested in exploring in order to strengthen the CG. At the same time, the evaluators' use of participatory methods and tools, and the fact that they collected data on two occasions in the same communities, also allowed for inductive inquiry whereby themes that were identified by participants could be explored in depth and theories of change and well-being further expanded.

The qualitative component of Ethiopia's Social Cash Transfer Pilot Programme (SCTPP) included two rounds of fieldwork (Berhane et al. 2012a,

2012b, 2012c; Devereux and Roelen 2012; Institute of Development Studies 2014b). In round one, the qualitative component focused on perceptions, awareness, and effectiveness mostly pertaining to operational features such as targeting processes, payment delivery, grievance mechanisms, and interactions and effects of the SCTPP on informal social safety net mechanisms of support. The second round followed up on issues examined during the first round and also explored some new questions identified during baseline. The new questions concerned views and perceptions of the SCTPP's retargeting exercise, use of cash with an attempt to 'track' the transfer beyond the beneficiaries, and perceptions of impact on children from both beneficiary and non-beneficiary households, and communities.

4.2.3.3 Methods, Timing, and Sequencing

In South Africa, the qualitative research included FGDs with beneficiaries and non-beneficiaries and KIIs. The qualitative fieldwork covered four of the five provinces where the programme was being implemented; within each province, three localities were chosen for fieldwork. The localities were stratified across rural, urban, and peri-urban to capture geographic diversity. In each locality, seven FGDs and four KIIs were conducted. The seven focus groups included adult and youth beneficiaries and non-beneficiaries and were single sex. Key informant interviews were conducted with CT programme staff, health workers, education workers, and community leaders. The data collection was conducted simultaneously by four teams with two fieldworkers, each spending one week in each locality. All FGDs and KIIs were audio-recorded and subsequently transcribed and translated into English.

In Zambia, there were three rounds of data collection. Preliminary fieldwork was conducted in April 2013 to establish relationships and prepare for the evaluation fieldwork. The first round of evaluation fieldwork was conducted in July 2013 with a second and more focused round of data collection conducted in November 2013. In the four months between the two rounds of data collection, significant changes were made to the national social protection policy, including shifting the CG to the 10 per cent inclusive model. As a result, the second round of data collection also served as an assessment of the perceptions and uncertainty related to the policy changes. Fieldwork was conducted in two districts with focus on three Community Welfare Area Committees (CWAC) in each district, two intervention and one control. Within each CWAC, qualitative methods included FGDs with participatory tools (eight), household case studies (ten), and KIIs (five). Stratified sampling was used at each level, starting with selection of CWAC, based on intervention participation and distance from the road. Primary criteria for selection of households for case studies were poverty level, followed by head of household characteristics, including gender and age. Key informants included traditional leaders, teachers, health workers, and payment managers. Data were recorded through fieldwork diaries and photographs of the products of participatory activities; these records were used to create transcripts following the fieldwork.

In Ethiopia, two rounds of qualitative fieldwork were completed, each one following a round of quantitative fieldwork. This was deemed highly useful to allow for quantitative preliminary findings to inform the design of qualitative data collection tools and for the qualitative research to verify and deepen results from the quantitative survey. The first round was implemented in August 2012, about one year after the initial targeting and about ten months after the first payment; a second round was conducted in April 2014. The qualitative evaluation during both rounds of fieldwork was conducted in four *tabias*,[4] of which one was urban. The fieldwork was carried out over three days per *tabia* and comprised a range of methods, including FGDs, KIIs, and household case studies. Purposive sampling was used in selecting informants with the assistance and guidance from the Woreda Social Welfare Officer. In each *tabia*, FGDs were conducted at both rounds with Community Care Coalitions (CCC), beneficiaries, and non-beneficiaries (in both intervention and control communities). In addition, KIIs (thirteen) were conducted at the regional, *woreda*, and community levels. The participatory tool of poverty profiling was also applied with a group of community members to examine SCTPP inclusion and exclusion among community residents. The participatory mapping tool was conducted with community members in both rounds to assess the use of the transfer, how use changed over time, and the transfer impacts on children (e.g., nutrition, health, education, and labour). A qualitative research interview and discussion guide was prepared outlining questions for field researchers to follow—including specific questions oriented to the respective informant (officials, etc.)—and explaining use of the community poverty profile tool.

4.2.3.4 Analysis and Reporting

In South Africa, a fieldwork report summarizing the data collection process and lessons learned was completed immediately after data collection. More in-depth data analysis was initiated following the completion of fieldwork within each locality. Analysis began with development of a coding scheme that was applied systematically to all of the interview and FGD transcripts. This coding scheme integrated deductive codes (informed by the topics covered in the interview and FGD guides), inductive codes (informed by themes identified by the research team during the data collection and coding processes), and structural codes, such as participant sex, to facilitate comparative analysis

---

[4] *Woreda* and *tabia* are administrative levels in Ethiopia, *woreda* being equivalent to a district, and *tabia* or *kebele*, a ward.

around key strata of interest. The team generated code reports to facilitate data reduction and the identification of themes, illustrative quotes, and analytic matrices to further refine the themes and key findings. The team developed a report to inform the design of the quantitative survey instrument.

In Zambia, although there were two data collection points, they were only four months apart and were therefore treated as one dataset. A thematic analysis approach was used to create codes and categories related to the key study objectives and to link back to the 3D framework. The analysis process was both deductive, in that it was guided by the constructs and hypotheses of the 3D framework, as well as inductive and iterative, in that it responded to findings from each wave of data collection. Given the stratified sample, analysis was highly comparative to identify differences between different categories of the population (e.g., transfer recipients and non-recipients) and socio-demographic characteristics. Qualitative and quantitative findings were reported jointly in reports, and key conclusions reflect an integrated interpretation of quantitative and qualitative data.

Reporting and analysis of findings in the SCTPP Ethiopia evaluation was presented through a mixed-methods IE framework. Presentation and discussion of qualitative findings from the first round was linked to quantitative data, specifically concerning informal community support mechanisms, and CCC operations and implementation. Findings in the baseline report highlighted concurrence and discrepancies between qualitative and quantitative findings, reflecting the highly integrated approach. This type of analytical presentation reflects effective integration of approaches and use of qualitative data, particularly to contextualize the set of quantitative results and analysis. Results from the first round of qualitative research and the overall baseline study were discussed during a dissemination workshop with main stakeholders in November 2012. This deepened analysis and, as noted, provided recommendations which generated new directions for the second round of qualitative research.

4.2.3.5 Critical Analysis

The three examples of thematic designs reflect the use of qualitative methods to address operational issues and to explore specific themes or topics. In the thematic design, there are examples of both breadth and depth. In the case of Zambia, the focus was on breadth by using a stratified approach to sample different categories of households. While having strata can facilitate comparative analysis and broad understanding of the context, a certain level of thematic saturation within each stratum is also required in order to be useful. It is extremely important to monitor this saturation, or lack thereof, during the fieldwork process to avoid coming up short by identifying themes but not being able to assess their salience beyond a few participants. In South

Africa, qualitative methods were used essentially for formative purposes to inform the quantitative survey; the findings reflected more of a breadth than depth perspective and also cut across several strata. In Ethiopia, attempts were made to combine depth,through a more deductive approach,with breadth, and with flexibility,through an inductive and open-ended approach. This flexibility has been emphasized by the researchers as vital to enabling exploration and capturing of unintended and unexpected impacts (Roelen and Devereux 2014). Also, the overall duration of the IE, and periods of time between rounds can also play an important factor in assessing types and quality of impacts and the processes and mediating factors bringing them about. Longer periods of qualitative study in IE can allow for better understanding of impacts that are genuinely sustainable and which emerge only over time.

4.3 CONCLUSION

The approaches to qualitative evaluation presented in this chapter demonstrate a range of strengths and trade-offs. Table 4.2 provides a summary highlighting core principles; timing, methodological approaches, and tools; analytical processes; and lessons learned. The PtoP comparative, cross-country approach provided a rigorous framework for analysing how and why varying types of CT programmes impacted households and wider communities across distinct contexts. Its strength lies in the replicability of a consistent, structured methodology—using a mix of approaches and tools—based on a common set of hypotheses. This enabled comparison of trends and patterns across countries. The comparative power of the PtoP evaluation ultimately was its most valued feature, generating useful lessons and recommendations concerning CT programmes—per country and overall—anchored in an expansive evidence base. Use of a consistent structural framework (protocol), as used in PtoP, simultaneously requires a well-grounded knowledge of reality and practical fieldwork experience, as well as allowing for degrees of adaptation. Reaching this balance between rigour and flexibility by use of in-depth inductive inquiry while carrying out a deductive-framed protocol is a challenge. Intensive nightly team debriefings provided the critical 'space' for ensuring iterative processes of inquiry and continuous sharpening of causal explanations. In PtoP, this was managed largely by having a strong qualitative team leader (as well as FAO) with high technical expertise and experience throughout the fieldwork; this is an essential condition for carrying out this type of fieldwork and IE.

The lack of follow-up rounds distinguishing the comparative approach can limit understanding of causal relations of impact processes and changes over

Table 4.2. Comparison of Qualitative Design Approaches

Design approach	Principles of approach	Timing, main methods, and tools	Data analysis and reporting	Key lessons
Comparative, cross-country	— Systematic, structured protocol based on five hypotheses within a theory of change. — Inductive and flexible with emphasis on contextual mediating factors that explain CT impact. — Establishing comparability within and across countries to reveal patterns, variations, and mediating factors. — Common sampling enabling comparability among countries.	— Inception workshop to optimize qual–quant alignment. — Intensive five-day training to practice guiding questions and tools. Research in two distinct regions and one comparison community to identify variations. — Methodological triangulation, including FGDs, using participatory tools, KIIs, and in-depth household case studies. — Presence of experienced team leaders/FAO expert.	— Intensive daily debriefings and analysis shaping conclusions iteratively. — Extensive integration of contextual dimensions and tools' results, triangulating data. — Feedback at community, district, and national levels to validate findings and to build consensus and 'buy in' of recommendations. — Findings of the six-country qualitative research consolidated into a synthesis report and brief, and incorporated in PtoP briefs and presentations.	— Retain a structured, consistent protocol for comparability and to garner lessons which inform design. — Undertake daily debriefings to strengthen analysis and guide follow-up inquiry, but this requires experienced leadership. — Establish protocol for quant–qual coordination and continuous sharing of findings to strengthen causal pathway analysis. — Collaborate with others' research programmes ('piggy backing') to increase research opportunities: but this can cause delays.
Longitudinal	— Inductive and iterative. — Multiple encounters to develop rapport. — Staged analysis to obtain initial impressions and then more in-depth understanding. — Focused on processes and mechanisms of change to add fuller understanding.	— In-depth interviews with the same participants at least at two time points. — Methodological triangulation for FGDs and KIIs for context and programme implementation assessment.	— Templates to systematically facilitate rapid analysis. — Audio recording to facilitate in-depth analysis. — Integration of qualitative findings in evaluation reports and briefs and standalone qualitative dissemination.	— Stage analysis to facilitate timely dissemination. — Overly ambitious and structured guide limits opportunity for extensive probing. — Consider loss to follow-up at initial recruitment.

| Thematic | — Focused evaluations on specific areas of inquiry.
— Prioritizing design and operations to inform future scale-up and re-design.
— Combination of inductive and deductive approaches. | — Initial findings from quantitative evaluation inform qualitative focus and data collection tools.
— Sequential rounds of fieldwork; methodological triangulation with FGDs, KIIs, case studies and participatory tools.
— Stratified sampling to capture diverse contexts of CT impacts. | — Analysis of findings emphasize trends and patterns.
— Analysis of first round of qualitative evaluation informs second round. | — Combining methods and joint reporting of findings contextualizes and strengthens evidence to inform programme and evaluation design.
— Different strata of participants facilitate comparative analysis, but adequate saturation within strata is critical to enable full understanding.
— Use exploratory mixed-method approaches and longer periods (e.g., panel studies) to capture unforeseen impacts and complex processes. |

time. As in the case of PtoP, it also might result in relatively patchy, somewhat unsystematic integration of mixed methods, reducing the power of the qualitative research in serving its primary functions of informing survey design, explaining findings from quantitative research, and defining causal pathways.

The longitudinal studies, in contrast, implemented through the UNC/Malawi and AIR/Zimbabwe evaluations, provided a diachronic perspective, allowing for greater explanatory analyses of change and greater context of causal linkages, largely through use of one primary method (longitudinal in-depth interviews with youth and caregivers in small samples of households) and smaller samples. Longitudinal qualitative research is relatively more costly than implementing one fieldwork round and, as cases in this chapter show, requires choices regarding which methods to use for follow-up rounds and how to manage the data.

An additional valuable feature of implementing a longitudinal approach, if timed correctly, is its potential to inform quantitative survey design, either at baseline, the case for AIR/Zimbabwe, or during quantitative survey follow-up rounds, the case for UNC/Malawi. As qualitative research typically highlights particular thematic areas meriting further exploration, these identified areas can then be incorporated into both future quantitative surveys as well as qualitative studies. This is a strength emerging also from the thematic approach implemented in several countries. In Zambia, for example, initial qualitative studies of the CG identified several thematic focus areas as priorities for follow-up qualitative research. This is now planned under the transformed programme—the 10 per cent inclusive programme. In Ethiopia, the workshops organized around discussion of the baseline report (Berhane et al. 2012b) directly influenced the revision and addition of thematic areas for the qualitative evaluation during the second round of qualitative fieldwork conducted in 2014.

Thematic studies enabled sharp and focused analysis of the more instrumental aspects of programme design and operations (e.g., effectiveness and impacts of operational arrangements and features). This is of particular interest to governments who are eager to better understand the performance and impacts of implementation processes—how they mediate impacts and where improvements can be made to best attain programme objectives. Qualitative findings and recommendations concerning operations added immediate and significant value by informing social protection programme and policy design and thereby contributed to advocacy efforts to increase national budget allocations. Thematic studies may be relatively low in cost, but can possibly risk compromising the breadth and longitudinal perspectives of impacts.

Each qualitative approach described in this chapter has its particular strengths, as well as costs and trade-offs. An ideal design would likely combine: (i) the PtoP comparative approach of breadth, richness, and comparative power; within a (ii) longitudinal design—ideally allowing for three rounds of fieldwork, that is at baseline to inform quantitative survey design, a first round following quantitative analysis, and a second follow-up round; and (iii) built-in flexibility to implement focused thematic studies of issues arising. This model would require a substantial budget to accommodate for sequential rounds of research, a team leader presence throughout fieldwork and analysis, and built-in flexibility to identify and research new thematic topics. Good knowledge of the context by the research team is an additional, particularly important, asset to qualitative study, contributing to deepening understanding of the experiences, perceptions, and reasons for change caused by CT programmes.

REFERENCES

American Institutes for Research (2013). 'Baseline Report for the Impact Evaluation of Zimbabwe's Harmonised Social Cash Transfer Programme' (December). Washington, DC: American Institutes for Research.

Barca, V., S. Brook, J. Holland, M. Otulana, and P. Pozarny (2015). 'Qualitative Research and Analyses of the Economic Impacts of Cash Transfer Programmes in Sub-Saharan Africa—Synthesis Report'. Available online at: <http://www.fao.org/3/a-i4336e.pdf> (accessed 12 January 2015). Rome: Food and Agriculture Organisation.

Berhane, G., S. Devereux, J. Hoddinott, F. N. Tegebu, K. Roelen, and B. Schwab (2012a). 'Evaluation of the Social Cash Transfers Pilot Programme, Tigray Region, Ethiopia: Draft Baseline Report' (11 November). Washington, DC: International Food Policy Research Institute.

Berhane, G., S. Devereux, J. Hoddinott, F. N. Tegebu, K. Roelen, and B. Schwab (2012b). 'Evaluation of the Social Cash Transfers Pilot Programme, Tigray Region, Ethiopia: Baseline Report' (5 December). Washington, DC: International Food Policy Research Institute.

Berhane, G., S. Devereux, J. Hoddinott, F. N. Tegebu, K. Roelen, B. Schwab, and A. S. Taffesse (2012c). 'Evaluation of the Social Cash Transfers Pilot Programme, Tigray Region, Ethiopia: Inception Report' (12 July). Washington, DC: International Food Policy Research Institute.

Bernard, H. R. (2011). *Research Methods in Anthropology: Qualitative and Quantitative Approaches* (5th edn). Lanham: AltaMira Press.Department of Social Development, South African Social Security Agency, and UNICEF (2011). *Child* 'Support Grant Evaluation 2010: Qualitative Research Report' (June). Pretoria: UNICEF.

Devereux, S. and K. Roelen (2012). 'Tigray Social Cash Transfer Pilot Programme (SCTPP): Revised Concept Note for Qualitative Evaluation' (9 July). Brighton: Institute of Development Studies.

Devereux, S., K. Roelen, K. Tsegazeab, and H. Miruts (2012). 'Tigray Social Cash Transfer Pilot Programme (SCTPP) Qualitative Fieldwork Report' (18 September). Brighton: Institute of Development Studies.

Garbarino, S. and Holland, J. (2009). 'Quantitative and Qualitative Methods in Impact Evaluation and Measuring Results', Issues Paper (March). Birmingham: Governance and Social Development Resource Centre.

Handa, S., G. Angeles, S. Abdoulayi, P. Mvula, M. Tsoka, C. Barrington, K. Brugh, M. J. Hill, K. Kilburn, F. Otchere, and D. Zuskov (2014). 'Malawi Social Cash Transfer Baseline Evaluation Report' (18 July). Chapel Hill: Carolina Population Center, University of North Carolina at Chapel Hill.

Handa, S., D. Seidenfeld, P. Matondi, and L. Zanamwe (2013a). 'Comprehensive Methodology Report for the Impact Evaluation of Zimbabwe's Harmonized Social Cash Transfer Program' (18 January). Washington, DC: American Institutes for Research.

Handa, S., K. Kilburn, C. Barrington, G. Angeles, P. Mvula, and T. Maxton (2013b). 'Impact Evaluation of the Malawi SCT Inception Report' (February). Chapel Hill: Carolina Population Center, University of North Carolina at Chapel Hill.

Institute of Development Studies (2012). 'Tigray Social Cash Transfer Pilot Programme (SCTPP) Qualitative Research Instruments' (8 August). Brighton: Institute of Development Studies.

Institute of Development Studies (2014a). 'The Wider Impacts of Social Protection: Research on the Views, Experiences and Perceptions of Social Cash Transfer Programme Recipients and Their Communities in Zambia, Report on the 10 per cent Inclusive SCT: Kalomo, Monze and Choma', Draft (June). Brighton: Institute of Development Studies.

Institute of Development Studies (2014b). 'Proposal: Qualitative Field Work SCTPP Evaluation—Round II' (3 March). Brighton: Institute of Development Studies.

Krishna, A. (2004). 'Escaping Poverty and Becoming Poor: Who Gains, Who Loses, and Why?' *World Development*, 32(1): 121–36.

Matondi, P., L. Zanamwe, D. Seidenfeld, and S. Handa (2012). 'Inception Report for the Impact Evaluation of Zimbabwe's Harmonized Social Cash Transfer Program' (August). Washington, DC: American Institutes for Research.

Oxford Policy Management (2013a). 'Qualitative Research and Analyses of the Economic Impacts of Cash Transfer Programmes in Sub-Saharan Africa, Zimbabwe Country Case Study Report' (November). Available online at: <http://www.fao.org/docrep/018/ar671e/ar671e.pdf?utm_source=website&utm_medium=link&utm_campaign=PtoPwebsite> (accessed 12 January 2015). Rome: Food and Agriculture Organisation.

Oxford Policy Management (2013b). 'Qualitative Research of the Economic Impacts of Cash Transfer Programmes in Sub-Saharan Africa: A Research Guide for the From Protection to Production Project. Available online at: <http://www.fao.org/docrep/018/aq662e/aq662e.pdf> (accessed 12 January 2015). Rome: Food and Agriculture Organisation.

Oxford Policy Management (2013c). 'Qualitative Research and Analyses of the Economic Impacts of Cash Transfer Programmes in Sub-Saharan Africa, Ghana Country Case Study Report' (February). Available online at: <http://www.fao.org/fileadmin/user_upload/p2p/Publications/Ghana_qualitative.pdf> (accessed 12 January 2015). Rome: Food and Agriculture Organisation.

Oxford Policy Management (2014a). 'Qualitative Research and Analyses of the Economic Impacts of Cash Transfer Programmes in Sub-Saharan Africa, Ethiopia Country Case Study Report' (December). Available online at: <http://www.fao.org/3/a-i4276e.pdf> (accessed 12 January 2015). Rome: Food and Agriculture Organisation.

Oxford Policy Management (2014b). 'Qualitative Research and Analyses of the Economic Impacts of Cash Transfer Programmes in Sub-Saharan Africa, Kenya Country Case Study Report' (March). Available online at: <http://www.fao.org/docrep/019/i3721e/i3721e.pdf> (accessed 12 January 2015). Rome: Food and Agriculture Organisation.

Oxford Policy Management (2014c). 'Qualitative Research and Analyses of the Economic Impacts of Cash Transfer Programmes in Sub-Saharan Africa, Lesotho Country Case Study Report' (March). Available online at: <http://www.fao.org/docrep/019/i3616e/i3616e.pdf?utm_source=website&utm_medium=link&utm_campaign=PtoPwebsite> (accessed 12 January 2015). Rome: Food and Agriculture Organisation.

Oxford Policy Management (2014d). 'Qualitative Research and Analyses of the Economic Impacts of Cash Transfer Programmes in Sub-Saharan Africa, Malawi Country Case Study Report' (November). Available online at: <http://www.fao.org/3/a-i4188e.pdf> (accessed 12 January 2015). Rome: Food and Agriculture Organisation.

Patton, M. Q. (2002). *Qualitative Research & Evaluation Methods* (3rd edn). Thousand Oaks: SAGE Publications, Inc.

Roelen, K. and S. Devereux (2014). 'Evaluating Outside the Box: Mixing Methods in Analysing Social Protection Programmes'. Centre for Development Impact, Practice Paper 6 (January). Brighton: Institute of Development Studies.

Warr, D. J. (2005). 'It Was Fun … but We Don't Usually Talk about These Things': Analyzing Sociable Interaction in Focus Groups'. *Qualitative Inquiry*, 11(2): 200–25. doi:10.1177/1077800404273412.

World Bank (2011). 'Participatory Methods'. *Poverty Reduction and Equity*. Available online at: <http://go.worldbank.org/PCECWZHFS0> (accessed 12 January 2015). Washington DC: World Bank.

5

Local Economy-Wide Impact Evaluation of Social Cash Transfer Programmes

J. Edward Taylor (University of California, Davis), Karen Thome (USDA Economic Research Service), and Mateusz Filipski (International Food Policy Research Institute)

5.1 INTRODUCTION

The stated goals of social cash transfer (SCT) programmes described in this book are social: to improve the welfare of the beneficiary or 'treated' households, by providing cash and encouraging changes in behaviour related to nutrition, education, and health. But by providing poor households with cash, SCT programmes also treat the local economies of which these households are part, by stimulating the demand for goods and services.[1]

Targeting strategies in sub-Saharan Africa generally limit SCT eligibility to resource-constrained and labour-poor households, so the design of these programmes would seem to work against the creation of positive production impacts. Despite this, the evaluation findings presented in this book point to a number of positive production impacts in the beneficiary households. From a local economy-wide perspective, the households that receive SCTs are a conduit through which new cash enters the local economy. As beneficiaries spend their cash, they unleash general equilibrium (GE) effects that transmit programme impacts to others in the local economy, including non-beneficiaries.

Most households that do not receive SCTs are poor—just not poor enough to qualify for transfers. Most SCT-ineligible households fail to meet asset-poverty-related criteria and are not labour constrained; thus, they may be better positioned to expand their production when SCTs stimulate the local demand for goods and services.

---

[1] The views expressed in this information product are those of the author(s) and do not necessarily reflect the views or policies of the United States Department of Agriculture.

Why evaluate the local economy impacts of SCTs? There are several reasons.

Often, looking at SCTs through a local-economy lens reveals impacts missed by other approaches. Documenting positive impacts outside of the households directly affected by a development programme can tip the cost–benefit scale in favour of funding or expanding the programme. More and more, governments and donors want to know that a development project not only benefits targeted households and sectors but also creates positive economic spillovers—and they want to know what can be done to enhance those spillovers. Documenting impacts beyond the treated can be critical in order to garner political and institutional support for projects and policies.

Local economy-wide impact evaluation (LEWIE) links models of treated and non-treated households to GE models of project-area economies, explicitly capturing interactions among households while evaluating the *total* economic impacts of SCT programmes. LEWIE models are estimated with microdata from surveys carried out as part of programme evaluations. Thus, they provide the micro focus needed to realistically simulate programme impacts. LEWIE simulations can be complemented by experimental and non-experimental estimates of programme impacts. As described in Chapter 1 and evident in the country chapters, LEWIE uncovers important spillovers that result from SCTs.

LEWIE has been used to evaluate a wide variety of policies. The general LEWIE methodology is detailed in Taylor and Filipski (2014). This chapter describes the theory and methodology of LEWIE as it is applied to the evaluation of SCT programmes as part of the PtoP (From Protection to Production) project in Ethiopia, Ghana, Kenya, Lesotho, Malawi, Zambia, and Zimbabwe, which has been detailed in this book. Here, we show LEWIE models constructed for each of the seven African countries for which a local-economy evaluation was carried out, and what considerations shape differences in local economy outcomes of SCTs across countries. The local economy impacts for each country appear in the country chapters of this book.

5.2 LEWIE THEORY AND METHODOLOGY

A cash transfer generates spillovers if it affects households other than the intended recipients in any way, for example, by changing their incomes, production, consumption decisions, access to information, perceptions, or even social interactions. In our LEWIE models, we focus exclusively on local economic spillovers that are generated when a SCT-recipient household spends its cash transfer—referred to as GE spillover effects. In economic systems, prices transmit the influences of market shocks from one actor to another. Prices are central to LEWIE models because these models simulate the way local economies work in order to uncover SCT impacts.

If the local economy were perfectly integrated with outside markets (i.e., all goods were tradable with the rest of the world), increased spending from the recipient households would have no impact on prices or on local production. The recipient household would be able to use its SCT to purchase goods and services from suppliers outside the local economy at prevailing market prices. In this case, the SCT would not create spillovers. The SCT recipients' demand would not be large enough to affect prices in the larger economy, so prices would not convey impacts to local producers.

Some goods and services are tradable between poor rural economies and the outside world. Obvious examples include Coca Cola, Kleenex, and dish soap. Others obviously are not, for example haircuts, construction, and foods too perishable or too bulky to buy or sell in distant markets. Imported goods and factors may be imperfect substitutes for local ones (e.g., black versus white teff in Ethiopia; family versus hired labour in agricultural production). Goods that are obviously tradable have a non-tradable component. For example, the purchase of a bar of soap in a local grocery store will have a tradable (wholesale price plus transport cost to the village) and non-tradable (grocery mark-up, from which wages and profits come, and possibly within-village transport cost) component. Poor roads, communications, and marketing infrastructure easily can turn what might be a tradable good—for example, livestock or cassava—into a non-tradable, produced to supply local demand.

The existence of non-tradable goods and services with locally determined (endogenous) prices is necessary in order for SCTs to general local income spillovers. If goods and services are non-tradable, their supply will not be perfectly elastic (i.e., supply curves will slope upward), because goods and services will not rush in from outside markets to meet changes in local demand. Increases in local demand from SCTs will put upward pressure on local prices. Whether and to what extent local prices actually increase depends on the local supply response.

Figure 5.1 illustrates how an SCT can create spillovers. Initially, the transfer creates excess demand for goods in the local economy, represented by an outward demand shift from D to D'. The supply of the good increases along the supply curve, S, to meet this new demand, creating income for the owners of the factors of production for the good. LEWIE is designed to measure these spillovers.

The magnitude of the supply response compared with the inflationary effect depends on local suppliers' ability to respond to the increase in demand. The diagram illustrates three different possibilities, which result in three different market equilibria after the demand increase.

If the local supply response is very elastic (the supply curve is flat, like curve S_1), production of the good increases from Q_1 to Q_2, but the price does not change. This is the best possible outcome, because in this case the SCT is purely expansionary and not inflationary.

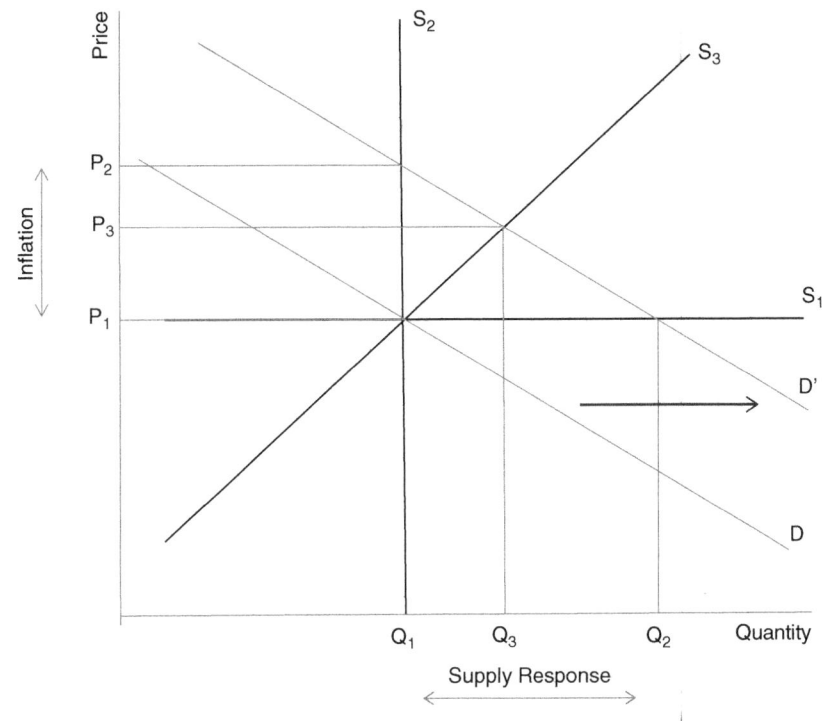

Figure 5.1. Illustration of Possible Impacts of SCT in a Local Market

At the other extreme, the local supply could be totally unresponsive (inelastic), as depicted by supply curve S_2. The price increases, from P_1 to P_2, but there is no real effect on the economy: the quantity produced and consumed stays the same, at Q_1. This is the worst possible outcome, because in this case, all of the impact of the SCT programme is inflationary. An inelastic supply response can result if local markets and prices do not function properly to convey impacts from recipient households to producers, or if producers face constraints that prevent them from responding to price signals.

In between these two extremes lie many other possibilities, in which the SCT creates both local economic expansion and inflation. The expansionary versus inflationary impact depends on the slope of the supply curve. Supply curve S_3 depicts one of these many possibilities. The increase in demand results in a production increase from Q_1 to Q_3, and a price increase from P_1 to P_3.

The good or service in question as well as the circumstances shaping the supply response are critical in determining how the SCT affects a local market. In the very short run, it may be difficult for local producers to increase their output, because crop and livestock production and investment in new activities take time, even under ideal conditions. Households are also likely to face constraints with respect to access to land, cash to purchase inputs or invest in new activities, technologies to raise productivity, capital, and markets to acquire inputs in a timely fashion. Price inflation is not inevitable, however. In an economy with high levels of unemployment, a stimulus programme like cash transfers may increase the local labour demand without exerting significant upward pressure on wages. If land is abundant, it will not impose constraints on local production. In a sector like retail, which obtains most of its merchandise in markets outside the local economy, increased demand might not push up local prices noticeably.

5.3 DESIGNING THE SCT-LEWIE MODELS

LEWIE models are structural GE models that nest different groups of households within a local economy, where they interact in markets. Each household may participate in different income generating activities and spend its income on goods and services within and outside of the local economy. The household and business survey data tell us which activities households participate in, to what extent, and how households and local businesses spend their income.

Sections 5.3.1–5.3.4 describe the general structure of LEWIE model for the analysis of SCT programmes, defines the Zone of Influence (ZOI) for which the LEWIE evaluation is carried out, discusses model assumptions and how to test them, and shows how data from surveys of households and businesses are incorporated into LEWIE.

Household groups, activities, and factors form the backbone of the LEWIE model. We chose which household groups, activities, and factors to model based on their significance in the local economy and their importance to the stated goal of the SCT programmes themselves.

5.3.1 Households

Defining the household groups is straightforward in evaluating SCT programmes. The SCT-LEWIE model simulates impacts of the SCT on two households groups: the eligible households who receive the cash transfer, and the non-eligible households who live in the same communities and do not receive the transfer but may benefit from spillovers. It is possible to further disaggregate the household groups to focus on a specific vulnerability or economic activity, for example, but that was beyond the scope of the SCT evaluations.

The LEWIE contains models of representative households of each type (eligible and non-eligible). Because eligible households are considerably less than half the population, we weight the representative households' income and expenditures by population size (so the modelled eligible household represents all eligible households in the ZOI). The relative population sizes of the two household groups are determinants of the scale of the transfer within the economy, and also of how business (and factor) ownership is allocated among eligible and ineligible households.

5.3.2 LEWIE Activity and Factor Accounts

The LEWIE model structure is centred on the principal economic activities in which the households participate, the households' income sources, and the goods and services on which households spend their income. These constitute the accounts in the LEWIE model. Households participate in productive activities (crop and livestock production, retail, service, and other production activities), which produce these commodities for sale within the ZOI and for export outside the region. The productive activities use a combination of factors, including hired and family labour, land, capital, and purchased inputs, to produce their output. They can also purchase commodities (such as retail items or crops) to use as intermediate inputs. The activities, commodities, and factors modelled in the SCT-LEWIEs are summarized in Table 5.1.

On the expenditure side, households can purchase any of the commodities in Table 5.1 or goods purchased outside the local economy. They can also give transfers to other households, or spend money on healthcare or savings. In addition to income from productive activities and factor ownership, households can obtain income from transfers from other households and from other exogenous sources (like the SCT programme itself).

5.3.3 Zones of Influence

We designate a 'Zone of Influence' as the geographic boundary of the local economy; this is the area over which LEWIE simulates the SCT programme's impacts and across which we calculate the SCT multipliers. In the SCT-LEWIE studies featured in this book, the ZOI varies from a representative village (Ghana) to an entire district (Zimbabwe). The classification of goods as tradable or not depends on whether their prices are determined within the ZOI (these are non-tradable, or local, goods), or if prices are exogenous, determined in markets outside the ZOI (tradable goods).

There are two major considerations that guide the definition of the ZOI. The first is the programme evaluation itself: over how large an area do we wish to document the impacts of an intervention? For example, many of

Table 5.1. Accounts in the SCT-LEWIEs

Activities[a]	
Crop	Crops
Live	Livestock
Ret	Retail
Ser	Services
Prod	Other Production Activities

Commodities	
Crop	Crops
Live	Livestock
Ret	Retail
Ser	Services
Prod	Other locally produced goods
Outside	produced outside the local economy

Factors[b]	
HL	Hired Labour
FL	Family Labour
Land	Land
K	Capital/Physical Assets
Purch	Purchased Input
Herd[c]	Herd (livestock)

[a] Malawi: Included maize and fishing activities and commodities
[b] Malawi: Hired labour was disaggregated into HL and GL (*ganyu* labour), as well as into gendered labour factors; included Inventory factor
[c] Ethiopia, Kenya, and Lesotho: Herd factor was represented by K

the SCT programmes were randomized at the village cluster (VC) or ward level. In those cases it made sense to define the ZOI as a village cluster and simulate a multiplier for this economic space. Table 5.2 relates the ZOI definition to the study design for each country.

The second consideration in defining the ZOI is the structure and organization of local markets. If there is a market that we think may be important in transmitting spillovers among households, that market should be included in the ZOI. For example, we might know that households in a particular region spend a large percentage of their cash at a weekly market. We will want to define our ZOI such that it captures the weekly market, inasmuch as it may represent an important mechanism for creating expenditure linkages within the local economy.

In some country case studies, there were plans to scale up the SCT programmes to entire regions, and the original study areas included some communities with recipient households and some without (Table 5.2). In these cases, we defined a second, scaled-up ZOI that linked the two types of communities, often through a shared market.

Table 5.2. ZOI Definitions and Evaluation Designs

Country	Core Design	Randomization of Treatment[a]	Base Model ZOI	Scaled-Up ZOI
Ethiopia	PSM	Household level within a village	Village (regional models)	NA
Ghana	Longitudinal PSM (propensity score matching)	Village	Representative Village	Representative programme district
Kenya	Location RCT (randomized control trial)	Village Cluster (VC)	Representative VC (regional models)	Representative programme district
Lesotho	ED RCT	Village Cluster (VC) [ED Level]	Representative VC	Programme region
Malawi	VC RCT	Village Cluster (VC)	Representative VC	NA
Zambia	CWAC RCT	Village Cluster (VC) [CWAC]	Representative VC	Representative programme district
Zimbabwe	District matched case-control	District	Representative district	NA

[a] The term Village Cluster (VC) represents the different names for administrative units in the programme countries: Electoral District (ED) in Lesotho; Community Welfare Assistance Committee (CWAC) in Zambia; Location in Kenya.

5.3.4 LEWIE Model Assumptions

The SCT-LEWIE models, like the SCT experimental studies, evaluate impacts of cash transfers in the relatively short run. Because we do not simulate long-run programme impacts, our LEWIE modelling assumes that land and capital are fixed at their initial levels.

Other goods and factors are marketable. Assumptions about market closure—that is, where prices are determined—reflect how well integrated households and businesses are with local and regional markets. Households' and businesses' answers to survey questions about where they buy and sell different goods and services informed our assumptions about market closure. Goods with high transaction costs tend to be non-tradables, with prices determined inside the ZOI. In a poor village without access to good roads, public transportation, and communications, it is difficult to access distant market centres or obtain information about market prices and other information needed to buy inputs, obtain new technologies, sell output, or purchase consumption goods. Transaction costs are likely to be particularly high for perishable and bulky, difficult-to-transport goods like fruits and vegetables.

Table 5.3. Market Closure Assumptions

	Local/ZOI Markets	Integrated Markets
Crop	ALL	
Live	ALL	
Ret	ALL	
Ser	Ethiopia, Kenya, Lesotho, Ghana, Zambia, Malawi	Zimbabwe
Prod	Ghana, Zambia, Malawi	Ethiopia, Kenya, Lesotho, Zimbabwe
HL	ALL	
FL	ALL	
Purch		ALL
Herd	Ghana, Zambia	Malawi, Zimbabwe

Note: For Malawi, fish is local, Maize and inventory factor are integrated

They also tend to be high for prepared foods and services like construction activities or labour.

Because all of the SCT evaluations in this book took place primarily in similarly poor, rural areas, we made similar assumptions about the tradability of most goods and factors (Table 5.3). In all cases, we used information from qualitative fieldwork plus our own surveys to determine where transactions take place.

It is useful to keep in mind the role of prices and the local supply response while thinking about the market assumptions underlying our LEWIE models. The role of prices is determined to an important extent by the market closure assumptions in Table 5.3. The LEWIE model assumes that there is an elastic labour supply in all countries (elasticity = 100), reflecting the high-unemployment environments characterizing the programme areas.

Households in poor economies often are cash-constrained and have difficulty purchasing inputs (Purch in Table 5.3), like fertilizer. We explicitly model this constraint in the agricultural sector in Ethiopia and Malawi. It is reasonable to assume that households underinvest in the purchased input (fertilizer), so we simulate the SCT's impact on the constraint by fixing a percentage spent by households on the purchased input. Without the constraint in place, households spend all cash on consumer goods (and not factors for their businesses); the change in demand for factors due to the SCT is determined by prices of those factors and the change in local demand for the good.

Where liquidity constraints limit the local supply response, SCT income and production multipliers generally are smaller, and complementary interventions (e.g., micro-finance programmes) may be required to increase the productive impacts of SCTs in local economies.

5.4 ESTIMATING THE LEWIE MODELS

Household and business surveys have two main purposes for the construction of LEWIE models. First, they provide data to econometrically estimate parameters of interest and their standard errors. We estimate Cobb–Douglas production functions for each activity, assuming shared technologies across all households (households have the same production function for a particular activity). We also estimate marginal budget shares for each household group, corresponding to a Stone–Geary utility function with no subsistence minima. The consumption items here include all the commodities produced by the local activities, plus outside goods, transfers to other households, and so on.

Data also provide initial values for all variables in the model including production and input levels, household demands, the value of transfers, other exogenous income, and labour market income received by each household group. The values of all of these variables differ—often substantially—across household groups.

Estimates of parameters and their standard errors along with the starting values for all variables are entered onto an EXCEL data input sheet that interfaces with GAMS, where LEWIE resides.[2] LEWIE uses the initial values and estimated production and expenditure functions to create a base GE model of the project-area economy, in which all actors' incomes equal their expenditures and supply equals demand. The base model, in turn, is used to simulate the impacts of the SCT programmes. The LEWIE model generates a social accounting matrix (SAM) of the local economy as an intermediate output.

5.4.1 Modifying Surveys for LEWIE

The household survey questionnaires for the impact evaluation of the SCTs in this book are based in large part on living standards measurement surveys (LSMS). They include detailed information on household expenditures, income sources, and inputs and outputs of each productive activity. The information gathered to evaluate productive and social impacts of the SCT programmes was generally sufficient to estimate production functions and find initial values of intermediate inputs and outputs in agricultural activities, as well as to recover initial values of incomes from different sources and estimate expenditure functions.

However, some adaptations of the survey instruments were necessary to construct the LEWIE models. First, because the SCTs target a specific group of

---

[2] GAMS stands for General Algebraic Modelling System. It is a high-level modelling programme that is particularly useful for general-equilibrium analysis.

households eligible for transfers, impact evaluation typically focuses only on the eligible households (Both the treatment and control groups consist of households that are eligible for the SCT programmes.). However, to uncover spillovers, we need to measure impacts not only on the eligible households but on the local economy as a whole. This requires collecting information on ineligible as well as eligible households within the communities in which transfers are given out. Ideally (and in many of the cases described in this book), this meant using the same household survey instrument to survey a sample of ineligible households in the treated communities. However, in some cases this was not possible, and we based our model of ineligible households on data collected in other national LSMS-type surveys.

The second major adaptation in data collection for LEWIE is the inclusion of questions about where economic transactions take place. Adding a 'Where / with whom?' question to surveys captures which expenditures and sales happen within the ZOI. For example, it is not sufficient to know that a household spends 30 per cent of its income on retail items. We also need to know what share of these retail purchases were within the ZOI and thus have the potential to create spillovers within the local economy, contributing to local income and production multipliers. Expenditures outside the ZOI represent a programme leakage. Information on where and with whom expenditures and sales occur permits us to estimate expenditure functions that disaggregate goods purchased within and outside of the ZOI.

Finally, a business enterprise survey (BES) was added to the household surveys at each of the study sites. Most businesses in the rural areas where the SCT programme evaluations took place are associated with households, and thus can be captured in the household surveys. However, household surveys do not necessarily pick up all types of businesses. Moreover, due to time and cost constraints, the business modules in the household surveys only captured sufficient information to measure household income from each business type. We conducted separate BESs to obtain information on gross income, the value of intermediate inputs produced inside and outside of the ZOI, payments to factors (wages, capital costs, profits), and other expenses. We used this information to estimate quantities of intermediate inputs used in each business and to estimate production functions for each business type.

5.4.2 Timing of Data Collection

Ideally, all the data described in the data section and listed in the first row of Table 5.4 would be collected at the same time, before the first transfer payment to eligible households (i.e., at 'baseline'). When this is the case, the simulated LEWIE multipliers are predictions about the impacts of the SCT on the local economy. This was not possible in all of the case studies, and data were collected at follow-up, after the transfers had begun.

5.4.3 Combining Multiple Data Sources

Ideally, all the household data necessary for parameterizing LEWIE would come from the same source (each cell in Table 5.4 would read 'baseline'). In this scenario, eligible and ineligible households would reside in the same communities and respond to the same questions, making it easier to classify questions into particular income and expenditure categories, and ensuring all households faced the same set of weather and political conditions.

In some cases, however, the SCT evaluation designs did not collect information on the ineligible households, which are a crucial part of the LEWIE model (see Table 5.4). In this case we sought out other national LSMS-style surveys to provide information on the ineligible households' income and expenditure patterns. In each case, we were able to identify a subset of the

Table 5.4. Data Sources and Timing

Country	Business Enterprise Surveys (BES)	Eligible HHs (Expenditures and Incomes)	Ineligible HHs (Expenditure and Incomes)	Locations and Sources of Economic Transactions	Agricultural Production Functions
Ethiopia	Baseline (2012)	Baseline	Baseline		baseline
Ghana	Follow-up (2012)	Baseline (2010)	Institute for Statistical, Social and Economic Research (ISSER) (2010) (rural households)	Follow-up, locations collected for eligible households only, trading partners from Zambia	ISSER (rural households)
Kenya	Follow-up 2 (2011)	Follow-up 1 (2009)	2005 KIHBS	Follow-up 2, collected for eligible households only	
Lesotho	Baseline (2011)	Baseline	Baseline	Baseline	Baseline
Malawi	Baseline (2013)	Baseline	Baseline	Baseline	Baseline
Zambia	Follow-up (2012)	Baseline (2010)	LSMS (2010) (rural households)	Follow-up, collected for eligible households only	Baseline (eligible households only)
Zimbabwe	Baseline (2013)	Baseline	Baseline	Baseline	Baseline

surveyed households that would have been ineligible for the SCT. Additionally, we narrowed the subset of surveyed households to the smallest possible geographic area, while still ensuring a sufficient sample size.

There are still several concerns from combining multiple data sources to model the different household groups. First, the national LSMS we used to fill in information on the ineligible households were not always conducted in the same year as the SCT surveys used to model the eligible households. If there was a shock (e.g., drought or flood, political unrest) captured by either set of surveys, this would affect the income of the households surveyed in that year. Depending on the direction of the shock and the household group affected, it would affect (shrink or magnify) the difference in size of income and value of factors owned by the two household groups. If the shock was big enough, the allocation of the spillover income across the two household groups could be misleading.

Secondly, we use the household data to estimate expenditure functions and to initialize the values of productive factors in the LEWIE input sheet. If the questions asked in our SCT survey and the LSMS where we source information on the ineligible households is very different, it may require aggregating expenditure categories so that we estimate the same function for both household groups; certain expenditures of interest, especially health and education expenses, are not always captured as in depth by the LSMS surveys. The potential issues here were mitigated because the SCT surveys were designed to mirror national LSMS/DHS (Demographic and Health Survey) data as much as possible, in order to provide a comparison dataset for and to be more useful to the government/CT (cash transfer) programme administrators.

Thirdly, national LSMS do not contain the location module designed for the SCT household survey instruments, and it was necessary to impute location and sources of economic transactions for the ineligible households using data on the eligible households. This means we assumed that the household groups purchased items from the same sources. In countries where a comparison was possible, the locations of purchases of specific goods were similar across household groups. However, the bundle of goods ineligible households buy is different than that of eligible households, and the location questions were not asked item by item, but were instead aggregated into categories representing the commodities modelled in LEWIE. Specifically, we might expect richer households, if anything, to travel outside the ZOI to shop more frequently because they have more money to pay for transport and may want to access a more diverse bundle of goods. If we impute their spending locations using the eligible households, we may underestimate the amount of leakages outside the ZOI.

The final concern is how to interpret the SCT multipliers if the ineligible households are drawn from a different population than the eligible households. In cases where the two households groups are surveyed in the same location, the multipliers are representative of the programme ZOI. However, in cases with mixed data sources, the ineligible households may be representative of ineligible rural households, a group which does not have the same region-specific characteristic of the eligible population. In most of the case studies in the book, the programme was rolled out specifically targeting the poorest regions first thus the study area is poorer than the rural average.

A similar concern is when the programme evaluation took place in multiple regions. When we did not have access to data on ineligible households in all regions, we created an aggregate model of the programme area, which was representative of the rural region, not the specific programme regions. In the case of Ghana, we were able to use the fact that there were multiple data sources used to model the eligible and ineligible households, including those in non-treated communities, to test the robustness of the model to the selection of the households used to model each household group. We constructed two LEWIE models with the same group of ineligible households, but with one eligible group in the programme region and the other in a currently non-treated region. The empirical differences using the two eligible populations were not great enough to affect the overall multiplier, and the small differences in overall multiplier implied that the LEWIE models were reasonability representative of rural Ghana.

When we did have information on both household groups in different programme regions, as in Kenya and Ethiopia, we created regional models. This allowed us to make different market closure assumptions for each region, and to account for differences in livelihoods.

5.4.4 Populations

The relative sizes of the two household types matters, but this information is not always easy to come by. Some programmes conduct full censuses as part of the targeting process, making it straightforward to get population numbers and find the relative sizes of the two household groups. In other programmes, targeting is community-based, and no censuses are conducted. If there are no recent local census numbers from other sources, it can be difficult to pin down the percentage of the population that is eligible and will receive the SCT.

Getting the relative population size wrong can yield misleading multipliers. In LEWIE, spillover income accrues to households proportionally to their share of ownership of factors of production. Inaccurate population shares of each group will result in misallocation of the spillover income across household groups. In the case of Zambia, the districts in the programme evaluation were geographically far apart and had different economic characteristics, but because data on ineligible households came from an outside source, making regional models didn't make sense. Thus, the Zambia LEWIE was representative of a rural district. However, the regions had different percentages of households eligible for the programme. We ran two separate LEWIE models for each of the population groups in order to study the impact of the relative sizes of the household population on the size and distribution of SCT programme spillovers.

5.4.5 Asking About Locations

While the location questions themselves are not complex, the choice of location and trading partners to include in the questions is. The location questions are closely related to the ZOI definition and the information we collect must be sufficient to determine which transactions take place within the ZOI and which take place outside of it.

After a time, it also became clear that information beyond transaction location was important as well, and we added questions to the location modules in the household and business surveys about whether the trading partner was another household, a roving trader, or a business. The identity of the trading partner, along with the location of the trade, helped us to trace the cash from recipient household back to other households in the local economy. It is not sufficient to know the locations of stores where recipients spend money; we also want to know where the owners live. If the owners reside in the ZOI, the money will continue circulating and creating more spillover income, but if they reside outside the ZOI, it will be a leakage.

The second challenge with writing the location and trading partner questions is that they are intrinsically linked to the definition of the ZOI and the tradability of the different commodities. It is necessary to have an idea of the geographic coverage of the ZOI when writing these questions, but the information from the location modules can help to reinforce our assumptions about the tradability of goods and whether or not certain markets should be included in the ZOI. When qualitative fieldwork was conducted before the quantitative work, those study results proved very useful in making a preliminary ZOI definition and designing the location modules.

5.4.6 Selection of Businesses

Selecting the businesses to interview for the BES was one of the trickier aspects of the fieldwork. Censuses of household businesses did not exist, and it was too costly to create a complete list of businesses. The issue was compounded because we use the BES to estimate production functions for retail, service, and other productive enterprises, meaning selection would have to be stratified across the three groups. Thus, we needed to develop a way to classify businesses into the three categories before selection for the BES. Finally, it was important to consider the mix of businesses within each category. Estimating aggregate crop production functions that included diverse crops like maize and cassava was possible because we had a random, representative sample of households.

However, without knowing the prevalence of diverse businesses in, for example, the service industry—including tailors, millers, phone chargers, bike taxis—it is difficult for the business surveys to be completely representative of that industry in the ZOI. We ended up with a selection method that was replicable across countries. We used information from the qualitative surveys or from community surveys to make a list of the types of businesses that were most important in the community. We then selected the three most important of each type to survey in each community and picked the most common business type to survey when we had additional surveys to conduct.

5.5 LEWIE EXPERIMENTS AND CALCULATION OF SCT MULTIPLIERS

The principal use of the LEWIE models was to estimate SCT programme multipliers by simulating the impacts of income transfers to eligible households upon income, production, and other outcomes in the local economy and each household group.

LEWIE multipliers are calculated by dividing the impact on the value of the outcome of interest (income, production, etc.) by the amount transferred to eligible poor households. Income multipliers take the total change in recipient and non-recipient household incomes and divide it by the amount transferred, which is the cost of the SCT programme. The interpretation of the multiplier is the income generated for each dollar transferred to a recipient household. If this total income multiplier exceeds one, it means that the SCTs created positive spillovers in the local economy, such that one dollar of SCT payment to poor households increased local income by more than one dollar. LEWIE income multipliers can also be calculated for each household group, by taking the group's income change divided by the total cost of the SCT programme. A LEWIE income multiplier greater than zero for non-beneficiary households is evidence of positive spillovers from treated to non-treated households. A LEWIE income multiplier greater than one for beneficiary households is evidence of positive feedback effects of these spillovers on programme-eligible households.

In a similar manner, LEWIE multipliers can be calculated for production, employment, food consumption, prices and wages, or other outcomes of interest in the whole local economy or in specific household groups.

Unless the local supply is perfectly elastic, the price of goods will increase as a result of the higher local demand. In this case, real (inflation-adjusted) income may be a more accurate way to describe the SCT's impact than nominal (non-inflation-adjusted) income. We adjust for inflation by dividing income before and after the SCT by a consumer price index (CPI) calculated within the LEWIE simulation. Real income multipliers generally are smaller than nominal multipliers for SCT programmes, which stimulate local demands, because income gains are partially offset by inflation. The more flexible the local supply, the more nominal and real multipliers will tend to converge with one another.

5.6 RESULTS AND VALIDATION

Validation is always a concern in GE (and all simulation) modelling. Econometric estimation of production and expenditure function parameters opens up a new and interesting possibility in this regard, because we have standard errors along with parameter estimates. We used the distribution of estimated parameters and Monte Carlo methods to construct confidence intervals (CIs) around the LEWIE multipliers obtained from our simulations. If the model's parameters were estimated imprecisely, this will be reflected in wider CIs around our multipliers. Structural interactions within the model may magnify or dampen the effects of imprecise parameter estimates on simulation confidence bands.

This novel method of constructing confidence intervals allows us to compare results from different modelling scenarios and test the robustness of multiplier estimates to model assumptions. We can use confidence intervals to test for the significance of SCT impacts, that is, to test the null hypothesis that spillover effects on production are zero and that income multipliers are unitary: a dollar transferred to a recipient household adds no more than a dollar to the local economy. Similarly, we can use the CI to compare real and nominal income multipliers.

In addition to testing the sensitivity of the LEWIE model results to parameter estimates, we can conduct robustness checks on the modelling assumptions we have made, including on model closure, labour supply elasticities, and liquidity constraints. Table 5.5 summarizes these robustness tests as well as the SCT multiplier experiments in the seven countries for which LEWIE models

Table 5.5. Robustness Tests and Experiments

	Experiments and Robustness Checks
SCT	Impact of a one-unit increase in eligible-household income from SCTs (local currencies, all countries)
Factor Supply	Elasticity of labour (Kenya, Lesotho), liquidity constraint on purchased factors (Kenya, Lesotho, Ghana, Zambia, Malawi), injection of capital (Kenya)
Market Closure	Commodities tradeable in village or integrated markets (Ghana, Malawi), shared markets in scale-up (Zambia)
Regions	Define regions with distinct economic characteristics (Kenya, Ethiopia)
Scale-Up	Treat more villages in the region (Lesotho, Zambia), or more households in the village (Kenya)
Populations	Model control region (Ghana), population share of eligible (Zambia)

were constructed (Ethiopia, Ghana, Kenya, Lesotho, Malawi, Zambia, and Zimbabwe).[3]

The results of sensitivity experiments give us insights into the importance of local production and market constraints in transmitting impacts and creating spillovers. For example, we can test the effect of a low labour elasticity instead of the very elastic labour supply used in our base models. If the new multiplier is not significantly different than the base, we can conclude that labour supply constraints do not play a large role in transmitting programme impacts.

We find that the seven SCTs modelled for PtoP project generate spillovers in the local economy. Because of these spillovers, each dollar transferred to an eligible household generates more than a dollar of income in the local economy—that is, SCTs create income multipliers. Figure 5.2 shows the nominal and real income multipliers at each of the study sites. The horizontal line in the figure represents the dollar transferred. The difference between the multiplier and this dollar line is the local spillover. The confidence interval around the multiplier is shown at the top of each bar.

The nominal income multipliers range from 1.27 (in Malawi) to 2.52 (Hintalo, Ethiopia). They imply income spillovers of 0.27 to 1.52 per dollar transferred to eligible households. Real income multipliers range from 1.08 (Nyanza, Kenya) to 1.81 (Hintalo, Ethiopia). All of the multipliers are significantly greater than 1.0 (that is, spillovers are positive), indicating that each dollar transferred to a poor household adds more than a dollar to total income

---

[3] For the detailed country reports see Kagin et al. (2014) for Ethiopia; Taylor et al. (2013) for Kenya; Taylor, Thome, and Filipski (2014) for Lesotho; Thome et al. (2014a) for Ghana; Thome et al. (2014d) for Malawi; Thome et al. (2014b) for Zambia; and Thome et al. (2014c) for Zimbabwe.

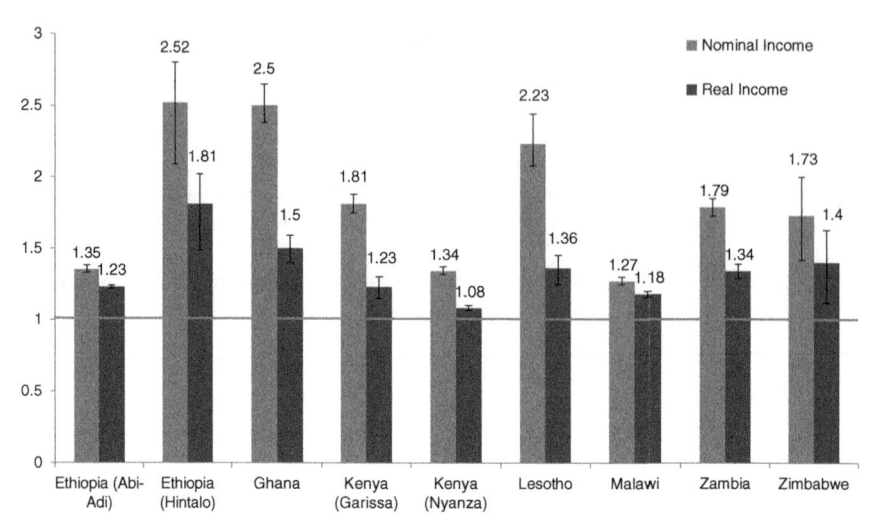

Figure 5.2. Real and Nominal Income Multipliers with Confidence Bounds for SCT Programmes in Seven Countries

in the local economy. The SCT programmes are first and foremost charged with social protection, and their success at achieving that goal is not captured by the multiplier metric. The SCT multipliers do, however, illustrate the potential for cash injections to stimulate growth in the rural economy.

The relative magnitudes of multipliers within and across countries reflect differences in programme targeting, expenditure patterns, business composition and production functions, and market integration in each country. A detailed comparison of multipliers across countries and household groups, as well as a discussion of why they vary, can be found in Thome et al. (2015).

5.7 CONCLUSIONS

LEWIE methods highlight impacts not only on the households directly affected by SCT programmes (that is, eligible households), but also the spillover impacts on other (ineligible) households within the local economy. Documenting SCT spillovers is important, because policy makers and donors want to know about the impacts of their programmes beyond the households that are affected directly by them. They also want to know what sorts of complementary interventions might be needed in order to make sure that their programmes are successful. Answers to these questions are needed before programmes are expanded to include new households and regions.

We find that SCTs have impacts beyond what experimental comparisons of treatment and control groups reveal. Documenting these impacts may tip a cost–benefit analysis in favour of expanding SCT programmes. LEWIE simulations offer insights into what can be done to enhance those spillovers. Documenting and enhancing the impacts beyond the treated can be critical in order to garner political and institutional support for SCT programmes.

Here's a recent example: Our LEWIE of LEAP (Ghanaian Livelihood Empowerment Against Poverty Program), Ghana's flagship social cash transfer programme, found that each cedi transferred to a poor household could increase local income by as many as 2.5 cedi (a summary of this evaluation can be found in Chapter 8). Ghana's President John Dramani Mahama, opening the Pan-African Conference on Inequalities in April 2014, stated: 'LEAP has had a positive impact on local economic growth. Beneficiaries spend about 80 per cent of their income on the local economy. Every GH1 transferred to a beneficiary has the potential of increasing the local economy by GH2.50.'[4]

President Dramani's goal was clear: to demonstrate that social protection and economic growth can be complements. LEAP could accomplish both. LEWIE changes the way we think about impacts, direct or indirect, of poverty programmes on people who are so vulnerable that we cannot risk being wrong.

REFERENCES

Kagin, J., Taylor, J. E., Alfani, F., and Davis, B. (2014). 'Local Economy-Wide Impact Evaluation (LEWIE) of Ethiopia's Social Cash Transfer Pilot Programme'. PtoP Project Report, FAO and The World Bank.

Taylor, J. E., Kagin, J., Filipski, M., Thome, K., and Handa, S. (2013). 'Evaluating General Equilibrium Impacts of Kenya's Cash Transfer Program for Orphans and Vulnerable Children (CT-OVC)'. PtoP Project Report, FAO and The World Bank.

Taylor, J. E., Thome, K., and Filipski, M. (2014). 'Evaluating Local General Equilibrium Impacts of Lesotho's Child Grants Program'. PtoP Project Report, FAO and The World Bank.

Taylor, J. E. and Filipski, M. (2014). *Beyond Experiments in Development Economics: Local Economy-Wide Impact Evaluation.* Oxford: Oxford University Press.

Thome, K., Taylor, J. E., Kagin, J., Davis, B., Darko Osei, R., Osei-Akoto, I., and Handa, S. (2014a). 'Local Economy-wide Impact Evaluation (LEWIE) of Ghana's Livelihood Empowerment Against Poverty (LEAP) Program'. PtoP Project Report, FAO and The World Bank.

---

[4] The President's speech as available at <http://www.presidency.gov.gh/node/532> (accessed 26 October 2015).

Thome, K., Taylor, J. E., Davis, B., Handa, S., Seidenfeld, D., and Tembo, G. (2014b). 'Local Economy-Wide Impact Evaluation (LEWIE) of Zambia's Child Grant Program'. PtoP Project Report, FAO and The World Bank.

Thome, K., Taylor, J. E., Davis, B., Seidenfeld, D., and Handa, S. (2014c). 'Evaluating Local General Equilibrium Impacts of Zimbabwe's Harmonized Social Cash Transfer (HSCT) Program'. PtoP Project Report, FAO and The World Bank.

Thome, K., Taylor, J. E., Tsoka, M., Mvula, P., Handa, S., and Davis, B. (2014d). 'Evaluating Local General Equilibrium Impacts of Malawi's Social Cash Transfer (SCT) Program'. PtoP Project Report, FAO and The World Bank.

Thome, K., Taylor, J. E., Filipski, M., Davis, B., and Handa, S. (2015). 'The Local Economy Impacts of Social Cash Transfers: A Cross-country Analysis'. PtoP Project Report, FAO.

Part II

Assessment of Cash Transfer Programmes: Country Case Studies

6

The Cash Transfer Programme for Orphans and Vulnerable Children

The Catalyst for Cash Transfers in Kenya

Joanne Bosworth (UNICEF), Carlos Alviar (Independent), Luis Corral (UNICEF), Benjamin Davis (FAO), Daniel Musembi (Government of Kenya), Winnie Mwasiaji (Government of Kenya), Samuel Ochieng (Government of Kenya), Roger Pearson (UNICEF), Pamela Pozarny (FAO), Patrick Ward (Oxford Policy Management), and Will Wiseman (World Bank)

6.1 INTRODUCTION

In 2003, faced with rising child vulnerability due to HIV (Human-Immunodeficiency Virus), orphanhood, and the breakdown of family and community social protection mechanisms, Kenya decided to trial a cash transfer to families taking care of orphans and vulnerable children (OVC) as part of its OVC Plan of Action. The programme commenced as a partnership between the Ministry of Home Affairs and UNICEF (United Nations Children Fund); Government leadership and ownership was key from the start, as was high level political backing (Pearson and Alviar, 2009).

The immediate objective was to encourage fostering and retention of orphans and vulnerable children within their families and communities, and to promote improved educational and health outcomes for these OVCs, by strengthening households' capacities to care for the children via regular cash transfers. The programme was highly relevant as the number of orphans in Kenya was approaching 1.6 million, of whom approximately 892,000 were estimated to be due to HIV and AIDS (Acquired Immunodeficiency Syndrome) (UNAIDS, UNICEF, and USAID, 2002).

From small beginnings of 500 households in three Locations in 2004,[1] the Cash Transfer Programme for Orphans and Vulnerable Children (CT-OVC) has expanded to a nationwide programme reaching 250,000 households by 2014. It has inspired numerous other cash transfers targeting other groups including the elderly, severely disabled, the urban poor, and those facing chronic poverty in Kenya's arid lands. Over the ten-year period, it has become progressively integrated into government policy and budgets as one of government's 'flagship' publicly funded social programmes, and is now one of the core components of Kenya's emerging social protection system. Over this period, public and political acceptance of social assistance in the form of cash transfers to the vulnerable has been transformed, and the right to social protection and obligation of the state to provide it has been recognized in the Constitution and under a National Social Protection Policy (NSPP). Most importantly, evidence on the feasibility and benefits of cash transfers has been demonstrated, and myths about negative impacts have been countered, sustaining the programme and allowing its progressive expansion.

From the outset, evaluation was an important component of the design and development of the CT-OVC. When the programme began in 2004, evidence on the feasibility and impacts of cash transfers in Africa was limited. There was a great deal of scepticism about whether cash transfers could be implemented effectively, about whether they were affordable or sustainable within the severe fiscal constraints of the time, and about whether they would be effective in achieving developmental impacts given the multiple deficits in public service provision.

Evaluation has played an important role throughout the progress of the programme. A participatory evaluation was conducted during the pre-pilot phase, followed by a rigorous impact evaluation during the pilot phase, with a second round after four years giving a longer-term perspective on the impacts of the programme. A further evaluation is currently underway to consider specific policy issues.

Evidence from the evaluations has been used by implementers, managers, and policy makers to modify design and operational aspects of the programme, to protect it from attacks, and to advocate for expansion with public funds. The length of time the CT-OVC has been running, together with the availability of longitudinal data on the programme households, means that it is one of the best-evaluated of Africa's cash transfers, making a rich contribution to national and global evidence on the effectiveness and impact of cash transfers, and to consideration of the role of evaluation evidence in social policy making.

---

[1] A Location was the lowest administrative division in Kenya prior to the constitutional reforms of 2010. The three Locations were selected by the Steering Committee to present different potential contexts for a scaled-up programme—arid lands, poor rural areas, and poor urban areas.

6.2 CHRONOLOGY OF PROGRAMME DESIGN, IMPLEMENTATION, AND EXPANSION

The development of the CT-OVC can be outlined in three broad phases: the 'pre-pilot' (2004–6), the pilot (2007–9), and the expansion (2009–14). Evaluations were completed in each of the three phases: pre-pilot (evaluation); pilot (baseline and twenty-four-month follow-up impact assessment); and expansion (forty-eight-month follow-up impact assessment; second evaluation of development conditions).

The *pre-pilot phase* was essentially a test or proof of concept. In 2004 the Government of Kenya submitted a proposal to the Global Fund for HIV, TB (Tuberculosis), and Malaria to provide cash transfers to households taking care of OVC. The proposal was not accepted, on the basis that this type of intervention had not been tested before in the country. Therefore, the Department of Children Services, within the Ministry of Home Affairs, and UNICEF, supported by SIDA (Swedish International Development Agency) and the Norwegian National Committee for UNICEF, started an initiative to demonstrate the feasibility of cash grants to respond to the OVC crisis in three geographic areas with different socio-economic and cultural characteristics: a pastoralist district in the northern semi-arid lands, an urban slum in the country's capital, and a coastal agricultural district. For around one year, 500 poor households taking care of OVC received $6 per month.

Monitoring and assessment, including community monitoring, was integral to the pre-pilot phase, and was highly participatory, involving recipients, communities, implementers, and political leaders. This resulted in strong local buy in and ensured a high level of programme acceptance within the community from the outset.[2] The following lessons and recommendations were drawn from the pilot phase: i) the programme had a positive impact on the welfare of children, with the expenditure of the funds mainly on items such as school uniforms, food, and medical expenses; ii) there was need to review the value of the subsidies (the transfer was not sufficient to cover minimum basic needs) and improve the payment delivery system, until now, the responsibility of the District Children Officers; iii) there was little evidence of misuse in expenditures (a persistent concern); and iv) facing resource constraints, it was felt, including by communities themselves, that certain conditions could be imposed on those receiving cash subsidies to ensure that these funds were used to promote children's welfare and to introduce the possibility of replacing those misusing the funds received.

Beneficiaries and communities consistently supported the need to expand the programme to more families taking care of OVC. The lessons from the

---

[2] Personal communication, Sumaira Choudhury, December 2014.

pre-pilot and the additional support encouraged the Ministry of Home Affairs to increase the pre-pilot's coverage to 2,500 additional households in ten new districts in different provinces of the country. At the same time, it was decided to scale up the transfer from three to seven districts with support from UNICEF, SIDA, and DFID (Department for International Development, UK).

During the *pilot phase* the foundations of the CT-OVC as a nationally viable programme were laid. This included the establishment and testing of systems that would be capable of being scaled up, building capacity and institutions, and a rigorous impact evaluation which would provide evidence to inform the expansion and identify and quantify the developmental impacts in order to convince policy makers of the value of the approach.

The pilot phase implied a change from the ad-hoc procedures of the pre-pilot to systematic standardized procedures. As the CT-OVC expanded, a comprehensive Operations Manual was produced, tested, and adjusted with clear guidelines, instruments, and step-by-step procedures for every actor involved in the programme implementation cycle. Training materials were also produced for every process and actor in order to guarantee the quality of their implementation. A Management Information System (MIS) was developed to process all programme data. Among other processes the system supported first a poverty scorecard then an improved Proxy-Means Test (PMT) targeting mechanism, registered beneficiaries, produced ID cards, and generated payments and reconciled them on regular basis. At enrolment, the beneficiary households received information about their responsibilities and entitlements related to the programme. The Kenya Postal Corporation (PCK) was contracted to deliver cash every two months (calculated at around $20 per household per month) with operational guidelines and instruments for standard service delivery and transparent operational fees.

Another important feature of the pilot phase was its Capacity Building Strategy (CBS) that aimed at strengthening the capacity of the OVC Secretariat (at the Department of Children's Services—DCS) to manage the pilot's expansion and assure the allocation of the necessary human and financial resources. The structure for implementation evolved in time from three individuals undertaking various DCS activities, including cash transfer operations, to a more organized OVC Secretariat with the required human resources and clearer roles and responsibilities assigned to different aspects of programme implementation (Management, Operations and Training, M&E (Monitoring and Evaluation), MIS (Management Information System), Finance and Administration, and Communications). During this period the OVC Secretariat became an organization that stood out within the institutional context of the Kenyan public administration due to its capacity to plan and execute activities and report on expenditures.

During this period the Kenyan OVC team, officials from the Ministry of Finance, and political leaders were exposed to cash transfer trainings, international fora, and study tours which also contributed to knowledge of how to manage cash transfers as well as their potential impacts.[3] One particular study tour, to Colombia, was a milestone both technically and politically, crystallizing a vision of what was possible technically, reinforcing the role of the vice president as an ambassador and champion for increased budget allocations for the programme, and strengthening the understanding of the Ministry of Finance through involvement of Treasury officials. From 2007 to 2010 government and donor funding for the CT-OVC multiplied almost ten times as it became more widely known and politically acceptable.

During the *expansion phase*, the CT-OVC was scaled up nationwide, reaching 150,000 households by 2013, 250,000 households by 2014, and a further 90,000 households planned in 2015. According to current government plans, all eligible households should be enrolled in the programme by 2018. Over time the level of funding provided by government has expanded rapidly while the proportion provided by development partners has reduced. The scale-up is part of the government's larger plan to establish a national social protection system comprising of social assistance, social insurance, and social health insurance. Under the social assistance arm, four cash transfer programmes targeting different groups (CT-OVC, Older Persons Cash Transfer (OPCT), the Hunger Safety Net Programme (HSNP), and the Cash Transfer for Persons with Severe Disability (CT-PWSD)) will be progressively harmonized as they scale up to reach around one and a half million households in total by 2018.[4] From the financial year 2014–2015 direct development partner support to the CT-OVC stopped, although the World Bank continued to support the overall National Safety Net Programme (NSNP) including the CT-OVC through a form of sector budget support.[5]

---

[3] This included the then Permanent Secretary of Treasury and the then Head of Macroeconomics, who was later to become the Cabinet Secretary for Finance. Some observers have suggested that these trainings and exposure have been a significant factor inducing longer-term buy-in to the cash transfers at senior level, and ultimately played a role in facilitating the scale-up.

[4] A fifth transfer, the Urban Food Subsidy with a coverage of ten thousand poor households in urban informal settlements in Mombasa was to be part of this expansion. However, at the time of writing this transfer was not expected to continue after financial year 2014–15.

[5] From 2014–15 UNICEF and SIDA ceased direct support to households in favour of technical assistance; DFID's support transitioned to technical assistance to the NSNP with direct support to households under the HSNP; while the World Bank shifted to the 'Programme for Results' modality, under which the Bank transfers resources to the Treasury based on the programme accomplishing certain disbursement criteria, one of which is the scale-up of support to a larger number of beneficiaries including the CT-OVC.

6.3 IMPACT EVALUATION—ORIGIN, PROCESS, AND METHODS

The focus of this chapter is the rigorous impact evaluation of the CT-OVC which commenced under the pilot phase with a baseline in 2007 and a first follow-up in 2009, and continued under the expansion phase with a second and expanded follow-up. A further evaluation focusing on the impact of development conditionalities is currently underway but has yet to report results.[6] The availability of the longitudinal data from the three rounds covering the same beneficiaries over the period from 2007 to 2011 means Kenya is able to assess the longer-term benefits of cash transfers for vulnerable children (Figure 6.1).

There were several components to these evaluations. The pre-pilot evaluation was conducted through a single round of a survey of beneficiary and non-beneficiary households in the three programme Locations. The first-round twenty-four-month and second-round forty–eight-month impact evaluations used mixed methods. For the twenty-four-month evaluation, this comprised of two rounds of quantitative sample surveys of households (beneficiaries and non-beneficiaries), once before the programme was introduced to the areas in 2007, and again two years later. Households interviewed

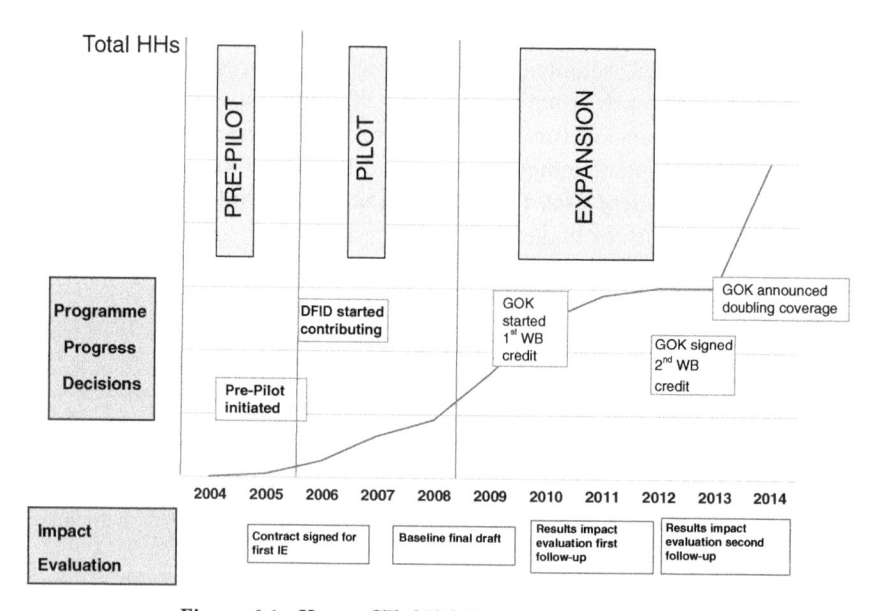

Figure 6.1. Kenya CT-OVC Programme Expansion

---

[6] A baseline report was produced in early 2015 (Acharya et al., 2015).

at baseline were re-interviewed for the follow-up survey. This was complemented by qualitative data collection through focus groups and in-depth interviews undertaken in 2008 and again in 2009, and a costing study undertaken in 2009. The baseline survey conducted in 2007 was the basis for an analysis of the effectiveness of initial programme targeting using a poverty scorecard method. At the request of government, a team from UNICEF undertook additional quantitative analysis of the targeting in order to provide a more contextual assessment of the effectiveness of targeting. Following the impact evaluation, a team from UNICEF and the World Bank again undertook additional analysis of the differential impacts of the transfer on households of different sizes in order to inform the debate on the value of the transfer.

For the forty-eight-month follow-up, a further round of the household survey with re-interview of the same households was undertaken in 2011 for longitudinal quantitative analysis. In addition, a qualitative study was undertaken in two Locations, one covered by the quantitative follow-up and one outside the quantitative sampled area. Focus group discussions were held in each Location with groups of participants stratified by social criteria, and utilizing a range of participatory tools. Key informant interviews (at district and community levels) and in-depth household case studies were also undertaken. A further component of the forty-eight-month follow-up was a Local Economy Wide Impact Evaluation (LEWIE). More details of these methodologies are found in Chapters 3, 4, and 5.

The original decision to conduct an impact evaluation was taken by the Department of Children's Services and UNICEF with support from SIDA,[7] with the aim of addressing the need for evidence of impact from Kenya to justify investment by government, other partners, and potential donors, including potentially the Global Fund, the World Bank, and DFID. It was also considered prudent to gather evidence that might protect the programme from political or media attacks given the high profile of the launch of the pre-pilot. Critical audiences for the evaluation were various government institutions, the Parliamentary OVC Committee, donors and funding agencies, and the Kenyan press.

During the preparation for the pilot phase starting from 2006, both DFID and the World Bank became involved in the design of the pilot and in the impact evaluation. The participation of a wider group of stakeholders had important consequences for the development of the programme and for the design of the impact evaluation. In particular, at the time, there was intense debate about the relative effectiveness of cash transfers with and without development conditionalities including educational attendance and adherence

---

[7] UNICEF programming principles, which require an evaluation wherever UNICEF is supporting a pilot, also played a role in this decision.

to health conditions. The pilot phase CT-OVC Operational and Impact Evaluation was initially intended to assess a programme designed to deliver cash transfers with health and education conditions in three districts. Ultimately, it was decided to use the Kenyan case as a trial to test the effectiveness of Conditional Cash Transfers (CCT) versus Unconditional Cash Transfers (UCT). Substantial changes in the programme's design and scale were agreed among partners and the evaluation was transformed to cover seven districts with a bigger sample testing the two types of design. Its objectives were to establish the overall efficacy and efficiency of the programme and its impact on children, households, and communities.

The pilot phase impact evaluation was designed specifically to assess the following questions.

1. How much of an impact are cash transfers having? Are cash transfers reaching the most vulnerable children and having a substantial impact on their welfare, in terms of both human development for the child and wider social benefit for the household?

2. Does the impact justify the cost of the programme? Would a national programme be affordable and fiscally sustainable? On that basis, should the programme, or a variant of it, be scaled up to a national level?

3. If the programme were to be scaled up, which aspects of its operation must be modified or strengthened for it to operate effectively at a national level? Which aspects of good practice should remain the same and be replicated?

4. What is the impact or incentive effect of imposing conditions with penalties on recipients, compared with not imposing them? What is the cost of imposing conditions, for both households and the government? Does any additional impact warrant the additional cost? If households fail to comply with conditions, why is this so?

The main component of the evaluation followed a panel design in a longitudinal impact evaluation of beneficiary households with matched controls, with information collected using a household survey and including anthropometric measures on children. The original design of the impact evaluation, carried out by Oxford Policy Management (OPM), compared households and children in treatment and control groups at baseline, with one follow-up twenty-four months later. A second follow-up was later added on to the evaluation, forty-eight months after baseline. The conditional or unconditional status was allocated randomly to each district in the seven-district sample: conditions were imposed in three of the seven districts plus one Location in Nairobi, while the other three districts and other Nairobi Locations did not have conditions. Given the desire to test two types of design, two treatment Locations and their respective control groups were selected randomly in each district after excluding those Locations with particularly low poverty rates, inadequate capacity to supply the relevant health and education services, or with large existing OVC support programmes. Beneficiaries were selected using standard targeting guidelines. Since the programme was not scheduled to be implemented during this phase in the control Locations, it was not possible to use the targeting guidelines. Instead, programme targeting was 'simulated' in order to identify a sample of households that were comparable to those identified as eligible in treatment Locations. Statistical modelling was therefore necessary to control for differences that emerged between treatment and control households at baseline. The baseline data was utilized to evaluate the programme's targeting effectiveness comparing treatment and control households. Information on operational effectiveness was captured in the follow-up quantitative survey through the addition of an extra module asking about beneficiaries' experience with programme operations. The quantitative evaluation was complemented by a qualitative evaluation in two rounds (2008 and 2009), and by a costing study.

The initial two-year evaluation was extended to four years under the Transfer Project. The second, forty-eight-month follow-up was financed with a grant from the National Institutes for Health (NIH), and was implemented by the University of North Carolina at Chapel Hill in conjunction with the From Protection to Production (PtoP) project of the FAO (Food and Agriculture Organization of the United Nations). In addition to investigating the longer-term impacts on consumption, diet, health, nutrition, and education, the follow-up survey included additional modules to facilitate assessment of the impact of the programme on adolescent behaviour and household economic activities. The household survey was accompanied by a business enterprise survey in order to facilitate estimation of the local economy income multiplier, and additional qualitative fieldwork which focused on perceptions of the household economy and decision making, social networks, local community dynamics, and operations.

Finally, a separate impact evaluation was commissioned in 2012 by the World Bank and is being implemented focusing on districts and households brought in during the expansion of the programme. This study aims to revisit the issues of targeting and conditionality.

6.4 IMPACT EVALUATION—ISSUES AND RESULTS

The impact evaluation and further analysis has provided evidence on many of the main policy and implementation debates for cash transfers in Kenya, although the evaluation evidence has not yet conclusively addressed some policy questions to the satisfaction of all partners.

6.4.1 Cash Transfers are a Practical Policy Option in Kenya

Before the implementation of the pre-pilot there was a high degree of scepticism over whether cash transfers could be implemented in Kenya. The pilot phase set out to demonstrate and assess whether transfers could be implemented effectively at a larger scale, in particular the operational effectiveness of systems for targeting, payments, and complaints. The evaluation confirmed that these systems were functioning adequately, and that the programme was achieving its primary purpose in that beneficiaries were receiving regular payments, without excessive demands for unofficial payments. It also identified some areas where operations could be improved. On payments, it highlighted the costs to beneficiaries, particularly those from remote areas, in transport for collecting payments; and beneficiary concerns over waiting times and security. It found there were weaknesses in communication around the programme rules and in monitoring of conditions; and that community 'volunteers' were playing an important role, supporting beneficiaries to obtain and fill out forms and comply with the various programme requirements. The subsequent qualitative evaluation from 2011 also found that there were some difficulties associated with irregularity and late payments.

6.4.2 Targeting of the Programme Has Been Successful Despite Some Challenges during Scale-Up

The importance of a legitimate and transparent targeting mechanism for gaining and sustaining public support for the programme and for maximizing the effectiveness of transferred resources was clear almost from the outset of the pre-pilot. During the pre-pilot phase, targeting was carried out by community targeting committees made up of elders in the Location, half of whom had to be female. Households had to be the very poorest and include children, preferably orphans or children otherwise judged to be vulnerable. Committees proposed households for inclusion up to a maximum determined by budget ceilings, and the final list was discussed in a public forum with residents in the target area, in the presence of the District Children's Officer.

Criticism of the targeting mechanism arose in part from operational difficulties, but the principal challenge was related to the lack of an objective mechanism to differentiate the poverty level of the eligible households. The definition of poverty was agreed with each community according to its characteristics and the opinion of its members. According to the pre-pilot evaluation, this resulted in a small but significant inclusion error. The evaluation recommended development of a universal definition of who qualified as an 'OVC', together with 'locally relevant definitions of vulnerability and poverty' (Acacia Consultants Ltd, 2007). In response, a means-testing element was developed for the targeting under the pilot phase, based on a survey of all eligible households in the target Locations.

The initial means test was based on the use of proxy variables to assess the household's relative poverty status (identifying assets and housing conditions). The variables were identified in focus groups with community representatives and verified using national household survey data. All proxy variables had the same weight in the poverty assessment formula. A number of innovative elements of the targeting mechanism have been described elsewhere (Alviar, Ayala, and Handa, 2010; Handa et al., 2011).

A targeting analysis was conducted with the data from the 2007 baseline survey (Hurrell, Ward, and Merttens, 2008). The CT-OVC targeted households within a location that met eligibility criteria of caring for an orphaned child or containing a chronically sick adult, and meeting a poverty test. At the time of the targeting analysis, following community identification of households meeting the basic eligibility criteria, an initial poverty test was applied, based on a simple score on a list of predetermined indicators relating to household assets and housing conditions. The targeting analysis assessed whether the programme was effectively identifying households that met the eligibility criteria and was selecting those households that were poorest. The evaluators reported that while 96 per cent of beneficiary households met the programme criteria of having an orphan or vulnerable child, it was not directing resources at the poorest OVC households as successfully as it might. Specifically, 'an estimated 43 percent of the poorest OVC households in programme areas are not supported; while some 13 percent of Programme recipients were in the top (best-off) consumption quintile' (Ward et al., 2010: iii–iv). The explanations provided for this were at all levels of the targeting process: the geographic quota system that meant households with OVCs in some locations had a greater probability of being targeted than in others; the initial community listing omitted some potential beneficiaries either due to lack of knowledge, resources, or time on the part of the Location committees or because the Location committee members did not consider some households deserving; and the criteria within the poverty scorecard which did not effectively discriminate between poor and non-poor households.

The reported results of the targeting analysis undertaken using the 2007 data were among the most controversial of the evaluation. The results were presented in such a way as to suggest substantial inclusion and exclusion errors, with many households in programme areas who qualified not receiving the transfer, while some programme recipients were judged to be ineligible based on the poverty test. The validity of this analysis was hotly contested on the basis that it mainly arose due to the allocation of households between districts and because the initial coverage was low, at only 21 per cent of eligible households. The division of beneficiaries and non-beneficiaries from the programme areas into wealth quintiles was also misleading since the programme areas themselves were among the poorer areas of Kenya. Thus, the targeting analysis had effectively ranked families from the worst-off to the better-off in a context of existing extreme poverty. It was also argued by implementers that the manner in which the targeting results were reported by the evaluation team was not sensitive to the Kenyan context or to the relatively early stage of development of the programme, putting it at risk from policy makers who might misinterpret the findings.

The perception of risk to the programme from the targeting result led to additional efforts by government and UNICEF to translate and contextualize the evaluation results in line with evidence on the targeting performance of cash transfers around the world. Further analysis of the programme's targeting performance compared the profile of beneficiaries with those of the population at large using two sources of quantitative data: the 2007 baseline database and the Kenya Integrated Household Budget Survey (KIHBS) database. Household poverty among CT-OVC recipients (78 per cent) was found to be over double that of the national rate (38 per cent). CT-OVC households were much less likely to be in the two top quintiles compared with all Kenyans. According to this analysis, 'among CT-OVC programme households, 51 percent are in the poorest quintile and only six percent appear in the top two quintiles' (Handa et al., 2011). Comparing the targeting performance of the CT-OVC with some of the other more established programmes around the world that were also poverty targeted (Mexico's Oportunidades, Colombia's Familias en Acción, and Jamaica's Path Programme), 'targeting in the Kenyan Programme was at least as good as those well-known programmes'. The conclusion from this analysis was that contrary to the initial targeting findings, the CT-OVC targeting experience was highly encouraging in terms of the potential to implement rigorous poverty-based targeting in African countries with relatively low capacity. The demographic eligibility requirement of OVC status had widespread public support and provided a transparent way to select a sub-group of poor households given the context of widespread poverty and limited programme resources (Handa et al., 2011). At the same time, the poverty test could be conducted relatively successfully due to the substantial investment in operations including the advanced MIS, training, and capacity building.

6.4.3 Transfers Have a Range of Positive Development Impacts in the Medium and Longer Term

The successive rounds of the CT-OVC evaluations offer a number of findings related to the medium- and longer-term impacts and heterogeneous impacts based on household size and composition.

Programme impacts were estimated from a comparison between treatment and control groups through a standard difference-in difference-model.[8] The results, presented in Table 6.1, have been mixed but on the whole indicate the programme has a positive impact on beneficiaries in several areas.

After twenty-four months, significant impacts were found on household consumption, food consumption, and poverty reduction. The study reported an increase in the consumption levels of programme households, with average consumption levels per adult equivalent to Ksh 232 higher in real terms in 2009 than in 2007, and a programme impact of Ksh 274 per adult equivalent. Consumption of meat, milk, fruit, fats, and sugar increased significantly among beneficiary households compared with non-beneficiary households. The increase in consumption led to a reduction in poverty; the programme led to a 13 percentage point reduction in the proportion of households living below a (nominal) $1-per-day poverty line (Ward et al., 2010). These results demonstrated that the programme significantly increased household consumption levels, increasing food consumption, allowing dietary diversity, and increasing resilience.

Analysis of the programme impacts after forty-eight months found that the initial gains in household consumption among the beneficiary households compared to controls were later offset by high levels of inflation. Nevertheless, positive and significant effects persisted over four years in terms of reduction of poverty and the severity of poverty, as well as in terms of shifting consumption to more nutritious foods (particularly meat and fish and dairy), especially for beneficiaries who were poorest at baseline (Romeo et al., 2014).

The programme also had a significant impact on children's education. After twenty-four months, the programme had resulted in a 4.5 percentage point increase in the proportion of children aged 6–17 years enrolled in school in beneficiary households. However, when broken down into the standard age for basic and secondary schooling, the impact was not significant for primary level education. Instead, programme impact was found on young children with an 11.6 percentage point increase in basic education enrolment for children aged 6–7 years. The programme's major educational impact was at secondary level, where it led to a 7.19 percentage point increase in enrolment in secondary school. This impact at the secondary level is comparable to that found for other conditional and unconditional cash transfer programmes (The Kenya CT-OVC Impact Evaluation Team,

---

[8] Two model approaches were used, cross-section and cohort models. Cross-section models provide an estimate of the effect of the programme on children belonging to a determined age group (comparing same age groups but different children over time). Cohort models estimate the effect of the programme on a determined group of children as they grow older (comparing the same group of children but of different age group all the time).

Table 6.1. Summarized Key Impacts of CT-OVC Impact Evaluation Round 1 and 2

Impact Evaluation Cash Transfer for Orphans and Vulnerable Children Results First and Second Follow-Up		
	First follow-up March/July 2007–March/July 2009	Second Follow up March/July 2007–March/July 2011
Poverty Reduction		
Poverty: mean total monthly household consumption expenditure per adult equivalent below $1 per day (real)	−0.132**	
Poverty: mean total monthly household consumption expenditure per adult equivalent below $2 per day (real)	−0.103*	
Food Consumption and Household Welfare		
Mean total monthly household consumption expenditure per adult equivalent (Ksh—real)	274.4**	
Mean monthly food consumption expenditure per adult equivalent (Ksh—real)	153.0*	157.6*
Food Security	Improvement in food security, diet diversity	Improvement in food security, diet diversity
Schooling		
Proportion of children aged 14–17 years currently enrolled in secondary school	0.0719**	
Schooling impacts by age — Age 12–17		0.055
Age 14–18		0.085
Health		Suggestive effects on sickness and curative care but not significant
Reduction in diarrhoea frequency in last month — Age 3–5		−0.95*
HH size 1–4		−0.185*
Sought care of diarrhoea? — Age: 0–5		0.151*
Age: 3–5		−0.28*
Had Measles Vaccination? — Age: 0–5		0.122*
Age: 3–5		−0.14*
Nutrition	No impact on nutrition status	No impact on nutrition status

HIV-Related Risk Behaviour		
Sexual Debut (had sex)	Age 15–20	−0.078*
Mental Health	Female 15–20	−0.082*
Reduction in odds of dispalying depressive symptoms	Age 15–24	−0.15*
Productive		
Increase in ownership of small livestock	small HH Female-headed	0.149* 0.59*
Child Labour		
Proportion of children doing paid work	Age: 6–13 Age: 14–17	−0.034* −0.0193
Proportion of children doing unpaid work	Age:10–15 Boys 10–15	−012*** −0.131***

Notes: ***p < 0.01, **p < 0.05, *p < 0.1
Sources: Asfaw et al. (2012); Romeo et al. (2014); Handa et al. (2012); Ward et al. (2010).

2012b). Nevertheless, the qualitative evaluation in 2011 found OVCs still facing significant challenges in transitioning from primary to secondary school, and some households preferred to have their children attend private primary schools that were believed to provide a better chance of accessing free state secondary education (OPM, 2014).

These findings were further confirmed and qualified after forty-eight months. Although school enrolment dropped among the older age group which included individuals who, at twenty-one years of age, were by this time beyond normal school age, the programme was successful in reducing the decline and maintaining older children in school, and also eliminated differences between boys and girls in enrolment, school progression, and grades behind (Romeo et al., 2014).

The health impacts of the programme took longer to emerge. While, after two years the programme led to a significant increase in health spending, this did not translate into significant impact on health and nutrition outcomes for children under five, including anthropometric measures, immunization status, vitamin A supplements received, common illnesses, and use of health services. This lack of impact could be attributed to constraints in the provision of health services or the role that cash plays as only one of multiple factors influencing some of these outcomes.

By the time of the forty-eight- month follow-up, however, beneficial health impacts for children in the beneficiary households had emerged, and for the first time the study found impacts on the health of young children (0–5 years old).

Use of a well-baby clinic increased by 15.8 percentage points for children under thirty months of age, while the incidence of diarrhoea among children aged 31–59 months decreased by 13 percentage points. Health card ownership of children under the programme increased by 15.6 percentage points for children under 60 months of age, while the share of children with full immunization increased by 14.8 percentage points, compared with the controls (Romeo et al., 2014).

Thus while inflation eroded overall household consumption, and weakened the income effect of the transfers on household human capital accumulation, the provision of a predictable and regular source of income combined with the social marketing component (soft conditions)[9] appeared to have positively altered household behaviour towards investing in the education and health of young children, many of whom were not even born at the time of the baseline. In other words, the CT-OVC appears to have led to long-term behavioural change that persisted even in the face of a decline in the real value of the transfer.

The first round of the impact evaluation found that impacts vary substantially between small households and larger households, with many positive effects being limited to the small households. These results include total household consumption expenditure per adult equivalent, which increased to Ksh 368.9 for smaller households with no significant impact for larger households. Similarly, the rate of households in poverty fell by 17.3 and 13 percentage points for smaller households living below a $1 and $2 per day poverty lines, respectively, with again no impact on larger beneficiary households. Similar findings were found for the proportion of children 7–13 years old enrolled in basic education, the proportion of children 1–3 years old fully vaccinated, the proportion of children under 5 who had been ill with cough, and the proportion of children under 5 who had been ill with diarrhoea (Ward et al., 2010).

Some of the programme objectives were related to improving conditions for orphans and vulnerable children and protecting them from other rights violations. The twenty-four-month impact evaluation found no evidence that the programme enhanced fostering and retention of OVCs among programme households and communities because this was already occurring at a high rate, attesting to strong community norms. However, other important changes occurred: the proportion of children in beneficiary households with birth certificates or registration forms increased by 12 percentage points, while a significant reduction in child labour, by 3.3 per cent, was also observed among beneficiary households (Ward et al., 2010). After forty-eight months, the programme had led to a 12 percentage point reduction in child

---

[9] 'Soft' conditions are conditions that are encouraged through communication, but not rigidly enforced through a system of monitoring compliance and penalties for non-compliance.

labour on the farm, particularly among boys aged 10–15 years (Asfaw et al., 2014).

The forty-eight-month follow-up also offered findings in areas where impact had not previously been measured, including adolescent behaviour, productive activities and labour allocation, the local economy, and community dynamics. The study for the first time evaluated the impacts of the programme on adolescent social behaviours that increase their vulnerability to HIV, and on adolescent psychosocial status. Programme beneficiaries aged between 15 to 21 years were 7 percentage points less likely to have had sex (indicating a postponement of sexual debut) as well as significantly less likely to have unprotected sex. In terms of psychosocial status, the programme significantly reduced depressive symptoms and these effects were stronger for 15-to-19-year-olds (Handa et al., 2014).

The forty-eight-month evaluation also indicated that the CT-OVC programme impacted some aspects of the livelihoods of beneficiaries and their communities in rural Kenya, particularly for female-headed and smaller-sized households. Receipt of the CT-OVC led to a 15 and 6 percentagepoint increase in the share of smaller-sized and female-headed households, respectively, owning small animals. While the study did not find consistent evidence using direct indicators of crop and animal production such as fertilizer and land use, the study found robust indirect evidence of impact on production. Beneficiary households—primarily smaller sized and female-headed households—consumed a significantly larger share of dairy/eggs, meat/fish, fruit and other foods derived from their own production. This impact was substantial, reaching 20 percentage points in the case of dairy/eggs for smaller sized households (Asfaw et al., 2014).

The programme also influenced the flexibility of beneficiary households and individuals in terms of the type of income generating activities in which they participate, most of which involve casual or informal labour. For adults, the CT-OVC was associated with a 7 percentage point increase in participation in household-run, non-farm business enterprises for female-headed households, and a similar sized decrease was recorded for male-headed households. For those individuals (particularly women) that lived farther from markets, the receipt of the transfer helped facilitate engagement in casual wage labour activities. The programme was associated with an increase in work in casual non-agricultural wage labour (particularly for males), compared with a decrease in work in agricultural wage labour. These impacts on work were stronger with increasing age. However, the programme appears to have led to a reduction in the intensity of casual wage labour. The study was unable to determine, however, whether individuals increased time spent on domestic chores or child care (Asfaw et al., 2014).

Many of the quantitative findings of the second round evaluation were confirmed and contextualized through the inclusion of the qualitative study.

This study confirmed the positive effects on household income, education, and local economies, but also found perceptions of high exclusion error, in particular in areas with high burdens of HIV and AIDS. The CT-OVC was found to increase social capital and to strengthen informal safety nets and risk sharing arrangements. Though this is contrary to what might be expected, this is largely explained by the effects on increased self-esteem and increased ability to engage in community groups and religious activities, even for the poorest households. These positive effects on trust-based reciprocity within communities are, however, sometimes undermined due to jealousy of similarly poor non-beneficiary households and the perception of targeting errors (OPM, 2014).

When beneficiaries spend the cash transfer they transmit the impact to others inside and outside the local economy, more often to households not eligible for the cash transfer, who tend to own most of the local businesses. The regional LEWIE for the CT-OVC found income multipliers of KSh1.34 and 1.81 in the West and East regions, respectively—that is, every KSh transferred to poor households in the East region raised local income by KSh 1.81. These income multipliers, however, are potentially limited by poorly functioning labour, capital, and land markets which may constrain the supply response of local producers (Taylor et al., 2013).

There are two aspects of transfer value that the successive evaluations have highlighted: first, the absolute value of the transfer and whether it is adequate to have beneficial effects even when eroded by inflation; and second, the issue of variability of the transfer with household size. The value of the transfer under the initial pre-pilot was KSh 500. This was increased following feedback from communities, and there was some debate over whether to opt for a variable level of transfer, with one level for households with only one child and another value where a household had three or more children, or whether to opt for a uniform level of transfer. A uniform flat rate of KSh 1,500 was agreed, based on the analysis of poverty levels (Allen et al., 2007). The impact evaluation identified that by 2011 the real value had declined by over 38 per cent and recommended that the value of the transfer be indexed to inflation to protect future payments. Given the differential impacts between small and larger households, consideration of a variable transfer was also recommended.

6.4.4 Cash Transfers do not Lead to Undesirable Behaviours or to Dependency

As in many other countries, policy makers and the public in Kenya have been concerned that recipients of cash transfers will 'misuse' the transfers (spending them on alcohol, for example, or on having additional wives), or that people will become dependent on the transfer. In the Kenya case, the value of the transfer was never more than 22 per cent of average beneficiary household consumption (and fell to 11 per cent by mid-2011), so the possibility of a household becoming wholly 'dependent' on the transfer is unrealistic. However, there is still a question of how the beneficiaries use the cash, its effect on incentives to work, and the extent to which the transfer facilitates different forms of social or productive investment.

The evaluation's findings on education suggested many beneficiaries do use the transfers to invest in human capital, but other findings have also given important indications that the cash is being utilized effectively. The twenty-four-month evaluation found increases in both food expenditure and dietary diversity, but subsequent analysis of the changes in consumption patterns identified changing preferences among programme recipients—that is, the CT-OVC led to behavioural changes, beyond the income effect, in terms of the composition of household spending. This included reductions in spending on alcohol and tobacco. Evidence of significant changes in expenditure elasticities was found for alcohol and tobacco, and to a lesser extent for food, health, and transportation and communication (Kenya CT-OVC Impact Evaluation Team, 2012a). The forty-eight-month evaluation showed an increase in savings and investment in livestock assets, and that households were more able to hire labour for farm production—essential given the composition of many of the households composed of elderly grandparents and orphans.

6.4.5 Conditions are Difficult to Implement in Kenya, and the Value of Conditions is Therefore Difficult to Assess

While the first round evaluation was able to provide evidence to address most of the critical questions for the programme at the time, it was not able to adequately resolve the questions posed under the test of development conditions. This issue initially arose as a result of the community consultations undertaken during the pre-pilot, when some communities indicated that beneficiaries should be required to do something in return for the money. It also coincided in 2005 and early 2006 with a debate between different sections of the development partner community. To a certain extent this debate had begun to take on aspects of an 'ideological' character, linked to perceptions of poverty and the reasons why poor households were not sending their children to school or participating in health programmes.

On the one hand, it was argued that development conditions would improve programme impact while enhancing the political acceptability and legitimacy of the transfer with both communities and policy makers. On the other hand, it was argued that imposing development conditions would not significantly affect programme outcomes, and would be likely to be costly and complicated to implement, in particular in the context of sub-Saharan Africa, where service access and quality was uneven and capacity for monitoring compliance likely to be weak, and this could also risk penalizing more vulnerable households who already encountered more difficulties accessing services.

This debate threatened to delay implementation of the pilot phase until it was agreed among financing partners to undertake a trial to determine whether conditions would lead to improved outcomes. Conditions were to be implemented in selected Locations chosen at random, and households in areas with conditions were required to take all children under one year for immunizations and growth monitoring and older children up to five years for Vitamin A administration and growth monitoring; and to enrol all children from 6 to 17 years in school and to register 80 per cent attendance; and caregivers had to attend annual awareness sessions.

Overall, the evaluation was unable to assess the effect of conditions because there had been major challenges in implementation. First, there was little difference in awareness and knowledge of some form of condition between areas with programme conditions and those without, largely due to the way in which the programme was explained on enrolment. Overall, 84 per cent of all beneficiaries enrolled believed that they had to follow some conditions in order to continue benefiting—ranging from providing adequate food, nutrition, and clothing for orphans to ensuring children attended school. At the same time, in areas with conditions, there was poor knowledge of some of the conditions, weak monitoring of compliance, and lack of understanding of the reasons when payments were deducted.

One conclusion drawn from this has been that the attempt to implement conditions was premature, that the programme in Kenya was not ready to implement conditions as part of the pilot phase, where implementation was largely in the hands of government agencies with understandably little control over uniformity of communication messages at enrolment. However, others now draw the conclusion that hard conditions were proved unnecessary, either for the programme to have impact, or for community and political acceptability. The fact that the vast majority of beneficiaries believed the transfer was linked to them taking care of the OVCs led to a form of 'soft' conditionality which did not need to be backed up with sanctions and penalties.

6.5 INFLUENCE OF THE EVALUATION ON POLICY AND ON PROGRAMME EXPANSION

The CT-OVC was among the first of the new generation of cash transfer pilots to be implemented and the impact evaluation was integral to design and to setting the foundations for a nationally scaled-up programme. There is no doubt that the evaluation has provided findings of significant interest both in Kenya and in other countries in the region. It is also clear that the programme as a whole has been highly successful in attracting resources, expanding coverage, and influencing the development of several other cash transfers in Kenya, culminating in the decision to expand four cash transfers into a nationwide 'National Safety Net'. To what extent did the evaluation contribute to this success, and what specific aspects of scale-up can be attributed to either the evaluation findings or the use and dissemination of these findings to various audiences?

One area where evaluation was clearly influential was in providing evidence for the operational effectiveness of the cash transfer in the Kenyan context, including in remote and low capacity environments. In particular, evidence of the ability of the programme to deliver cash on a regular and predictable basis was critical and has underpinned all subsequent expansion and the emergence of other cash transfer programmes. In addition, evidence from the twenty-four-month follow-up showing beneficiaries were not subject to excessive demands for unofficial payments was vital in the context of high levels of petty corruption and mistrust in Kenya.

Specific operational findings and recommendations, sometimes supported by additional analysis, were also influential in the design and roll-out of the programme. In particular, further analysis of the evaluation data was used to advocate revision of the targeting process and an increase in the transfer value.

The additional analysis of targeting conducted in 2009 indicated differences in the relative importance of the proxy variables in determining welfare and also showed the relative importance of the indicators differed between regions, with livestock possession and availability of lighting fuel being much more important in rural areas while schooling and toilet facilities were much more important correlates of welfare in urban areas. This prompted an adjustment to the Proxy Means Test (PMT) and introduction of differential weights to the variables utilized (including urban and rural differences), based on the most recent national household budget survey. The PMT developed as a result has continued as the basis for selection of programme beneficiaries since then, and is now part of a wider debate on targeting in Kenya, including consideration of the geographical distribution of beneficiaries between locations, and the role of communities and other agents in identification of beneficiaries. Programme coverage is still a minority of those who are caring for OVC, and given this there continues to be substantial dissatisfaction with the targeting process particularly from those who have not been included. Since the 2007 targeting analysis, however, there has not been another attempt to conduct a rigorous analysis of the effectiveness of targeting based on poverty criteria.[10]

Additional analysis and lobbying was also conducted during 2011 on the level of the transfer in order to develop a clear recommendation on the level of increase. A policy note was prepared jointly by the World Bank and UNICEF, with options for increasing the value of the transfer. Ultimately a new value of KSh 2,000 per beneficiary household, with no adjustment for the size of the household, was agreed with the Ministry of Finance and has been effective since the September–October 2011 payment cycle. However, there is still no mechanism for regular uprating of the transfer value.

The evaluation is also reported to have had indirect effects on the programme success and scale-up. Interviews with those connected with the pilot phase suggest there were important indirect effects from the knowledge that an evaluation would take place which led to increased commitment to good quality implementation, with adherence to programme procedures and a determination to demonstrate success and impact. This influenced the decision to engage long-term technical assistance and to develop the Operational Manual, and the adoption of the capacity building strategy that ultimately has served as the basis for a relatively robust implementation structure. In the case of the qualitative study as part of the forty-eight-month follow-up, the process itself was important in stimulating interest and understanding of the programmes by implementers at decentralized levels, and the need to link the beneficiaries of CT-OVC with other development programmes at field level.

Some observers also credit the fact that an evaluation was to take place incorporating the issue of conditions, with allowing the programme to move forward in 2006 with support of the different funding agencies. At the same time the fact that the programme was subject to a rigorous impact evaluation was also a factor in the decision of the World Bank to commence financing of the programme expansion in 2009 with a $50 million credit.[11] Although the evaluation of conditionalities has not yet been able to assess the impact of conditions for the reasons noted earlier, the agreement for testing and evaluating them was important in 2006–8 for keeping the partner groups—DFID,

---

[10] The separate evaluation currently ongoing is attempting to assess this, but is subject to significant methodological challenges and has not yet provided a report.

[11] World Bank support at a lower level of funds had been under discussion for some time. The availability of evaluation evidence meant it was possible to pursue a specific large-scale credit for programme expansion.

Kenya Orphans and Vulnerable Children Cash Transfer 139

World Bank, UNICEF, and SIDA—together. This also means sustained technical and financial support has been available to the government for more than eight years, and facilitated the expansion of the programme to its current status.

Turning to the broader policy influence of the evaluation, while it is more difficult to attribute wider policy change to the evaluation, many observers and participants are clear that the role of the evaluation evidence in demonstrating that cash transfers are viable, affordable, and have beneficial developmental impacts has also been significant within the broader political process. Starting from 2007 with the inclusion of cash transfers within Kenya's Vision 2030 'development roadmap', moving through debates around Kenya's constitutional revision during 2009 and 2010, and then into the development of the NSPP in 2011 and 2012, the role of cash transfers and social protection in general in Kenya's development policy has become progressively more embedded in the domestic policy, legislative, and fiscal arenas. The expansion of the CT-OVC and its ability to demonstrate results also influenced the emergence of other cash transfers including the Hunger Safety Net, Older Persons Cash Transfer, and Persons with Disability Transfer, which collectively have built wider support for the principle of government-funded income transfers. In the 2013 presidential and parliamentary elections both of the main contenders endorsed cash transfers and pledged their expansion. From July 2013 government funding of cash transfers expanded hugely, with KSh 8 billion ($100 million) allocated for the CT-OVC alone.

According to programme managers, evidence from the evaluation, in particular the finding on 13 per cent poverty reduction, has played a role in facilitating the expansion phase, particularly in persuading Treasury officials to increase public investment in cash transfers under the NSNP, and in garnering support from parliamentary committees and from the Senate. Frequently quoted as a '13 percent reduction in poverty', this result is somewhat misleading given that it applied only to programme beneficiaries who were a very small proportion of Kenya's poor. Nevertheless it has been one of the most widely cited and helpful findings for mobilizing support for the programme. Development partner financing is also an important element, in particular a $250 million Programme for Results (PfR) credit from the World Bank covering the period 2013–17,[12] and continued support by DFID and Ausaid to the HSNP. In particular, the mode of financing from the World Bank, under which disbursements are made in arrears, following achievement of targets including scale-up, has

---

[12] Resources under this modality do not directly support the programme but support the overall government budget based on the achievement of specific milestones linked to the expansion and harmonization of the cash transfer programmes.

enabled expansion and a permanent increase in the government budget for cash transfers. The evaluation evidence from the forty-eight-month-follow-up, particularly on the impacts on adolescent sexual behaviour and HIV risk, has also been significant in leading to the inclusion of social protection as part of the national HIV prevention and response strategy.

These developments cannot be attributed solely to the influence of the evaluation evidence. A large number of other influences appear to have played a part, rooted principally but not exclusively in domestic politics. By 2013 cash transfer programmes including the CT-OVC had expanded into all areas of the country and demand from citizens for their expansion played a part in campaigns around the country. Members of parliament and other political leaders were thus supportive of scaled up coverage of these programmes. At the same time, government was pursuing taxation reform which involved restructuring and extending VAT (value-added tax), a policy that was likely to impact more on the poorest. Expanding social protection coverage was a means to cushion the poorest from the effect of this policy.

One of the issues raised in discussion of the influence of the evaluation is the fact that, until 2013, there had been limited dissemination of or access to the first round evaluation report or evaluation data beyond the programme managers, particularly to the public. The evaluation report was a large and highly technical study that was not thought to be suitable for dissemination, yet it took several years before more 'reader friendly' summaries of the policy findings could be produced. Several of those involved in managing the evaluation and the public dissemination of information have suggested that the way in which the evaluation results were initially presented by the independent evaluators was perceived as misleading and a potential risk to the programme. In the absence of a theoretical framework, reference to comparable international experience, or an elaboration of the type of results that could be expected in the short or longer term, there was a risk that the evaluation could undermine confidence in the programme. This generated some internal resistance and reduced the desire to disseminate the findings.

While the full report was not made widely available, the major findings including the validation of the payments system and the positive developmental impacts became well known among key policy makers through various channels including discussions on the NSPP, and the process of a Social Protection Sector Review, as well as exposure of many key individuals to social protection training and exposure at various international events. Eventually, in 2013, policy briefs were developed highlighting some of the main findings but a clear communication strategy on the outcomes of the first and second round evaluations has not been developed, and as a result the Kenyan public has not benefited from the information. The process of commissioning, managing, and disseminating the evaluation results has revealed the need for greater clarity in ownership of the information and transparency in management of the public dissemination of results.

In the same way that the overall development of political support for social protection cannot be clearly attributed to the evaluation and yet the existence of robust evidence has influenced the process, there are some specific policy areas where political realities have meant that technical evaluation evidence and recommendations have not yet led to policy change. The two most obvious are on the issue of conditions and in connection with the value of the transfer, both in indexing the level of transfer to inflation and in linking the transfer to the size of the household. With respect to conditions, although an evaluation is currently underway, there is limited interest in policy circles in this issue given that the programme is seen as successful in achieving a range of impacts without conditions or at least with 'soft' conditions. Evidence on the differential impacts of the transfer in smaller and larger households has not yet translated into a policy decision in support of a variable transfer. Reasons for this include that increasing the value for larger households would cost more, unless there was a corresponding reduction for smaller households, and there is now pressure to have harmonized levels of benefit for all the four transfers. The current political preference is for expanding coverage to more households. There is also a belief among policy makers that this could encourage expansion of households, in particular potentially through incentives to higher fertility. Evidence has not clearly addressed this concern.

As Kenya embarks on the process of building a national social protection system, founded on a constitutional right to social protection and income support, evaluation evidence including that from the forty-eight-month follow-up is beginning to inform policy and operational decisions. At Kenya's First National Social Protection Conference Week in January 2015, the evidence on the impact of the CT-OVC and HIV prevention, on the productive benefits of the CT-OVC, and on the need for greater complementarity with other programmes was presented. Conference outcomes signed by the Cabinet Secretary include commitments to consolidation and further expansion of the cash transfers, to reviewing payment levels and linking them to economic conditions, and to developing improved links with complementary social services and productive livelihood programmes. Furthermore, a commitment to the use of evidence and evaluation, and to the sharing and dissemination of information, has been made.[13]

---

[13] Joint Call to Action, First Kenya Social Protection Conference Week, Nairobi, 27–30 January 2015.

6.6 CONCLUSIONS

The CT-OVC has been successful in achieving its objectives of supporting the development of orphans and vulnerable children, and has also catalyzed the expansion of cash transfers as a viable and legitimate policy tool in Kenya. The expansion from 2004 has been clearly accompanied by robust evidence of the operational effectiveness and impact of the programme, responding to many of the major management and policy concerns. While many of the issues addressed in the evaluations are most relevant at a technical level, the headline findings have influenced the scale-up of the programme through influential individuals and policy processes, and without this evidence it would not be clear that the programme would have had so much success.

There are a number of lessons to be learned from Kenya's experience of impact evaluation through the CT-OVC. First, the decision to incorporate evaluation in the programme right from the outset of the pre-pilot phase was prescient and ensured there was some evidence available to protect the programme right from the early days. Even where there was debate over the validity or applicability of the findings, the debates were thus always framed on the basis of the evidence rather than on anecdotes and hearsay. During the pre-pilot phase, a simple and less costly form of evaluation relying heavily on community participation was adequate to address basic questions and convince policy makers to enter the formal pilot phase. This avoided the higher cost of a rigorous impact evaluation until the basic elements of the transfer were operating and the major questions relating to a national programme were clarified. At the same time, the fact that there has now been a rigorous impact evaluation with two rounds of data collection has been a great benefit in confirming the longer-term impacts, highlighting areas of impact that take longer to emerge, and bringing in new evidence to inform wider policy debates and bring on board a larger range of actors.

The second lesson relates to the decision to embed both the programme and the evaluation within government structures. This ensured a high level of government ownership of both processes, which was a clear advantage in influencing the development of other cash programmes and in utilization of the evaluation findings to improve operational effectiveness. However, the experience with the results of the first round also highlights the need for clarity on the roles of those commissioning and managing the evaluation and for clear communication with the evaluators concerning the expectations of the evaluation and the presentation of results.

A further lesson relates to the value of evaluation evidence over the longer term. While the pre-pilot evaluation and twenty-four-month impact evaluation provided evidence of immediate value to managers and policy makers, and led to relatively rapid changes to the design of the CT-OVC itself, other issues can take longer to surface and begin to influence policy. The issues of indexing the transfer value and creating stronger links with complementary services and programmes are now rising up the policy agenda, and the evidence from the evaluations is a critical tool to further these ideas. Even where evaluation evidence is not immediately demanded by policy makers, Kenya's experience demonstrates that the availability of robust evidence that can be brought to bear at key moments in the policy process is an enormous advantage. Over the ten-year time horizon, continuous availability of evaluation evidence has been a critical element facilitating the CT-OVC to move from a tiny test project to the mainstream of Kenya's social policy and catalyzed the emergence of an integrated social assistance programme for Kenya's poor and vulnerable.

The next steps in the development of Kenya's social protection system were debated during the first Kenya Social Protection Conference Week in January 2015, resulting in a Joint Call to Action with twelve commitments that reflect Kenya's aspiration to move towards an integrated social protection system, based on consolidation of existing programmes and enhancing complementarity between cash transfers and other social and economic empowerment programmes. The CT-OVC remains a core component of the NSNP, but its success in enhancing the status of its target group needs to be extended to the wider group of vulnerable children in Kenya, recognizing both that orphans are a minority of the children living in poverty in Kenya and that Kenya currently spends a relatively small proportion of GDP (gross domestic product) on social protection.

REFERENCES

Acacia Consultants Ltd. (2007). 'Evaluation of Cash Transfer Programme in Nairobi, Kwale and Garissa Districts'. Nairobi, Kenya : UNICEF.

Acharya, A., Martinez, J., Marinda, E., Pearson, M., Dube, B., Bello, B., Nel, A., and Johnson, S. (2015). 'Kenya Orphans and Vulnerable Children Cash Transfer Programme, Impact Evaluation: Baseline Report', January. Nairobi, Kenya: World Bank.

Allen, K., Campbell, P., Chatterjee, S., Ismail, O., Pearson, R., and Renshaw, M. (2007). 'Can the Kenyan State Put the 300,000 Most Vulnerable Children in the Country on a Cash Transfer by the End of 2010?'. New York. UNICEF. Available at: <http://www.unicef.org/socialpolicy/files/Can_the_Kenyan_State_put_300K_Most_Vulnerable_Children_on_Cash(3).pdf> (accessed 22 November 2015).

Alviar, C., Ayala, F., and Handa, S. (2010). 'Testing Combined Targeting Systems for Cash Transfer Programmes', in Lawson, D., Hulme, D., Matin, I., and Moore, K. (eds), *What Works for the Poor. Poverty Reduction Programmes for the World's Ultra Poor*. Rugby: Practical Action.

Asfaw, S., Davis, B., Dewbre, J., Federighi, G., Handa, S., and Winters, P. (2012). 'The Impact of the Kenya CT-OVC Programme on Productive Activities and Labour Allocation', PtoP Project Report. Rome: FAO. Available at: <http://www.fao.org/fileadmin/user_upload/p2p/Publications/KenyaCT-OVCproductivImpactjan13.pdf> (accessed 22 November 2015).

Asfaw, S., Davis, B., Dewbre, J., Handa, S., and Winters, P. (2014). 'Cash transfer programme, productive activities and labour supply: evidence from a randomized experiment in Kenya'. *Journal of Development Studies*, 50(8): 1172–96.

Handa, S., Alviar, C., Musembi, D., and Ochieng, S. (2011). 'Targeting of Kenya's Cash Transfer Program for Orphans and Vulnerable Children', in Handa S., Devereux S., and Webb D. (eds), *Social Protection for Africa's Children*. Routledge Studies in Development Economics, published online.

Handa, S., Huang, C., Kilburn, K., Halpern, C., Pettifor, A., Rosenberg, M., and Thirumurthy, H. (2012). 'Impact of the Kenya CT-OVC on the Transition to Adulthood', University of North Carolina, Chapel Hill.

Handa, S., Halpern, C., Pettifor, A., and Thirumurthy, H. (2014). 'The government of Kenya's cash transfer program reduces the risk of sexual debut among young people aged 15–25'. *PLOS ONE*, 9(1): 1–9.

Hurrell, A., Ward, P., and Merttens, F. (2008). 'Kenya OVC-CT Programme Operational and Impact Evaluation, Baseline Survey Report'. Oxford: Oxford Policy Management. Available at: <http://www.opml.co.uk/sites/default/files/Kenya%20OVC-CT%20Programme%20Operational%20and%20Impact%20Evaluation_0.pdf> (accessed 22 November 2015).

Oxford Policy Management (2014). 'Qualitative Research and Analyses of the Economic Impacts of Cash Transfer Programmes in sub-Saharan Africa, Kenya Country Case Study Report', FAO, Rome.

Pearson, R. and Alviar, C. (2009). 'Cash Transfers for Vulnerable Children in Kenya: From Political Choice to Scale Up', UNICEF Social and Economic Policy Working Paper. New York. UNICEF. Available at: <http://www.unicef.org/socialpolicy/files/Postscript_Formatted_PPCI_cash_transfers_in_Kenya_Final_Dec_15.pdf> (accessed 22 November 2015).

Romeo, A., Dewbre, J., Davis, B., and Handa, S. (2014). The Long Term Impacts of Cash Transfers in the Context of Inflation: The Case of the CT-OVC Programme in Kenya. Mimeo, unpublished. Rome: FAO.

Taylor, J. E., Kagin, J., Filipski, M., Thome, K., and Handa, S. (2013). 'Evaluating General Equilibrium Impacts of Kenya's Cash Transfer Programme for Orphans and Vulnerable Children (CT-OVC)', PtoP Project Report. Rome: FAO.

The Kenya CT-OVC Evaluation Team (2012a). 'The impact of the Kenya cash transfer programme for orphans and vulnerable children on household spending'. *Journal of Development Effectiveness*, 4(1): 9–37.

The Kenya CT-OVC Evaluation Team (2012b). 'The impact of Kenya's cash transfer programme for orphans and vulnerable children on human capital'. *Journal of Development Effectiveness*, 4(1): 38–49.

UNAIDS, UNICEF, and USAID (2002). 'Children on the Brink 2002: A Joint Report on Orphan Estimates and Program Strategies'. Available at: <http://data.unaids.org/topics/young-people/childrenonthebrink_en.pdf> (accessed 22 November 2015).

Ward, P., Hurrell, A., Visram, A., Riemenschneider, N., Pellerano, L., O' Brien, C., MacAuslan, I., and Willils, J. (2010). 'Cash Transfer Programme for Orphans and Vulnerable Children (CT-OVC), Kenya—Operational and Impact Evaluation, 2007–2009'. Oxford: Oxford Policy Management. Available at: <http://www.opml.co.uk/sites/default/files/OPM_CT-OVC_evaluation_report_july2010-final_Kenya_2010-019.pdf> (accessed 22 November 2015).

7

Social Protection and the Livelihood Empowerment Against Poverty (LEAP) Programme in Ghana

Generating Positive Change through the Power of Evidence

Luigi Peter Ragno (UNICEF and University of Manchester), Sarah Hague (UNICEF), Sudhanshu Handa (University of North Carolina at Chapel Hill and UNICEF), Mawutor Ablo (Government of Ghana), Afua Twun-Danso (University of Sheffield), Lawrence Ofori-Addo (Government of Ghana), Carlos Alviar (UNICEF), Benjamin Davis (FAO), Pamela Pozarny (FAO), and Ramla Attah (Oxford Policy Management)

7.1 INTRODUCTION

As earlier chapters of the book have proposed, conservative estimates suggest that about one billion people are currently targeted by cash transfer schemes—an important component of social protection interventions in developing world (Barrientos, 2013: 4). An increasing number of developing and middle-income countries are launching or expanding cash transfer schemes to target the poorest and most vulnerable households (Conway et al., 2002; World Bank, 2001).

Ghana is no exception. Since 2007 Ghana has launched new initiatives in line with these global trends, including completion of the National Social Protection Strategy (NSPS) and the launch of the cash transfer scheme, the Livelihood Empowerment Against Poverty (LEAP) programme.

The aim of this chapter is providing a critical exploration of social protection and the LEAP programme in Ghana, its impacts on beneficiary households, and how the robust evaluations and evidence produced over time are contributing to adjust its operation and the 'narrative' surrounding the programme.

This chapter begins by presenting what social protection means in Ghana, describes the LEAP programme, its implementation challenges, its expansion over time, and also provides an explanation for the triggers that may have contributed to social protection's development and expansion. The chapter continues by presenting the role of recent rigorous evaluations, which, firstly, contribute to creating a new narrative for the LEAP programme enabling it to expand and become considered one of the main poverty reduction instruments in Ghana, and, secondly, prioritize practical implementation issues, such as payment and communication with beneficiaries.

7.2 SOCIAL PROTECTION IN GHANA

First we examine the emergence and, to some extent, the evolution of social protection in Ghana, before assessing the main drivers that favoured this and specifically led to the development of the LEAP programme in Ghana.

In the early 2000s, several factors played a major role in promoting social protection and cash transfers in Ghana. First, the Ghana Poverty Reduction Strategy (2002–2005) and a Poverty and Social Impact Assessment identified and called for the need to initiate special and targeted programmes for the vulnerable and excluded. The documents also identified the need to develop a coordinated Social Protection Framework that would guide the design and implementation of such initiatives.

During this period the government launched a series of new social protection interventions in both the health and the education sector—such as the National Health Insurance System (NHIS), the capitation grant, and the school feeding programme—and, between 2005 and 2007, developed the National Social Protection Strategy (NSPS) as an attempt to move towards an integrated forward-looking national framework (Sultan and Schrofer 2008). The NSPS takes the view that social protection is an integral part of the overall development architecture of Ghana as a key principle of the 1992 Constitution. The strategy, approved by the cabinet in 2007 (and revised in 2012), aimed to direct the prioritization of sector-wide social protection interventions and to facilitate collaborative implementation of social protection across the country. The Strategy also framed and institutionalized the beginning of the cash transfer scheme LEAP in Ghana, which will be the discussed in Section 7.3.

Second, key individuals in the Ghanaian government became national 'champions' and initiated and continued to promote over the years the importance of social protection and specifically of LEAP from within the system, notwithstanding the initial low political support and political space. These advocates, well-trained and committed civil servants already equipped with international exposure, were further supported and exposed to overseas training, exchange trips, and international workshops on social protection and cash transfers.

The third major factor that contributed to the emergence of social protection in Ghana was the global focus on such interventions and new robust evidence on their impacts from countries like Mexico and then Brazil as well as regional calls for action such as the Livingston Conference in 2006.

Many countries, often financially and technically supported by development partners such as the World Bank, Department for International Development (DFID), and the United Nations Children Fund (UNICEF), initiated the development of similar interventions adapted to local contexts. In the African region, Kenya, South Africa, and Ethiopia are the best-known examples. Ghana followed with a new partnership forged with Brazil, promoted by development partners, namely World Bank, UNICEF, and DFID. Donors acted as a global learning hub for successful initiatives and actively engaged the Government of Ghana in initiating such interventions. They played a major role by providing technical expertise and financial support as well as by taking advantage of horizontal (south–south) cooperation with countries like Brazil. This is a continuing strategy and is evident even throughout recent developments in social protection in Ghana.

This critical mass of national champions and trusted external development partners proved to be the right mix to contribute to create an enabling environment for social protection and cash transfers to develop effectively in Ghana. However, the importance of the critical mass should not be overestimated.

As also discussed widely in the literature (De Haan, 2014; Niño-Zarazúa et al., 2012), politics played a major role in Ghana. The evidence on how interventions like Brazil's Bolsa Familia (Zucco, 2013) can impact on voting behaviour demonstrates that such programmes are prone to political interests. Ghana, again, is no exception. The design and 'rushed' roll out of the LEAP cash transfer scheme just a few months before the December 2008 presidential election suggests that politics clearly may have been an influencing factor,[1] as suggested by some international experts involved in the design of LEAP and other political commentators in 2008, though this was strongly denied by government officials.[2] It was suggested that the LEAP programme was an attempt by government to showcase new efforts to reduce poverty after the release of the 2006

---

[1] The design of the LEAP was completed on the 27 November 2007; the LEAP was launched in March 2008, four months after its design.

[2] 'The objection that a welfare programme is dubious because it is an election year is a very unworthy objection. If pursued, then indeed, all development activity (building of roads, hospitals, schools, rural electrification, pay increase, etc.) should all cease in an election year. It is an unimagined absurdity', Nana Akomea Minister of Manpower, Youth and Employment,

national household survey data, the Ghana Living Standard Survey 5 (GLSS5) in order to shift consensus ahead of the imminent election. What matters since then is, firstly, that the LEAP programme survived the resulting change of government in 2008 and has since expanded and rolled out from 1,654 households in 2008 to 140,000 in 2015 (November), and secondly, that an increasing proportion of government resources have been allocated to LEAP.

Since 2008, an increasing number of social protection schemes and programmes have been instituted by various government ministries. As a result, the social protection landscape in Ghana is fragmented with a multiplicity of social protection schemes and programmes.

In 2012, the revised draft NSPS identified forty-four schemes and programmes that were loosely categorized as social protection. A recent study, attempting a more precise inventory of interventions (ILO, 2014), found that out of the forty-four programmes only nine had social protection as the primary objective, with others focusing more broadly on education, health, employment, and other such sector-specific objectives. In addition to the LEAP programme, the main social protection interventions in Ghana are the National Health Insurance Scheme (NHIS), Free School Uniforms, Free Exercise Books, the Ghana School Feeding Programme, the Capitation Grant for basic education, and the Labour Intensive Public Works Programme (LIPW). However, in the majority of cases, these schemes and programmes are not targeted well to the poor and vulnerable, are not well designed, and are often implemented inefficiently with significant gaps in geographical and demographic coverage (ILO, 2014). As is the case for many developing countries, the rationalization study suggested that Ghana is far from having a well-structured and coordinated social protection system. There is no national policy document, the governance and institutional framework is weak, and there is no sector-wide social protection monitoring and evaluation system with standardized definitions and consistent concepts and classifications.[3] The study also noted that most programmes were not clearly designed in terms of eligibility criteria and benefit levels, operated as discreet entities unconnected to other programmes, were unable to provide detailed information on expenditure, number, and characteristics of beneficiaries (by sex, age, etc.) over time, and did not have a credible M&E (Monitoring and Evaluation) system in place (ILO, 2014).

In 2013 and 2014 attempts were made to address some of these issues raised in the rationalization report. In January 2013, after the December 2012 presidential election, which the incumbent party also won, the Government of Ghana underscored the importance of social protection in its poverty

---

said at a press conference in February 2008. Available online at: <http://allafrica.com/stories/200802010131.html> (accessed 28 October 2015).

[3] A Sector Working Group on Social Protection involving all actors in the area was the only official and functional platform for coordination.

reduction efforts by restructuring the Ministry of Women and Children into the Ministry of Gender, Children and Social Protection (MoGCSP). The new ministry is charged with three primary responsibilities: (i) providing and managing family support services, social work, and alternative care; (ii) leading efforts to mainstream gender in national policies and interventions; and (iii) to coordinate all social protection interventions across multiple implementing agencies, as well as implementing the LEAP programme.

In mid-2014, the MoGCSP submitted and obtained the approval of a Cabinet Memo laying out the vision for Ghana's social protection system. The Memo paved the way for accelerating improvements in social protection in several ways. It improved the effectiveness and coordination of social protection by strengthening the strategic, oversight, and monitoring roles of the MoGCSP to coordinate social protection initiatives. It also proposed and agreed to a definition of social protection and a social protection floor; laid down an institutional framework for coordination of social protection; and validated the establishment of a national targeting system for poor households. The MoGCSP has also taken advantage of the political significance of the cabinet memo to further strengthen its pivotal role and develop a National Social Protection Policy. The new policy has now been approved by the cabinet (December 2015).

7.3 GHANA'S FLAGSHIP SOCIAL PROTECTION PROGRAMME: THE LEAP CASH TRANSFER PROGRAMME

Introduced in 2008 with the aim to empower the poorest of the poor in Ghana to exit poverty, LEAP is a cash transfer programme now reaching more than 140,000 poor households in all the ten regions of Ghana (as of November 2015), from an initial coverage of 1,654 extreme poor households in 21 districts in 2008. The roll-out of LEAP to increase its coverage was phased in the original LEAP design document to ensure the availability of financial resources as well as to build consensus over time.

The programme is managed by the MoGCSP through its Department of Social Development. It is largely funded from the domestic budget of the Government of Ghana (some of which originates from a World Bank loan) and a grant from DFID, and receives technical support from the UNICEF Ghana social protection team.

LEAP is designed to provide social protection for the poorest and most marginalized people in Ghanaian society, notably those that fall under the national extreme poverty line. According to the new Ghana Living Standards Survey (2013), this group now makes up 8.4 per cent of the country's population, equalling 2.2 million people.[4] Within this category of extreme poor, the programme further targets those households which include one or more beneficiaries who are either over sixty-five years of age, or living with a severe disability, or caregivers of orphans and vulnerable children (OVC). From 2016, as result of a new initiative known as the LEAP 1000, LEAP will also target households with a pregnant woman and children below one year of age.

The programme's objective is to increase long-term human capital development among Ghana's extreme poor and vulnerable by increasing consumption and promoting access to services and opportunities. The specific objectives of the programme are as follows (MESW, 2012: A2):

1. To improve basic household consumption and nutrition among children under the age of two, the elderly (aged sixty-five and over without productive capacity) and people with severe disability and thus unable to work;
2. To increase access to health care services among children below five years of age, the elderly (aged sixty-five and above without productive capacity), and people with severe disability;
3. To increase basic school enrolment, attendance, and retention of beneficiary children between five and fifteen years of age;
4. To facilitate access to complementary services such as welfare, livelihood, and improvement in productive capacity.

The LEAP grant is unconditional for the disabled and the elderly. However, although not part of an enforceable monitoring system, carers of OVC are expected to adhere to certain conditionalities/corresponsabilities, which include:

1) Enrolment and retention of school-age children in school;
2) Birth registration of new born babies and their attendance at post-natal clinics;
3) Full vaccination of children up to the age of five;
4) The non-trafficking of children and ensuring their non-engagement in the 'worst forms' of child labour (MESW, 2012: A5)

The implementation of LEAP over the years has been far from homogenous across districts or consistent with operational guidelines. The lack of a detailed operational manual that described in detail the different processes from targeting to information management and payment was

---

[4] The national extreme poverty line is set at the level at which households cannot even support their daily food needs.

at the root of this heterogeneous and often inconsistent implementation and has only been partially addressed since 2012, due to the relentless work of the LEAP management unit and its development partners. Inconsistent implementation affected many processes such as manual payment to beneficiaries, monitoring and reporting, and payment reconciliation documentation.

LEAP's implementation has, however, evolved towards more structured processes over time. Payment and Targeting are good examples. Payments, from the first time since LEAP was launched in 2008, have been regular since August 2013. In the case of targeting, from using multiple approaches in selecting LEAP beneficiary households, which left great discretion to local elites to capture the process, in 2010 LEAP initiated the development and later on adopted a more transparent and objective mechanism to reach the poorest households in Ghana.

LEAP now uses Ghana's common targeting mechanism, which though agreed upon by five ministries as the national system to be used jointly across governments to select beneficiaries for social assistance programmes, has only been adopted and rolled out by LEAP.[5] Originally the mechanism involved the selection of potential beneficiaries through geographical targeting to identify districts and communities,[6] then through a Community Based Targeting (CBT) process to discuss the identification of the poorest households in a community,[7] and then finally by applying Ghana's Proxy Means Test (PMT).[8] With this information, the Management Information System (MIS) then carried out PMT score calculation on the selected households to determine their poverty level using a cut-off point based on the national extreme poverty line. Depending on which side of the line households fall, they are then designated as 'extremely poor' or 'not extremely poor'. However, this lengthy selection approach has now been revised within a national targeting system. This system is primarily based on the PMT, which will be

---

[5] Ministry of Employment and Social Welfare/Ministry of Gender, Children and Social Protection, Ministry of Health, Ministry of Education, Ministry of Food and Agriculture, and Ministry of Local Government and Rural Development

[6] The purpose of this geographical targeting is to select regions, districts, and communities that have large concentrations of extremely poor, vulnerable, and excluded sections of the population. Data used includes regional poverty rates from the national household survey as well as data available at district level and in coordination with district officials.

[7] For the Community-Based Targeting (CBT), the District Social Welfare Officer (DSWO) supervises the formation of the Community Committees (CCs), which are made up of key opinion leaders of the community. The CC is sensitized by the DSWO and the District Committees (DCs) on the CBT. They support the DSWO in identifying the extremely poor and vulnerable households within their communities.

[8] The PMT has been developed and is regularly revised by the World Bank, which has led the efforts in improving the targeting effectiveness of LEAP.

applied directly and more extensively across the country in order to compile a comprehensive Ghana National Household Registry. This national registry will eventually form the basis for selection of households for all Ghana's social protection programmes.

The grant amount has been revised twice, in 2012 and 2015. From September 2015,[9] the monthly amount per household ranges from thirty-two GHS with one beneficiary, thirty-eight GHS with two beneficiaries, forty-four GHS with three beneficiaries, and fifty-three GHS for four or more beneficiaries.[10] Beneficiaries are paid once every two months through Ghana Post, though a new electronic payment is being rolled out.

A key feature of LEAP is its integration into complementary services to connect beneficiaries with a wider range of social services, and provide beneficiaries with opportunities to build their capacity to exit poverty as a result of their own efforts. As of 2015, the linkage to complementary services is only well established for health insurance. LEAP families are entitled to free health insurance through the NHIS and are encouraged to access post-natal clinics and birth registration as well as complete the Expanded Programme on Immunization.

As mentioned earlier in the chapter, since 2008, LEAP has expanded from 1,654 in 2008 to more than 140,000 households in November 2015, with plans to expand it further to reach at least 250,000 households by the end of 2016 (see Figure 7.1).

The expansion of LEAP was described in the original design document in 2007 under two scenarios which aimed at achieving 164,000 households by the fifth year of implementation (by 2013). Nevertheless, the roll-out plan was never fully implemented and LEAP expanded at a much lower and more irregular pace than planned.

The slower pace of the expansion can be explained by the low political traction and the subsequent lack of resources allocated to implement the planned roll-out in LEAP's initial years. Also, the inability to expand the LEAP management unit with human resources to cope with the increasing number of beneficiary households may have played a major role.

The irregularity of the expansion is interlinked to external factors such as the financial, fuel, and food crisis of 2009 (3F Crisis),[11] political elections, as well as major government policy shifts, such as the creation of a dedicated

---

[9] The baseline evaluation workshop held in Akosombo in October 2011 was a particularly important moment when the low value of the transfer and irregular payments were highlighted to the minister and his deputy, and triggered an advocacy effort which led to the subsequent tripling of the transfer level in 2012.

[10] 1USD=3.8GHS (November 2015).

[11] In 2009, the Government of Ghana, with the support of the World Bank, expanded LEAP to reach about 20,000 new households with a LEAP emergency package. These households, have since then been incorporated into LEAP.

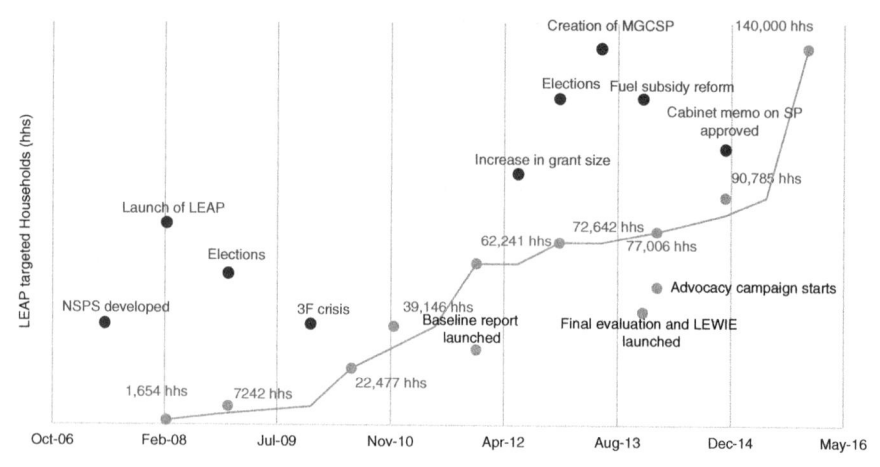

Figure 7.1. The Expansion of LEAP
Source: the Authors

ministry to deal with social protection issues (MoGCSP), and more recently, the fuel subsidy reform and fiscal adjustments with the new International Monetary Fund (IMF) programme.

The fuel subsidy reform and its importance in LEAP's expansion require further explanations. The increasing proportion of government resources allocated to LEAP, and the subsequent major expansion in 2015, has its roots in economic changes and challenges that several countries in Africa, including Ghana, face. Governments across Africa have implemented fuel subsidies over recent decades as politically appealing subsidies to the cost of living. However, their escalating cost as fuel prices rise and concerns over their efficiency have brought the use of fuel subsidies into question. In Ghana, with an almost 12 per cent fiscal deficit in 2012, their burgeoning cost drew attention to questions of fiscal sustainability as well as their overall efficiency and effectiveness. In 2013, the Ghanaian Government would have spent over 1 billion USD on fuel subsidies, equalling 3.2 per cent of GDP—more than half of Ghana's allocation to the entire education sector. In early 2013 the Ghanaian Government introduced the removal of fuel subsidies over the first half of the year. Prices of petrol, kerosene, diesel, and LPG (liquefied petroleum gas) saw rises of between 15 per cent and 50 per cent, until prices reached their market level in mid-September 2013 (Cooke et al., 2014).

Since fuel subsidies around the world have been proven to be generally regressive, benefiting largely the richest group with very little reaching those living below the poverty line, their removal was seen as progressive if the diverted resources were reallocated well. In Ghana, UNICEF and the Partnership for Economic Policy carried out research to determine the impact of fuel subsidies on poverty and inequality and compared this to expansion of the

LEAP programme (Cooke et al., 2014). The research found that almost 78 per cent of fuel subsidies benefited the wealthiest group, with less than 3 per cent of subsidy benefits reaching the poorest quintile. However, it was estimated that the removal of the subsidies would have the biggest negative impact on the poorest quintile, and push almost 400,000 additional people into poverty. Following extensive advocacy before the 2013 budget was finalized, the Government agreed to scale up social protection spending, particularly LEAP. LEAP's budget rose from 8m GHS in 2012 to 20m in 2013 and to 38m GHS in 2014.

7.4 IMPACTS OF LEAP ON THE HOUSEHOLDS' WELL-BEING

In terms of LEAP's impact on well-being, a number of recent research studies and evaluations have been conducted using a range of qualitative and quantitative methods—these are described in Chapters 3, 4, and 5 of this book.[12] While the first rigorous evaluation was only completed in 2013, the need for generating evidence on the impacts of LEAP was a key concern highlighted in the LEAP design document and fully supported by government officials. Nevertheless only when resources became available and development partners, notably DFID, also became interested in producing rigorous evidence on the impacts of the programme and of their support to the government, the evaluation was implemented.

At a glance, the evidence generated between 2010 and 2013 on LEAP was the product of a quantitative impact evaluation implemented by the University of North Carolina at Chapel Hill and the Institute for Statistical, Social and Economic Research (ISSER, University of Ghana), a qualitative research of the economic impacts of LEAP by the Oxford Policy Management Institute, and a Local Economy-Wide Impact Evaluation (LEWIE) of LEAP by FAO (Food and Agriculture Organization of the United Nations).

Most notably, the quantitative impact evaluation was completed to determine the benefits of the programme on beneficiaries and their communities. This study (Handa et al., 2013), conducted by the University of North Carolina at Chapel Hill and ISSER compared LEAP families with other families who had the same socio-economic profile but who did not receive LEAP. The quantitative impact evaluation for LEAP is a longitudinal propensity score matching (PSM) design where baseline data was collected from future beneficiaries in three regions (Brong Ahafo, Central, and Volta) who were part of a larger nationally representative sample of households surveyed as part of a research study conducted by ISSER and Yale University (USA) in the first quarter of 2010

---

[12] Thome et al. (2013); OPM (2013); Handa et al. (2013).

(N=699), with the purpose of exploiting the national survey to construct a non-experimental comparison group.

Overall, notwithstanding the heterogeneous and often inconsistent implementation of LEAP, these rigorous studies show that the LEAP cash transfer programme is reaching the poorest households in Ghana,[13] and is having a significant impact both on beneficiaries and their families, particularly in relation to food security, health, education, savings, and investments, as well as on their wider communities in terms of community development and economic growth (see Table 7.1).

7.5 LEAP ENSURES THAT HOUSEHOLDS SURVIVE AND MEET BASIC FOOD NEEDS

A key setback with the LEAP in earlier years was its irregular payment as the central release of funds to the programme was often delayed. The effect of this was captured in the impact evaluation, which did not find an impact on overall food consumption levels as households were using bulk payments to make bulk purchases, instead of adding to daily spending and smoothing consumption. However, perceived food insecurity significantly reduced for LEAP families (by 25 percentage points) especially for those headed by women (by 32 percentage points) between 2010 and 2012 (Handa et al., 2013: 14).[14] Families in the northern regions explained how it helped them to avoid hunger during the lean season. Furthermore, LEAP has led to an increase in the consumption of fats (by GHS 0.88) and food eaten out (by GHS 4.12) and a reduction in starches (by GHS 2.58) and meats (by GHS 1.99), particularly for smaller families. While the decline in meats could raise concern, this might be explained by the increase in the number of LEAP families being able to eat a wider range of food prepared outside of the home.

7.6 LEAP ENABLES FAMILIES TO FOCUS ON THEIR HEALTH NEEDS

One of the features of the LEAP programme is free enrolment in the NHIS. As of early 2012, 90 per cent of LEAP families had been enrolled to

---

[13] A recent World Bank study on the targeting of social transfer programmes (Wodon, 2012) assessed the LEAP programme to be the best-targeted social transfer programme in Ghana. This finding (concluded even before the PMT was refined) demonstrates that LEAP is reaching the poorest households in Ghana.

[14] The food security situation of LEAP households has improved dramatically, nevertheless the improvements observed cannot be interpreted to be due to participation in LEAP alone.

Table 7.1. LEAP's Impacts Summary Table

Summary table—LEAP impacts		Impacts—final evaluation 2013
Food Security		
Perceived food insecurity		−0.245
Child food insecurity		−0.702
Female-headed households food insecurity		−0.321
Adult consumption food		No impact
Healthcare		
LEAP HH enrolment into the NHIS		90% of Household enrolled
Enrolment of children into the NHIS	Age 6–17	0.16
	Age 0–5	0.34
Likelihood of falling ill (for children aged 6–17)		−0.05
School Enrolment and Attendance		
Likelihood of missing any school	Age 5–17	−0.08
	Girls-Age 13–17	−0.11
Grade repetition	Age 5–17	−0.11
	Age 13–17	−0.10
Chance of missing an entire week of school	Age 5–17	−0.05
	Age 13–17	−0.11
Secondary school enrolment	Age 13–17	0.07
Household Productive Activity		
Loan re-payment		0.234
Savings		0.108
Own farm labour	General LEAP HH	8–9 days
	Smaller LEAP HH	13 days
Social Inclusion and Happiness		
Self-reported happiness, self-esteem and feelings of hope	General LEAP HH	0.158
	Female-headed HH	0.233
Support for others	General LEAP HH	GHC 1.60
	Female-headed HH	GHC 1.80
Local Economic Growth		
Every 1 GHS transferred to a beneficiary family could increase local income by 2.5 GHS (multiplier effect)	Production of crops	GHC 0.27
	Livestock	GHC 0.16
	Retail	GHC 0.78

Source: Handa et al. (2013).

the NHIS, which was an increase of 25 percentage points compared to 2010 (Handa et al., 2013: 8). In comparison, the enrolment of other poor households (with a similar profile to LEAP beneficiaries) in the NHIS increased by 18 percentage points.

LEAP has led to a significant increase in the number of children aged 6–17 (16 percentage points) and aged 0–5 (34 percentage points) enrolled in the NHIS. In addition, children in the age group 6–17 are less likely than non-LEAP households to be ill (5 percentage points): this is an important point as healthy children are more able to attend school on a regular basis (Handa et al., 2013: 24). Another main outcome is the increased number of beneficiaries seeking preventative care especially for young girls aged between 0 and 5, which is crucial given the importance of this stage of life for cognitive development and longer-term well-being.

LEAP has also enabled beneficiaries to maintain their health, paying for prescriptions and medicines and even operations. The outcome of linking LEAP to the NHIS is that beneficiaries are spending less on health than previously—LEAP households have reduced their health out-of-pocket spending by up to 7 GHS monthly. This is important to note as this reduction in health expenditure is an outcome not of the LEAP cash grant itself, but rather the enrolment of beneficiaries in the NHIS (Handa et al., 2013).

7.7 LEAP INCREASES SCHOOL ENROLMENT AND REGULAR ATTENDANCE

Both the quantitative and the qualitative impact evaluations conducted on LEAP have shown that the programme has positively impacted children's education in terms of enrolment, grade repetition, and absenteeism. Regular school attendance, in particular, has improved at all levels.

While LEAP has not had a significant impact on the already high primary school enrolment rates, the programme has reduced school absenteeism (by 8 percentage points), grade repetition (by 11 percentage points), and the chance of missing an entire week of school (by 5 percentage points) (Handa et al., 2013: 26).

LEAP had a greater impact for older children's schooling. For children aged 13–17 the programme significantly increased secondary school enrolment rates (by 7 percentage points), particularly for boys, and reduced grade repetition (by 10 percentage points) compared to children in non-LEAP households (Handa et al., 2013: 27). LEAP also reduced the likelihood of older girls missing school (by 11 percentage points). Hence, while girls already in school experienced an improvement in their attendance, boys experienced an increase in secondary school enrolment. Children's ability to attend and remain in school increases their chances of entering effectively into employment and increases their future earnings (UNICEF, 2012). This causal effect has a great potential of reducing inter-generational poverty and the enhancement of livelihoods of future generations.

According to the qualitative research, beneficiaries in the Northern Region say they are now much more able to pay the required levies and to provide their children with the essentials required to keep them in school such as uniforms, pencils, exercise books, and food. As a result, their children are missing school less often. Similar findings were identified in the Central Region. According to beneficiaries and key informants in Dompoase, school attendance has increased due to LEAP, with beneficiary families now able to not only keep up with school levies, but also spend more on school textbooks and uniforms (OPM, 2013: 30). Furthermore, the evidence suggests that there has also been a reduction in child labour as children from beneficiary families who used to work all day now worked on farms and stalls only after school and on weekends.

7.8 LEAP PROVIDES OPPORTUNITIES TO INCREASE PRODUCTIVITY

In line with its overall objective to empower poor families to 'leap' out of poverty, the programme has also provided opportunities for beneficiaries to transform their lives in the long term. Specifically, LEAP families have felt sufficiently empowered to use their cash to increase loan re-payment (by 23 percentage points) (Handa et al., 2013: 20) or savings (by 10.8 percentage points) (Handa et al., 2013: 15–16). The LEAP transfer also increased the capacity of beneficiaries to access credit.

Additionally, a number of beneficiaries used their LEAP payments for investment activities. For example, in both the Central and Northern regions beneficiaries mentioned that they had used the cash for petty trading, investing in animals, household items, and kerosene. Others had started vegetable gardens or increased on-farm productivity by hiring labour, purchasing farm assets and inputs (Korboe, 2011).

With regard to own farm labour, LEAP beneficiaries work 8–9 days more on average over the season than equally poor non-LEAP households. Smaller families work an extra thirteen days over the season (Handa et al., 2013: 18). In addition, those who are not able to work on their own farms are now able to hire labour. For example, in South Natinga (Northern Region), those who lack the physical ability said they are now able to pay for tractor services or hire labour to work on their land (Korboe, 2011: 51).

7.9 LEAP BUILDS THE CAPACITY OF BENEFICIARIES TO BECOME ACTIVE PARTICIPANTS IN THEIR COMMUNITIES—SOCIAL INCLUSION AND HAPPINESS

In a society where the value of reciprocity remains critical to the maintenance of traditional social welfare mechanisms, being able to provide support to extended family and community members is central to ensuring that one receives support in return when needed. Social ties through contribution are generally emphasized and the LEAP impact evaluation reiterated that. It was shown that amongst the Fante of the Central Region, there was a belief that 'if you do not contribute then you are easily prone to being side-lined in the community'. As a result, 'extended family support for the most vulnerable was very patchy or non-existent' (OPM, 2013: 39). Similarly, in the Northern Region prior to LEAP, beneficiaries were not able to borrow from community members because they were not perceived to be creditworthy (OPM, 2013: 42).

As a result of the introduction of LEAP within these communities, perceptions and attitudes towards beneficiaries have changed. In particular, LEAP has enabled households to contribute to various groups in their communities such as extended family risk-sharing arrangements and savings groups such as *susu*. In this way, beneficiaries were able to move from a position of isolation and vulnerability to one of greater inclusion within their communities. Specifically, beneficiary families have increased the amount they spend on providing support to others (by GHS 1.60 annually). This development has been particularly noted among families led by women (increase of GHS 1.80) (Handa et al., 2013: 15–16).

These effects mean that beneficiaries are more able to contribute to ceremonies and other key social events that take place. This has improved their self-esteem as well as increased their visibility and social status in their communities. For example, in Dalung (Northern Region) prior to the introduction of LEAP, beneficiaries felt excluded and marginalized as they were not invited to participate in decision-making in the community and were also not well received during social gatherings and other events. This function of cash transfer programmes improving social networks and community resilience is often overlooked when focusing only on consumption benefits, but it is critical to consider for a holistic approach to the impact of social protection on communities.

Active participation in their communities also contributes to an increase in self-reported happiness, self-esteem, and feelings of hope amongst LEAP families who are 16 percentage points more likely to feel happy about their life than in non-LEAP households (Handa et al., 2013: 13). This figure increases for female-headed families (23 percentage points). According to one key informant in Dompoase, 'before LEAP they [the beneficiaries] looked miserable but [they now look] happier and hopeful' (OPM, 2013: 40).

7.10 LEAP: A BOOST TO LOCAL ECONOMIES

A recent study (Thome et al., 2013) found that the LEAP programme could have multiplier effects by channeling cash into the local economy through the increased purchasing power of beneficiary families. As beneficiaries spend their cash (80 per cent of which is spent within their local economy), the impact of the transfers immediately spread from the beneficiary families to others in the area. The study estimated that every 1 GHS transferred to a beneficiary family could increase local income by 2.5 GHS (multiplier effect) and that most of this would go to non-beneficiary households. In this way the impact of the cash transfer on the local economy is likely to significantly exceed the amount transferred to beneficiaries provided payments were made regularly.

These indirect benefits to the wider community are set in motion by petty trade and purchases in stores and markets within targeted villages as well their surrounding areas. The programme also has a significant impact on production. For every one GHS transferred, the production of crops increases by GHS 0.27 and livestock by GHS 0.16. The largest effect is on the retail sector, which has a multiplier effect of GHS 0.78.

This particular impact of LEAP has been especially noted in communities with relatively small local markets (OPM, 2013: 36–37). The local economy of Dompoase is a good example. Here, local traders and beneficiaries confirmed that trading activity has increased due to LEAP transfers as they have enabled beneficiaries to buy more in the local shops especially after payment day. Traders and vendors described a more vibrant local economy, with vendors' food bowls now being finished at the end of the day. In addition, in the same area, informants reported that there are now more food vendors and petty traders than before, leading to a stabiliztion, rather than an increase, in prices.

The rigorous evidence collected in these evaluations tells that LEAP is having positive impacts on people's lives and on all members of the community, effects that could be even higher if some important operational obstacles could be resolved. The evidence of the impacts of LEAP also contributed to changing a common perception that LEAP was only 'handout' to the poor. When the studies were released, the 'narrative' on LEAP, the discourse on LEAP's role in the national development strategy, began to change.

7.11 A NEW EVIDENCE-BASED NARRATIVE ON THE EFFECTIVENESS OF THE LEAP PROGRAMME

This section of the chapter describes how the impacts of the LEAP programme have contributed to shape a new and more positive narrative on the LEAP programme itself. This has occurred in two ways. First, effective advocacy was undertaken, which translated the evidence into clear and digestible messages for a variety of stakeholders. Second, the studies helped to present LEAP as an improving programme that is refining its operations.

The LEAP studies provide evidence that the programme works and is contributing to reducing poverty in the targeted households and beyond. This evidence helped to break down a preconception that saw LEAP as a small-scale, charitable handout creating dependency in poor households. Such notions were fuelled by occasional writings based on anecdotal evidence (e.g. Debrah, 2013) or uninformed media coverage that hyped the risk of fraud or dependency.

The studies and evaluations themselves alone did not overcome this narrative. It was *the way in which they were used* that created the change. Several nationwide events were organized in late 2013 and early 2014 by the MoGCSP with support of partners. The media were engaged substantially in these events, which resulted in a series of more realistic, positive, and evidence-based media coverage.[15]

The studies' results were also transformed into easy-to-digest briefing papers and factsheets on specific impacts and widely distributed at major events and meetings. This material became the basis of any interview or television debate given by the MoGCSP's staff and by the minister herself. Media were proactively engaged and outreached by the MoGCSP to promote the role of social protection and LEAP, and not just to react to events. In addition, a wide range of actors were engaged on their own terms and invited to contribute to the dialogue—emerging civil society was invited to sector meetings, the national-university-led research activities, and alliances forged and maintained between disparate social protection programmes.

Beyond communication on LEAP's positive impacts, the studies helped to demonstrate to both decision-makers and the public that LEAP is also an *evolving* programme, *improving* itself based on operational weaknesses identified. The operational studies suggested that, despite the significant and proven achievements of LEAP, its impact on the lives of the poorest communities in Ghana has been limited by a number of functional factors. These issues were highlighted in LEAP's Operational Evaluation in 2012 and are broadly related to payments (size and regularity) and beneficiary information.

In relation to payments, as mentioned in Sections 7.3 and 7.5, the pattern of payments had been highly erratic, preventing households from viewing LEAP

---

[15] Available online at: <http://graphic.com.gh/news/general-news/243-leap-improves-lives-of-vulnerable.html> (accessed 28 October 2015) and <http://graphic.com.gh/news/politics/16127-system-to-monitor-leap-launched.html>; <http://graphic.com.gh/business/business-news/16889-leap-pilots-electronic-payment-system.html> (accessed 20 November 2015).

grants as predictable and factoring them into their regular spending and investment plans. In 2011, LEAP households received an amount equivalent to only four payments (instead of six) in three irregular instalments (instead of six)—with two instalments at the beginning of the year and one instalment (equalling a double payment) in the middle of the year. In 2012, LEAP's households received an amount equivalent to nine payments instead of six to help overcome arrears. But again these were often grouped together, with an amount equivalent to three payments transferred in one instalment in February 2012. In 2013, an amount equivalent to five payments (out of the required six) was disbursed in three instalments, but with no payments received at all until August. The studies have confirmed that this operational issue limited the full poverty reduction potential of the programme. In particular, as a protective social protection scheme, LEAP sought to have an impact on the consumption expenditure of beneficiaries especially in relation to food. This objective was not fully achieved in earlier years as a result of the irregularity and delays in the payment process. However, at the time of writing, following intense advocacy, the programme had received regular funding enabling it to resolve this issue and provide regular payments to households since August 2013.

The low value of the cash transfer was also identified to be limiting the potential positive impacts of the programme. In 2010 the value of the transfer was 7 per cent of consumption, which did not compare favourably with other successful programmes elsewhere which transferred at least 20 per cent of consumption to beneficiaries (Handa et al., 2013: 8). To address the low value of the cash grant, the transfer value of LEAP was tripled in late 2012, and again revised in 2015.

Poor beneficiary information on eligibility and conditions has also been a key shortfall identified in the studies. Households were not receiving all the necessary information regarding the programme and eligibility criteria. LEAP beneficiaries believe that the programme is for the old, very poor, sick, and those unable to work. Only 28 per cent of LEAP households know that OVC is an eligible category. Confusion about conditionality and payment expiry rules also remains. Of households receiving LEAP payments, 83 per cent said that households do not have to follow any rules or conditions, 13 per cent said that there are rules or conditions, and 4 per cent did not know. Among those who believed there were conditions, the most frequently reported conditions were NHIS and children's school enrolment. Such difficulties with payments and beneficiary communication are symptomatic of a programme that has not been able to develop core systems, such as a monitoring and evaluation system to track payments, or a case management structure to initiate two-way communication with the targeted households.

These shortfalls defined the key priorities for improving the programme and important steps have recently been undertaken to address them. With the technical, advocacy, and financial support of development partners, the LEAP programme has designed and operationalized a new M&E system which has led to the generation, in 2014, of the first LEAP quarterly report. To aid communication and beneficiary awareness, the programme has developed and distributed 80,000 booklets and posters on what LEAP is and households' rights and responsibilities, and a case management system has been designed.

To modernize payments, LEAP has piloted a new electronic payment system and is now planning a nationwide roll-out.[16] Payments have become regular since August 2013.

The way in which both the impact evidence and the operational evidence was used and communicated contributed directly to the creation of a new, positive narrative for the LEAP programme based on robust, validated evidence. A range of channels were effective in this: workshops to present and research findings by the technical team and the minister and the subsequent personal advocacy of the minister,[17] research on the impact of fuel subsidy removal on the poor (Cooke et al., 2014), and south–south cooperation with Colombia and Brazil, all played an important role. The dynamism, resourcefulness, and networking of the new Minister of Gender, Children, and Social Protection was central in pushing forward the LEAP and social protection agendas. As a result, the Ministry of Finance and the presidency have been actively speaking on the impacts and role of LEAP, its potential safety net effect in mitigating the impact of fuel subsidy reform on the very poor, and, as a result, committing increased resource allocation to expand the programme to cover substantially more households. In the 2014 Pan-African Conference on Inequalities, hosted in Accra, the president resonated key findings from LEAP impact studies and hailed the role that LEAP plays in reducing poverty and inequality and promoting growth.

South–south cooperation was instrumental in enhancing a conducive environment to promote both social protection and LEAP specifically. Senior representatives from different ministries visited Colombia in 2012 and Brazil in 2014 and experienced first hand as well as discussed with peers the role of social protection and cash transfer schemes in reducing poverty, achieving equity, and contributing to the national growth. The 2014 high level mission to Brazil involved senior parliamentarians from the government and opposition party as well as an advisor to the president, who had not been part of previous attempts to build consensus. Development partners again provided the required support, both financial and technical, and impetus to these initiatives.

---

[16] A pilot of the new e-payment system has been completed and assessed.
[17] See footnote 8.

7.12 WHAT IS NEXT FOR LEAP AND SOCIAL PROTECTION IN GHANA?

How social protection will evolve in Ghana over the coming years is dependent upon several factors. However, this chapter demonstrates that the deliberate crafting of an evidence-based, positive narrative on the role of social protection in national development can have a direct influence on the sector's development. In Ghana, this has occurred through the following key stages.

First, Ghana's flagship social protection programme, LEAP, works. The solid and broad evidence is now available, highlighting its targeting efficiency, its impacts on well-being, and its operational value. The studies involved covered this full range of issues and were completed through a variety of different partnerships that strengthened buy-in as well as independence. The research also confirmed that the LEAP programme is not perfect. LEAP has evolved over the years from a heterogeneous and often inconsistent implementation towards more robust systems. Operational analyses have enabled a frank identification of key weaknesses, which consequently are being addressed. However, one of this chapter's central conclusions is that it is not just 'what' is communicated that matters, but 'how'. Numerous social protection programmes in Ghana and in many other countries around the world exist and even expand rapidly without being supported by any evidence base at all. The focus of donors and external commentators on LEAP, and the production of evidence on its impact would not, alone, have changed the national perception of the programme. Rather, we conclude, the accompanying strategy to actually use the evidence, communicate it, translate it into advocacy, and integrate it directly into national dialogue has been instrumental. This strategy has ranged from briefing papers, factsheets, media briefings, and national events to press interviews and innumerable informal meetings on a continuous basis with a very wide range of actors. Strategic partnerships with countries such as Brazil have been important in strengthening understanding and support.

As a result, it was this combination of the LEAP evidence as well as its active use that contributed to creating a new narrative for LEAP and, increasingly, social protection more broadly. This more positive and engaging narrative has gradually replaced a more neutral or even negative perception of the programme based on anecdotal evidence and occasional newspaper articles.

In addition, by mobilizing and bringing together key champions from within and outside government, the narrative becomes self-perpetuating. In Ghana, a small group of development partners was key in engaging with the government and encouraging their support of key initiatives. The personal drive and commitment of the new Minister of Gender, Children and Social Protection, as well as outreach to the Minister of Finance and the president, were crucial in building support at the highest political level.

Lastly, it is evident that politics matters. It may have been a central factor in the decision to establish the LEAP programme in 2008. It is central to the increasing dialogue on tackling inequality. More recently in Ghana, political debate around the current fiscal crisis, the new IMF programme, and the need to 'mitigate' negative impacts of a range of shocks are clearly founded, to some extent, on political calculations. The issue is to recognize and understand these drivers and contribute constructively to the political dialogue, providing evidence and buy-in which can set the tone of the debate. Raising LEAP's profile and scale, particularly as a programme which has already survived a change of government once, can only help to further embed it within the national development landscape.

These key factors—the evidence, its proactive strategic use, key champions, and understanding politics—have led to a new narrative on LEAP and social protection in general, which is shaping national dialogue on development, transformation, and equity. As a result, additional resources are being allocated for LEAP's expansion to more households and new groups ('LEAP 1000'),[18] new donor support was agreed to initiate major nationwide initiatives such as the new National Targeting System, and the new National Social Protection Policy on the future of social protection in Ghana has been approved.

Going forward, the success of LEAP as a showcase programme with ever-improving operations needs to spread more rapidly to other social protection schemes in Ghana. LEAP has acted as a catalyst for test-driving innovative new features which will now need to impact more broadly on Ghana's national development strategy. LEAP's electronic-payments system, for example, is setting the agenda for a national e-payment framework. Its M&E system is being replicated within transfer programmes in the education sector. And its targeting approach is the basis for the new national targeting system.

Most importantly, the dialogue around the role of social protection in the national development agenda needs to continue. Social protection should no longer be viewed as an add-on social service. Rather the success of the LEAP programme in building human capital, promoting productivity, increasing economic growth, and reducing inequality is helping to secure social protection a more permanent position in Ghana's development vision. As LEAP's success spills over into other programmes, and the poorest are empowered to engage productively in the economy and protect their own futures, social protection must become institutionalized into a true national social protection system, made up of a complementary package of programmes that protect and promote households across the life cycle.

---

[18] The 'LEAP 1000' is a modified component of the national LEAP programme, integrated in its existing operations, to target and provide cash grants to households with pregnant women and women with children aged 0–12 months for a period of three years. The project is implemented through a UNICEF partnership with the Government of Ghana with funds from United States Agency for International Development.

REFERENCES

Barrientos, A. 2013. *Social Assistance in Developing Countries*. Cambridge University Press, Cambridge.

Conway, T. and Norton, A. 2002. 'Nets, ropes, ladders and trampolines: the place of social protection within current debates on poverty reduction'. *Development Policy Review*, 20: 533–40.

Cooke, E. F. A., Hague, S., Cockburn, J., El Lahga, A.-R., and Tiberti, L. 2014. 'Estimating the Impact on Poverty of Ghana's Fuel Subsidy Reform and a Mitigating Response'. Policy Paper, PEP-UNICEF.

De Haan, A. 2014. 'The rise of social protection in development: Progress, pitfalls and politics'. *European Journal of Development Research*, 26: 311–21.

Debrah, E. 2013. 'Alleviating poverty in Ghana: the case of Livelihood Empowerment Against Poverty (LEAP)'. *Africa Today*, 59: 40–67.

Handa, S., Park, M. J., Darko, R. O., Osei-Akoto, I., Davis, B., and Diadone, S. 2013. 'Livelihood Empowerment against Poverty Impact Evaluation'. Carolina Population Center, University of North Carolina.

ILO. 2014. 'Rationalizing Social Protection Expenditure in Ghana: Consolidated Version: Draft for Comments'. International Labour Office, Social Protection Department, Geneva.

Korboe, D. 2011. 'Participatory Poverty Vulnerability Assessment (PPVA): Understanding the Regional Dynamics of Poverty with a Particular Focus on Ghana's Northern, Upper East and Upper West Region'. Government of Ghana, Accra.

MESW. 2012. 'LEAP Operations Manual'. Ministry of Employment and Social Welfare, Government of Ghana.

Niño-Zarazúa, M., Barrientos, A., Hickey, S., and Hulme, D. 2012. 'Social protection in Sub-Saharan Africa: getting the politics right'. *World Development*, 40: 163–76.

OPM. 2013. 'Qualitative Research and Analyses of the Economic Impacts of Cash Transfer Programmes in sub-Saharan Africa: Ghana Country Case Study Report'. Oxford Policy Management, FAO.

Sultan, S. M. and Schrofer, T. T. 2008. 'Building Support to have Targeted Social Protection Interventions for the Poorest—The Case of Ghana'. Paper Presented at the Conference 'Social Protection for the Poorest in Africa: Learning from Experience', 8–10 September 2008, Kampala, Uganda.

Thome, K., Taylor, J. E., Davis, B. and Darko Osei, R. 2013. 'Local Economy-Wide Impact Evaluation (LEWIE) of Ghana's Livelihood Empowerment Against Poverty (LEAP) Program'. FAO, Rome.

UNICEF. 2012. 'Integrated Social Protection System: Equity for Children'. UNICEF.

Wodon, Q. 2012. 'Improving the Targeting Of Social Programs in Ghana'. World Bank, Washington DC.

World Bank. 2001. 'Social Protection Sector Strategy: From Safety Net to Springboard'. World Bank, Washington, DC.

Zucco, C. 2013. 'When payouts pay off: conditional cash transfers and voting behavior in Brazil 2002–10'. *American Journal of Political Science*, 57: 810–822.

8

The Role of the Tigray Pilot Social Cash Transfer Programme and its Evaluation in the Evolution of the Tigray Social Protection Policy

Roger Pearson (UNICEF), Solomon Afaw (FAO), Angela Baschieri (UNICEF), Beyene Birru (UNICEF), Guush Berhane (IFPRI), Ted Chaiban (UNICEF), Benjamin Davis (FAO), Stephen Devereux (IDS), John Hoddinott (IFPRI and Cornell), J. Hoel (IFPRI), J. Kagin (University of California, Davis), Natasha Ledlie (IFPRI), Heshe Lemma (Bureau of Labour and Social Affairs, Government of Tigray), Djanabou Mahonde (UNICEF), Remy Pigois (UNICEF), Pamela Pozarny (FAO), Keetie Roelen (IDS), Benjamin Schwab (Kansas State University), Peter Salama (UNICEF), Ibrahim Sessay (UNICEF), Fredu Nega Tegebu (HESPI), Yalem Tsegay (Bureau of Labour and Social Affairs, Government of Tigray), and Douglas Webb (UNDP)

8.1 INTRODUCTION TO CASH TRANSFERS IN ETHIOPIA AND POLICY DIALOGUE ON SOCIAL PROTECTION

Tigray borders Afar to the east, Amhara to the south, and Sudan and Eritrea in the west and north, and is divided into six zones and forty-six *woredas*.[1] Some 4,314,456 million people were counted in the 2007 census (CSA, 2007), growing at 3 per cent per year, with a total fertility rate of 4.8 in 2011 per woman aged fifty (CSA, 2012). Under-five mortality rates declined from 106

---

[1] A *woreda* is akin to a district; the sub-woreda is called a tabia in Tigray.

to 85 between the 2005 and the 2011 Demographic and Health Survey. Social service quality improvements have been steady for the last twenty years resulting in, inter alia, higher levels of education, better health care, better roads, greater access to electricity, and more productive agriculture.

Economic growth has been stifled by years of civil war and war with Eritrea starting in 1998, the latter resulting in the border still being closed in 2015. Rain-fed agriculture underpins the economy; rains are erratic, possibly due to a combination of climate change, soil erosion, and deforestation. Reliance on migration and remitted income is increasing.

In 2009 Tigray had Ethiopia's lowest GDP (gross domestic product) per capita by region; 36.4 per cent of people were living on less than 1 US$ per day. Largely as a consequence of war, both civil and against Eritrea, 30 per cent of households were headed by women according to the 2007 census, the highest in the country; 1.5 per cent of people were disabled, 10 per cent of children under eighteen were orphans, and 6.5 per cent were elderly. In 2009 the estimated adult HIV/AIDS (Human Immunodeficiency Virus/Acquired Immunodeficiency Syndrome) prevalence rate was 2.9 per cent.

Nationwide, over the last thirty years, the number of people estimated to be drought-affected reached 13.2 million in 2003; 30 per cent of the country's woredas were affected. Other droughts resulted in emergency operations reaching between 10 and 18 per cent (1980, 1982, 1983–84, 1985, 1986, 1988, 1991, 1992, 2000, 2002) (Ministry of Finance, Ministry of Women, Children and Youth Affairs and United Nations, 2012). Between 1997 and 2002 emergency food aid average annual cost was $US 265 million (World Bank, 2003). In June 2003, the government issued its food security strategy. It had three strands: a) resettling households from overpopulated environmentally degraded highlands; b) developing a safety-net for chronically food insecure households; and c) supplying agricultural and financial services to poor households to promote their growth.

International development partners to the Government of Ethiopia have not supported all elements with equal vigour. Resettlement efforts have received little support; the Productive Safety Net Programme (PSNP) has been well supported with international contributions of approximately $US 360 million per year since 2005 (PSNP Secretariat, 2010). The third element receives increasing support from a number of different sources. The PSNP guarantees work for the six months of the year when agricultural activities are minimal; over 5 million people work in exchange for either food or cash and a further 1.5 million receive cash or food without working (direct support beneficiaries (DSB)). By definition DSBs are households where no one over eighteen is able to carry out manual labour. Pregnant and lactating women are also categorized as temporary DSBs. The geographic area between 2005 and 2015 included only those rural woredas that required emergency food aid for all of the three years leading up to 2005; most of Tigray thus qualified. The PSNP has reduced the scale of emergency humanitarian emergency responses to drought and is helping to protect and help households grow their assets (Berhane et al., 2011); for example, in 2011 government estimated that of the 7.5 million people enrolled in the PSNP only 4.5 million people would need humanitarian food assistance. What is not clear in 2015 is the pace with which non-DSB households enrolled in the PSNP can be expected, on aggregate, to protect and grow assets sufficiently to be resilient to drought over the medium term.

The Africa Union's adoption of a social policy framework in 2009 led Ethiopia's prime minister to assign the Minister of Labour and Social Affairs and the Minister of Agriculture to prepare a national social protection policy. One element of this discourse centred on the possibility of building a professional social worker cadre that could liaise with community-based social protection committees with the power and resources to step in where community efforts were inadequate.

Late in 2009 the President of Tigray region wrote to UNICEF requesting assistance to explore and possibly pilot test options for the case of Tigray, where the Bureau of Labour and Social Affairs (BoLSA) had local level capacities in the form of tabia level social protection committees known as 'Community Care Coalitions' (CCCs). These committees are chaired by the elected tabia chairperson and include salaried woreda-based social workers, health extension workers (salaried and managed by the Ministry of Health with 2 servicing every 5,000 households), schoolteachers and local businessmen. The origins of the CCCs date from early in the millennium when World Vision worked in a number of countries to set up community-led child care groups as a strategy to address the Orphans and Vulnerable Children (OVC), an issue that was growing as a result of the HIV/AIDS epidemic (Germann et al., 2009).

While World Vision's involvement ended in 2006 the self-help ethos of the CCCs appealed to the Tigray People's Liberation Front (TPLF), the ruling party in Tigray, and thus the CCCs have gradually been scaled-up until in 2009 they were present in virtually all tabias. In 2010, the regional council ordered all tabias to constitute CCCs issuing a manual (BoLSA, 2011a) to guide their responsibilities including raising resources locally for funding social protection actions. A 2012 review of the performance of CCCs found that a third were working well, a third were making some progress and a third were starting up. In 2011 amongst all CCCs combined, on top of voluntary support of time and labour to vulnerable households, $US 750,000 in cash and US$1.8 million in kind was collected and reinvested in social protection actions (BoLSA, 2012).

The year 2010 saw consultations under the direction of the Tigray president's office to discuss how the region would move responsibility for DSBs from Ministry of Agriculture (MoA) to Ministry of Labour and Social Affairs (MoLSA). International and national members of the National Social Protection Platform were invited to help the regional government deliberate the issue. The conclusion was that a pilot would test the capacity of the

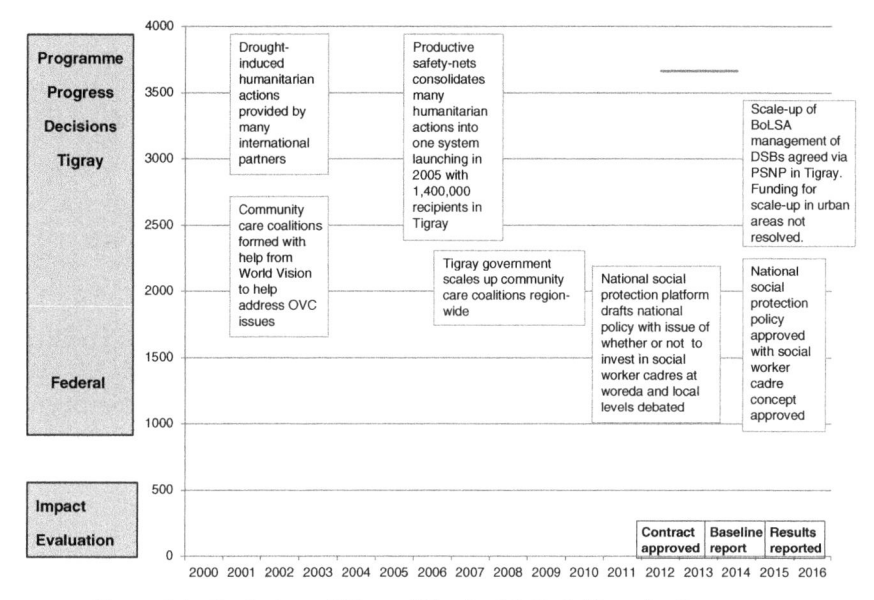

Tigray Pilot Evaluation and its Link to Policy Dialogue

Figure 8.1. Evolution of Tigray Pilot Social Cash Transfer Programme

CCCs to take over responsibility for the DSBs in rural areas and set-up a system to care for social welfare cases in urban areas where there was no PSNP. A contribution to this decision was a trip to Kenya by a team of officials from federal government and the Tigray regional government. They saw how Kenya's Children's Department had built its capacities from virtually zero in 2004 to the point where they were on the way to managing a nationwide cash transfer programme in 2010. On the request of the president of Tigray UNICEF agreed to provide technical and financial support on the condition that UNICEF's financial commitment would end after the three-year life of the pilot (Figure 8.1).

8.2 PILOT OBJECTIVES

The objectives of the pilot were to a) reduce poverty, hunger, and starvation in all extremely poor labour-constrained households; b) increase access to basic social welfare services; and c) generate information on the feasibility, cost-effectiveness, and impact of a social cash transfer (SCT) scheme.

While not explicitly stated, the underlying focus of (b) and (c) was to test MoLSA's capacity to take on responsibility for cash transfers at scale and whether the social worker with CCC programme model would provide a sufficiently more sensitive service than the PSNP to warrant the extra investment needed to scale up social worker numbers. This was a key point of dialogue in the drafting of the national social protection policy.

8.3 PROGRAMME DESIGN, FUNDING, AND IMPLEMENTATION

The design took eighteen months with first payments in August 2011. Funding for the programme came from the regional government budget, UNICEF, and Helpage International. In the course of the pilot Irish Aid started to contribute. The pilot was scheduled to run for three years during which time the evaluation would be carried-out with a baseline taking place before the first payment and a second survey at the end of three years of payment (BoLSA, 2011b).

8.3.1 Selecting Geographic Areas

Two woredas, Abi-Adi, a small market town of less than 20,000 people, and Hintalo-Wajirat woreda, a rural area, were selected. The budget available was not high enough to cover all tabias in the rural woreda but it was high enough to cover all tabias in Abi-Adi. In Hintalo-Wajirat, the seven poorest of twenty-two tabias were selected.

Abi-Adi is 2.5-hour drive from the regional capital Mekelle. It had been the home of an Ethiopian army base during the war with Eritrea. With the end of hostilities early in the new millennium the base was shut leading to the biggest source of jobs and revenue leaving town. Perhaps as a consequence of the army base, HIV/AIDS rates are higher than average for Tigray. The 2010 pilot baseline assessment found 5,316 family heads, 2,550 female headed. Average household size was 4.3. Female-headed households were the poorest category and especially lacked capital for small-scale business. The 2007 census found 280 persons living with disabilities and 882 single and double orphans in Abi-Adi town. According to the Abi-Adi Office of Labour and Social Affairs, based on their local knowledge, there were 525 elders with no reliable family support.

In Hintalo-Wajirat during a 'normal' agricultural year, typical families can feed themselves for about six months if only their own production, and not income from other sources, is included. Incomes from wage migration and working on public works (the PSNP) are the two main ways in which the gap is closed. The 2007 census counted 153,505 people; those less than 18 years numbered 79,594, those over 60 were 10,855, orphans 6,878 (8.64 per cent of total child population), and 2,420 persons living with disabilities. Based on the Labour and Social Affairs baseline assessment carried out in preparation for the pilot, the woreda had 53,365 family heads, and out of this 24,006 (45 per cent) were female-headed. The average household size was estimated at four persons. Over 45 per cent were estimated to live below the poverty line, that is, one dollar per day/person.

8.3.2 One Cash Transfer System for Poor Vulnerable Children, the Disabled, and the Elderly

The pilot targeted households that were either poor and labour constrained, ultra poor, elderly, sick, disabled, and/or female-headed, or had a dependency ratio of more than 3 up to a maximum of 10 per cent of households per tabia. In part this decision to merge categories was inspired by the 2009 study tour to Kenya, where separate schemes for each category were managed by different teams in the same ministry, a situation which seemed inefficient. CCCs would ensure the targeted households did not benefit from any other major social protection support, for example enrolment in the PSNP, or remitted income from a family member; for households previously enrolled in the PSNP, their participation would be switched to the pilot.

8.3.3 Community-Based Targeting

The regional steering committee decided to identify eligible households entirely through community-based targeting, depending on the local knowledge of the CCC members with a cross-check supervised by woreda-based social workers in public meetings. In essence the steering committee was confident that the CCCs were immune to elite capture. Use of a proxy means test was thought to be too complex and something that would be difficult to scale-up; there was also precedence in Ethiopia in that the PSNP uses community-based targeting. This assumption would be reviewed in the course of the pilot.

CCC members were inducted into the pilot via a pre-service seminar on case assessment which included case planning, interview techniques, documentation, data collection, mapping, and referral. The targeting procedure was designed as follows: a) CCC members were to list, visit, and interview all households that seemed to meet the targeting criteria. They were to rank them according to whether or not they had a fit adult or a dependency ratio of more than 3. b) The CCC were then to present the list of households selected in a community meeting asking the meeting to look for inclusion and exclusion error and reach a consensus on the list. c) They were to verify the information gathered by the CCC, woreda social workers, and the woreda civil society network visiting each household selected and reporting their findings independently to the woreda social cash transfer secretariat (WSCTS) providing an independent check on fairness and transparency. d) After receiving the list of households recommended for approval by the CCC and the results of the verification visits by the woreda social workers, the WSCTS were to prepare the approval meeting. The secretariat would then cross-check each application form for completeness and consistency, household social situation and structure (dependency ratio), and the correctness of school enrolment status. e) After checking if a household conformed to the eligibility criteria, the WSCTS were to indicate, for each household, if they recommended approval or disapproval of the application. The woreda social workers were then to tell the households the payment level for which they would be eligible. f) Finally, the WSCTS were to conduct an approval meeting in the course of which a final list was to be agreed.

8.3.4 Cash Transfer Value

The value of the transfer was based on the transfer delivered by the PSNP in 2011, itself based on an examination of cash required to cover approximately 20 per cent of the resources needed to reach the food poverty threshold. The transfer would be distributed throughout the year, not only for the six months that the PSNP applies. The basic household grant was Ethiopian Birr (ETB) 155;[2] on top of that extra grants were awarded in the following way: child grant ETB 25; child disability grant ETB 40; adult disability grant ETB 50; and elders grant ETB 60. For each child enrolled in primary school a bonus of ETB 25 was added with up to four children being eligible; for each disabled child going to school 50 birr/40 birr was added depending on the level of disability.

Due to inflation, the pilot steering committee discussed the advisability of indexing the rates so that their value could be maintained. However, no action was taken so that by the end of the evaluation period the value had been eroded as a proportion of the transfer required to reach the food poverty level (see Table 8.3).

8.3.5 Delivering the Cash

The head of the WSCTS submitted the list of households to the Tirgay BoLSA SCT Secretariat who issued a payment order requesting the Micro Finance Institution (Dedebit Microfinance) to pay the monthly amount. The Dedebit

---

[2] 1 US$ varied in value from approximately 16 Birr in 2011 to 19 Birr in 2014.

is a parastatal entity partly owned by the regional government. The bank entered the names of beneficiary households into their financial management system. It produced a list of beneficiary households with their respective transfer amounts per month and sent it to the BoLSA SCT Secretariat for approval. The Woreda SCT Secretariat informed the beneficiary households through the Woreda SCT social workers and the Tabia CCC members of the payday. Before paying the transfers for the first time, the beneficiaries were assembled at the pay point by members of the Woreda SCT Secretariat. The beneficiaries were then informed of the objectives of the pilot and why they were selected and were provided with beneficiary cards.

8.3.6 Administration of Changes in Beneficiary Households and Retargeting

The pilot was designed to adapt to changes in households by adding additional households due to changing circumstances, for example because breadwinners have passed away, dissolution of households due to deaths, graduation of households when children pass their eighteenth birthday, and changes in the numbers residing in a household. To administer these changes the CCCs would have to inform the WSCTS.

8.3.7 Monitoring

The pilot had three types of monitoring activities: a) an internal monitoring system, providing monthly reports compiled by Woreda SCT Secretariats; b) monitoring and assistance trips to the implementing districts organized by the BoLSA Secretariat; c) Rapid appraisals organized by BoLSA focusing on specific issues like the quality of targeting or the impact of transfers on school enrolment. Based on the information derived from monitoring BoLSA would submit quarterly reports to the Steering Committee.

8.4 EVALUATION ORIGINS, PURPOSE AND ITS CHAMPIONS

8.4.1 Origins

UNICEF policy requires it to commission evaluations when it supports partners to pilot test programme strategies (UNICEF, 2015). Thus evaluation, as a core element of UNICEF's support for the regional government's pilot, was on the table from the beginning of negotiations with the president of Tigray. This also suited the president's aims of using the pilot to foster more senior policy maker debate, both in his region and at federal level, on what capacities would be needed to implement the as yet draft national social protection policy. As a member of the federal level executive council for Ethiopia the president of Tigray was sensitive to the value of evaluation results to stimulate dialogue on the nature of greater state involvement in social protection. The Tigray regional council was of the view that the CCC model, at least for the case of Tigray, was a viable way of both fostering a more organized system of local responsibility for social protection while also serving as a way for regional government to take more responsibility.

Another factor in favour of organizing a pilot was the potential source of financing from the social welfare fund generated by the Endowment Fund for the Rehabilitation of Tigray (EFFORT), which was established soon after the end of the civil war in the early 1990s by the TPLF (Tigray People's Liberation Front) as an agglomeration of sixteen companies operating in the industrial, mining, construction, agro-processing, trade, and service sectors; it is still managed by a board made up of senior TPLF officials and contributes 60 per cent of regionally collected taxes (Vaughan and Gebremichael, 2011). According to decisions made by EFFORT's board, 10 per cent of profits are channelled towards the social welfare of Tigrayans, which amounted to approximately $US4 million in 2013. When the pilot was being designed most of the resources were being channelled towards construction of social service delivery points, a legacy of underinvestment and destruction caused by years of civil war. The evaluation results would help the board in their investment decisions once the construction programme started to wind down regarding a possible long-term investment in building the CCC system.

Discussants agreed that the steering committee for the pilot, chaired by the representative of the president, would finalize the evaluation terms of reference, that UNICEF would tender and cover the costs, and that the evaluators, subsequent to the adoption of their inception report by the steering committee, would act independently in their implementation, reporting back to the steering committee.

8.4.2 Evaluation Purpose and Its Champions

The overall purpose of the evaluation was to provide the steering committee with the information they needed to take decisions regarding programme model modifications and to provide information to facilitate a discussion with the regional council and the EFFORT board regarding possible scale-up of SCTs managed by BoLSA rather than BoA (Bureau of Agriculture) as part of the regional social protection plan of action.

Another audience was the National Social Protection Steering Committee, whose members had an open invitation to observe the pilot and take part in the steering committee meetings. The aim was to bring the results to the federal level and to other regions to help foster discussions related to the development of the National Social Protection Policy and especially on the potential role of the BoLSA and CCCs across the county.

The key champions of the evaluation were therefore the regional president of Tigray, himself a member of the coordinating committee for the ruling party of Ethiopia, the members of the pilot steering committee in Tigray, the Minister of Labour and Social Affairs, the co-chairs of the National Social Protection Platform together with key partners in that platform.

8.4.3 Evaluation Questions

The evaluation set out to answer the following questions: a) What is the extent of impact on participants attributable to the pilot programme? b) Has the pilot programme reached the intended beneficiaries and has it had a substantial impact on their welfare? c) Have welfare improvements, if any, been commensurate with the investments made? d) Would region-wide and national programmes be affordable and fiscally sustainable? e) On that basis, should the programme, or a variant of it, be scaled up to a regional/national level? f) To what extent has the programme created dependency? g) To what extent has the programme relieved social and financial costs borne at community level? h) If the programme is to be scaled up, which aspects of its operation must be modified or strengthened for it to operate effectively at a regional/national level? i) Which aspects of good practice should remain the same and be replicated? j) What is the impact or incentive effect of imposing soft conditions on beneficiaries, versus not imposing conditions? k) What is the cost of doing so, for both households and the government? l) Does any additional impact warrant the additional cost? m) If households fail to comply with the soft conditions, why is this so?

8.4.4 Accountability for Evaluation Quality and Linking Findings to Action

The president of Tigray's taskforce advising him on the evolution of social protection policy became the core of the steering committee for the pilot's evaluation. It consisted of senior membership of the social sector bureaus in Tigray together with civil society representatives, including Civil Society Organisations (CSOs), active in the social sector. Members of the federal national social protection platform had an open invitation to join the

178   *Roger Pearson et al.*

deliberations of the regional committee. The regional social protection committee was responsible for the approval of the pilot design including the operations manual and for oversight of the roll-out of the pilot. This committee approved the terms of reference for the evaluation.

8.5 EVALUATION METHODS

Three types of information were needed to answer the key evaluation questions: impact on participant households, especially impact on children; design, especially the targeting approach; operational performance, including costs broken down by capital and recurrent costs and how they change in start-up and maintenance phase. Several research protocols were devised to answer these questions: a) quantitative surveys: household and community surveys (baseline, follow-up, and endline); b) qualitative surveys: focus group discussions and household case studies, with a range of different groups in beneficiary and comparison communities, and in-depth interviews, with key programme stakeholders; c) cost analysis; and d) a survey of local businesses and modelling to track the flow of money once spent by the households to calculate the multiplier effect.

8.5.1 Quantitative and Qualitative Surveys and Measuring Impact

The first report based on data collected as part of the evaluation included information from a quantitative household survey (HH1) as well as qualitative work (key informant interviews, focus group discussions) and case studies (Berhane et al., 2012). Subsequently, the evaluators fielded a number of monitoring surveys to focus on issues of interest with a seasonal topicality. Food security and nutrition outcomes are examples of these. Table 8.1 gives the dates when these were fielded.

For the purpose of the impact measurement the treatment group was the Social Cash Transfer Pilot Programme (SCTPP) beneficiaries. The comparison households were households that appear in the control sample and who are not receiving benefits from other programmes. As much as possible, double-difference impact estimates were used. Inverse probability weighted regression adjustment estimators were used to generate impact. This addressed the problems of non-random selection into the programme as well as the problem of the counterfactual.

The household survey had a statistical power to detect the following impacts: a one-month reduction in the food gap; a 10 per cent increase in

Table 8.1. Survey Timing by Round

Survey	Start Date	Finish Date
Household Survey 1 (Baseline)	6 May 2012	26 June 2012
Monitoring Survey 1	6 October 2012	27 October 2012
Monitoring Survey 2	9 March 2013	29 March 2013
Monitoring Survey 3	20 July 2013	11 August 2013
Monitoring Survey 4	6 November 2013	26 November 2013
Monitoring Survey 5	3 March 2014	25 March 2014
Household Survey 2 (Endline)	16 May 2014	17 July 2014

Table 8.2. Sample Sizes, by Location and Treatment Status

Beneficiary status	Abi–Adi	Hintalo-Wajirat (excluding Bahr Tseba)	Bahr Tseba	Totals
Beneficiary (treatment sample)	599	829	202	1,630
Control (eligible, not selected)	548	826	215	1,589
Random sample	132	266	48	446
Total	1,279	1,921	465	3,665

livestock holdings; a 10 percentage point increase in the use of fertilizer; a 10 percentage point increase in the use of credit; and a 50 birr increase in net transfers to other households. Initial sample size by location and treatment status is presented in Table 8.2.

During each survey, the team monitored attrition (the loss of households from the sample). This varied from round to round averaging about 150 households with the endline survey including 3,351 households, 91.3 per cent of the initial sample. There were three reasons for attrition: i) death of respondents; ii) whole household migration; and iii) refusal to be interviewed. Religious reasons were given for the majority of refusals, which were concentrated in two localities.

The following subjects were investigated at:

A) Baseline only: hired labour, labour sharing.

B) Baseline and endline only: production equipment and consumer durables; housing stock; social capital; transfers and remittances; credit; cash transfer targeting and the operation of the transfer programme; participation in PSNP or other safety nets; non-food and food expenditures and consumption; shocks, trust, control agency, and respect; access to ante-natal care.

C) In the course of one or more of the monitoring surveys and sometimes either in the baseline or in the endline only or in both the baseline and the endline. Demographic composition: listing and updates; in and out migration; schooling and child labour; land characteristics and tenure; crop production; sales; agricultural practices and technology; livestock ownership; wage employment; own business activities; payments; food availability, access, coping strategies; child food consumption, frequency, and diversity; cash transfer payments; food availability, access, coping strategies; time preferences; child health; infant feeding; nutrition knowledge and practices; maternal health; access to antenatal care; anthropometry; water and sanitation; heart rate variability.

For reasons not in the control of the evaluation the baseline took place several months after first payments, in May 2012 when first payments had been made in August 2011 in most woredas, while a true baseline took place in the extra woreda added on with funding from HelpAge International. These were the only significant changes to the design of the pilot.

There were three rounds of qualitative fieldwork, one in August 2012 and one in April 2014 by the IDS (Institute for Development Studies) team, and one in 2013 by the OPM (Oxford Policy Management)/FAO (Food and Agriculture Organization of the United Nations) team (FAO, 2014). In both 2012 and 2014, this work was undertaken in Abi-Adi and in purposively selected tabias in Hintalo-Wajirat: May Nebri, Senale, Bahr Tseba, and in the town of Adi Gudem, where the Woreda office of Labour and Social Affairs (WoLSA) Secretariat is based. Fieldwork took approximately three days to complete in each tabia. A total of fifty-three data collection activities were undertaken including Key Informant Interviews, Focus Group Discussions, Case Studies, and Participatory Rural Appraisal.

The 2012 qualitative fieldwork elicited perceptions of participants, non-participants, programme staff, and other stakeholders on targeting criteria, procedures, and outcomes; assessed the performance of the SCTPP in terms of receipt of payments and grievance procedures; assessed how the SCTPP interfaces with informal social protection mechanisms and changes community dynamics; and looked at the functioning of CCCs. The 2014 qualitative fieldwork examined the same issues as in 2012 and also investigated the impact of the SCTPP in terms of spending, household and children's outcomes; continued to review how CCCs functioned in terms of implementing the SCTPP as well as complementary services, and what role CCCs could play after the SCTPP ends; and assessed how the SCTPP interfaces with informal social protection mechanisms and changes in community dynamics.

8.5.2 Local Economy-Wide Impact Evaluation

The local economy-wide impact evaluation (LEWIE) methodology captures the impact of cash transfers on local economies, including on the income and productive activities of both beneficiary and non-beneficiary households (Kagin et al., 2014). From a local economy-wide perspective, households that receive cash transfers are the conduit through which new cash enters the economy. As they spend their cash the beneficiary households generate general equilibrium effects that transmit programme impacts to others in the economy, including non-beneficiaries. The LEWIE estimates the extent of this impact on the local economy. LEWIE model parameters are estimated using econometric techniques.

Two data sources were used to construct the models: the 2012 baseline household impact evaluation survey, used to obtain data on household expenditures including location of expenditure and incomes, and the 2012 business enterprise survey. Data were gathered on income derived from wages and the location of wage work, various family enterprises in agriculture, livestock, and non-agricultural businesses, and transfer income from the government, local residents, and people outside of the woreda. These data allowed the estimation of crop and livestock regressions that provided the parameters for the LEWIE models.

The business enterprise survey took place in December 2013. The survey provided information on costs and revenues from a selection of businesses operating in the programme districts needed for the construction of the LEWIE model. The underlying technology and intermediate demand shares from the business enterprise survey and the income from household businesses were estimated from the household survey. The business enterprise survey provides the inputs to estimate production functions for each business.

8.6 LESSONS FROM PROGRAMME IMPLEMENTATION

Programme implementation did not deviate from the operations manual guidelines (BoLSA, 2011c). Using mobile banking to reduce travel times for cash pick-up was explored. However, at the time, licences had not been granted to the companies working on launching this service. Licences were granted and operations started to roll out mid-2014 after the endline survey for the impact evaluation.

A pilot goal was to see to what extent PSNP DSBs were transferred to the BoLSA pilot system in the rural woreda. The initial targeting revealed that 70 per cent of households enrolled had been PSNP DSBs. Yet the other 30 per cent had not been enrolled in the PSNP although they were not distinguishable from the former PSNP DSBs. The budget caps on proportion of overall households in the PSNP that could be enrolled, officially 20 per cent of total enrollees but sometimes locally interpreted as being lower, meant that, for the case of Hintalo, a sizable portion of genuine welfare cases were not being supported by the state. However, since the SCTPP also had a quota of not more than 10 per cent of all households, while the coverage of the vulnerable was an improvement on PSNP, significant numbers of families categorized by the CCCs as genuine welfare cases could not be included. Since a number of the CCCs were also collecting their own limited resources from local donors some chose to use these resources to add a modest number of households to the roster beyond the 10 per cent cap.

8.7 EVALUATION RESULTS

The results are categorized by the four pilot objectives. For details refer to the independent evaluators endline report (Berhane et al., 2015). Results are summarized in Table 8.3.

8.7.1 Objective 1: Reduce poverty, Hunger, and Starvation in all Extremely Poor Labour-Constrained Households

8.7.1.1 Poverty, Diets, Expenditures, and the Proportion Covered by the Transfer

The transfer represented an increase in household income of 10 per cent and food consumption expenditure of 17 per cent. The mean monthly food consumption in the comparison households was around 900 birr at the time of the baseline in May 2012 and mean total monthly consumption was 1070 birr. The household survey found that 61 per cent of households received 155 birr, 16 per cent received between 180 birr and 200 birr and less than 1 per cent received more than 300 birr. The mean transfer was 187 birr at endline. Table 8.4 shows that the majority of the transfer was used on food purchases in the period before the endline survey.

Across a wide range of measures, household food security of SCTPP beneficiaries improved. The food gap was reduced by approximately 0.50 months in both Abi-Adi and Hintalo-Wajirat. Adults and children ate more meals. Both diet quantity (as measured by caloric availability) and diet quality (as measured by the Dietary Diversity Index and the Food Consumption Score (Wiseman et al., 2009) also improved. The impact evaluation results indicate that: a) the SCTPP reduced the food gap by 0.24 months in May 2012; b) increased the availability of calories at the household level, increasing them by 94 kcal per adult equivalent in May 2012 and 158 kcal per adult equivalent in May 2014; c) relative to comparison households, this represented an increase of 3.6 and 6.0 per cent respectively; d) improved diet quality, as measured

Table 8.3. Impact of SCT on Development Outcomes in the Tigray Pilot

Source of data	Baseline survey (May 2012) and endline survey (May 2014)
Poverty Reduction	
Poverty: mean total monthly household consumption expenditure per adult equivalent below $1 per day (real)	Transfer represented an increase in household income of 10 per cent and food consumption expenditure of 17 per cent.
Food Consumption and Household Welfare	
Mean total monthly household consumption expenditure per adult equivalent (birr—real)	Per capita monthly household consumption expenditure by SCT beneficiaries rose from 341 birr (May 2012) to 375 birr (May 2014). Note, however, that the May 2012 result is measured eight months after the SCT began. There is no statistically significant difference in the change in consumption expenditure between SCT beneficiaries and matched non-beneficiaries. Results are not adjusted for inflation.
Mean monthly food consumption expenditure per adult equivalent (birr—real)	Per capita monthly food consumption expenditure by SCT beneficiaries rose from 278 Birr (May 2012) to 284 birr (May 2014). Note, however, that the May 2012 result is measured eight months after the SCT began. There is no statistically significant difference in the change in consumption expenditure between SCT beneficiaries and matched non-beneficiaries. Results are not adjusted for inflation.
Food security	Food gap reduced by 0.24 months by May 2012; calories consumed increased by 94 kcal in May 2012 and 158 kcal by May 2014; relative to comparison households an increase of 3.6 and 6.0 per cent respectively.
Schooling	Large positive impact on girls aged 6–11 in rural area; likelihood of enrolment increased by 13 per cent; school efficiency by 14 per cent; grade attainment by half a grade.
Health	Suggestive effects on sickness and curative care but not significant.
Nutrition	No impact on nutrition status (note that the evaluation may not have had the power to measure impact on these indicators).
Maternal Physical and Mental Health	No impact on maternal physical or mental health or body mass index (note that the evaluation may not have had the power to measure impact on these indicators).
Productive	
Increase in ownership of small livestock	7 per cent increase in chance of owning any form of livestock compared to controls in rural areas; no impact in urban area.
Child Labour	
Proportion of children doing paid work	No significant impact on child labour outcomes except for girls' work on family businesses in Abi Adi.
Proportion of children doing unpaid work	Had a significant reduction in labour hours for girls in urban area working in family businesses.

Table 8.4. Self-Reports on Use of Last Transfer

	All beneficiaries	By location	
		Abi-Adi	Hintalo-Wajirat
Mean payment (birr)	187	187	188
Mean expenditures by item (birr)			
Food	105	110	101
Rent, house repairs	19	26	15
Non-food goods that directly benefit children (school expenses, clothes, books, toys, etc)	6	5	7
Non-food goods that directly benefit adult males in the household (clothing, alcohol, tobacco, etc)	3	2	4
Non-food goods that directly benefit adult females in the household (clothing, cosmetics, etc)	12	5	16
Goods related to crop production	1	1	1
Given to other household members for their own private consumption	15	12	16
Not yet spent	24	22	26
Shared with other households	2	2	2

Source: Calculated from endline survey data.

by the Dietary Diversity Index, in May 2012 and May 2014 by 13.4 and 11.7 per cent respectively; e) in Hintalo-Wajirat, it reduced seasonal fluctuations in children's food consumption.

8.7.1.2 Household Income Generation

Overall, farmers in Hintalo shifted land from sharecropping out to operating it by themselves. In line with that, an increase in long-term land investments and visits by extension agents was observed. All these together, with other possible factors, seemed to push cereal yields up. The per cent of households providing livestock service and selling livestock products also increased. Although most of the increase came from households in the random and control group, an increasing trend in terms of per cent of households participating in own business and wage employment was also observed. Transfers from the government in terms of per cent of pensioner households increased but most of them were households in the control group. Rather, transfers from friends and relatives, specifically in Hintalo, increased in favour of beneficiary households. All these changes cannot be attributed to the SCTPP as many other possible factors could also have contributed.

The impact estimation results indicate that the SCTPP brought about significant impacts on different indicators in Hintalo and Abi-Adi. In Hintalo, the SCTPP helped beneficiaries by significantly increasing cereal yields. It also significantly increased the proportion of beneficiary households receiving transfers from friends and relatives. In Abi-Adi, the SCTPP seems to have helped beneficiaries significantly reduce the proportion participating in wage employment and significantly increased participation in selling livestock products.

8.7.1.3 Social Networks

Even though the households targeted were very poor, the cash transfer allowed them to enhance their social connectedness, enabling them to join rotating savings groups, which helped to improve confidence and self-esteem and reduce feelings of social isolation.

8.7.1.4 Asset Holdings

SCT beneficiaries accumulated assets in a variety of forms at a modestly greater rate than controls. In Hintalo, the SCTPP increased holdings of farm productive assets by 2 per cent and consumer durables by 0.8 per cent. It increased the likelihood that they own any form of livestock or animals by 7 per cent with this driven largely by increases in poultry (chickens). In Abi-Adi, we find no consistent evidence of impacts on assets.

8.7.1.5 Multiplier Effects

The LEWIE model was applied using information from a local market survey to simulate the wider impact. The simulated results found that each birr distributed in Hintalo could have generated an extra 1.52 birr via local economic linkages, for an estimated total income multiplier of 2.52. Similarly, each birr distributed in Abi-Adi could have generated an estimated additional 0.35 birr, for an estimated total income multiplier of 1.35. Thus the initial transfer of 5.58 birr million in Hintalo-Wajirat and 1.62 birr million in Abi-Adi potentially generated 14.06 birr million and 2.19 birr million respectively. However, when credit, capital, and other market constraints limit the local supply response the increase in demand brought about by the cash transfer programme may lead to increased prices and consequently a lower income multiplier. Simulations incorporating such constraints estimate a 'real' or price-adjusted income multiplier of 1.84 birr for Hintalo-Wajirat and 1.26 birr for Abi-Adi. In both cases non-beneficiaries and the local economy benefit from cash transfer programmes via trade and production linkages. Maximizing the income multiplier may require complementary interventions that target both beneficiary and non-beneficiary families. The proof that the SCTPP led to this economy-wide impact can only come from a follow-up survey that is being carried out in 2015.

8.7.2 Objective 2: Increase Access to Basic Social Welfare Services

8.7.2.1 Maternal Health

Improving children's outcomes is a primary objective of the SCTPP, and because mother's health may impact children's outcomes, the impact of the SCTPP on mothers was also assessed. No statistically significant difference was found in maternal body mass index between those receiving the transfers and controls. In the course of the pilot the data showed a worsening of mental health in both Abi-Adi and especially in Hintalo in beneficiary and control groups with no significant differences detected.

8.7.2.2 Schooling

Data on schooling (enrolment, attendance) and grade attainment were collected for all children aged 6–18 in all survey rounds. These data show rising rates of enrolment and grade attainment in both Abi-Adi and Hintalo-Wajirat. In Abi-Adi especially, by endline enrolments approach 100 per cent for children aged 9–15. There are many factors that could account for these changes including steady access and quality improvements within the schools. No statistically significant difference was found in school outcomes in Abi-Adi. SCTPP had a modest effect on enrolment and schooling efficiency in Hintalo-Wajirat. It had large, positive, and statistically significant impacts for girls 6–11 years of age and living in Hintalo-Wajirat. It raised the likelihood of enrolment by 13.3 percentage points, schooling efficiency by 14 percentage points, and grade attainment by a half grade.

8.7.2.3 Anthropometry

In the baseline and endine surveys as well as each monitoring survey, data were collected on the heights and weights of all children sixty months and younger. These data were used to construct four anthropometric measures: height-for-age z scores (HAZ); stunting; weight-for-height z scores (WHZ); and wasting. Under-nutrition in these localities is high, with the prevalence of stunting in excess of 45 per cent at baseline. There is no evidence of impact of the SCTPP on stunting, HAZ, wasting, or WHZ in either Abi-Adi or Hintalo-Wajirat. However, these results should be treated cautiously. The targeting of the SCTPP was such that there are relatively few children in the age range where the SCTPP might be expected to have an impact (those children under twenty-four months of age) and even fewer children were exposed to the SCTPP for a reasonably lengthy period of time. There is suggestive evidence of a dose-response relationship with respect to HAZ but the small sample precludes drawing strong conclusions.

8.7.3 Objective 3 and 4: Capability of BoLSA and CCCs, for Scaling Cash Transfers Tigray-Wide

8.7.3.1 Community Care Coalitions

Evidence from the qualitative investigations indicates that CCCs understand and execute the roles assigned to them. They are well regarded by SCTPP beneficiaries. They exerted considerable effort to raise additional funds and were able to identify and distribute these to households in need of assistance. It is also clear that CCCs are not a substitute for a formal social safety net. Reflecting the poverty of the localities in which these CCCs operate, the resources they raise benefit only a relatively small number of households. Especially in rural areas, it appears that many CCCs are operating at the limit of volunteerism and are not able to take on additional commitments.

8.7.3.2 Targeting

Targeting processes in the SCTPP work well. Woreda and tabia officials, CCC members, and SCTPP participants demonstrated sound knowledge of the eligibility criteria and confirmed that the targeting procedures had been correctly applied in all communities surveyed. At baseline, there is little evidence of inclusion error. However, there is substantial exclusion error, or under-coverage. Many households that do satisfy the eligibility criteria were excluded from the SCTPP because a budget constraint meant a quota had to be applied. Although there was acceptance of the eligibility criteria and the targeting decisions, these households that were initially selected, but later cut, were most likely to perceive the targeting process as unfair. The CCCs played an important role in explaining the eligibility criteria and increasing acceptance of targeting processes among non-selected households.

There were few instances where households were subsequently dropped from the SCTPP either because they had been erroneously included or because their living conditions had changed so much that assistance was no longer needed. Given a fixed budget, this meant that the number of new entrants was limited to the number of places on the programme that opened up subsequent to the death of a beneficiary; this was not infrequent given the age of some of the older beneficiaries. Inclusion of new households was based on existing targeting criteria.

8.7.3.3 Payment Process

SCTPP payment processes worked well across the two years studied. At baseline, virtually all beneficiaries reported that they received their payments on time with more than 90 per cent reporting full payment, and 82 per cent reporting that programme staff treated them courteously. This performance was maintained throughout the life of the programme. SCTPP payments are regular. Once the programme was operational, more than 95 per cent of beneficiaries received payments each month with few complaints.

At baseline, there were concerns over distances that beneficiaries in Hintalo had to travel to reach pay points. While the use of designates provided some advantages, in 2012 designated persons were often rewarded in cash or in kind and sometimes conflicts arose. The 2012 data indicated that in 21 per cent of cases when the beneficiary sent someone else to collect payment, that person was paid. Both issues had been resolved by endline; the additional pay point in Hintalo, along with improvements in the road network, led to reduction in travel times and by May 2014, designated persons were increasingly likely to be household (and nearly always family) members and thus less likely to be paid. The proportion of designates who received a payment fell to 7.6 per cent and out of the 563 beneficiaries who reported using a designate, only 18 (3.5 per cent) reported paying more than 50 birr. Problems with designating someone else appeared to be exceptions to the rule. When problems were encountered, different arrangements for collection were made, usually with the help of the CCCs.

8.7.3.4 Impact on Trust and Non-Government Financed Social Protection

The evaluation tested the possibility that the SCTPP may have had unintentional negative effects on informal social financial protection, on trust, and on social cohesion. Via the qualitative element of the evaluation through focus group and key informant interview there is evidence that beneficiaries received fewer transfers from their family and friends due to the SCTPP, particularly in Abi-Adi, and that this gave them a feeling of greater dignity and respect because they no longer needed to ask their family members for support.

No evidence was found in either the quantitative or the qualitative research that the SCTPP negatively affected trust and social cohesion in Abi-Adi, and while there was some evidence of weakened social cohesion in Hintalo, overall levels of reported trust and social cohesion were rising for all groups. Also being beneficiaries meant they found it easier to access credit and to become members of elder associations. Only a few respondents indicated that they thought the long-term formalization of social protection would undermine community networks.

The level of knowledge among tabia social workers, tabia officials, CCC members, and SCTPP participants about when the programme would end and what would happen afterwards was mixed across tabias with many having incorrect or partial information. When asked about what would happen if the programme were to stop, almost all participants were wary about the future of the programme and felt that they would fall back to their old situation without any support. While some expressed a strong belief that government would continue their support in one way or the other, others were less convinced. Despite the positive role of the CCCs in implementation of the SCTPP, their role in supporting all poor and vulnerable households on their own without external support was known to be limited.

8.7.3.5 Role of the Social Workers

The evaluation observed the work of the social workers based at woreda level and working with the CCCs. While the Tigray social workers have university degrees they do not have specialized training in social work. At the time of the evaluation a federal committee was working on developing recommended accreditation standards and job descriptions for different levels of social workers. The vision for the social workers is that, together with the CCCs, they would be able to provide more nuanced social welfare support than the food security committees that manage the DSB support in the PSNP programme model. Yet the qualitative evaluation didn't find much evidence of the social workers doing more than the important job of administering the SCTPP, including managing targeting and dealing with complaints and grievances. Most of the extra support of a social welfare nature was being provided by the 'para social workers' who make up the CCC committees themselves including the tabia chairperson, the health extension workers, businessmen, and schoolteachers.

8.8 ASSESSMENT OF THE EVALUATION AND ITS CONTRIBUTION TO THE EVOLUTION OF TIGRAY'S AND OTHER REGIONAL SOCIAL PROTECTION STRATEGIES

8.8.1 Knowledge Gains from the Evaluation

The evaluation showed that channelling small amounts of money to poor labour-constrained households allowed an increase in the standard of living, food security, and dignity of participants; it also improved some social outcomes, notably school retention. It demonstrated that CCCs supported by woreda level social workers can maintain an efficient cash transfer programme over a wide area in urban and rural areas. It demonstrated that the pilot served poor welfare cases in Hintalo that had been overlooked by the PSNP because of the cap on households with no manual labourers. Even with a cap of 10 per cent of households enrolling in the pilot 30 per cent of those households had been excluded from participation by the PSNP.

8.8.2 Evaluation Implementation Problems

Although fieldwork and analysis went smoothly, political expediency led to the pilot being launched before the contracts with the independent evaluators were finalized. First payments for most of the pilot area started in August 2011, whereas the first household survey did not take place until May 2012. The envisioned three years of implementation between baseline and endline surveys ended up being cut down to two years and that, for many welfare indicators, there were no data on pre-intervention levels.

8.8.3 Informing Tigray's Regional Social Protection Steering Committee About Impacts

The regional social protection committee that had commissioned the pilot became the steering committee for the evaluation, thus key decisions regarding the evaluation such as agreeing on the terms of reference, approving the evaluators inception report, and reviewing the results of the baseline and follow-up surveys were committee agenda items. A circulation of reports electronically to give members time to review findings would precede such meetings. The meeting to review the endline report of the independent evaluators took place in June 2015, two months after the report became available. It is probably that the stream of information coming from the evaluation to the committee was an impetus for the committee to meet and discuss broader issues related to the future of social protection in Tigray than might otherwise have been the case.

8.8.4 How a Combination of Results from Evaluation and Monitoring Stimulated Dialogue on Future Social Protection Policy

Some findings from steering committee monitoring of progress (findings later confirmed by the evaluation) became apparent early in the pilot. It became clear relatively early, from monitoring visits, that the BoLSA and CCC system, in the pilot areas, did indeed have sufficient capacity to manage a relatively complex system. The data from the evaluation confirmed the monitoring reports including the high quality maintenance of the service throughout the pilot period.

The evaluation findings, including information from the baseline and study tours from other regions and federal level to the pilot, fed into the wider objective of the Tigray regional government, namely stimulating debate within the region, at federal level, and in other regions on whether it was time to increase the level of investment in social worker capacities from the federal and regional development budget across the country.

It seems that the Tigray government was successful in that the approved national social protection policy issued in 2014 did indeed endorse the need to scale up social worker numbers with a role for government in training such a cadre and also encouraged regional governments to ask communities to form CCC committees who might have responsibility for cash transfers if the resources could be found to finance them. The policy also noted that government should be expected to allocate resources to social protection in the budget, a departure from the 1996 Developmental Welfare Policy, which noted that government expected communities to address their own social protection issues with little support from government (MoLSA, 1996).

8.9 ENDING THE PILOT

In supporting the pilot UNICEF agreed with the office of the president of Tigray that the arrangement would end after three years of transfers (the evaluation found that the exit plan had not been well communicated to pilot households). Based on the lessons from the pilot UNICEF and other development partners would then help to implement the scale-up of the regional social protection strategy whether it included cash transfers or not.

Finalizing the regional policy and strategy. However. depended on the steerage provided by the federal policy. The policy was agreed to by the federal council of ministers in 2014 thus opening the door for detailed work at regional level only towards the end of the pilot period. Thus funding for participants continued as an interim measure including that from the regional government's own funds. In 2015, rural beneficiaries from the SCTPP will become PSNP direct support beneficiaries with twelve-month transfers. Since the PSNP is not active in urban areas as of the second quarter of 2015 the Tigray's regional council had not decided if or how it would support cash transfers in those locations.

8.10 SCALING CASH TRANSFERS MANAGED BY BOLSA IN TIGRAY

8.10.1 The Value of the Transfer

The regional social protection committee knew that it must pilot a transfer that could, over the medium term, be affordable when scaled-up. They understood that too low a transfer could result in little impact thus risking closure. From initial briefings they were familiar with the rule of thumb that transfer levels should amount to not less than 15–20 per cent of the value needed for households to reach the poverty line. They chose, with an eye to future coherence across social protection actions, to follow the transfer levels agreed for the PSNP but to extend the transfer period from six months (PSNP) to a year thus effectively doubling the transfers offered to the poorest households via PSNP.

While the evaluation revealed that the impacts, after two years of transfers, in terms of changes in social outcomes detected, given the power of the survey (see methods), were modest, the gains in terms of increased dignity for the very poorest were thought to be worth the value of the transfer.

8.10.2 Financing and Building Social Worker Capacity for Scaling Up

How many people might a region-wide scaled-up Tigray-wide cash transfer programme aim to enrol? Based on an estimated headcount poverty rate of 32 per cent there are about 1.5 million people living below the poverty line. The budget required including salaries and the transfers is estimated to cost around US$5 million once scaled up, which amounts to 2–3 per cent of the current Tigray budget depending on the value of the transfer. If it is assumed that only the very poorest 10 per cent are to be targeted with a scale-up over five years, starting with the very poorest locations, then a more realistic requirement for the first year is closer to 30 million birr.

Finding these resources is a matter of political choice. International development partners have been supporting PSNP across the region for several years and with the approval of phase four of the PSNP in 2014, including agreement to help build BoLSA capacity to manage transfers to the DSBs, a good portion of the resources needed for scale-up are secured over the medium term. However, the PSNP does not cover urban areas for now. Where could those resources come from for the urban areas? The obvious source is from the regional budget envelope; the newly agreed national policy stipulates that finances for social protection should be allocated from government budget although the details have not been agreed to date. Another potential source is from the approximately US$4 million per year social welfare budget of the Endowment Fund for the Rehabilitation of Tigray, a regionally owned conglomeration of sixteen companies operating in the industrial, mining, construction, agro-processing, trade, and service sectors. While in the immediate term these resources are earmarked for helping to fund social sector infrastructure improvements (e.g., school classrooms and health centre extensions), a choice could be made to start investing in channelling some of this cash through the cash transfer system to the very poorest Tigrayans. The CCCs raise modest amounts of resources from community contributions; it is possible that urban CCCs could raise more resources, especially in the wealthier area such as in the regional capital and in the successful sesame exporting west of Tigray. Finally, the Tigray economy is likely to continue to grow in the coming years increasing revenue and thus fiscal space available to the regional government.

The endorsement of the national social protection policy (MoLSA, 2014) and encouragement for regions to build BoLSA, social welfare workforce, and CCC capacities opened the door for international development partners to help regional governments plan for a full scale-up. This will take some time since it is likely that each woreda needs two experts with assistant social workers to cover two tabias each; this means the recruitment and training of 500 more BoLSA staff for the case of Tigray. In the design of the next phase of the PSNP (PSNP phase 4), it is envisaged that MoLSA and BoLSAs will become gradually more responsible for the permanent direct support beneficiaries caseload.

8.11 CONCLUSION AND MEDIUM-TERM ACTIONS

The value of the pilot in helping the regional governments understand current BoLSA and CCC capacities and thus system investment needs has led two other regions, SNNP (Southern Nations and Nationalities) and Oromia, to launch SCT pilots in 2015, with stronger linkages with nutrition-sensitive activities and the social protection system approach, and evaluations as part of their design. In these two additional regions, in line with the PSNP phase 4 and the social protection policy frameworks, the social workers, the development agents, and the health extension workers will work together to coordinate and provide access to basic social services linkages for PSNP beneficiaries; with additional specific support to pregnant and lactating women and households with malnourished children.

The evaluation contributed to the social protection policy dialogue on a number of key points. The most important findings were that the BoLSA had the capacity to manage a complex programme at some scale efficiently and effectively. The results contributed evidence to important policy issues. Finally, the following conclusions and discussion points are its most important issues highlighted by the pilot and enhance the evaluation: a) the importance of the extent to which dignity is increased for the poorest by channelling a small amount of cash to their household and how living in a society where resources are set aside for this purpose make people proud to be part of that society; b) The modest increase in development outcomes such as reductions in malnutrition and child labour one can expect to see from a modest transfer; c) That CCCs supported by social workers enhance social cohesion at local level to the extent that the regional government is keen to further invest in this capacity; d) That work is needed to fine-tune the job descriptions of woreda-based social workers and amount of work one can expect from a voluntary cadre of community level para social workers; e) That more dialogue is needed to agree on what proportion of regional resources will be allocated to the regional social protection strategy, and especially in urban areas now that funding has been secured via PSNP phase 4 for rural areas.

In terms of the value of spending resources on evaluation the cost of this evaluation was about 10 per cent of the total pilot budget. This expenditure created space for more evidence-based policy dialogue on Tigray's and other regions' social protection strategies than would otherwise have been the case. Indeed the value of evaluation is confirmed in the eyes of two other regions in Ethiopia since they have recently commissioned similar support for evaluated pilots starting in 2014.

REFERENCES

Berhane, G., Hoddinott, J., Kumar, N., Taffesse, A. S., Diresses, M. T., and Yohannes, Y. (2011). 'Evaluation of Ethiopia's Food Security Program: Documenting Progress in the Implementation of the Productive Safety Nets Programme and the Household Asset Building Programme'. International Food Policy Research Institute, Institute of Development Studies, and Dadimos Consulting.

Berhane, G., Devereux, S., Hoddinott, J., Tegbu, F. N., Roelen, K., and Schwab, B. (2012). 'Evaluation of the Social Cash Transfers Pilot Programme, Tigray Region, Ethiopia'. Baseline Report. International Food Policy Research Institute, Institute of Development Studies, University of Sussex, and University of Mekelle, Tigray.

Berhane, G., Devereus, S., Hoddinott, J., Hoel, J., Kimmel, M., Ledlie, N., and Roelen, K. (2015). Endline Report. 'Evaluation of the Social Cash Transfer Programme, Tigray Region, Ethiopia'. International Food Policy Research Institute, Institute of Development Studies, and University of Mekelle.

BoLSA (2011a). 'Community Care Coalition Working Manual'. October 2002 (Ethiopian Calendar), Mekelle, Tigray, Regional Government of Tigray.
BoLSA (2011b). 'Design, Budget and Logical Framework of the Tigray Social Cash Transfer Pilot Program April 2011–March 2014'. Tigray BoLSA in collaboration with UNICEF, Regional Government of Tigray.
BoLSA (2011c). 'Manual of Operations for the Tigray Social Cash Transfer Pilot Programme'. Tigray Bureau of Labour and Social Affairs, Mekelle, Tigray, Regional Government of Tigray.
BoLSA (2012). 'Status Report on Community-Based Social Protection and Social Cash Transfer', Mekelle, Tigray, Regional Government of Tigray.
CSA (Central Statistical Agency) (2007). 'Population and Housing Census'. Central Statistical Agency, Government of Ethiopia, Addis Ababa.
CSA (2012). 'Ethiopia Demographic and Health Survey 2011'. Central Statistical Agency, Government of Ethiopia, Addis Ababa.
FAO (2014). 'Qualitative Research and Analyses of the Economic Impacts of Cash Transfer Programmes in Sub-Saharan Africa'. Ethiopia Country Case Study Report, FAO, Rome.
Germann, S., Ngoma, F., Wamimbi, R., Claxton, A., Gaudrault, M, and the Community Care Coalitions Study Teams (2009). 'Mobilizing and strengthening community-led childcare through community care groups and coalitions: a study from Ethiopia, Mozambique, Uganda and Zambia'. *International NGO Journal*, 4(1) (January): 1–6.
Kagin, J., Taylor, J. E., Alfani, F., and Davis B. (2014). 'Local Economy-Wide Impact Evaluation (LEWIE) of Ethiopia's Social Cash Transfer Pilot Programme'. PtoP Project Report, FAO and The World Bank.
Ministry of Finance, Ministry of Women, Children and Youth Affairs, and United Nations. (2012). 'Investment in Boys and Girls: Past, Present and Future', Addis Ababa.
MoLSA (1996). 'Developmental Social Welfare policy'. MoLSA, Addis Ababa, Government of Ethiopia.
MoLSA (2014). 'National Social Protection Policy'. MoLSA, Addis Ababa, Government of Ethiopia.
PSNP Secretariat (2010). 'Designing and Implementing a Rural Safety-Net in a Low-Income Setting: Lessons Learned from Ethiopia's Productive Safety-Net Programme 2005–09'. PSNP Secretariat, Addis Ababa, Ethiopia.
UNICEF (2015). 'Programme policy and procedure manual'.
Vaughan, S. and Gebremichael, M. (2011). 'The Role of EFFORT, the Endowment Fund for the Rehabilitation of Tigray in Ethiopia'. Reserch Report No. 2, Africa Power and Politics Programme (APPP), the Overseas Development Institute, Funded by DfID and Irish Aid.
Wiseman, D., Bassett, L., Benson, T., and Hoddinott, J. (2009). 'Validation of Food Frequency and Dietary Diversity as Proxy Indicators of Household Food Security'. International Food Policy Research Institute Discussion Paper 00870, Washington, DC.
World Bank (2003). 'Securing Consumption While Promoting Growth: The Role of a Productive Social Safety Net in Ethiopia'. An Issues Note, World Bank, Washington, DC.

Annex 8.1. Summary Impacts of SCT on Development Outcomes in the Tigray Pilot

Source of data	Baseline survey May 2012 and End line survey May 2014
POVERTY REDUCTION	
Poverty: mean total monthly household consumption expenditure per adult equivalent below $1 per day (real)	Transfer represented an increase in household income of 10 per cent and food consumption expenditure of 17 per cent
FOOD CONSUMPTION AND HOUSEHOLD WELFARE	
Mean total monthly household consumption expenditure per adult equivalent (Birr – real)	Per capita monthly household consumption expenditure by SCT beneficiaries rose from 341 Birr (May 2012) to 375 Birr (May 2014). Note, however, that the May 2012 result is measured eight months after the SCT began. There is no statistically significant difference in the change in consumption expenditure between SCT beneficiaries and matched non-beneficiaries. Results are not adjusted for inflation.
Mean monthly food consumption expenditure per adult equivalent (Birr – real)	Per capita monthly food consumption expenditure by SCT beneficiaries rose from 278 Birr (May 2012) to 284 Birr (May 2014). Note, however, that the May 2012 result is measured eight months after the SCT began. There is no statistically significant difference in the change in consumption expenditure between SCT beneficiaries and matched non-beneficiaries. Results are not adjusted for inflation.
Food Security	Food gap reduced by 0.24 months by May 2012. Calories consumed increased by 94 kcal in May 2012 and 158 kcal by May 2014, Relative to comparison households an increase of 3.6 and 6.0 respectively
SCHOOLING	Large positive impact on girls 6–11 in rural area; Likelihood of Enrolment increased by 13 per cent, school efficiency by 14 per cent; grade attainment by half a grade
HEALTH	Suggestive effects on sickness and curative care but not significant
NUTRITION	No impact on nutrition status (note that the evaluation may not have had the power to measure impact on these indicators).
Mental Health	No impact on maternal health or body mass index (note that the evaluation may not have had the power to measure impact on these indicators).
PRODUCTIVE	
Increase in ownership of small livestock	7 per cent increase in chance of owning any form of livestock compared to controls in rural areas; no impact in urban area.
CHILD LABOUR	
Proportion of children doing paid work	No significant impact on child labour outcomes except for girls' work on family businesses in Abi Adi.
Proportion of children doing unpaid work	Had a significant reduction in labour hours by girls in urban area working in family businesses.

9

The Role of Impact Evaluation in the Evolution of Zambia's Cash Transfer Programme

Paul Quarles van Ufford (UNICEF Zambia), Charlotte Harland (Independent Consultant), Stanfield Michelo (Ministry of Community Development, Mother and Child Health, Zambia), Gelson Tembo (University of Zambia and Palm Associates), Kelley Toole (DFID Zambia), and Denis Wood (Independent Consultant)

9.1 INTRODUCTION: POVERTY CONTEXT IN ZAMBIA AND THE ROLE OF SOCIAL PROTECTION

Social cash transfers (SCTs) have been part of Zambia's social protection response to poverty roughly since the start of this century. Since the early 2000s, a number of pilots, the introduction of new targeting models, gradual scale-up, increased government financing, and the realization of a series of impact evaluations have characterized the progressive consolidation of cash transfers in the social protection portfolio. The aim of this chapter is twofold: first, to document the evolution of Zambia's cash transfer programme and to put critical milestones into the perspective of the broader socioeconomic development and policy context; and second, to explore the range of factors that led to critical decisions in the life of the programme with emphasis on the role of impact evaluations that have accompanied its implementation. In other words, it addresses the interaction and dynamics between the evolving programme and the evaluation process and findings. In view of the special nature of the most recent and ongoing impact evaluation, a dedicated section presents an overview of main findings as these have emerged. Hence, the chapter aims to contribute to the discussion about the extent to and ways in which the interaction between impact evaluations and the broader political economy environment leads to change in scale, scope, and operational design of cash transfer programmes.

9.1.1 Poverty and Inequality in Zambia

Although the mining sector has been a critical contributor to the Zambian economy, for the large majority of the working-age population agriculture remains the basis of livelihoods. On- and off-farm activities, both in rural and in urban areas, take place to a large extent in the informal economy, which employs up to 85 per cent of Zambia's 13 million population (CSO 2012a). Over the past decades, poverty and vulnerability have been driven by the variable climatic conditions, the HIV (Human-Immunodeficiency Virus) pandemic, and limited access to economic opportunity in an economy dominated by mineral exports. Despite consistent economic growth since the mid-2000s, driven by favourable global copper prices, poverty levels in Zambia have remained high. In 2010, headcount poverty stood at 60 per cent (up to 80 per cent in rural areas) and extreme poverty at 42 per cent (CSO 2012b). This situation reflected a near status quo as compared with figures from 2006, mainly as a result of urban-centred and non-labour-intensive growth not spilling over into Zambia's rural areas (World Bank 2012). This has sharpened the geographical and consumption dimensions of inequality (United Nations in Zambia 2013).

9.1.2 Zambia's Policy Response to Poverty and Vulnerability

The nature and intensity of Zambia's policy response to poverty and vulnerability have varied over the years. Factors such as fiscal space and changing conceptions of effective policies to address poverty and vulnerability have been influential in determining policy intentions and budget allocations.

Zambia's longest established social assistance scheme is the Public Welfare Assistance Scheme (PWAS). Launched before Independence in 1964, the PWAS originally provided support for a range of needs to people recommended for assistance to a central government committee. However, the economic downturn that resulted from falling copper prices and rising cost of oil, in a landlocked country severely constrained by regional independence struggles, created an upsurge in demand. An increasing population and declining revenues led to significant falls in spending on poverty reduction and welfare, and the PWAS was no exception. By the 1980s, much of public expenditure was allocated to debt service, wages, and subsidies. Agricultural subsidies, mainly for fertilizers, have always constituted a major component of social policy but their capacity to reach the poorest rural farmers has been weak.

In the mid-1990s, however, and following the removal of agricultural subsidies, the new multiparty government decided to re-launch the PWAS. In particular, the aim was to do something to support the increasing number of orphans being cared for by impoverished grandparents, largely as a result of

HIV and AIDS (Acquired Immunodeficiency Syndrome). A new design moved decision making to the community level, and provided for a partnership between government and communities that were already critical in providing support to destitute households. The initial roll-out established Community Welfare Assistance Committees (CWACs) in most districts across Zambia. However, the early years of implementation remained hampered by very low budgets and disbursements.

Although cash was originally not given directly to beneficiaries, the PWAS provided for flexible use of resources, as agreed by recipients and communities. In time, however, the notion of giving cash directly to beneficiaries was proposed as a simplified approach. While some did not fully trust recipients to use resources to good effect, a pilot programme in one district began to provide some evidence that such fears were unfounded (see Section 9.2.1). From this point, a consensus that social transfers should be expanded, and that cash offered the best means of doing so, began to grow.

While Zambia's Poverty Reduction Strategy Paper (PRSP), developed in the early 2000s, still only made scanty reference to social assistance, under the auspices of the Ministry of Community Development a National Social Protection Strategy (NSPS) was drafted in 2005. It was the first policy document in this field and it has strongly influenced the thinking of social protection within government, including the conceptual differentiation between incapacitated households, with labour constraints, and the so-called *vulnerable but viable* households, with the potential capacity to benefit from productive support (Tembo, Michelo, and Zulu 2009). The strategy was adopted by the Ministry of Community Development and its text formed the basis of a dedicated social protection chapter in the Fifth National Development Plan (FNDP) for 2006–2010. This had significant implications as it paved way for: 1) the establishment of a Social Protection Sector Advisory Group (SP-SAG), with reporting obligations to the Ministry of Finance; 2) a clear mandate for the Ministry of Community Development (chairing the SAG); 3) the inclusion of social protection in the Joint Assistance for Zambia (JAZ) framework that guides donor support; and 4) the establishment of a dedicated donor coordination group on social protection. In sum, it brought social protection to Zambia's policy agenda. Whereas the social protection chapter remained in the Sixth National Development Plan (SNDP, 2011–15) in a very similar way, changes in the social protection response to poverty happened on the ground and mainly through the developments in cash transfer programming. These are described in Section 9.2. Initially, the changes were taking place at a small scale, both geographically and financially. In fact, despite a recommendation in the FNDP's mid-term review, to move away from fertilizer subsidies towards cash transfers, public expenditure remained largely confined to agricultural subsidies. For instance, Whitworth (2015) estimates that between 2005 and 2011, expenditure on the Farmer Input

Support Programme (FISP), government purchase of maize, and consumer subsidies of maize meal (through the Food Reserve Agency) increased by 0.5 per cent and 1.6 per cent of GDP (gross domestic product), respectively. During the same period, expenditure on PWAS and cash transfers remained negligible when expressed as a percentage of GDP.

In June 2014, the government approved a National Social Protection Policy (NSPP), which is based on five pillars: social assistance, social security, livelihood and empowerment, protection, and disability. The NSPP can be seen as reflecting a next stage in social protection policy in Zambia, after the release of the FNDP in 2005. It integrates and consolidates cash transfers as a flagship programme and aims to provide a broad foundation for improved coherence and coordination between the proposed pillars. This is described in more detail in Section 9.4, which addresses the role of the 2010–14 cash transfer impact evaluations in policy development. Before that, Section 9.2 provides an overview of the main milestones in the evolution of Zambia's cash transfer programme. This section, together with the broad poverty and policy context outlined earlier, points to an increasingly conducive environment for the introduction of an expanded cash transfer programme accompanied by a rigorous impact evaluation. The main findings of this impact evaluation are presented in Section 9.3. Section 9.4 then analyses the contribution of the evaluation to policy development, that is the Zambian Government's decision to significantly scale up its cash transfers from 2014 onwards. This is followed by a brief analysis of the role of targeting assessments in shaping cash transfer policy (Section 9.5). Section 9.6 concludes and identifies remaining questions for further analysis and research.

9.2 THE EVOLUTION OF ZAMBIA'S CASH TRANSFER PROGRAMME

This section presents an overview of main milestones in the evolution of Zambia's cash transfer programme, distinguishing between an initial period up to 2010 and a subsequent phase between 2010 and 2013. Figure 9.1 presents on overview of critical points in time for the evolution of Zambia's cash transfers and distinguishes between evaluation- and policy-related events. It also presents trends in terms of number of districts covered and programme caseload.

9.2.1 The Period up to 2010

With regard to the origin and development of social welfare programmes in Zambia, three phases can be distinguished in the period leading up to 2010.

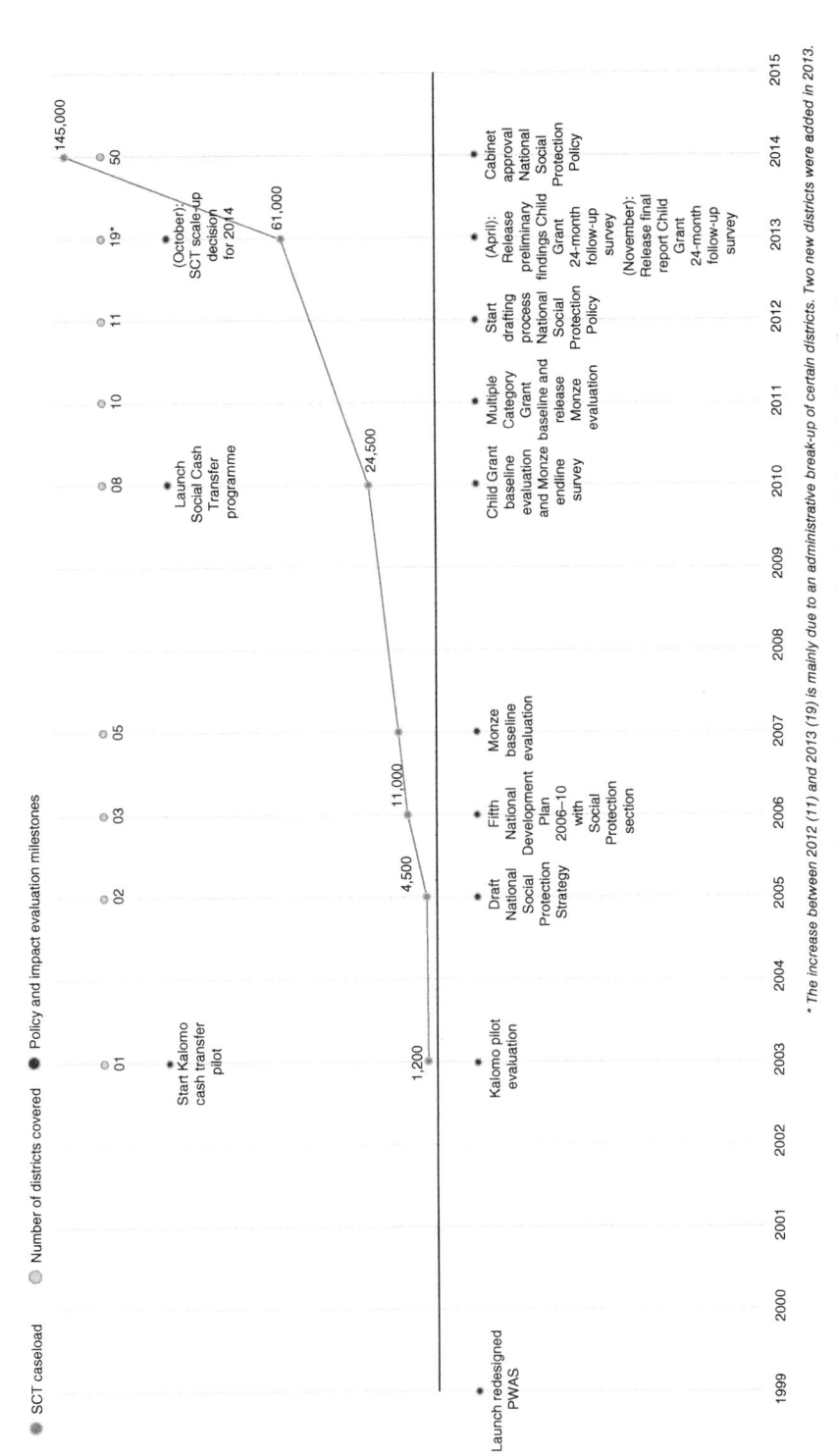

Figure 9.1. Timeline with Main Policy and Evaluation Milestones Related to Zambia's Cash Transfer Programme

* The increase between 2012 (11) and 2013 (19) is mainly due to an administrative break-up of certain districts. Two new districts were added in 2013.

First, the period before the second half of the 1990s during which levels of service delivery were low and little fiscal space existed for allocations to welfare programmes. Also, in this period, support to social welfare programmes typically remained outside the scope of official development assistance portfolios. This changed somewhat with the emergence of poverty reduction strategies in the 1990s. The start of what can be considered as the second phase was marked by the 1999 launch of the re-designed PWAS, which provided for one-off social assistance transfers, in cash or in kind, to incapacitated or extremely vulnerable families. The re-designed version of the PWAS established volunteer social welfare structures below the district level for the delivery of social assistance.[1] The PWAS was not supported by donors. The move towards offering cash to beneficiaries and the basis of future expansion in partnership with multiple donor countries in Zambia's social welfare sector can be said to have started in 2003, with the GTZ (German Agency for Technical Cooperation)-supported SCT pilot in Kalomo district in southern Zambia (phase 3). Although administered through the PWAS mechanism, the scheme was funded by GTZ and received significant outside technical assistance. It covered approximately 1,200 households and its objective was to reduce extreme poverty, hunger, and starvation. Beneficiary identification took place through a community-based targeting process that put strong focus on the incapacitation criterion in a context where HIV/AIDS had led to high mortality and morbidity among caregivers as well as a large number of orphans to be taken care of. Clearly, the scheme reflected the evolving thinking about the most appropriate response to humanitarian crises such as the southern Africa food shortages in 2002 and 2003.

The Kalomo pilot has been subject of several studies and evaluations, but given the level of attention that the project received it is notable that all fell well short in terms of research design and methodological rigour. The main evaluation of the Kalomo pilot had a 'before and after' design but did not include a control group, which appeared problematic in view of the drought that hit the region during the evaluation year (Tembo et al. 2014). The evaluation, after following beneficiary households for one year, found improvements in a number of indicators, including school enrolment rates (up by 3 per cent), nutrition (improvements in quantity and quality of meals), asset endowments, ownership of small livestock, and self-perception of social status (Schuring, Michelo, and Boonstoppel 2007). The difficulty of attributing observed changes to the cash transfer was considered its main limitation. The ministry was only very marginally involved in the leadership, design, and management of the evaluation.

---

[1] These included Area Coordinating Committees at ward level and Community Welfare Assistance Committees at community level. These structures exist till today and have specific roles in targeting and monitoring payments of transfers to cash transfer beneficiaries.

Around 2005, the UK Department for International Development (DFID) took over the funding of the Kalomo pilot and assisted with expanding cash transfers to a few new districts. Though officially implemented through the structures of the Ministry of Community Development, the schemes remained donor-funded and received significant outside assistance, from DFID, GTZ, and CARE in particular. Between 2005 and 2010, however, a transition took place in the sense that the role of Zambian technical assistants became stronger compared with international technical assistants. The role of the Ministry of Community Development in the implementation gradually increased as well. This was also reflected in an overall stronger interest in the functioning and impact of cash transfer programmes. Piloting remained a major driver behind implementation, which was reflected in the choice of districts and targeting criteria: urban environment (Chipata, from 2006 onwards), low density population and remote rural environment (Kazungula, from 2005 onwards), old age (Katete, from 2007 onwards), and district-wide scale-up (Kalomo and Monze, from 2007 onwards). With the exception of Katete district, which used a social pension type model, targeting was done using the incapacitation criterion of the Kalomo model, with communities selecting the 10 per cent poorest households on the basis of a ranking. Finally, an Oxfam-sponsored pilot was implemented in two districts (Kaoma and Mongu) to test relative effectiveness, efficiency, and market impact of cash and in-kind (food) assistance, following a major 2004–5 drought (Tembo and Tembo 2009).

The idea behind these various designs and variations was that they should offer an opportunity to understand how best and most effectively to deliver SCTs. However, two significant problems existed in this regard. First, the objectives of the various programmes were not articulated in any quantified or specific terms. Rather, the cash transfer was thought to offer general and variable 'good', which would be detected and understood at a later point. Hence, in the absence of any objectives, the idea that some programmes could be said to be better or more effective than others was inevitably rather weak. Second, with close and localized arrangements for management supplemented by NGOs (non-governmental organizations), technical assistants, and consultants, it was hard to know whether any of the pilot variations were sufficiently 'hardy' to be implemented in the real-world setting of a national programme under the Ministry of Community Development, or what that might cost.

The implementation of the programme in Monze district was accompanied by an impact evaluation, which, for the first time, aimed at using an experimental design (with a baseline in 2007 and a follow-up survey in 2010, both among treatment and control groups) in order to address weaknesses in the Kalomo impact evaluation. The purpose of the Monze impact evaluation was to garner support for expansion of cash transfers. The report was released in

2011, shortly after the government and donors had consolidated ongoing and new targeting models into the SCT programme, which marked the fourth phase in the history of cash transfer programmes in Zambia. Apart from the release coming after the completion of discussions on the new phase, the report of the Monze impact evaluation had little policy influence. The evaluation design was considered complex, partly as a result of different evaluation teams doing baseline and follow-up surveys, and the report considered rather technical in nature. The findings highlighted impacts on education enrolment and livestock ownership but the questions in the consumption module were too few to allow analysis of poverty and food expenditure (Seidenfeld and Handa 2011).

9.2.2 Zambia's Social Cash Transfer Programme: 2010–2013

In 2010, the government launched the SCT programme. A number of factors influenced the design of this programme. First, the perceived limitations of the ongoing cash transfer pilots, which used a targeting model that identified the 10 per cent poorest households in the community (the so-called 10 per cent inclusive model). The main observed bottleneck here was the difficulty of applying a poverty criterion with a 10 per cent cap in communities, which had poverty rates often well above 60 per cent.[2] The second factor was the increasing availability of evidence on the impact of cash transfers in Africa and elsewhere as well as emerging corporate priorities in donor and development organizations, such as DFID and UNICEF (United Nations Children's Fund), which were leading social protection cooperating partners in Zambia at that time. They made a case for using categorical targeting models with a strong focus on children. Third, the design of the new SCT programme was shaped by the strong belief in the Ministry of Community Development and Social Services that although cash transfers were a potentially strong response to poverty and vulnerability in Zambia, broader support in government for the expansion of social assistance was far from a 'given', in particular in a context in which cash transfers were still commonly perceived as handouts and prone to creating dependency. Finally, the progressive recovery of the Zambian economy, with consecutive years of steady economic growth, had translated in a positive outlook on fiscal growth for the coming years. It were these factors combined that sparked a constructive and extensive dialogue between

---

[2] The discussion about using categorical targeting in districts with high poverty rates (geographical filter) was also a recommendation from a 2008 targeting assessment. Following intensive discussions, including through a workshop with an international expert, it was eventually decided to leave out the means-test in the new Child Grant and Multiple Categorical Targeting Grant models. It came back in the targeting model adopted in 2014.

the Ministry and cooperating partners, in particular DFID and UNICEF, and which, during the period between 2008 and 2010, led to the design of the SCT programme and an accompanying implementation 'package' that had the following main features:

1. Continuation of the programme in the 10 per cent inclusive model districts and in the social pension district;
2. Expansion of the programme into districts with high poverty, malnutrition, and child mortality rates, using two new targeting models: a Child Grant (for mothers with children under five years old) and a Multiple Categorical Targeting Grant (MCTG) for households with orphans or disabled members. The adoption of this new approach, in particular the Child Grant, represented a significant shift away from the hitherto used targeting of 'incapacitated households', which strongly linked poverty to prevailing labour constraints. The adoption of categorical targeting criteria in locations with very high poverty and malnutrition rates, as informed by the 2008 targeting assessment, represented another shift. This geographical filter justified the categorical targeting approach, which was strongly pushed by development partners. In all, the discussion around the new targeting approach amplified the consensus that a solid impact evaluation was required to demonstrate the impacts of these investments (see point 5);
3. A scale-up plan for the 2010–2015 period, with an initial 2015 target of 70,000 households in fifteen districts, which was later increased to a target of 100,000 households with additional resources from partners and budget commitments from government;
4. A joint financing plan for ten years, with donor contributions (at around 70 per cent in 2010) gradually reducing and government allocations gradually increasing;
5. An impact evaluation of the two new targeting models (the Child Grant and the MCTG);
6. A technical assistance plan for the development of robust targeting, payment, and management information systems required for when the programme would scale up to the national level; and
7. An overall SCT programme objective—reduce extreme poverty and the intergenerational transmission of poverty—and the following specific objectives:
    – Supplement and not replace household income,
    – Increase the number of children enrolled in and attending primary school,
    – Reduce the rate of mortality and morbidity of children under five,
    – Reduce stunting and wasting among children under five,
    – Increase the number of households having a second meal per day,
    – Increase the number of households owning assets such as livestock.

> **Box 9.1. Key features of the Social Cash Transfer Programme for the Period 2010–2013**
>
> — Main target groups: (1) Children below five years, (2) Orphans and Vulnerable Children, (3) Elderly above sixty-four years, (4) 10 per cent poorest population in the community, and (5) Children with a disability.
> — Transfer value: 60 Kwacha up (approximately 10–12 US$ per month, paid bimonthly, and double transfer value for households with a disabled member).
> — Flat transfer rate and unconditional.
> — Number of districts covered: 08 (2010), 10 (2011), 11 (2012), 19 (2013).
> — Caseload: 24,500 (2010), 61,000 (2013).

Box 9.1 presents an overview of selected parameters of the programme as it gradually expanded over the 2010–2013 period.

The discussion on programme objectives (point 7) influenced the key features of the conceptual framework that was eventually used as a basis for the design of the evaluation, which included variables on poverty, food security, child health, nutrition, schooling, assets, and production. The purpose of the impact evaluation was to further build a case for cash transfers, in particular for the new categorical targeting approach (Child Grant and MCTG). The ministry strongly felt that this was a requirement to gathering sufficient support for the scheduled scale-up. The ministry was strongly involved in the development of the evaluation design, both conceptually and methodologically. The proposed use of a Randomized Control Trial (RCT), with delayed entry after three years for those communities that were part of the control arm of the study, required leadership of the ministry in implementing the randomization and communicating with districts and communities participating in the study. The randomization process was also used during the 2014 scale-up when it was decided to proceed with partial coverage in a relatively large number of districts. The extensive involvement of the ministry in the early stages of the impact evaluation and the constructive relationships with the evaluation research team are likely to have laid a solid foundation for confidence in using the findings and communicating these to other stakeholders in government at a later stage (see Sections 9.4–9.6).[3]

---

[3] It is worth noting that the design of the evaluation for the SCT programme from 2010 onwards also reflects an attempt to incorporate evaluation design lessons from the Monze district impact evaluation, published in 2011. Clearly, the Monze impact evaluation experienced significant difficulties and baseline and follow-up surveys were conducted by different contractors. This was detrimental to its credibility and it is commonly acknowledged that the Monze

The following sections of the chapter will focus on the impact evaluation findings and the role the evaluations played in influencing policy decisions, in particular the government decision to significantly scale up the SCT programme from 2014 onwards.

9.3 MAIN FINDINGS FROM THE IMPACT EVALUATIONS

This section provides an overview of the main findings of the impact evaluations of the SCT programme in Zambia, which have been implemented since 2010. Details on the methodology of impact evaluations have been provided elsewhere in this book. Section 9.3.1 and Box 9.2 provide a summary.

9.3.1 SCT Impact Evaluation Methodologies

A longitudinal, randomized, controlled evaluation with repeated measures was used to measure quantitatively the impact of the SCT intervention at the individual and household levels. This was done by using a differences-in-differences (DD) statistical model, which compares changes in outcomes between baseline and follow-up and between treatment and control groups. The DD estimator is the most commonly used estimation technique for impacts of cash transfer models. For some programmes and waves, where attrition was significant, the analysis was refined by using inverse probability weights. The SCT programmes provide the same transfer size to a household, regardless of the household size. Therefore, the analysis also included investigating differential impacts by household size for each outcome.

In addition to the RCT, a mixed-methods assessment was used to gauge perceptions, opinions, and experiences of cash transfer recipients and communities. This wider impacts research combined a Quality of Life questionnaire to capture perceptions on well-being with a mix of participatory and qualitative methods among key informants and stakeholder groups.

An influx of cash into a region may influence non-beneficiary households as well, a phenomenon that is estimated through a local economy model. In Zambia, such economy-wide impacts were estimated for the Child Grant using the Local Economy-Wide Impact Evaluation (LEWIE) model, the main parameters of which are described elsewhere in this book.

---

evaluation findings did not significantly influence the SCT programme as it was designed in 2010.

> Box 9.2. Key Features of the Social Cash Transfer Impact Evaluation Methodologies
>
> Longitudinal RCT impact evaluation (2010–2014):
>
> - Child Grant: baseline, and twenty-four-, thirty-, thirty-six-, and forty-eight-month follow-up surveys. Sample size of 2,459 households in ninety CWACs in three districts, of which 1,221 in the treatment group and the rest (1,238) in the control group. Selection into the treatment or control groups was done through a community-level randomization process. The same study households were interviewed in all the five survey waves—a five-wave panel design.
> - MCTG: baseline, and twenty-four- and thirty-six-month follow-up surveys. Sample size of 3,077 households in ninety CWACs in two districts, of which 1,522 in the treatment group and the rest (1,488) in the control group. Selection into the treatment or control groups was done through a community-level randomization process. The same study households were interviewed in all the three survey waves—a three-wave panel design.
> - Evaluation team: American Institutes for Research, University of North Carolina, and Palm Associates.
>
> Research on wider impacts and perceptions, opinions, and views of cash transfer beneficiaries and community members (2012–15):
>
> - 10 per cent inclusive model: 1 round of fieldwork in 2 districts and a control district (2013) and 1 round of fieldwork in 3 districts in 2014.
> - Child Grant: 2 rounds of fieldwork in 2 districts in 2013.
> - Well-being approach using Quality of Life questionnaire and mix of participatory and qualitative research methods.
> - Evaluation team: Institute of Development Studies (Sussex-UK), Rural Net Associates Zambia and University of Zambia.

The purpose of this section is to share the main 'story lines' emerging from the various evaluation reports to gauge the type of change the cash transfer brings into the livelihoods and communities of poor and vulnerable households in Zambia. Apart from representing significant learning about the role of cash transfers in socioeconomic development, these story lines are gradually influencing or appear to have the strong potential to influence the understanding and perception of policy makers on cash transfers. In fact, the nature of findings strongly contrasts with common perceptions of handouts and dependency. Section 9.6 attempts to assess the extent to which the impact evaluations and the nature of their findings have influenced recent policy decisions. Irrespective of the extent to which this was the case, the evaluation findings have an inherent potential to change the narrative around cash transfers. Beyond this, they carry a similarly large potential to ignite a policy discussion around complementary policy and programme interventions that would optimize the impact of transfers and contribute to sustainable poverty reduction.

From the impact evaluation data that are currently available, the following story lines emerge:

9.3.2 Cash Transfers Smoothen the Consumption of Poor Households and Enhance Food Security

The original value of the transfer was set to represent the amount required to purchase, on average since the transfer is a flat rate irrespective of household size, an extra daily meal (maize meal portion) for each household member. The findings reveal that two to three years after being launched, the programme had not only enhanced food expenditure but also expenditure on clothing, health, and transport/communication services (Table 9.1). Further analysis reveals that cash recipients also diversified their diet, consuming more meat, fats, cooking oil, and sugars.

Overall, the food security objective of the cash transfers has largely been achieved under both CG and MCTG models. Table 9.2 shows that significantly more households eat more than one meal per day, and do not consider themselves very poor or severely food insecure as a result of the cash transfers. Besides having a significantly greater food security scale, cash recipients are also more likely to consider themselves better off than they were twelve months before the interview than their non-beneficiary counterparts.

More importantly, however, the findings of all impact evaluations point to the fact that recipient households are able to smoothen their consumption within seasons and between years. This is a critical finding because shocks and instability are the ones that typically sustain the vicious cycle of poverty. The three-wave evaluation of the CG (baseline, twenty-four-month and thirty-six-month) also revealed that many households at some point stop increasing consumption further but instead prefer investing the additional cash in a range of productive and livelihood domains referred to in Section 9.3.4 (American Institutes for Research 2014b, 2014c). Consumption smoothening can be interpreted as a sign of enhanced resilience. Yet, it is important to understand in more detail in what domains investments were made.

The poverty-reducing effects of the cash transfers are also very apparent in both the CG and the MCTG (see Table 9.3). Apart from improving food security, the programmes reduced poverty, albeit predominantly by moving households closer to the poverty line and not above it. This was reflected in greater reductions in the poverty gap than in the poverty head count (Table 9.3).

Table 9.1. Statistically Significant Impact of the CG and the MCTG on Per-Capita Monthly Expenditures (in ZMW)

Outcome variable	CG		MCTG (24-month)
	24-month	36-month	
Total	14.44 (4.82)	10.44 (4.45)	12.29 (3.49)
Food	11.15 (4.68)	7.56 (3.86)	10.75 (3.91)
Clothing	0.84 (5.80)	0.54 (3.43)	0.49 (2.60)
Health	1.02 (4.23)	0.60 (2.17)	1.31 (3.07)
Transport/Communication	0.87 (2.54)	1.14 (3.60)	—

*Robust t-statistics clustered at the CWAC level in parenthesis
Source: American Institutes for Research (2013, 2014a, 2014c).

Table 9.2. Statistically Significant Impacts of the CG and the MCTG on Food Security

Outcome variable	CG		MCTG (24-month)
	24-month	36-month	
Eat more than one meal a day	0.058 (5.12)	0.055 (3.47)	0.113 (4.14)
Ate meat/fish 5+ times last month	—	0.108 (2.22)	—
Does not consider itself very poor	0.293 (5.89)	0.216 (4.59)	0.255 (4.49)
Food security scale	2.310 (3.90)	2.256 (3.36)	1.780 (3.76)
Is not severely food insecure	0.222 (3.98)	0.266 (4.06)	0.117 (2.07)
Better off than 12 months ago	0.459 (10.84)	0.296 (7.40)	0.400 (10.28)

*Robust t-statistics clustered at the CWAC level in parenthesis
Source: American Institutes for Research (2013, 2014a, 2014c).

Table 9.3. Statistically Significant Impacts of the CG and the MCTG on Poverty Indicators

Outcome variable	CG		MCTG (24-month)
	24-month	36-month	
Head count	−0.058 (−3.13)	−0.041 (−2.545)	−0.043 (−2.804)
Poverty gap	−0.108 (−4.47)	−0.084 (−4.66)	−0.079 (−3.64)
Squared poverty gap	−0.106 (−4.13)	−0.076 (−3.92)	−0.074 (−3.52))

*Robust t-statistics clustered at the CWAC level in parenthesis
Source: American Institutes for Research (2013; 2014a; 2014c).

9.3.3 Cash Transfers Stimulate Child Development Although Impacts Are Capped by Supply-Side Constraints

The two evaluations have shown significant impacts on a number of child development indicators. These include, for example, a statistically significant improvement in infant and young child feeding (IYCF) among CG households

Impact Evaluation and Cash Transfers in Zambia 211

Table 9.4. Statistically Significant Impacts of the CG and the MCTG on Children

Outcome variable	CG 24-month	CG 36-month	MCTG (24-month)
IYCF	0.180 (2.99)	0.183 (2.88)	n/m
Material well-being (5–17 years)			
All needs met	0.387 (5.61)	0.297 (5.07)	0.227 (4.52)
Shoes	0.353 (5.19)	0.279 (5.08)	0.226 (4.20)
Blanket	0.149 (5.87)	0.145 (5.04)	0.165 (4.68)
Two sets of clothing	0.083 (4.82)	—	0.048 (2.05)
Currently enrolled (males 7–14)	—	—	0.088 (3.49)
Currently enrolled (females 15–17)	—	—	0.185 (3.10)

Robust t-statistics clustered at the CWAC level in parenthesis
*n/m = not measured
'–' = impact not statistically significant
Source: American Institutes for Research (2013, 2014a, 2014c).

(Table 9.4) although this is yet to translate into significant improvements in the more long-term anthropometric scores. Primary and secondary school enrolment effects were also apparent among boys and girls in MCTG households. However, health and educational effects seem to be capped by supply-side constraints as schools and health facilities are not easily accessible in most study communities.

The results also show that both programmes (CG and MCTG) have had unambiguously positive effects on material well-being among children 5–17 years old (see Table 9.4).

9.3.4 Cash Transfers Allow Poor Households to Invest in Livelihoods and Enhance Resilience

It is clear that the complex interactions of household and individual preferences on the one hand, and the livelihood circumstances and opportunities on the other, have led to important productive and economic impacts of cash transfers among beneficiary households. Compared to households in the control group, cash transfer recipients over a 2–3-year period significantly increased ownership of both non-agricultural and agricultural assets, including livestock (Table 9.5).

In addition, it appears that recipient households invested in crop production and non-farm enterprises, thereby strengthening sources of income. This translated into increased harvests in terms of both quantity and value. The hiring of labour, in particular for labour-constrained households, and the purchase of agricultural inputs such as fertilizer contributed strongly to generating these effects. Finally, recipient

Table 9.5. Statistically Significant Impacts of the CG and the MCTG on Asset and Livestock Ownership

Outcome variable	CG 24-month	CG 36-month	MCTG (24-month)
Non-agricultural asset index	0.416 (6.73)	0.458 (6.05)	0.292 (3.56)
Agricultural implements index	0.230 (2.97)	0.208 (3.01)	—
Livestock index	0.392 (5.13)	0.403 (6.19)	0. 552 (7.82)

*Robust t-statistics clustered at the CWAC level in parenthesis
Source: American Institutes for Research (2013, 2014a, 2014c).

households were able to reduce their debt level and financial dependence. In all, the combined impacts point to strengthened livelihoods and increased resilience to shocks and stress.

9.3.5 Cash Transfer Have Significant Economic and Social Ripple Effects in the Wider Community

One of the key areas of investigation under the SCT impact evaluations in Zambia has been to explore the wider community effects of cash transfers, in both the social and economic spheres. Clearly, there is an unambiguous story of strong economic multipliers as a result of cash transfers. For instance, estimates from a local economy impact model reveal that every dollar worth of cash transfer generates a 0.79 dollar multiplier. Out of this, non-recipient households get a share of 0.62 dollar (American Institutes for Research 2013). Local purchases and enhanced bartering have contributed to an economic stimulus. With the exception of temporary price increases occurring during payment periods, there is no evidence that the cash transfers have led to inflation.

The use of a Quality of Life survey, implemented to assess subjective well-being, confirmed this observation, revealing that non-recipient households in cash transfer communities rated themselves much higher on a goals satisfaction scale than non-recipient households in communities where the programme was not yet rolled out (IDS et al. 2014a).

The understanding of community-wide social impacts of cash transfers is still at an early stage. Qualitative research has demonstrated that recipient households rely less on informal support mechanisms and in some cases brought out a reversal in support patterns. Importantly, the same research has highlighted the connection between poverty and social exclusion. It revealed that the overall improvements in well-being facilitated recipient households to 'reconnect' with the community. On the one hand, this came about by the ability

Impact Evaluation and Cash Transfers in Zambia 213

to pay monetary contributions and hence reconnect with community institutions such as churches or parent–teacher associations. On the other hand, reconnection has a less tangible manifestation, with the cash transfer recipients reporting a feeling of enhanced 'status' and perceptions of being more 'respected' than before by other community members (IDS et al. 2014a).

9.3.6 Impact and Targeting Model

Tables 9.1–9.5 presented impact results that are largely consistent between the CG and the MCTG. Overall, both have had impacts across an impressive range of indicators, covering consumption, food security as well as livelihoods. As such, both grants clearly contribute to the twin objectives of mitigating food insecurity and consumption deficits, and laying a foundation for breaking the inter-generational transmission of poverty by strengthening livelihoods and increasing human capital investment. Figure 9.2 compares the impacts of the MCTG with that of the CG after two years across a range of indicators. Impacts were measured as a proportion of the baseline mean for each individual indicator and are truncated at 2 (i.e., 200 per cent impact). Overall, both programmes have demonstrated impacts across a range of domains of interest to the Government of Zambia. The livelihood-related impacts appear stronger in the CG, but it should be remembered that those households are in a better position to use the cash transfer for productive purposes because of their demographic make-up. The MCTG, meanwhile, has had larger impacts on

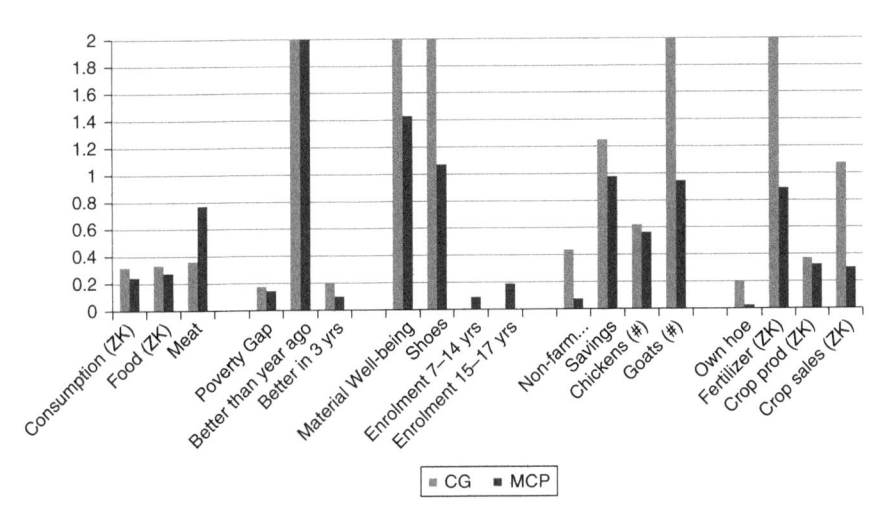

Figure 9.2. Comparison of Impacts between CG and MCTG
Source: American Institutes for Research (2014a).

schooling, again because of the demographic composition of MCTG households, which contain more school-age children. The consumption and food security impacts are comparable—a finding that was expected given that these effects are driven by poverty and both target groups are extremely poor.

9.4 LINKING IMPACT EVALUATION AND POLICY DEVELOPMENT: THE 2013 SCALE-UP DECISION

This section analyses the factors that influenced the Zambian Government's decision in 2013 to scale up the SCTs and explores linkages with the release of findings from the Child Grant impact evaluation. It argues that the impact evaluation definitely contributed to the scale-up decision albeit in a non-linear way. The section first briefly outlines the nature of the scale-up decision. It then describes the range of factors that contribute to it. Finally, it analyses the ways in which the Child Grant impact evaluation has been of influence. Figure 9.3 summarizes the various factors that contributed to the scale-up decision and highlights specific factors related to the Child Grant impact evaluation.

9.4.1 The 2013 Scale-Up Decision

In October 2013, parliament discussed and approved the 2014 government budget, which included a total allocation of ZMW 200 million (about US$33 million) to the SCT programme. The total allocation comprised a donor contribution of approximately ZMW 50 million. For the Ministry, this translated into a 2014 target of reaching 190,000 beneficiary households, up from about 60,000 in 2013. Apart from this leading to a tripling in size of the programme, the meaningfulness of this allocation was also that it represented a sheer eightfold increase in the government budget to the programme—ZMW 150 million, up from ZMW 17.5 million in 2013. The relative size of government expenditure to the total budget of the programme therefore increased from about one-third in 2013 to close to three-quarters in 2014. The donor contribution reduced concurrently.

9.4.2 Factors Influencing the Scale-Up Decision

In retrospect, it is evident that a number of factors came together to drive the scale-up decision. No single factor was by itself sufficient to trigger

Impact Evaluation and Cash Transfers in Zambia 215

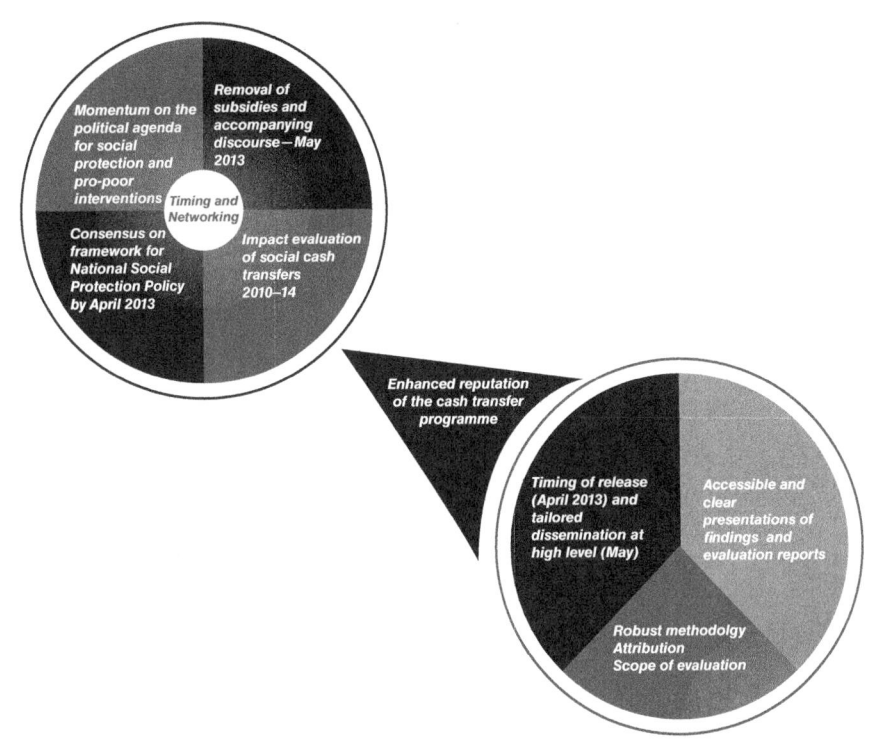

Figure 9.3. Overview of Factors Contributing to the Government's Decision to Scale Up Cash Transfers

the decision. At the same time, the various factors did not contribute to the decision in isolation. Rather, it was their coming together in time that created an environment conducive for an increased budget allocation. This section highlights the (formal and informal) contributing factors which shaped this environment and explains how each relates to the others. Section 9.4.3 will more explicitly delve into the role of the ongoing impact evaluation.

First, the new Patriotic Front (PF) government that had been elected in November 2011 put strong emphasis on social protection approaches to tackle poverty and inequality. Its 2011–16 Manifesto has a dedicated chapter on Social Protection, which announces an NSPP and mentions the importance of increased government budget allocations for sustainability of the cash transfer programme. In fact, the multi-year budget provisions for cash transfers in the 2011–16 SNDP reflect the attempt, at mid-term in 2013, to align Zambia's main socioeconomic planning document to the PF Manifesto.

Second, the scale-up decision was taken in a context of sustained criticism of Zambia's subsidy programmes for fertilizer, maize, and fuel. The regressive nature of these subsidies, whether highlighted through beneficiary or market analyses or under the influence of developments elsewhere in Africa, and the considerable strain they had exerted on the government budget for several years, eventually culminated in the May 2013 decision to fully remove subsidies on fuel and maize and to increase the farmer contribution to subsidized fertilizer. This decision was in line with the new government's *need* to address systematic budget overruns caused by subsidies and *intention* to align public expenditure to its Manifesto, notably with regard to poverty reduction. Importantly, the official communication from State House (the President's Office) that accompanied this decision repeatedly mentioned that this would be an opportunity to channel resources to pro-poor programmes.

Third, driven by the Party Manifesto, the Ministry of Community Development had launched the consultation and drafting process of the NSPP in December 2012. Following a series of consultations within an inter-ministerial Technical Working Group, a policy framework was agreed upon in April 2013 and presented to the Secretary to the Cabinet and a number of permanent secretaries in May 2013. The presentation focused on the opportunities that the comprehensive policy framework presented for enhanced coordination between social protection programmes and for improved efficiency of budget allocations, stipulating the low coverage of social assistance programmes, including SCTs. During this meeting, the Ministry of Community Development also presented findings from the Child Grant impact evaluation and from a World Bank study that revealed the low coverage and targeting challenges of Zambia's main social transfer programmes, including the Farmer Input Support Programme (World Bank 2013).

Fourth, with the previous three factors jointly setting the scene by May 2013, the subsequent months leading up to budget submission to parliament saw a process of intra-departmental advocacy and networking, which eventually resulted in the Ministry of Finance's budget department adopting the budget increase. An important role in the chain of events was played by the Cabinet Office, the Secretary to the Cabinet (who heads this Office) in particular. The latter had a commonly acknowledged favourable attitude towards expanding the social protection interventions of government and a special attention to the social protection policy formulation process, which was ongoing at the time. This confirms the often advanced thesis that major policy shifts require a political 'champion'. In addition to this, and in line with the prominent role of social protection in the Manifesto of the Patriotic Front, some analysts have attributed the 'triggering' of the scale-up decision to the favourable attitude of the president and his willingness to 'push' the social protection agenda. In all, the process culminated in the 2014 budget speech delivered by the Minister of Finance to parliament in October 2013, in which it was announced that 'Government policy is shifting to better designed social protection programmes such as the social cash transfer scheme [which] has proved more effective in targeting the most vulnerable members of our society'

(GRZ 2013). Clearly, this reflected the perception among sections of the political and bureaucratic elite about the effectiveness of the cash transfers. Section 9.4.3 will elaborate further on this.

9.4.3 Role of the Child Grant Impact Evaluation

This section analyses the extent to which the Child Grant impact evaluation influenced and shaped the 2013 scale-up decision.

First of all, it has become clear that the mere fact of having the SCT programme accompanied by a rigorous impact evaluation since 2010 significantly contributed to the enhancement of the reputation and credibility of the intervention among key audiences and stakeholders within the Ministry of Community Development as well as beyond it, including the Ministry of Finance. This has been the case since its launch but came specifically and more prominently to the fore during the period in which the preliminary findings from the twenty-four-month follow-up round on the Child Grant evaluation were released (April and May 2013). The RCT design, the multiple scheduled follow-up surveys, its accessible presentation to various audiences, and the well-explained fact that significant impacts can be attributed to the programme clearly resonated with different government audiences. Without reference to the nature of impacts per se, or the underlying pathways that explain these, the rigorous multi-year methodology design has enhanced the status of the SCT programme and, through this, made it a plausible option for scale-up.

Second, the *scope* of the evaluation has been instrumental in attracting an audience beyond the social welfare sector. In a country where cash transfers are still considered by many officials and policy makers as handouts that help families 'survive' but create dependency, demonstrating human capital but above all productive and local economy impacts—again through using a rigorous and credible measurement approach—has enlarged the understanding of and positive attitude towards the cash transfer programme and its attractiveness as an investment. The release of a comprehensive social protection policy framework, which explicitly reveals linkages between social assistance (e.g., cash transfers) and livelihood and empowerment programmes (including productive approaches) was helpful in understanding these linkages.[4] However, in the light of the above-mentioned official discourse that accompanied the removal of fuel and maize subsidies, it was the emphasis on *poverty impact of cash transfers* that was placed at the centre of the discussion, in terms of both findings highlighted by presenters (researchers first and later the Ministry of Community Development) as well as findings that caught the

---

[4] For instance, the term 'engine of inclusive growth' was used by the Ministry of Community Development when presenting findings from the evaluation.

attention of different audiences in the government, the Cabinet Office, and the Ministry of Finance in particular. A specific policy brief on poverty impact was produced to support this emphasis. And the crux of the accompanying advocacy message used by the Ministry of Community Development was that if current poverty reduction programmes in Zambia are so poorly targeted, there is now strong and reliable evidence that the SCT programme actually *does* reduce poverty and can be scaled up.

Third, though not a deliberate strategy from the outset, the *timing of release of findings* appeared highly strategic to bring together a number of factors and *justify* a solution—scale up the cash transfer programme—to an issue—current poverty reduction interventions do not reach poor people—that had so far only led high-level decision-makers to make statements on channelling more resources to pro-poor programmes. In other words, at a point in time where the political will (through the PF Manifesto), the political requirement (need to invest in well-targeted pro-poor programmes following removal of subsidies), and the new policy framework (the NSPP announced in the PF Manifesto) had created an environment in which investment in a cash transfer programme had become a serious option, the release of evidence that the SCT, using a rigorous evaluation approach, was delivering on poverty reduction may well have been the final piece of the puzzle, convincing the Cabinet Office and the Ministry of Finance to endorse that budget allocation. Timing was crucial in view of the subsidy removal decision (May), the consensus on the NSPP framework (April), and the decision-making month in the budgeting process (June). Although the timing of the former two was not known at the time the preliminary evaluation findings became available (April), as soon as these were adopted, a policy brief and strategic presentations were produced in order to seize the momentum, which could easily be felt by all actors involved. Particularly instrumental was a 'social protection' briefing, by the Ministry of Community Development's Social Welfare Department, for the Secretary to Cabinet, and a number of permanent secretaries from key line agencies. The briefing provided a link between the poverty situation, the targeting deficiencies of current programmes, the new policy framework, the findings from the cash transfer programme, and the options for scaling up social assistance with a focus on cash transfers.

9.5 LINKING EVIDENCE AND PROGRAMME DESIGN: THE 2013 TARGETING DECISION

This section analyses the way in which a 2013 targeting assessment provided evidence that significantly influenced the SCT programme design, with reference to the political economy context. It argues that whereas the Child Grant impact evaluation influenced the broader policy decision to scale up cash transfers in Zambia, it was the 2013 targeting assessment, implemented separately from the impact evaluation, which strongly influenced the programme design. In fact, cash transfers in Zambia in 2014 used the new 'harmonized' targeting model that was adopted following the findings and recommendations from the 2013 targeting assessment.[5] This section will first briefly summarize the main findings from the assessment and then explain how these influenced the design of the SCT programme, in terms of targeting and beyond.

9.5.1 Main findings from the targeting assessment

In terms of targeting design, the 2013 assessment considered existing models (Child Grant, MCTG, and the older Inclusive Model) ineffective in targeting the extreme poor, which has always been the core SCT programme objective: 'The contribution of the criteria to identifying the poorest is negligible since they are only slightly correlated with extreme poverty' (Beazley and Carraro 2013). The study noted that criteria for the inclusive and multiple category models are most in line with people's perceptions about who the poorest are and therefore these schemes were found to be more acceptable. In fact, the study found that communities tend to believe that the extreme poor are those with no or reduced labour capacity. The Child Grant scheme did not correspond to this perception of poverty and hence its acceptability is much lower.

In terms of implementation issues, the three schemes were found to have been adapted to local circumstances and to essentially operate as targeted programmes, often with quota or ceilings, rather than as universal ones (both the Child Grant and MCTG were designed as universal categorical programmes). The selection of beneficiaries relied exclusively on CWACs and other local actors (i.e., headmen) but the involvement of the communities was negligible. The study noted reports that when CWACs had to identify only some of the poorest, they prioritized relatives and neighbours. This undermined the acceptability of the programme.

The study proposed parameters for a harmonized targeting methodology considered more aligned to the objectives of the SCT programme and the local context. A double-screening strategy was proposed with two filters: a categorical eligibility criterion, the intra-household dependency ratio (the incapacitation criterion), and a poverty filter based on selected living conditions

---

[5] At the time of writing, the Ministry was finalizing exit strategies for the Child Grant, MCTG, both introduced in 2010, and the older 10% Inclusive Model that had been used since the 2003 Kalomo pilot.

variables and focused on excluding the better-off. The poverty assessment would be informed by the registration form and implemented through the Management Information System (MIS). The dependency criterion means that households without fit-for-work members and households with dependency ratios of at least three dependents per able body are eligible. The new targeting model had no ceilings as was the case for the inclusive model, which always had a 10 per cent ceiling. It was estimated that at national scale the incapacitation criterion would have a potential coverage of about 25 per cent of the population, with a high proportion of these among the extreme poor. With a poverty filter that would exclude around 5 per cent of the better-off, this gave a target of 20 per cent coverage. This target was adopted by the Ministry and subsequently used in its scale-up plans.

9.5.2 Role of Targeting Assessment in Shaping Programme Design

The discussion about the findings and recommendations from the targeting assessment made it clear that the proposed option of an incapacitated households targeting model resonated very well with the Ministry of Community Development. This was certainly related to the study's finding that the incapacitation criterion constitutes a strong proxy for extreme poverty. Yet, the proposed model also connected well with the prevailing thinking about cash transfers and social assistance in the Zambian political economy, whereby labour constraints are commonly perceived as a cause for poverty and eligibility factor for assistance. In fact, this precisely explained why the Child Grant targeting model was difficult to accept for stakeholders at central as well as at local level—despite the demonstrated impacts of this model. Hence, the readiness of the Ministry of Community Development to adopt, with a few nuances, the targeting model recommended by the assessment report. In retrospect, the use of 'targeting acceptability' as an assessment criterion—besides effectiveness and efficiency—was critical in shaping programme design and in determining the nature of the scaled-up cash transfers in Zambia. The adoption of the new model meant a clear reversal of programme design to bring it in line with initial government preferences, whereas the new targeting models (Child Grant notably) had been influenced by donor preferences.

The targeting assessment also influenced programme design in other ways. Most prominently through initiating a reflection on the role of the CWACs, which play a critical role in programme delivery at the community level. Most notably, the findings on the role of CWACs in identifying poor households in general and the 10 per cent poorest households in particular (under the so-called 10 per cent inclusive model) contributed to a new targeting design in which the CWAC members only identify households that comply with the categorical criteria related to the dependency ratio.

9.6 CONCLUSION AND LESSONS LEARNED

The preceding sections have demonstrated that the evolution of Zambia's SCT programme since the year 2000 has been the subject of a complex constellation of mutually influencing factors. As a result, the development of the programme cannot be characterized as linear or according to plan, even though on an overall basis cash transfers have systematically solidified and expanded their role in the government's response to poverty and vulnerability. What started as a donor-driven district pilot for some 1,200 households has now become a largely domestically financed national programme that is implemented in half of the districts and reached 145,000 households by the end of 2014. This chapter has highlighted that it took up to 2010 for the government to take full ownership of the programme and start financing part of its cost. By that time, the exposure of Ministry officials to the implementation and lessons from the various pilots as well as the evolving regional and global environment in which cash transfers became more commonplace had created a conducive environment to support an expanded roll-out through the introduction of two new categorical targeting models.

In the discussions during the period leading up to the 2010 launch of the SCT programme, findings from (impact) evaluations had not played a significant role. The chapter has highlighted a number of factors that contributed to this lack of uptake. These include issues related to evaluation design (e.g., the absence of a (quasi-) experimental design did not allow attribution of findings), evaluation scope (e.g., too few variables used to capture the range of consumption impacts), evaluation management (e.g., weak connection or coherence between baseline and follow-up), or the presentation and timeliness of evaluation findings. In addition to this, the Ministry was not in charge of the evaluation management and learning process. Based on lessons learned specifically from Zambia but also from other countries, the design and management of the impact evaluations that were launched in 2010 to accompany the new programme have to a large extent addressed these weaknesses. The recent impact evaluations are considered by the Ministry as Government-of-Zambia-commissioned evaluations (even though procured through UNICEF) and the Ministry made a strong contribution to the conceptual framework and the randomization process. The evaluations themselves are characterized by a robust methodology with experimental design, a broad scope, and accessible and concise evaluation reports, which allow for a comprehensive overview of the full range of impacts in the domains of consumption, human capital, livelihoods, production, and economic activity.

The generally acknowledged solid design of the impact evaluations launched in 2010 made them a critical factor in the scale-up plan for the SCT programme. The latter entailed the introduction of two new categorical targeting models, the Child Grant and the MCTG, for which broad support for further scale-up was still required. The impact evaluations were designed in such a way as to deliver credible evidence on the multi-sector nature of the impact of these new targeting models, thereby paving the way for their expansion.

In retrospect, and linking with the main question this chapter aimed to answer, the impact evaluation has definitely changed the status and position of the cash transfer programme in the Zambian political and institutional landscape, a development that was less determined by the nature of specific evaluation findings and more by the overall exposure to evaluation, the credibility it conferred to the programme, the possibility it provided to attribute findings to the intervention, and the discourse that accompanied it. As such, and while the chapter acknowledges and underlines the role of other factors, the impact evaluation could make a contribution to the government's 2013 scale-up decision as it made policy makers more confident about the programme being a credible and solid destination for increased budget allocations. Apart from the specific influence on the scale-up, the various evaluation reports are thought to have enhanced the understanding of cash transfer impacts among a broader audience and made cash transfers more acceptable as part of the policy portfolio to reduce poverty.

The precise influence of impact evaluation on the *design* of the programme is shaped by a number of other factors, in particular in the political economy environment. In this regard, the chapter highlighted the role of targeting assessments and how they interact with prevailing conceptions about 'acceptable' target groups. It is clear that notions of 'deservedness' continue to influence the public acceptance of cash transfers, in particular as these scale up and expand targeted categories. 'Confrontations' with more conservative notions of who deserve to be beneficiaries are more likely to occur as programmes expand across the country and become more visible. Indeed, recent developments in Zambia have confirmed this and given the significance of this issue a brief account is given here about the challenges that occurred towards the end of 2014.

9.6.1 A Few Words on Recent Developments (End-2014)

During the last quarter of 2014 and the first quarter of 2015 a number of developments have emerged that allow further learning about the factors that contribute and impede consolidation and expansion of cash transfers. Although these are recent and ongoing developments, they are worth mentioning since they shed additional light on certain political economy factors referred to in previous sections.

First, the sudden scale-up in 2014 was not followed by further expansion in 2015 as the budget allocation for SCTs remained the same, even declining slightly. Even though the 2015 budget was made in the context of a fiscal shortfall, the factors behind the freeze in expansion deserve to be explored. In theory the freeze in cash transfer spending does not seem to relate to lack of fiscal space for transfers, since the budget allocation to the Farmer Input Support Programme (FISP) increased more than twofold. However, despite its inefficiencies, the FISP occupies a very important position in terms of its political influence, and the two programmes would be considered less interchangeable in practice than an external analysis might suggest. This raises the question of how evidence can further influence the long-range debate on relative importance of budget allocations between transfer programmes, in this case between subsidies and unconditional cash transfers.

Second, and reflecting an equally significant development, the SCT programme targeting model—adopted in 2013—has increasingly been challenged by various stakeholders, including senior government officials, traditional leaders, members of parliament, district councillors, and the general public. Critical articles have appeared in the press. The main concern of these stakeholders relates to the programme enrolling households with a household head who is fit for work. These households qualified for the cash transfer because of their high dependency ratio and poor living conditions. The stakeholders' concern therefore purely relates to an individual, the household head, and her/his ability to work whereas the targeting model identifies labour constraints at the level of the household through the dependency ratio. The community-based targeting model which has for long been used in Zambia did typically target incapacitated individuals (the poor elderly or disabled notably). The observation that targeting outcomes triggered these concerns seems to point to the resilience of the political economy, as reflected in the mindset of a variety of stakeholders carrying strong notions about who deserves to be a beneficiary of cash transfers. The debate raises questions about what drives and what changes perceptions on acceptability, deservedness, and targeting. This is an important area for further research.

When assessing these recent developments in the light of the evolution of cash transfers in Zambia since 2000, the patterns observed seem to be the product of a continuous interaction between impact evidence on the one hand and the political economy on the other. Whether it is the 2013 scale-up decision, the adoption of new targeting models in 2010, or the difficult transition from pilot (before 2010) to roll-out (after 2010), these programme milestones have all been driven by that interaction. And despite it being part of a larger set of influencing factors, the analysis of the evolution of Zambia's cash transfers did show the importance of impact evaluation and as the programme enters a critical stage it cannot be absent from the debate and policy-making process in the years to come.

REFERENCES

American Institutes for Research (AIR) (2013). '24-Month Impact Report for the Child Grant Programme'. Washington: AIR.

American Institutes for Research (2014a). 'Zambia's Multiple Categorical Targeting Grant: 24-Month Impact Report'. Washington: AIR.

American Institutes for Research (2014b). 'Zambia's Child Grant Program: 30-Month Impact Report'. Washington: AIR.

American Institutes for Research (2014c). 'Zambia's Child Grant Program: 36-Month Impact Report'. Washington: AIR.

Beazley, R. and L. Carraro (2013). *Assessment of the Zambia Social Protection Expansion Programme Targeting Mechanisms.* Oxford: Oxford Policy Management and Rural Net Associates.

CSO (Central Statistics Office) (2012a). 'Zambia Labour Force Survey'. Lusaka: CSO.

CSO (2012b). 'Living Conditions Monitoring Survey Report 2006 & 2010'. Lusaka: CSO.

Government of the Republic of Zambia (GRZ) (2013). 'Budget Address by Hon. Alexander B. Chikwanda, MP, Minister of Finance, delivered to the National Assembly on Friday 13 October 2013.

Institute for Development Studies (IDS), Rural Net Associates, Platform for Social Protection, and University of Zambia (2014a). 'Research on the views, perceptions, and experiences of Social Cash Transfer Programme recipients and their Communities: Child Grant study findings'. Sussex: IDS.

IDS, Rural Net Associates, Platform for Social Protection, and University of Zambia (2014b). 'Research on the views, perceptions, and experiences of Social Cash Transfer Programme recipients and their Communities: Report on the 10% inclusive SCT'. Sussex: IDS.

Tembo, G., Freeland, N., Chimai, B., and Schuring, E. (2014). 'Social cash transfers and household welfare: evidence from Zambia's oldest scheme'. *Applied Economics and Finance*, 1(1): 13–26.

Tembo, G., Michelo, S., and Zulu, M. (2009). 'Poverty and Social Transfers in Zambia'. Paper presented at an SACD conference in South Africa.

Tembo, G. and Tembo, A. (2009). 'Food aid, cash transfers, and local markets: evidence from Western Zambia'. *Zambian Journal of Agricultural Sciences*, 9(1): 1–7.

Schuring, E., Michelo, S., and Boonstoppel, E. (2007). 'Final evaluation report: Kalomo Cash Transfer Scheme'. Lusaka: MCDMCH/GTZ.

Seidenfeld, D. and Handa, S. (2011). 'Results of the Three-Year Impact Evaluation of Zambia's Cash Transfer Programme in Monze District: Final Report'. Washington: AIR.

United Nations in Zambia (2013). 'Addressing the multiple dimensions of Poverty and Inequality in Zambia'. *United Nations Signature Issues Series*, 1. Lusaka: United Nations.

Whitworth, A. (2015). 'Explaining Zambian Poverty: A History of (non-agriculture) Economic Policy since Independence'. *Journal of International Development*, 27(7): 953–986.

World Bank (2012). 'Zambia Economic Brief: Recent Economic Developments and the State of Basic Human Opportunities for Children'. Lusaka: The World Bank Group.

World Bank (2013). 'Using Social Safety Nets to Accelerate Poverty Reduction and share Prosperity in Zambia'. Washington: Human Development Department, Social Protection Unit, Africa Region, The World Bank.

10

Zimbabwe

Using Evidence to Overcome Political and Economic Challenges to Starting a National Unconditional Cash Transfer Programme

David Seidenfeld (American Institutes for Research), Lovemore Dumba (Ministry of Public Service, Labour and Social Welfare), Sudhanshu Handa (University of North Carolina at Chapel Hill and UNICEF), Leon Muwoni (UNICEF Zimbabwe), Hannah Reeves (American Institutes for Research), and Elayn Sammon (UNICEF Zimbabwe)

10.1 INTRODUCTION

Zimbabwe's national cash transfer programme, called the Harmonized Social Cash Transfer (HSCT), stands out from other cash transfer programmes in Africa because it started in a highly sensitive political environment, with a compromise government of national unity and immediately following one of the worst economic collapses on the continent. The Zimbabwean economy started showing signs of distress in 1998, plummeting at an accelerated rate between 2005 and 2010. Hyperinflation between 2007 and 2008 reached the highest ever recorded for any country, thrusting a large portion of Zimbabwe into extreme poverty. Zimbabwe experienced negative economic growth from 2000 to 2008 with a GDP (gross domestic product) growth rate of −5.7 per cent. The economy was characterized by an overvalued exchange rate, high unemployment (approximately 80 per cent of the labour force since 2005), an inflation rate which reached 26,470 per cent in November 2007, and a domestic debt in excess of ZW$1 trillion (April 2007). Approximately 80 per cent of the population was living below the food poverty line. The economic situation was worsened by recurrent droughts that reduced agricultural productivity and weakened the central management of social services such as health and education and diminished real per-capita spending in these sectors.

With tensions rising due to disagreements over the Zimbabwean government's decision to redistribute land to the poor and marginalized who had been dispossessed during the colonial era, and the UK and other Western governments' condemnation of the exercise citing allegations of human rights abuses in the forceful manner of the approach, it was generally inconceivable that Western governments and Harare authorities would converge on social protection. During this period political tensions rose between political leaders of Zimbabwe and Western countries, with leaders from both sides publicly admonishing each other's behaviour and policies. Thus, it is quite impressive that amidst these challenging conditions the Zimbabwean government, Western donors including the British government, and UNICEF (United Nations Children's Emergency Fund) collaborated to design and successfully implement a national cash transfer programme.

Evidence, research, and data enabled the stakeholders to overcome the lack of resources and lack of trust that could have prevented the programme's success. The stakeholders used evidence to overcome the lack of resources by demonstrating the effectiveness of the programme to justify why limited funds are a good investment. Stakeholders also used evidence from evaluations to tweak the programme and improve its delivery. Similarly, the stakeholders used evidence to overcome the lack of trust between donors and programme implementers by demonstrating transparency through an independent investigation of the programme. The programme includes four primary monitoring and evaluation activities: 1) a management information system (MIS); 2) A targeting assessment; 3) A rigorous mixed methods impact evaluation; and 4) A process evaluation. Monitoring of the HSCT is conducted through routine field visits undertaken during each payment cycle by UNICEF and the Ministry of Public Service, Labour and Social Welfare (MPSLSW) and an independent end user verification carried out after every payment cycle by a private audit firm, Deloitte Advisory Services. The MIS captures data on all beneficiaries and programme operations such as payments to provide close monitoring of the programme's daily activities. The targeting assessment provides evidence that the programme reaches the intended beneficiaries as defined by the stakeholders, while the rigorous mixed methods impact evaluation measures the effect of the programme on beneficiaries, enabling stakeholders to determine the cost-effectiveness of the HSCT and its impact on beneficiaries. The routine monitoring activities on the other hand provides programme-level evidence that the intended beneficiaries are indeed regularly receiving the cash on time, in the right amounts, and without being intimidated or victimized by those delivering the cash or by other community members including those in positions of power. The monitoring also keeps track of programme processes and adherence to established programme guidelines and protocols.

This chapter describes the design and results of the three primary monitoring and evaluation (M&E) activities that enabled Zimbabwe to successfully implement a cash transfer programme under difficult circumstances. We begin with a brief description of the programme and the steps that led to its creation. We then present the design and results for each research activity, discussing how the activity and its results served to keep the programme on track. The three M&E activities do not operate in isolation, but instead build on and rely on each other, generating a rich set of data and evidence about the programme. Ultimately, Zimbabwe's HSCT stands out as an example of how research and data can help a programme succeed by providing measurable results and transparency to enable stakeholders to make decisions based on evidence instead of ideology or politics.

10.2 THE HSCT PROGRAMME

The HSCT programme, which is positioned to become one of Zimbabwe's primary social protection programmes and a key pillar in its national social protection policy framework, provides cash to the most vulnerable households across the country. The programme targets labour-constrained households that are also food poor. It was introduced in 2011 by the MPSLSW working collaboratively with development partners and UNICEF. It was designed as a child-sensitive social protection programme whose main objectives include enabling beneficiary households to increase consumption above the poverty line, reduce the number of ultra-poor households, and help beneficiaries avoid negative risk-coping strategies. HSCT targets the 200,000 households that are food poor and at the same time labour constrained. By February 2014, 55,509 households in twenty out of sixty-five districts in the country were covered. Figure 10.1 highlights the evolution of the programme and key points in its development.

The households enrolled in the programme are mostly headed by elderly people (61 per cent) and children (3 per cent). Most household heads are female (61 per cent), mainly widows; 81 per cent of the households include children, many of them orphans (20 per cent). Household members are mostly children (62 per cent), elderly (18 per cent), and disabled and chronically ill (19 per cent) (Muwoni et al. 2013, and the food poverty rate is 81 per cent. These statistics show that HSCT reaches the neediest citizens of Zimbabwe, those that are unable to benefit from labor-market-based policies and interventions. Instead of having separate programmes for all the different categories of vulnerable groups like elderly people, disabled people, orphaned children, and people living with HIV/AIDS (Human Immunodeficiency Virus/Acquired Immunodeficiency Syndrome), HSCT covers all these categories focusing on those households that are too poor to care for the needs of their vulnerable members. Eligible households receive unconditional cash payments every other month that range from US$10 (for a single person household) up to $25 per month for households with four or more members).

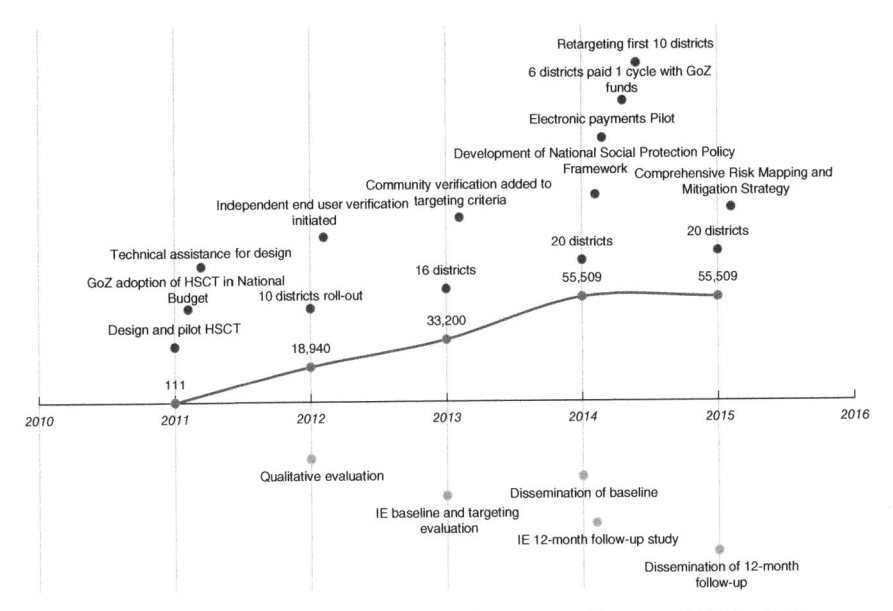

Zimbabwe's Harmonized Social Cash Transfer Programme 229

Figure 10.1. Timeline of Programme Milestones, Roll-out, and IE Activities

The HSCT is jointly funded by the Zimbabwean government and donors, with UNICEF providing additional financial and technical support in addition to managing the Child Protection Fund (CPF). The CPF is the funding mechanism for the HSCT embedded in a single sector policy and budget framework, the Zimbabwe National Action Plan for Orphans and Vulnerable Children (NAP). The Zimbabwean government, through fiscal funding to the MPSLSW, is supposed to match donor funds on a 50–50 basis for direct transfers to beneficiaries; while commitment has been demonstrated in budgetary allocations, actual releases have remained very low or non-existent since 2012 when government started budgeting for the programme. In 2014 for instance, the government budgeted US$3 million with only US$300,000 being released at the end of the year. This of course went a long way in boosting donor and other stakeholders' confidence as it bore testimony to a committed yet resource-constrained government. Indeed the HSCT continues to be a key programme in the government's medium-term economic blueprint, the Zimbabwe Agenda for Sustainable Socio-Economic Transformation (ZIMASSET).

10.3 HISTORY OF HSCT UP TO THE EVALUATION

The economic crisis between 2000 and 2008 had a considerable impact in weakening the rich array of social protection programmes in existence, particularly under social assistance (safety nets including cash and in-kind transfers, public works, fee waivers for health and education, and social care services). Similar negative impacts were felt in social insurance and labour market programmes, particularly those run by the state. The complex political and economic environment was compounded by an HIV epidemic with a 1997 peak prevalence rate of 29.3 per cent, resulting in an estimated 600,000 children orphaned by 2000. The acute economic downturn in Zimbabwe was accompanied by political uncertainty and international development partners' reluctance to engage bi-laterally with the government. The tensions arising out of the fallout on the land reform programme and growing internal strife fuelled by the rise in unemployment resulted in Western countries imposing 'smart' sanctions which they termed 'selective restrictive measures' while the Zimbabwean government considered these outright economic sanctions due to their far-reaching implications on the performance of the economy and Harare's ability to engage with the broader international economy.

The Ministry of Public Service, Labour and Social Welfare (hereafter 'the Ministry')[1] is the statutory authority mandated with implementing public assistance programmes and for the care and protection of children. Together with the National Aids Council and supported by UNICEF they introduced the first Cabinet-mandated NAP in 2004. The implementation mechanism for this government programme was the UNICEF-managed Program of Support (PoS) 2006–2010, a US$ 86 million multi-donor pooled fund which delivered direct support to children through more than 180 non-governmental organizations. By 2009 the receding gains in the education sector resulted in the PoS being expanded in scope specifically to revive government's once flagship BEAM (Basic Education Assistance Module) so that school fees were paid for more than half a million children.

During 2010 a re-designed programme to maintain the transition from emergency towards a national social protection framework in Zimbabwe was adopted in the revised NAP 2011–15 (NAP II). In order to promote child growth and development the NAP II proposed measures to both reduce household poverty through the provision of quality social protection (cash transfers) and deliver other critical child protection services within a national system of Case Management through significantly reduced partnership mechanisms.

In view of continuing donor restrictions on direct budget support to government, partnership with UNICEF remained the development partners' chosen option for maintaining support to the social sector. Commitment towards government leadership for sustainable development in this risk-averse and

---

[1] The Ministry of Public Service, Labour, and Social Welfare is the current name of the responsible ministry, although concurrent with changes in government it has also been referred to as the Ministry of Labour and Social Services.

politically sensitive context challenged UNICEF and partners to find new ways to support the poorest and most marginalized children to realize their rights.

In order to make the case for direct investments in social protection, UNICEF commissioned a 'Child Sensitive Social Protection Thought Paper' (Schubert 2010) to 'clarify the concepts and the terminology related to poverty,[and] vulnerability' and 'briefly analyse the social protection needs of children and other vulnerable groups and households in Zimbabwe'. This was succeeded by a review of past and ongoing and mostly small-scale or time-limited cash transfer programmes in Zimbabwe including lessons learned with regard to targeting, volume, and frequency of transfers, delivery mechanisms, and cost-effectiveness (Schubert 2011. Noting that most of the cash transfer programmes suffer from vaguely defined target groups and use eligibility criteria which may not necessarily be appropriate for identifying the neediest households, this report concluded that well-executed application of a simple well-defined targeting criteria would support a harmonized government system and reach the poorest and most vulnerable including orphans, elderly, and disabled people. The outcomes of both documents contributed to the development of a design document in full collaboration with the Ministry, for a national government-led cash transfer programme which considered risk mitigation through effective programme management. This programme plan proposed targeting labour-constrained and food-poor households and hypothesized that this methodology would corral households caring for the poorest and most marginalized children and HIV-affected families.

In view of the cautious approach being taken by donors, the report also suggested further evidence was needed regarding capacity of the Ministry to manage the programme efficiently and effectively and for CPCs (Child Protection Committees) to support its implementation locally. Two further data gathering exercises were commissioned: 1) DSS (Department of Social Services) Institutional capacity assessment, to assess the institutional capacity of the Ministry's DSS at national and sub-national levels (Wyatt et al. 2010); 2) CPC Rapid Assessment, to determine the numbers and current levels of functioning and capacity of CPCs to fulfil their statutory mandate for child care and protection including monitoring and verification of processes for the social cash transfers (Ministry of Labour and Social Services 2012).[2] Consequently, support for capacity development was included in the design, including provision of vehicles and bicycles to the DSS and CPCs as well as training and supervision support for monitoring and evaluation.

Intrinsic to the programme design, to support both efficiency and risk mitigation, was the concurrent development of an electronic Management

---

[2] This assessment commenced in 2010 and the data contributed to the design of the HSCT; however, the results were officially published in 2012.

Information System (MIS). This database was planned to support not only the cash transfer programme itself, but also to harmonize with the other existing programmes like BEAM and with the capacity to incorporate the Case Management System for child protection which was still under development. In parallel, a draft Manual of Operations for the HSCT was developed. This considered the Ministry emphasis on cost-effectiveness by streamlining targeting, delivery, and administrative procedures. To achieve this, the programme design was made as simple and undemanding as possible in order to function within a framework of limited infrastructure and scarce management resources.

In order to test and further refine the design of the programme, a test run of the whole targeting, approval, registration, and payment cycle as specified in the draft Manual of Operations was implemented in Goromonzi District, chosen because of its proximity to Harare and its mix of urban and peri-urban characteristics. The test run was necessary because the programme design incorporated a number of elements which had not previously been implemented in Zimbabwe. The outcomes contributed to further refinement of the Manual of Operations.

The test run process and results confirmed the effectiveness of the targeting criteria in identifying all vulnerable groups (very poor, children including orphans, elderly, disabled, and chronically ill). It confirmed the capacity of the MIS to effectively assist the targeting, approval, and payment process and to facilitate the analysis of the structure of beneficiary households. The outsourcing of targeting and delivery to private service providers supervised by the Ministry was found to be a feasible and effective mechanism which avoids the complications of community targeting and mitigates the potential for community politics (Schubert 2011).

Prior to moving to national scale, implementation district selection for a planned phased roll-out was considered. Again, related to the highly politicized environment, open and transparent criteria for selection were defined for approval by all of the partners involved. Agreement was reached by development partners, the Ministry, and UNICEF to initiate the programme in the poorest districts; however, this too presented a challenge in defining which those districts were since reliable poverty data was unavailable or outdated. Ultimately selection was made on the basis of triangulated data including the most recent Poverty Assessment Study Survey 2003, the Zimbabwe Vulnerability Assessment Committee Survey 2009, and the National Nutrition Survey 2010. This exercise ranked every district in Zimbabwe and provided the basis for staged implementation. Whilst initially envisaged as a rural programme, this exercise concluded with the inclusion of urban populations in the country's two metropolitan provinces of Harare and Bulawayo in order to assure a level political platform and in recognition of existence of urban poverty.

10.4 MONITORING AND EVALUATION

A monitoring and evaluation framework was developed to provide a structure, rationale, and narrative for monitoring outputs, outcomes, and impact. This framework was intended to ensure that government and donor reporting requirements were satisfied and that value for money could be gauged. It was designed to determine what changes are expected to be observed as a result of interventions and in order that findings can inform further programming and necessary policy reform and therefore required elements of independence and rigour. Three M&E activities were designed for the HSCT: i) MIS; ii) Targeting assessment; and iii) mixed methods impact evaluation including baseline and follow-up surveys.

As mentioned at the beginning of this chapter, the institutional and political environment in Zimbabwe was a key determining factor in setting up a comprehensive M&E framework and plan. Such a plan was seen as key to establishing trust and accountability of resources. The following sub-sections explain some of the key components of the M&E plan, how they served to build trust, and how they were used to strengthen implementation and inform programmatic changes.

10.4.1 MIS

The initiation and roll-out of the HSCT is supported by a vibrant MIS. The MIS serves two purposes, to implement the targeting process and to monitor the activities of the programme by capturing information about who is enrolled, when they are paid, and how much they received. The MIS has also been used to create an integrated case management approach to allow the Ministry to provide households with a suite of services depending on their needs—the 'H' part of the HSCT. Ultimately, the MIS helps stakeholders know that the cash is delivered to the intended beneficiaries in a transparent and unbiased reporting system. The HSCT targets households that are simultaneously food poor and labour constrained. The programme implements a targeting process to identify eligible households. First, census data, including demographic and poverty proxy indicators, are collected on every household in a specified area by ZIM-STATS (Zimbabwe National Statistics Agency). These data are entered into the Ministry's MIS and analysed to determine which households meet both the food-poor and the labour-constrained criteria (see next paragraph). Lastly a verification process is undertaken. The verification which takes cognizance of the importance of community participation in the process is done after the generation of the preliminary beneficiary list. This is done by the district social services officers and the CPCs.

The criteria that households must satisfy to be classified as food poor and labour constrained are defined on page 8 of the HSCT Operations Manual. A household is defined to be food poor if the household members are living below the food poverty line and are unable to meet their most urgent basic needs: they take only one or no meal per day, are not able to purchase essential non-food items such as soap, clothing, school utensils; live on begging or some piece work; have no valuable assets; and get no regular support from relatives, pensions, and other welfare programmes.[3] In operational terms, a household is considered food poor when it meets three or more of the poverty indicators given in Form 1R for rural households and in Form 1U for urban households. This cut-off was changed from 3 to 5 based on results from the baseline targeting analysis (see Section 10.4.3). A household is labour constrained when it has no able-bodied household member in the age group 18–59 who is fit for productive work; one household member in the age group 18–59 years who is fit for work and has to care for more than three dependents (household members who are under eighteen years of age or over fifty-nine or are unfit for work because they are chronically sick, disabled, or handicapped, or are still schooling); or has a dependency ratio between 2 and 3 but has a severely disabled or chronically sick household member who requires intensive care.

Though not normally considered a key element of a strong monitoring and evaluation framework, a sophisticated MIS is able to provide quick, accurate information about the number and characteristics of beneficiaries, payment schedules, and who received payments. This database can be triangulated with independent data gathered directly from households as part of the impact exercise to enhance the overall understanding of programme effectiveness as was done in the HSCT. In the specific context of Zimbabwe, this was an important part of the overall evaluation exercise and lead to immediate improvements in programme design. And the availability of beneficiary information increased the trust and transparency between government and donors that was essential to maintaining support for the expansion of the HSCT.

10.4.2 The Impact Evaluation Design

A rigorous mixed methods impact evaluation was commissioned to provide evidence about how the programme improves the lives of beneficiaries and

---

[3] A household is food poor when the total household expenditure is below the amount required to meet the minimal food energy requirements of the household members (2,100 kcal per adult equivalent). As households always have to spend some of their expenditure on non-food items, food-poor households suffer from chronic hunger and are unable to meet basic needs.

where there is room for improvement. The impact evaluation (IE) was conducted by an independent research team (American Institutes for Research (AIR) and UNC (The University of North Carolina at Chapel Hill)) in order to provide an unbiased and transparent assessment of the programme. The essential design of the quantitative component was a district-matched longitudinal study (a *non-experimental* design). The study compares cash transfer recipient households from Phase 2 districts (specifically Binga, Mwenezi, and Mudzi) with eligible households in Phase 4 districts (Uzumba-Maramba-Pfungwe [UMP] Chiredzi, and Hwange) that do not begin receiving the transfers during the period of the study. The comparison districts were selected by the Ministry to match the treatment districts by agro-ecological characteristics (they neighbour each other), culture, and level of development. The quantitative study included 3,000 households in ninety wards across the six districts, with sixty wards in the treatment sample and thirty wards in the comparison sample. This unbalanced design results from limited resources and time available to conduct targeting in the comparison districts. All wards receiving the HSCT in 2013 were targeted for the programme, regardless of the study, but the comparison wards were only being targeted for the purpose of the study. The qualitative component entailed an embedded longitudinal design, where sixteen households from the quantitative study were chosen for in-depth interviews (IDIs). IDIs were carried for the caregiver (recipient of the cash transfer) and one resident adolescent. Key informant interviews were also conducted at follow-up to understand programme operation and impacts from a broader set of potential stakeholders.

10.4.3 The Targeting Analysis

A targeting analysis was conducted at baseline using the evaluation survey which also incorporated a sample of 900 non-beneficiary households sampled from the targeting census that was conducted to identify eligible households. Data from three sources—the survey of eligible households, the survey of non-eligible households, and the MIS database—were used for the targeting report; the availability of census data from the MIS was extremely useful in helping understand the targeting performance of the programme and again underscores the importance of building a strong, computer-based system at the outset of the programme.

Results from the targeting analysis indicated that the programme's targeting were quite good, especially compared to other programmes around the world. The food poverty rate (individual level) among selected households was 81 per cent, and households appeared to be 'socially vulnerable', those with many adolescents (40 per cent of whom are orphans) and typically headed by an elderly woman who is widowed (37 per cent). These households can be viewed as 'missing generation' households, most likely AIDS affected, in the sense that they are missing prime-age able-bodied workers as a result of AIDS-related mortality. Selected households are significantly different from those of the rural poor in Zimbabwe and of the ineligible households from the same district, leading the report to conclude that the implementation of the labour-constrained criterion on the ground was successful. The unique demographic structure of HSCT households is shown in Figure 10.2, which compares the age distribution of residents in HSCT households (top) with those of the bottom quintile in rural Zimbabwe (taken from the Zimbabwe Demographic and Health Survey (ZDHS)) (bottom panel). There is a clear 'U' shape in HSCT households, with more members below eighteen and over sixty-five and fewer prime-age adults.

The targeting results, especially the comparison with other programmes such as Mexico's Progresa,[4] Colombia's *Familias en Accion*, and the PATH (Jamaican Programme of Advancement Through Health and Education) were extremely important because a key donor, DFID (Department for International Development, UK), felt that targeting was quite bad and threatened to pull funding for the programme in late 2013. A policy note based on the targeting results and incorporating the global evidence (see Figure 10.3) on targeting performance was prepared by the evaluation team at the request of the Ministry to both highlight the strong targeting and place the HSCT experience within a global context. The brief was presented to DFID and allayed their fears of programme leakage.

The targeting analysis also suggested ways to improve the targeting, for example suggesting that the poverty score cut-off be raised from 3 to 5, and that adjustments be made to the proxy means test. The poverty score was immediately changed based on these recommendations, though other changes to the proxy means test have not yet been implemented. The targeting report and associated policy note thus played a key role in influencing an important development partner to continue to support the programme.

10.4.4 The Baseline Report

The baseline survey for the IE was conducted in June 2013 and presented at a national workshop in February 2014. The workshop provided results on the success of the baseline survey, the targeting results described in Section 10.4.3, simulated impacts of the programme on beneficiaries, and simulated impacts of the programme on the local economy (Local Economy-Wide Impact Evaluation (LEWIE)). Collectively these results had an important influence

---

[4] Skoufias, Davis, and de la Vega, S (2001).

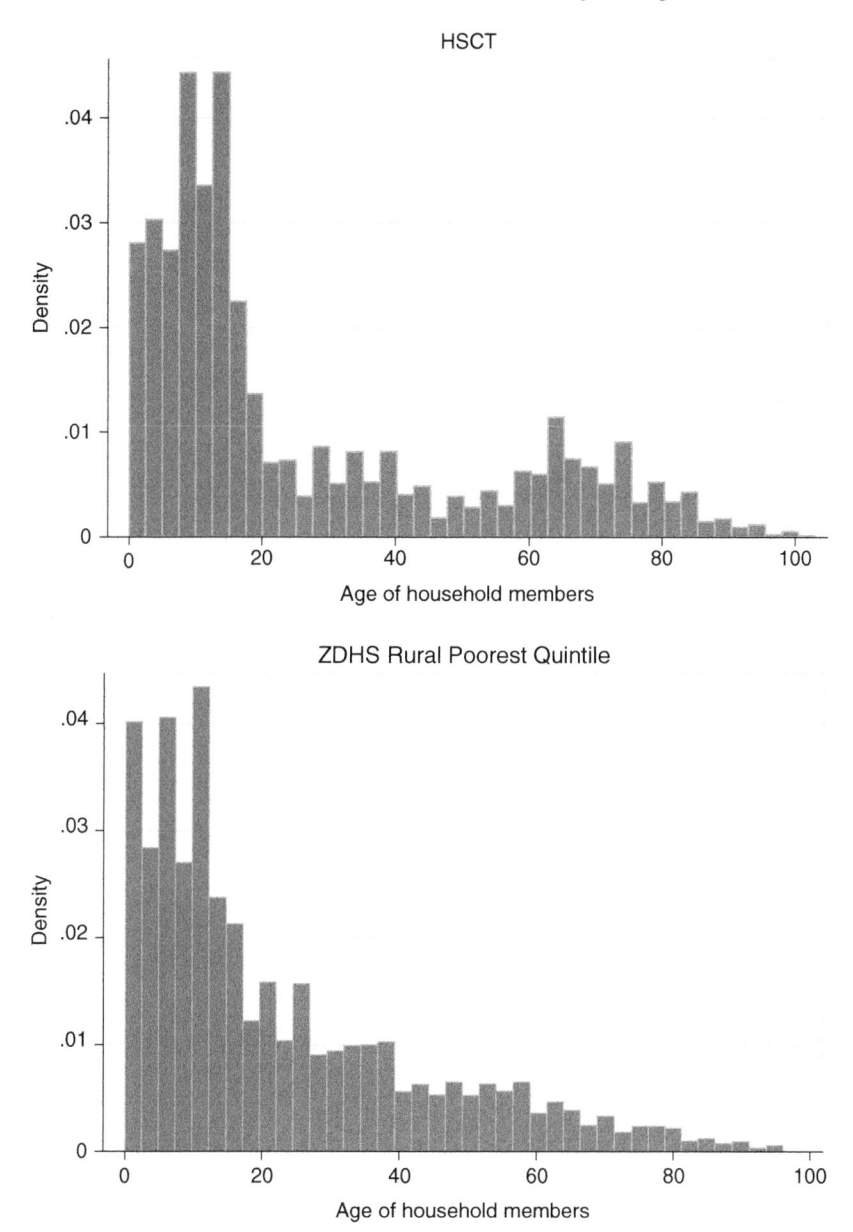

Figure 10.2. Age Distribution of Household Members

on the dialogue between the Ministry, development partners, and the Ministry of Finance. Both sets of simulations showed that the HSCT had the potential for significant positive impacts on both beneficiaries and the local economy. The LEWIE model predicted a potential 1.72 multiplier meaning each dollar

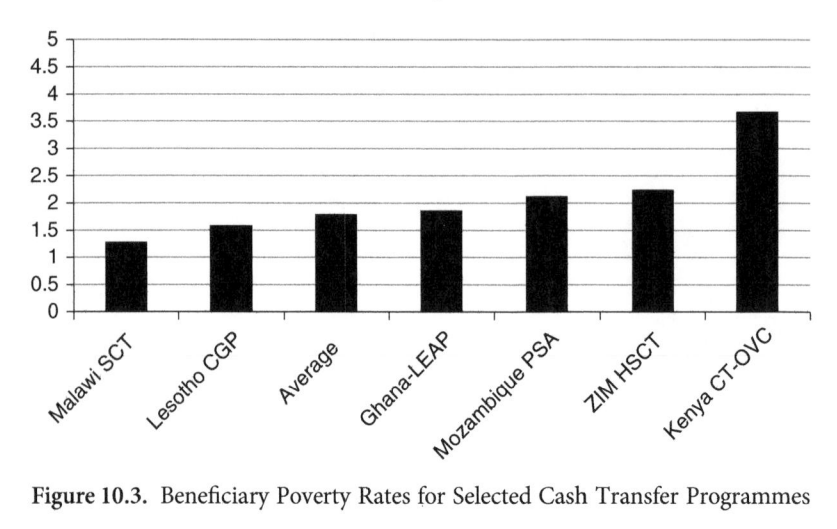

Figure 10.3. Beneficiary Poverty Rates for Selected Cash Transfer Programmes

of transfer would generate 0.72 cents of additional benefits to the local economy, primarily to non-beneficiaries. Similarly, simulated impacts on beneficiaries based on ex-ante income (or expenditure) elasticities showed the programme had the potential to improve food security, consumption, and children's material well-being. These results were summarized and presented to the Ministry of Finance by UNICEF and the Ministry, and resulted in the Ministry of Finance doubling the allocation to the HSCT from US$300,000 to US$600,000 in the subsequent fiscal year.

10.5 THE FOLLOW-UP EVALUATION STUDIES

The follow-up quantitative survey was supplemented by a qualitative study and a process evaluation to understand how the programme was functioning on the ground. Results from these three studies were presented at a national workshop in Masvingo, Zimbabwe, in January 2015. While it is too soon to report on the ultimate influence of these results, we nevertheless describe in Sections 10.5.1 and 10.5.2 the essential findings and the Ministry's response to those findings.

10.5.1 HSCT Process Evaluation

The process evaluation sought to determine fidelity of the programme implementation, in the context of how programme implementation has a strong bearing on the achievement or failure to achieve intended programme impacts. Furthermore, the process evaluation helped stakeholders understand how to scale the programme to larger populations, reproduce the programme in other contexts, and improve the harmonization component of the programme. The methodology adopted for the process evaluation involved a mixed methods approach that included both qualitative and quantitative approaches. Twenty focus group discussions (FGDs) were conducted with community members a year into the course of the HSCT implementation. These FGDs sought to gather information of value in determining how the HSCT implementation conformed to the set protocols of the programme. IDIs were conducted with nine youths and eight caregivers from beneficiary households in Binga and Mwenezi. These IDIs provided pertinent information about beneficiary perceptions and experiences with the HSCT which also informed the process evaluation. Furthermore, eighteen semi-structured interviews were conducted with key informants (community leaders) in the implementing districts and a total of nine staff from the Ministry and UNICEF were also interviewed to gather data of the programme fidelity. The qualitative components of the study were complemented by quantitative analysis of the household survey's Operational Performance Module. The Operational Performance Module included over sixty questions related to programme understanding, the payment process, use of funds, uptake of child protection services, and others. The key research questions were: 1) How was the communication of the HSCT roll-out conducted? 2) How is the Programme understood across the spectrum of the players within the HSCT? 3) What is the extent of HSCT harmonization with the other existing programmes? and 4) How are grievances being handled? The mix of quantitative survey data and qualitative information from interviews and focus groups generated robust process evaluation findings. The qualitative component allowed for in-depth exploration of nuanced issues measured in the household survey.

The results of the process evaluation showed that the Ministry had been generally very successful at implementing the HSCT programme. Survey data indicated that the vast majority of beneficiaries receive the correct amount of money, on time, and regularly, and did not face significant challenges with the payment process. Further to timely and correct payments, the beneficiaries considered the programme eligibility criteria to be fair. The programme communication strategy of having a pre-cash disbursement speech which outlined the key programme objectives and design was also viewed as having a contribution to the beneficiaries understanding of the programme.

The HSCT process evaluation also identified a few areas that required strengthening and the bulk of the session at the 2015 workshop was spent discussing these shortcomings among the district officers. The key areas for improvement included weak harmonization of the HSCT with other social programmes, underdeveloped HSCT grievance handling procedures, and inconsistent HSCT communication across the headquarters, provincial, district, and community levels.

While the design of the HSCT underpins the centrality of harmonization of the HSCT with existing social and protection services, results from the process evaluation pointed to some deviations from this ideal. The process evaluation survey data revealed that beneficiaries and implementing partners did not fully understand this programme objective and instead believed that HSCT beneficiaries are ineligible to receive other assistance programmes. This misconception ran counter to the very objectives of the HSCT (to harmonize assistance to Zimbabwe's neediest) and had the potential to undermine the programme's positive impact. Perceptions of social justice and the need to spread benefits across vulnerable households were viewed as impeding the goal of harmonization. Relatedly, the link between the HSCT and child protection services was also noted to be weak. Children in HSCT beneficiary households were found to be not deliberately targeted with child protection services. To correct this trend, the DSS, as part of programme refinement, resolved that the DSS cash delivery teams would be supported by the DCWPS (Department of Child Welfare and Probation Services) officers at all pay points to deliberately identify and respond to child protection issues. This resolution is expected to improve the provision of child protection services to the HSCT households.

The second key weakness identified was the HSCT grievance handling procedures. As few as 30 per cent of the beneficiaries reported being aware of someone to contact if they have problems with payments or any other aspect of the HSCT. The HSCT Operations Manual appeared to be weak in presenting a comprehensive grievance response mechanism, and a review of the inbuilt mechanism of having a complaints desk at each pay point (as per initial design) was also considered insufficient. At the workshop it was agreed to set up a neutral grievance handling procedure that did not place the DSS officer as the key arbiter in grievances that might ordinarily be directed against the system that the DSS officer managed.

The process evaluation gathered information on how the programme staff, especially at the district implementation level understood the programme and the effects of this understanding on implementation. Findings from the evaluation pointed to how the communication was mostly top-down, with the HQ providing direction to the Districts, while district staff indicated that information was mostly confined to the HQ, limiting the potential and opportunities for low level staff to contribute, laterally, to clear understanding of the programme at the district level. While there was consensus at the workshop that this was an issue, there was no immediate action plan developed to address the problem.

10.5.2 Impact Evaluation

The quantitative evaluation investigated the impact of the HSCT on a wide range of economic and social domains of beneficiary households. Two contextual features of the programme and the study are important to understand when interpreting the results. First, while other Transfer Project evaluations measured impacts after two years this study was done after only one year. This shortened timeline gave less opportunity for recipients to understand and internalize a change in their permanent income because they had only received five or six payments while changes in permanent income are typically what induce permanent shifts in consumption and other long-term behaviours. As a result, the evaluation showed behaviour patterns that were more similar to people who receive acute and 'transitory' injections of cash into the household, such as debt reduction and large item purchases for investment. Secondly, 50 per cent of recipient households had more than four residents—for these households the transfer was a flat $25 and there is a significant difference in the per capita value of the transfer between small and large households ($4.1 versus $7.50). Finally, as highlighted by the Process Evaluation, the harmonization feature of the HSCT was not implemented and in fact the opposite occurred with other programmes purposely distributed to other households to 'spread the wealth'.

The overall results of the twelve-month evaluation, summarized in Table 10.1, were consistent with these contextual and institutional features. Impacts on consumption were mostly found for small households, and in fact, across most domains studied, there were often positive impacts among smaller households and no impacts on the full sample or among larger households. This pattern was true, for example, for food poverty rates, diet diversity, subjective welfare, school attendance, asset ownership, and exposure to shocks. The impacts on consumption for small households were quite prominent, but for large households were relatively small compared to other cash transfer programmes. Meanwhile the programme increased livestock holdings (goats, donkeys) and reduced debt exposure—such lumpy spending typically occurs when households receive a perceived 'windfall' in their revenues. The decrease in debt, the average increase of eight goats per household, and the increase in consumption together 'accounted' for the average size of the transfer received by households over this period. These were deemed to be important and meaningful impacts given the short evaluation window.

Three key aspects of the results were of particular interest at the workshop and garnered much discussion and proposed actions. First and foremost was the result that secondary school-aged children in the HSCT saw a reduction in their access to BEAM of 6 percentage points (pp). This 'negative' impact of the

Table 10.1. Summarized Key Impacts of Zimbabwe HSCT

		Impact Evaluation Cash Transfer Results, Small and Large Households		
		Programme Impact	Small Households HH Size ≤ 4	Large Households HH Size > 4
Food Consumption and Household Welfare				
Subjective Well-being (SWL)		1.13**		
Headcount—Food poverty line		−0.10*		
Diet diversity score		0.70***		
Experience of any shock			−0.13*	−0.02
Proportion owning agricultural assets	Hoe	−0.94		
	Sickle	10.06**		
Percentage of households raising or owning livestock	Goats		8.07	9.22*
	Donkeys, mule		3.81*	1.13
Debt	Amount of credit outstanding	−17.19**		
Schooling				
School attendance	Primary Attendance	−0.04	0.01	−0.05*
	Secondary Attendance	−0.07**	−0.25***	−0.02
School enrolment	Enrolment in primary	0.01	0.05	−0.00
	Enrolment in secondary	0.03	0.05	0.06
	Grade progression primary	0.01	0.07**	−0.02
	Grade progression secondary	−0.02	0.02	−0.04
BEAM Scholarships	Received BEAM primary	0.00		
	Received BEAM secondary	−0.06**		
HIV-Related Risk Behaviour				
Sexual debut (had sex)	Age 13–20		−0.14**	−0.13**
Adolescent marriage and co-habitation	Age 12–20		−0.04	−0.02**
Adolescent pregnancy	Female aged 12–20		0.01**	−0.03*
Condom used at first sex	Age 13–20		−	0.22*
Ever experienced forced sex	Age 13–20	−0.03**	−	−0.03
Physical Violence				
Experienced physical violence, last 12 months	Age 13–20		0.39*	0.11
Slapped/pushed, last 12 months	Age 13–20		0.34*	0.12

Notes: ***p<0.01, **p<0.05, *p<0.1

programme on BEAM receipt was fully attributed to the actions at local level to distribute scarce resources across as many households as possible (also highlighted in the process evaluation), and so those receiving the HSCT were less likely to also get BEAM. This of course was in direct contrast to the stated Ministry policy. The key operational challenge was that BEAM targeting was community-based and done independently of HSCT targeting, and so district and provincial officers could not dictate who should get BEAM at the community level. As a result of this behaviour, the HSCT showed no positive impact on school enrolment at the secondary school level (though there were positive impacts at primary level). The evaluation thus highlighted a key implementation issue that led to an open discussion within the Ministry (at the workshop) on possible responses.

The second key results area was on resiliency (that is, the capacity of households to withstand or recover from a shock). The evaluation results showed that after only twelve months the HSCT was already enabling households to strengthen their resiliency. Specifically, the programme led to improvements in a number of domains that are typically associated with strengthening resiliency, including increased agricultural assets (hoes, sickles) and livestock (goats, donkeys), diversifying income sources (different cropping patterns, more non-farm enterprises), and a reduction in debt (improvement in credit market position). The programme also lead to a reduction in exposure to shocks among smaller households, a somewhat surprising result given that the most important shocks faced by households were covariate shocks such as price increases, crop failure, and drought. Nevertheless, given that the programme had only been operating for one year in the evaluation sample, there were clear positive indications that the HSCT was helping households become more resilient. These results were thought to be quite important for advocacy among both development partners and also within government itself, and a series of steps were discussed in order to disseminate these particular set of results to various stakeholders.

The third major set of results that attracted attention at the national workshop were those related to adolescent development—the Zimbabwe evaluation is one of four Transfer Project evaluations that include a special adolescent module. After only twelve months of operation, the results suggested that the HSCT was supporting the safe transition to adulthood through a number of different domains, including delaying marriage and sexual debut, as well as decreasing the likelihood of early pregnancy among female youth in large households. In addition, the programme positively impacted safe sex practices among sexually active youth (i.e., condom use at first sex) as well as decreased the probability of lifetime reports of forced sex. A particularly noteworthy aspect of the results was the heterogeneous impact by sex of the youth and the household heads. In nearly all cases where significant positive impacts were found, these were driven by samples of female youth and female-headed households.

The Zimbabwe evaluation is the only Transfer Project study that explicitly asked about violence among young people, using a set of questions taken from the Zimbabwe Violence Against Children survey. Surprisingly, the evidence showed increased reporting of violence among HSCT youth relative to those in the comparison areas, a result driven by the least severe form of violence reported on (slapped/pushed). This violence was driven by authority figures, with an interesting decline in violence perpetrated by peer among the treatment group. The discussion around this unexpected result cantered around the fact that violence awareness campaigns had been running in treatment areas as part of a package of complementary child protection interventions, which may have resulted in increased awareness and sensitivity to physical violence; such increased awareness typically leads to increased reporting though the underlying incidence itself remains the same. It was decided that the evaluation team would be provided a list of child protection interventions for each ward in the study areas to see if these could account for the increased reporting of violence in treatment areas.

A final key decision taken at the evaluation workshop was to postpone the next round of data collection to 2016 (thirty six months after baseline) rather than conduct it in June 2015 in order to give the Ministry time to adjust the implementation of the programme in response to the results of the evaluation, particularly the harmonization aspect, but also the communication and grievance components.

10.6 CONCLUSION

So what lessons can we draw from Zimbabwe on the interface between evidence generated by the evaluation on the one hand, and programming and policy on the other hand? While the IE is still ongoing, there are already some clear examples of how evidence fed directly into programme design and in defending the programme in the face of criticisms. And a key lesson here is that ancillary evidence and studies that do not have to do with impacts per se but which are generated from evaluation data or from the evaluation exercise as a whole can play an important role in advocacy and policy. This is certainly the case with the process evaluation of the HSCT programme which is already affecting policy.

In the Zimbabwe case, the targeting study, which used baseline evaluation data as well as data from the MIS, was crucial to building confidence among the development partners that leakage rates were acceptable and that the programme's targeting was robust. This study also fed into an immediate decision to improve the targeting performance by adjusting the poverty cut-off score. Finally, a series of simulations using baseline data also played a key role in allowing UNICEF and the Ministry to advocate for more resources from the Ministry of Finance. The LEWIE simulations showed an important multiplier effect on the local economy ($1.72) while econometric simulations showed large impacts on food security and children's material well-being.

At the time this chapter was written, the initial twelve-month evaluation results (including both impact and process evaluation data) had just been presented to the Ministry and stakeholders, and provided some clear areas for programme improvement, especially around harmonization. It is of course too early to tell whether this will lead to actual changes in programme implementation, but the Ministry has recognized this as a problem, a necessary first step towards change. Moreover, it was only through a comprehensive, mixed methods external evaluation that the challenges with harmonization (a crucial component of the HSCT) were exposed and elucidated.

Perhaps the biggest lesson from the Zimbabwe case is how a rigorous evaluation, including the entire suite of ancillary studies that emanated from the evaluation exercise, served as a vehicle to build trust and accountability among key stakeholders (development partners and government) within a politically tense atmosphere. As stated in the beginning of this chapter, the existence of a credible evaluation allowed all parties to base their discussions and dialogue around a strong and indisputable evidence base, rather than assertions or anecdotes. In that sense, then, the evaluation initiative in Zimbabwe has been an essential component to solidifying and expanding the HSCT. Further, the evidence base generated through the research and evaluation of the HSCT better positions the programme to fine-tune service delivery and continue to receive financial support for programme operations.

Moving forward, the Zimbabwe government hopes to continue expansion of the HSCT if they can secure funding from donors. The results from the evaluation will help the government solicit funds as they have demonstrated the ability to successfully implement the programme and have begun to see promising results. The research study will continue with a second round of data collection planned in 2016 to measure the three-year effects. The next round of the study will help the government and stakeholders understand the longer-term impact of the programme and learn how the effects of the programme evolve over time, especially since the twelve-month results occurred after only six bimonthly payments. Everyone is excited to see how this successfully implemented programme can help improve the lives of poor and labour-constrained households in rural Zimbabwe.

REFERENCES

Ministry of Labour and Social Services (2012). 'Rapid Assessment of Child Protection Committees in Zimbabwe'.

Muwoni, L., Sammon, E., Rumble, L., Mhishi, S., and Schubert, B. (2013). 'Building Resilience to Environmental Shocks and Hazards: Zimbabwe's Harmonized Social Cash Transfer (HSCT)'.

Schubert, B. (2010). 'Child Sensitive Social Protection Thought Paper'. UNICEF.

Schubert, B. (2011). 'Lessons Learned from Ongoing Social Cash Transfer Programmes in Zimbabwe'. UNICEF.

Skoufias, E., Davis, B., and de la Vega, S. (2001). 'Targeting the poor in Mexico: an evaluation of the PROGRESA selection mechanism'. World Development, 29(10): 1769-84.

Wyatt, A., Mupedziswa, R., and Rayment, C. (2010). 'Institutional Capacity Assessment: Department of Social Services, Ministry of Labour and Social Services: Zimbabwe: Final Report'. UNICEF—Ministry of Labour and Social Services.

11

Does Evidence Matter? Role of the Evaluation of the Child Grants Programme in the Consolidation of the Social Protection Sector in Lesotho

Luca Pellerano (Oxford Policy Management), Silvio Daidone (FAO), Benjamin Davis (FAO), Mohammad Farooq (UNICEF), Mariam Homayoun (Delegation of the European Union to Lesotho), Andrew Kardan (Oxford Policy Management), Malefetsane Masasa (Ministry of Social Development of Lesotho), Ousmane Niang (UNICEF Lesotho), Bettina Ramirez (UNICEF Lesotho), and Naquibullah Safi (UNICEF Lesotho)

11.1 INTRODUCTION

In spite of sustained growth—at an average annual 3.9 per cent rate over the past two decades (World Bank, 2013)—the triple threat of poverty, the HIV (Human-Immunodeficiency Virus) epidemic, and chronic food and nutrition insecurity has dealt a serious blow to the survival, development, and protection of the most vulnerable in Lesotho. Poverty rates remain high—57 per cent of the population are estimated to live below the basic needs poverty line—and income distribution is highly unequal (Government of Lesotho, 2013). With growth concentrated primarily in the textile, mining, and public sector, agriculture has lagged behind in a context, where about 90 per cent of the farmers depend on subsistence agriculture for their livelihoods. Between 10 and 30 per cent of the population suffers from food insecurity and poverty rates in rural areas are about double that of urban areas (Ministry of Health and Social Welfare, 2009). The additional burden of AIDS (Acquired Immunodeficiency Syndrome) falls disproportionally on women and the elderly, who care and provide for sick relatives and orphans. HIV/AIDS prevalence in Lesotho is estimated to be the second highest in the world, and one out of three Basotho children have been left orphaned as a result of the epidemic (UNICEF, 2011a).

In response to the challenges of poverty, vulnerability, and social exclusion, the Government of Lesotho (GoL) indicated in the National Strategic Development Plan 2012–17 its commitment to promote social protection. Spending on social protection grew remarkably in recent years. The country spends about 9.6 per cent of GDP (gross domestic product) on transfer programmes, well above the 1–2 per cent allocated by most developing countries (Grosh et al., 2008; Gentilini et al., 2014). However, almost 93 per cent of resources is taken up by three programmes only: the Old Age Pension (OAP), school feeding, and tertiary bursary (WB, 2011).

One recent intervention in the social protection landscape is the Child Grants Programme (CGP): an unconditional cash transfer programme targeted to poor and vulnerable households. By providing beneficiary household quarterly payments of between M360 (US$30) and M750 (US$65),[1] the primary objective of the CGP is to improve the living standards of Orphans and other Vulnerable Children (OVC) so as to reduce malnutrition, improve health status, and increase school enrolment among OVC.

The introduction of the CGP in 2009, and subsequent takeover by the GoL, has been an important element of recent progress towards a systemic and inclusive social protection system. A brief recollection of the history of the CGP reveals a process of change that was unanticipated by many. In a relatively short period of time the CGP went from a small-scale donor-led pilot to a national programme with strong government ownership and solidly embedded into a national policy. The process of consolidation involved a significant expansion of coverage, an increase in domestic funding, and the creation of institutional capacity and operational systems, as well as favoured the elaboration of a new policy framework. The establishment of a Ministry of Social Development (MOSD) in 2012 was a significant milestone and achievement, signalling strengthened government ownership and leadership of the sector. A new National Social Development Policy (NSDP) as well as a National Social Protection Strategy (NSPS) that recognize CGP as an important component of the national social protection system were approved on 14 December 2015 by the GoL with support from UNICEF (United Nations Children's Fund) and the European Union (EU).

---

[1] The transfer value for CGP was originally set at a flat rate of M120 per month per household and was disbursed every quarter. Effective from April 2013 the cash transfer has been indexed to number of children as follows: (1) Households with 1–2 children M360 quarterly; (2) Households with 3–4 children M600 quarterly; and (3) Households with 5 and more children M750 quarterly.

As many programmes of similar nature in the region, the implementation and progressive expansion of the CGP was accompanied by a comprehensive evaluation that was set from the early stages of the pilot implementation. The objective of this learning agenda was to document independently and rigorously the impact of the programme on the ground and generate evidence to improve its effectiveness and efficiency. Rather uniquely in the region, the conditions allowed for an experimental quantitative evaluation to be conducted in Lesotho, accompanied by extensive qualitative research focusing both on implementation and impact dimensions, as well as general equilibrium modelling of local economy effects, a rapid appraisal, and a costing feasibility study.

But what was the role—if any—of this ambitious learning agenda in achieving the aforementioned high-level policy progress? Were the evidence and evaluation results generated throughout the life of the CGP the main driver of key decisions leading to its expansion and embedding into government policy? Or what other factors influenced change? And did the evaluation results effectively contribute to making the CGP a better functioning programme?

This chapter analyses the conditions that made it possible for the CGP to be consolidated from a pilot into a nationally owned social protection programme in such a short spell of time, and how this process of change was interweaved with the results emerging from the evaluation.

11.2 THE CONTEXT: EVOLUTION OF THE CGP—FROM PILOT TO POLICY

The CGP has been praised for its extraordinary evolution from a small donor-funded pilot, into a public-owned national programme in a relatively short period of time. By undertaking a review of key milestones along the course of development of the CGP (see timeline in Figure 11.1), this chapter provides an overview of the efforts of all stakeholders involved, the technical challenges they faced, and their response to ensure the financial and operational sustainability of the programme.

11.2.1 The Genesis of the Child Grants Programme (2005–2009)

The CGP originated from a four-year project funded by the European Commission (EC) in response to the HIV/AIDS pandemic and the increasing number of OVC in Lesotho. At the end of 2005 the EU commissioned a consultancy mission in order to assess the HIV/AIDS response and suggest possible courses of action for an EDF (European Development Fund 9) funded

250   *Luca Pellerano et al.*

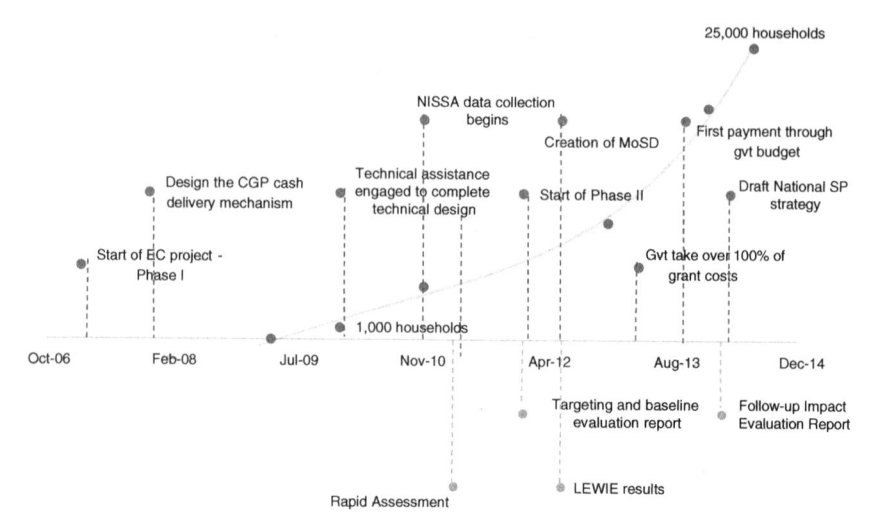

Figure 11.1. Child Grants Programme Timeline

Timeline events:
- Oct-06: Start of EC project - Phase I
- Feb-08: Design the CGP cash delivery mechanism
- Jul-09: Technical assistance engaged to complete technical design; 1,000 households
- Nov-10: NISSA data collection begins; Rapid Assessment
- Apr-12: Creation of MoSD; Start of Phase II; Targeting and baseline evaluation report; LEWIE results
- Aug-13: First payment through gvt budget; Gvt take over 100% of grant costs
- Dec-14: 25,000 households; Draft National SP strategy; Follow-up Impact Evaluation Report

initiative. Within the framework of the EU's priority focus areas, OVC support was identified as one of the HIV/AIDS-related fields where government's response was most lacking.[2]

In March 2007, the EU and UNICEF signed an agreement to implement a response. The main focus of the project was to build capacity in caregiver groups, to enable them to support OVC, including psycho-social support, HIV/AIDS prevention, and access to small grants for material support (Kardan et al., 2011). It was the small grants for material support through a network of caregivers that quickly evolved into a pilot cash transfer programme: the CGP.[3]

The first CGP payment was made in April 2009 in a single community council, with two additional councils being added in October for a total of three pilot councils.[4] A very slow onset undermined the confidence in the

---

[2] The GoL's response to OVC needs had been embodied in the National AIDS Strategic Plan of 1999 and the 2006–2010 National OVC Strategic Plan, but had been limited, fragmented, and lacked sufficient focus as a result of institutional weaknesses. An OVC Rapid Needs Assessment conducted in 2005 corroborated findings of other studies, which among other things, indicated that only 25 per cent of OVC households received some kind of support (UNGASS, 2005).

[3] Following a commissioned study (Samson et al., 2007) that provided a set of design recommendations on how to design the programme.

[4] Households caring for children under eighteen were selected using a community-based targeting approach that identified the poorest amongst them. Beneficiaries subsequently received a transfer of M360 (approximately the equivalent of US$40, the exchange rate at the time) on a quarterly basis.

wider EU project and the move to complete the four-year targets was driven primarily by the CGP's rapid expansion.[5] By January 2010, the CGP had expanded to six community councils, reaching 1,250 households caring for over 2,700 OVC.

11.2.2 Systems Building (2010–2011)

At the time, the CGP was housed at the Department of Social Welfare (DSW) within the Ministry of Health and Social Welfare (MOHSW). As the programme gained momentum, UNICEF engaged international technical assistance to support implementation and capacity building. The technical assistance was contracted in early 2010 to complete the technical design and strengthen operational systems. Subsequent to roll-out in further communities, the programme was reviewed in March, leading to a substantial redesign of its parameters (Ayala Consulting, 2010).

The priority in 2010 was thus devoted to strengthening and completing the programme's design through the development of technical guidelines and a Management Information System (MIS). At this stage the CGP adopted a novel poverty targeting system, moving from a pure community-based system to a combination of community validation and a proxy means-testing (PMT).[6] It was also suggested that the CGP's revised targeting approach could be used to establish a National Information System for Social Assistance (NISSA) (see Box 11.1). The redesign also contemplated the commissioning of an articulated evaluation strategy.[7]

The redesigned programme was rolled out in September 2011. By the end of that year—the end of Phase I—the CGP was present in twenty-one community councils, supporting almost 10,000 households caring for 27,737 children. All the expansion activities helped staff gain familiarity with the pilot's

---

[5] The first two years were spent almost exclusively on preparatory activities. Project staff was recruited at central and district levels of government and two studies were commissioned, one on cash delivery mechanisms and a second to develop an implementation plan.

[6] While previously existing programmes—most notably the OAP—were perceived to have positive outcomes and enjoy strong popular and political support, some studies indicated that the majority of the transfers are received by people who are not among the extreme poor (World Bank, 2011).

[7] An Organizational Development Strategy was also completed and demonstrated that the Department of Social Development would not be able to deliver effectively on its mandate unless its capacity was substantially improved at national and district levels (Ministry of Social Development, 2010). As an interim measure to assist the DSW to support the implementation of project activities, several temporary staff positions were funded to work mainly on the implementation of the CGP. The programme also used collaboration with civil society organizations—specifically World Vision International (WVI)—to organize and train Village Assistance Committees (VACs) in all beneficiary villages.

objectives, scope, tools, and procedures and by the start of 2012 the implementing capacity had considerably improved.[8]

Box 11.1. Building a Registry for Social Assistance Programmes in Lesotho

Although Lesotho has a number of social assistance programmes, traditionally they had been provided on a universal basis (e.g., OAP, school feeding, etc.). Programmes like the OVC Bursary had the goal of targeting the neediest, but had no formalized processes for doing so.

In this context, the introduction of the CGP's poverty targeting design was a first attempt to structure the poverty targeting process in a way that it could be applied and replicated at a national scale. It was planned that the programme would contribute to creating a national registry to identify the extreme poor which other social assistance initiatives could also access for targeting. This is what came to be known as the National Information System for Social Assistance (NISSA).

Socio-economic information of all households in a given area is collected and fed into the NISSA, the NISSA then filters household with children and applies a PMT formula that ranks each household according to a poverty score. As part of a separate exercise a VAC also selects poor from the household list generated through the NISSA (without knowing the PMT outcome). Only households identified through both means are invited to enrol in the programme.

NISSA data collection and the field supervision of the community validation process was outsourced to WVI due to the GoL's weak administrative capacities. This was instrumental for NISSA expansion, which to date has achieved a coverage of 103,000 households (approximately 25 per cent of all households) in all ten districts of the country.

11.2.3 Phase II—Government Takeover (2012–2014)

The focus of Phase II (2012–2014) was primarily on completing implementation of targets and then transitioning the full management and ownership of the CGP from UNICEF to the GoL. During Phase I, government ownership of the project was slow to develop, despite the participatory approach adopted,

---

[8] Still, the increasing complexity of processes and rapid growth of the programme's coverage continued to challenge the staff's capacity at all levels. At local level, implementation was constrained by the difficulty in recruiting and retaining experienced staff. At the central level, particularly, a lack of leadership, weak advocacy for the project, and inability to coordinate with other initiatives became apparent. At the policy level, lack of coordination between decision-makers and key top-tier stakeholders was also identified as a major limitation to the effective implementation of the CGP.

and the project was quite strongly supply driven. DSW was still dependent on short-term, project-funded positions to carry out its core CGP responsibilities; plans had been made to identify permanent staff to gradually replace the temporary positions but full implementation had not occurred. This raised a significant concern for the sustainability of the CGP and its district level implementation activities (UNICEF, 2012).

The CGP was only operational on a pilot basis and still needed to be more firmly embedded as a major element in the GoL's overall approach to social protection. The final EU project evaluation conceded that it was a huge challenge for the DSW to move from its current position to assume complete responsibility for the CGP in a period of three years (Thomson and Kardan, 2012). Yet a very rapid transition towards increased government ownership was fuelled by significant changes at three levels.

11.2.3.1 Creation of the MOSD

In 2009, a motion was tabled in parliament calling for the transitioning of the DSW into a standalone accountable unit separate from the MOHSW.[9] UNICEF assisted the DSW in identifying strategies for strengthening institutional and organisational arrangements, focused on realignment of standing social welfare activities and an appropriate functional arrangement, including a view on the option of setting up a standalone institution.[10] Further, the DSW commenced the process of developing a policy on social development, reflecting the change from a traditional welfare approach to a social development one.

The eventual creation of the MOSD in June 2012 strengthened engagement and leadership and was thus an important step forward on the road towards a strong social protection sector in Lesotho. Consequently, at the onset of Phase II the EU and UNICEF agreed to continue to provide financial and technical support for organizational development for the newly established MOSD and for continuing to strengthen the effectiveness of national and district level coordination structures for the protection and welfare of children.[11]

---

[9] Through parliament, government directed the minister to lead a process of strengthening the delivery of social welfare services. In November 2010 a principal secretary was appointed and charged with implementation of existing programmes including CGP and developing the capacity of the DSW. In the same year Ministry of Finance (MOF) declared the DSW as an independent accounting unit separate from Health. This indicated a formal separation between Health and Social Welfare.

[10] The report prepared to this effect recommended a separation of the DSW from the MOHSW as the first step towards strengthening social welfare service delivery (Bulwani, 2012). It also identified several social-welfare-related programmes managed by different ministries which could be merged with the DSW to form one institution on social development.

[11] Capacity development included innovations and development of IT (Information Technology) management systems to support CGP operations from targeting to payment of

11.2.3.2 Government Absorption of CGP Costs

Government's decision to take over the costs and administration of the CGP was crucial for the consolidation of the CGP. Development partners achieved this through a multi-tiered influencing strategy, at the core of which was relationship building (see Section 11.4).

In the context of the world financial crisis, donors had the foresight to include social spending commitments in their negotiations. A benchmark on social spending was included in the GoL's Extended Credit Facility negotiated in 2010 with the International Monetary Fund (IMF). OVC support—in the form of CGP expansion—was also was included as a performance indicator by the EU and GoL as part of negotiations on general budget support.[12]

It was finally agreed that halfway through Phase II, the CGP would be 100 per cent paid by the national budget and the EU support would continue to finance capacity building, technical assistance, and coordination efforts.[13] Besides progressively increasing MOSD allocation of staff to run operations independently,[14] in April the government successfully took over 100 per cent of benefit costs—contextually raising the value of the grant—and 70 per cent of operational costs.[15] Importantly, the change in government

beneficiaries. These investments include utilization of (i) a mobile research technology for data collection and treatment; (ii) a bar code system to facilitate counting of beneficiaries as well as financial reconciliation; and (iii) development of a new integrated MIS to better coordinate and harmonize programmes. Further investments in capacity building have more recently been provided to support the NISSA expansion and utilization of mobile phone to diversify methods of payment and also support the ministry to deliver an integrated and harmonized social protection system.

[12] A number of jointly agreed indicators and targets form the basis of a Performance Assessment Framework (PAF) that assesses the government's performance and commitment to achievement of certain economic and social objectives. The funds released through the budget support include a fixed as well as variable tranche, with the latter only being disbursed in the event of favourable performance in the PAF. During the budget support review of 2010, there was pressure on government to demonstrate it had children-focused interventions. The review pointed out that despite Lesotho's high spending on social transfers, there was no programme that exclusively targeted children. As part of the review process, the GoL agreed with the EU to consider taking over the costs of the CGP during a second phase of implementation of the project.

[13] Eventually the GoL indicated that instead of direct EC funding to scale up the CGP, they preferred a bigger direct budget support programme through which they committed themselves to gradually take over the payment of the CGP benefit costs.

[14] A revised establishment list adopted in 2012 provided for a significant increase in positions, including the recruitment of a large number of Auxiliary Social Welfare Officers (ASWO) to serve as frontline service providers, and in early 2013 the government took direct responsibility for all project staff positions. Likewise, by January 2014 great strides had also occurred in the handover of operational responsibilities from UNICEF to the GoL.

[15] This was a great milestone in the efforts towards a transition to full government ownership of the CGP, not least because the month of April also saw the introduction of differentiated payment levels which considerably raised the value of the grant for most beneficiary households.

of 2012 did not affect the sustainability and the buy-in towards national commitment to the CGP.

11.2.3.3 Coverage Expansion and Commitment to National Roll-Out

Such important institutional changes were achieved in the context of sustained expansion of the coverage of the CGP. Experience gained during Phase I allowed for a faster pace of growth. Activities related to the completion, development, implementation, and stabilization of CGP processes were largely marked by the aggressive expansion undertaken throughout 2013. By the end of 2013 the number of households enrolled in the programme was just under the target of 20,000.[16] Before the end of Phase II, the CGP was active in forty-five councils across all ten districts of Lesotho, and had reached its final target of 25,000 households in July 2014, directly supporting almost 80,000 children, or roughly 10 per cent of the total population of children. CGP budget has also been introduced in the MTEF (Mid Term Expenditure Framework), which represents an engagement for roll-out over the coming years.

11.2.4 Harmonization and Integration (2014–2015)

The implementation of the CGP has also contributed to engage government to move towards a more systemic approach which strengthens harmonization and integration of social protection programmes within a clear national vision.[17]

With the continued support of the EU and UNICEF, and benefitting from the engagement of new partners like the World Bank, in 2014 the GoL formulated an NSPS which uses the life-cycle approach to ensure comprehensive and coordinated service provision.[18] The approval of this strategy in December 2014 was an important step in the GoL's efforts to expand and

---

[16] Moreover, during this first year of Phase II, the programme expanded to an extra five districts and was from then on present in thirty-seven councils in every district of the country. Progress on the coverage of the CGP remained steady during the course of 2014.

[17] A major challenge of the sector is that existing safety nets are managed under different ministries and the lack of an umbrella framework for the coordination of transfers. The weak public monitoring and tracking system has allowed a situation whereby some households or areas benefit from multiple programmes while others who are similarly vulnerable receive none (World Bank, 2013).

[18] The human-rights-oriented life-cycle approach permits the government to propose a package of social protection services more adapted to the different types of vulnerabilities and also more linked with other social and economic services. The advantage of the life-cycle approach is then to address challenges in terms of harmonization of programmes, coordination among stakeholders and programmes.

diversify social protection provision to address the diversity of vulnerabilities and dimensions of poverty in Lesotho through: (i) the introduction of new interventions such as the Infant Grant Programme, a Disability Grant, and a Productive Safety Net; and (ii) the expansion of existing programmes such as the CGP and OAP.[19]

To facilitate integration, coordination, and harmonization, the government adopts a systems approach in which NISSA and the integrated MIS will be central tools for all programmes and interventions targeting the poor.[20] MOSD has also been supported in running a pilot project on the integration of the administrative mechanisms of all social safety nets, and on strengthening the link between supply and demand through community engagement and referral mechanisms.

11.3 THE EVIDENCE: MAIN FINDINGS OF THE CGP EVALUATION

The process that led to the consolidation of the CGP from a small-scale pilot into a government-owned national programme was mirrored by an ambitious evaluation agenda that contributed to producing a multifaceted range of evidence during the same time period (see bottom panel of Figure 11.1).

The overall purpose of the evaluation was to establish the efficacy and efficiency of the CGP. In particular, it had three core objectives: i) to evaluate the welfare and economic impacts of the pilot amongst those who benefit from it; ii) to evaluate the cost and operational effectiveness of the pilot programme, particularly the extent to which it reaches those in greatest need; iii) to evaluate local welfare, social, and economic impacts of the pilot in the community where it operates, beyond those who directly benefit from it.

The impact evaluation of the CGP employed a mixed methods approach and was structured around five components:

i. A *rapid assessment* of the results of the early phase of implementation of the CGP was conducted in 2010 on the basis of a mix of quantitative and qualitative evidence, although without a strong counterfactual design;

---

[19] The costing analysis undertaken during the formulation process informed government on all options of expanding social protection without distorting the current fiscal framework, ensuring the continued sustainability of the larger project.

[20] The strategy also proposes to strengthen integration and harmonization of social protection programmes as well as linking social protection with interventions in other sectors to increase efficiency and effectiveness as well as promote graduation from poverty and vulnerability.

ii. A *rigorous quantitative assessment* of the impact and operational effectiveness of the redesigned CGP (Round II) was subsequently conducted based on a randomized controlled trial (RCT) evaluation design, including a baseline survey in 2011 and a follow-up in 2013;

iii. The impact of the CGP on the *local economy* was simulated using a LEWIE (Local Economy-Wide Impact Evaluation) model, based on the baseline household survey data combined with a business enterprise survey that accompanied baseline data collection;

iv. *Qualitative research* using participatory methods and in-depth case studies was conducted in 2013 on beneficiary perceptions of the programme impact on household decision-making, community dynamics, and social networks;

v. A *costing and financial sustainability* study reviewed the historical costs of the CGP, simulated the likely future cost of the programme, and assessed the programme's affordability under the prevailing fiscal environment.

The main methodological characteristics of each component of the evaluation are reported in Annex 11.1, while the timing of the evaluation inputs vis-à-vis critical steps in the life of the CGP are reported in Figure 11.1.

During the same timeframe two other evaluation processes were conducted with significant implications for the Social Protection sector as a whole but less direct reference to the CGP. In 2012 UNICEF commissioned Oxford Policy Management (OPM) to prepare a review of the EC project (Thomson and Kardan, 2012). In 2013 the World Bank undertook a Social Protection Strategy Review (World Bank, 2013).

The World Bank review particularly has influenced the CGP design by shaping the overall policy debate in three main directions: (i) integration of safety nets; (ii) capacity development with creation of the social assistance unit; and (iii) committing government to formulate a new strategy.

11.3.1 Rapid Assessment

The Rapid Assessment (RA) was intended to give initial feedback information to assist the GoL and UNICEF in deciding whether and how to scale up the programme (Kardan et al., 2011). During this early phase, CGP households also received one food ration per child (maize, pulses, and oil) from the World Food Programme (WFP) for a cash value of approximately M180, while in subsequent pilot phases only cash was provided.

The RA drew on both quantitative and qualitative information. The absence of a baseline, the limited sample size imposed by time and budget restrictions, and the absence of a suitable control group acting as counterfactual impeded a traditional rigorous impact evaluation. Collected data were used to give statistically representative evidence: a) on the use of the transfer as reported by beneficiaries, and their perceived contribution of the CGP on well-being; and b) of the trends of indicators of interest and the change over time subjectively perceived by beneficiaries.

Overall, it was found that the CGP cash and WFP food had significant positive effect on recipients' well-being. Recipients typically used the food for consumption, and this tended to increase portion quantities, particularly in the period after the transfer was received. Households consumed more protein than previously and were also able to afford occasional purchases of rarer but preferred foods, such as meat. Recipients preferred cash to food, because it allowed them to meet their prioritized needs. The overwhelming majority of households spent the cash paying attention to the requirements of children, especially shoes, uniforms, and toiletries, resulting in children feeling more confident at, and enthusiastic about, school.

11.3.2 Baseline Survey

The analysis of the baseline evaluation survey was completed in September 2011 as a first piece of a rigorous evaluation to be conducted over the course of two years. By characterizing the study population and analysing livelihoods and living conditions of CGP beneficiaries, the baseline study was able to inform improvements of key programme design features (Pellerano et al., 2012).

The baseline report highlighted that value and frequency of the transfers were not optimally set up to achieve the desired outcomes of the programme, including sustaining the poorest and most vulnerable households containing children. As a consequence, it was suggested to revise the payment scale to move from a flat per-household amount to a variable amount indexed to the number of children.[21] It was also recommended to reinforce guidelines to ensure that unregistered children were enrolled in the CGP, while at the same time putting in place mechanisms to incentivize their prompt registration, given around 80 per cent of children aged 0–36 months were found not to have a birth certificate.

The study also unveiled the trends and seasonality of food security, a serious problem across all households, but particularly amongst eligible households who were found to face extreme shortage of food for four to five months during the year, mostly in the lean season. To address these problems, it was

---

[21] In this way it would have been possible to achieve a higher value of per-capita or per-child transfer in large households, and avoid the transfer dilution within households' overall expenditure, thus improving the progressiveness of the instrument.

suggested that the CGP should have considered increasing the transfer amount during the 'peak' food insecurity months of April and May.

11.3.3 Targeting Assessment

The evidence made available through the baseline survey constituted the basis for a review of the effectiveness of targeting. This aimed to determine whether the programme's targeting criteria and application process effectively led to targeting the poorest households. The analysis was based on the integration of qualitative and quantitative methods that allowed the measurement of targeting performance in terms of standard measures such as inclusion and exclusion errors, while also collecting in-depth information on households' involvement in the targeting processes and overall perceptions (Pellerano et al., 2012).

Households eligible to the CGP were shown to be significantly more likely to be poor than those not eligible, confirming a general indication that eligible households were worse off on all socioeconomic grounds, from food security, to access to public services, to livelihoods and assets. However, large exclusion errors were also registered, mainly as a result of financial constraints. The combination of targeting methods (PMT and community validation) was explicitly introduced in an attempt to minimize inclusion errors and the CGP performed similarly to other cash transfers in the region in this respect. Yet the study indicated that there was room for substantial improvement with the fine-tuning of the targeting design (both for the PMT and for the validation component) and the targeting process.[22]

11.3.4 Local Economy Results

The third block of evidence to become available as part of the evaluation agenda was an ex-ante simulation of the likely effects of the CGP on the local economy (Taylor, Thome, and Filipski, 2014) The impact on the local economy was simulated using the LEWIE model, which was based on the baseline household survey data combined with a business enterprise survey (see Chapter 5). The LEWIE simulation methods were used to assess the likely

---

[22] The review also highlighted that households did not have a good understanding of the detail of the selection process and there were no case management systems at the time of research. Households felt that setting up of a complaint mechanism would have been useful and suggested the use of existing local dispute resolution mechanisms as a means of addressing this.

impacts of the CGP on local markets in the treated clusters, and to understand the mechanisms by which project impacts were deemed to transmit to ineligible households. [23]

The LEWIE model for the CGP suggested that if households spend the transfer as they spend other cash, the transfers would lead to relatively large income multipliers. It was estimated that every Loti transferred to poor households has the potential to raise local income by M2.23. Ineligible households would receive the bulk of the indirect benefit through increased demand of local goods and services. This finding is not surprising given that the eligibility criteria for the CGP favour asset- and labour-poor households. The analysis also suggested that if land and capital constraints limit the supply response, the real expansion in the local economy is smaller, and higher demand for local commodities could put upward pressure on prices.

11.3.5 Impact Evaluation

The completion of the CGP rigorous impact evaluation required the collection of a second round of data in the summer of 2013 and results were available by the beginning of 2014. Findings from the experimental design impact evaluation (Pellerano at al., 2014; Daidone et al., 2014), complemented by qualitative fieldwork (OPM, 2014), indicated that the CGP has led to a broad array of impacts.

11.3.5.1 Increased Spending on Children Education and Enrolment

The messaging of the programme—that the transfer should have been used in the interest of children—was strictly followed by beneficiaries. The CGP contributed to a large increase in expenditures on schooling, school uniforms, clothing, and footwear for children, including a 26 percentage point increase (from a base of 46 per cent) in the share of pupils with uniforms and shoes (Table 11.1). The impact was particularly large for young boys and girls (aged 6–12). The CGP also led to an increase in school enrolment, especially by retaining boys aged 13–17 in primary school, who would have otherwise dropped out. The programme, however, did not have any noticeable impact

---

[23] The programme's immediate impact will be to raise the purchasing power of beneficiary households. As households spend the transfer, the impacts spread from the beneficiary households to others inside (and outside) of their village. Doorstep trade, purchases in village shops, periodic markets, and purchases outside the village potentially set in motion income multipliers within the village and beyond.

Table 11.1. Statistically Significant Impacts of the CGP on Children, Education, and Enrolment

Indicator	Treatment Group BL	Treatment Group FU	Control Group BL	Control Group FU	CGP Direct Impact Est.	CGP Direct Impact Obs.
% pupils with:						
Uniform and school shoes	46.3	68.8***	48	44.7	25.63***	4,874
Shoes	52	77.3***	54.1	58.9	20.41***	4,874
Uniform	71.6	81.9***	74.9	64.7***	20.06***	4,874
% children (aged 6–19) *currently enrolled* in school	84.6	87.4*	84.8	82.4	5.032**	5,913
Boys	82.2	84.2	84.2	77.7***	8.063**	3,044
Girls	87.1	90.9*	85.5	87.3	1.865	2,869
% children (aged 13–19) currently enrolled in *primary* school	54.7	56.9	53.3	48.4*	6.326*	2,864
Boys	56.8	58.7	57.8	44.7***	11.39**	1,512
Girls	52.5	55	47.7	52.4	0.887	1,352
% children (aged 13–19) currently enrolled in *secondary* school	17.5	19.2	20	18.7	3.429	2,864
Boys	12.4	12.5	14.9	14.7	1.006	1,512
Girls	22.9	26.6	26.3	23.1	5.737	1,352

The 'Obs' column denotes the overall sample size. The sample sizes for the disaggregated estimates in other columns are based on smaller sample sizes.
Asterisks (*) indicate that an estimate is significantly different to the relevant comparator: *** = 99%; ** = 95%; * = 90%.

on other important dimensions of school progression, like repetition or primary completion. This was not surprising, given the short term of the evaluation, the nature of the CGP, and the severity of challenges with service supply in the education sector.

11.3.5.2 Increase in Birth Registration and Child Health

The CGP led to an increase in birth registration by 37 percentage points amongst children aged 0–6 (from a baseline of 14 per cent). This is an anticipated effect of the programme, as there is a requirement for beneficiary children to have a birth certificate within six months of enrolment in the CGP. The CGP contributed to a 15 percentage point reduction (from a baseline of 39 per cent) in the proportion of both boys and girls aged 0–5 who suffered from an illness (generally flu or cold) in the thirty days prior to the survey, especially girls (Table 11.2). One possible cause of this reduction may be due to households buying more clothes and footwear for children, which in turn may be associated with a reduction of respiratory infections.

Table 11.2. Statistically Significant Impacts of the CGP on Birth Registration and Child Health

Indicator	Treatment Group BL	Treatment Group FU	Control Group BL	Control Group FU	CGP Direct Impact Est.	CGP Direct Impact Obs.
% children (aged 0–6) with birth certificate	13.9	55.4***	12.9	18.4	37.04***	1,747
% children (aged 0–5) who suffered from any illness in the last month	38.9	31.4	36.7	45.3	−15.38*	1,996
Boys	36.9	30.8	36.4	44.7	−12.87	1,016
Girls	41.4	32.1	37	46.1	−17.93*	980

The 'Obs' column denotes the overall sample size. The sample sizes for the disaggregated estimates in other columns are based on smaller sample sizes.
Asterisks (*) indicate that an estimate is significantly different to the relevant comparator: *** = 99%; ** = 95%; * = 90%.

11.3.5.3 Increased Protection against Food Insecurity

The CGP improved the ability of beneficiary households to access food throughout the year (Table 11.3). The programme reduced by 1.5 the number of months during which households experienced extreme food shortage. This translated into food security gains for both adults and children in beneficiary households. The proportion of children aged 0–17 that had to eat smaller meals or fewer meals in the three months previous to the survey because there was not enough food decreased by 11 percentage points. The proportion of adults who went to bed hungry because there was not enough food decreased 7 percentage points.

The evidence of the impact of the programme on poverty status, household consumption, food consumption, and dietary diversity was less compelling. Qualitative evidence suggest that the effects on food consumption and dietary diversity were mainly concentrated around pay dates, the last of which had taken place three months prior to follow-up data collection, and hence may have not been captured in the quantitative survey.

11.3.5.4 Impact on Household Livelihoods

The CGP impacted household livelihoods, especially agricultural activities. The programme increased the share of households using and purchasing crop inputs, like pesticides and seeds, especially among labour-unconstrained households, and led to a large increase in maize output and contributed to increasing the frequency of garden plot harvest among beneficiary households (Table 11.4). The fact that for a large number of beneficiaries the CGP was

Table 11.3. Statistically Significant Impacts of the CGP on Food Security

Indicator	Treatment Group BL	Treatment Group FU	Control Group BL	Control Group FU	CGP Direct Impact Est.	CGP Direct Impact Obs.
# months in which households had extreme shortage of food	4.7	4.0	4.3	5.2***	−1.534***	2,681
% households in the three months prior to the survey, in which:						
Any adult member went to sleep hungry	45.8	35.6***	51.9	49.1	−7.429*	2,702
Any child (aged 0–17) member had to eat fewer meals than felt needed	65.7	55.2**	70.8	71.7	−11.36**	2,659
Any child (aged 0–17) member had to eat a smaller meal than felt needed	69.1	60**	70.5	72.6	−11.21**	2,659

The 'Obs' column denotes the overall sample size. The sample sizes for the disaggregated estimates in other columns are based on smaller sample sizes.
Asterisks (*) indicate that an estimate is significantly different to the relevant comparator: *** = 99%; ** = 95%; * = 90%.

topped up with an additional transfer to deal with seasonality issues (the Food Security Grant) may have also played an important role in these productive impacts, as the latter was provided with the explicit objective to buy seeds and increase production.

Qualitative fieldwork indicated that some beneficiaries reduced the amount of piece work/casual labour around pay dates. The quantitative analysis found a reduction in the intensity of paid labour for adults in CGP households, but otherwise the impact of the CGP on adult labour activity and child labour and time use was mixed and inconclusive. The programme had little discernible impact on the accumulation of productive assets, with the exception of the ownership of pigs. Overall, beneficiary households seemed to be more resilient to shocks as they were less prone to engage in asset-depleting risk-coping strategies (Table 11.5).

11.3.5.5 Positive Impact on Social Networks

The CGP had a significant impact in strengthening the informal sharing arrangements in the community, particularly around food, affecting the probability of beneficiary households to both provide to and receive in-kind support from the rest of the community (Table 11.6). This change in the nature of reliance was also observed in the qualitative work, indicating the CGP has the potential to boost beneficiaries' self-esteem and sense of self-worth through engagement in reciprocal community-based sharing arrangement on less adverse grounds.

Table 11.4. Statistically Significant Impacts of the CGP on Livelihoods

	All		Unconstrained		Moderately		Severely	
	Impact	BL	Impact	BL	Impact	BL	Impact	BL
Use (% households)								
Any crop input	0.030	0.778	0.018	0.795	0.159**	0.767	−0.128	0.691
Seed	0.038	0.772	0.032	0.790	0.154**	0.753	−0.128	0.691
Pesticides	0.079**	0.122	0.127***	0.142	0.096	0.085	−0.256**	0.061
Organic fertilizer	0.074*	0.315	0.054	0.351	0.144*	0.263	−0.002	0.182
Purchase (% households)								
Any crop input	0.051	0.341	0.064	0.369	0.139	0.290	−0.185	0.254
Seed	0.074*	0.237	0.089*	0.251	0.073	0.221	−0.109	0.183
Pesticides	0.051	0.092	0.112***	0.105	0.020	0.064	−0.211**	0.061
Organic fertilizer	0.010	0.022	0.006	0.024	0.034	0.019	−0.012	0.010
Inorganic fertilizer	0.058*	0.104	0.043	0.124	0.070	0.071	0.171**	0.042
Harvested crops (kg)								
Maize	38.870**	37.099	62.349**	41.349	19.791	26.318	−34.887	30.607
Sorghum	9.817*	12.817	0.370	10.785	22.740**	18.706	49.324**	14.494
Wheat	6.866*	1.730	10.755	1.571	2.868	0.801	0.132	4.567
N	2,706		1,808		600		298	

The 'N' row denotes the overall sample size.
Asterisks (*) indicate that an estimate is significantly different to the relevant comparator: *** = 99%; ** = 95%; * = 90%.

Table 11.5. Statistically Significant Impacts of the CGP on Risk-Coping Strategies

Indicator	Treatment Group BL	Treatment Group FU	Control Group BL	Control Group FU	CGP Direct Impact Est.	Obs.
% households that in the last twelve months were forced to:						
Send children for wage employment		4.0		6.9	−2.883*	1,307
Send children to live elsewhere		3.9		9.4	−5.533***	1,307
Reduce spending on health care		6.7		13.9	−7.243***	1,307
Take children out of school		4.1		11.9	−7.785***	1,300

The 'Obs' column denotes the overall sample size. The sample sizes for the disaggregated estimates in other columns are based on smaller sample sizes.

Asterisks (*) indicate that an estimate is significantly different to the relevant comparator: *** = 99%; ** = 95%; * = 90%.

Table 11.6. Statistically Significant Impacts of the CGP on Community Networks

Indicator	Treatment Group BL	Treatment Group FU	Control Group BL	Control Group FU	CGP Direct Impact Est.	Obs.
% households borrowing or receiving support from other family members, friends, or neighbours:						
Cash	72.40	75.00	76.00	78.10	0.51	2,554
In-kind	71.20	84.40***	80.10	81.00	12.22**	2,554
% households providing support for other family members, friends, or neighbours:						
Cash	24.40	33.60**	31.10	28.50	11.83**	2,554
In-kind	46.30	59.10***	53.20	54.20	11.77**	2,554

The 'Obs' column denotes the overall sample size. The sample sizes for the disaggregated estimates in other columns are based on smaller sample sizes.

Asterisks (*) indicate that an estimate is significantly different to the relevant comparator: *** = 99%; ** = 95%; * = 90%.

11.3.6 Costing Review and Fiscal Sustainability

A last piece of evidence produced as part of the CGP evaluation consisted of a costing review and assessment of financial sustainability of the CGP expansion in the prevailing fiscal environment of Lesotho (Kardan et al., 2014). The total cost of the programme during its initial phase of implementation stood at M82 million, of which 38 per cent was transferred to beneficiaries.[24] Costs related to

---

[24] Between October 2007 and December 2012.

design and roll-out of the programme combined with institutional management and coordination accounted for the majority of the non-transfer costs. Once the initial investment costs were taken into consideration the share of administrative cost was substantially reduced: for every Loti given to beneficiaries the programme spent 50 Lisente.

The likely costs of the CGP in the future were explored under a number of scenarios. The lower-bound costs were projected under the hypothesis that the programme would maintain its current level of beneficiaries, while the upper-bound costs were given by the programme reaching national coverage by 2020.[25] The cost of the programme was projected to represent 0.2 per cent GDP in 2014–15 and range between 0.2 per cent and 0.8 per cent of GDP in 2020–1, suggesting that the expansion of the CGP would be affordable under the current macroeconomic framework in the medium term (2014/15–2017/18) and—with significantly less certainty about macroeconomic assumptions—in the years beyond that (2018/19–2020/1).

11.4 DRIVERS OF POLICY CHANGE. DID THE EVALUATION CONTRIBUTE TO ACHIEVING HIGH-LEVEL SOCIAL PROTECTION SECTOR REFORM?

The prospect for the CGP did not seem too rosy in the early days. From the government's side, the OAP was seen as an intervention that was already targeting the welfare of vulnerable children, so there was no understanding of the need of a specific intervention like the CGP, particularly since the OAP is universal. Moreover, the concept of the CGP as a poverty-targeted cash transfer was very new in the context of Lesotho, where existing programmes like the OVC Bursary and Public Assistance (PA) were reactive and self-targeted. Although the latter did have a cash component, it mostly delivered in-kind support. The government, particularly MOF, had serious concerns from a value–for-money perspective, and thus only committed to support the implementation of an externally funded pilot. The idea of providing cash transfers to poor and vulnerable households were perceived by the most sceptical as a way of creating dependency and not encouraging beneficiaries to work. With no evidence that it would be a valuable investment for human development it was a challenge to see the added value of the CGP.

---

[25] These scenarios assumed the benefit levels to be linked to inflation; for households to be retargeted in 2018 (i.e., every five years) and for the programme to reach the poorest 30 per cent of the households with at least one child.

Few years later the landscape surrounding the CGP is remarkably different. The CGP is firmly placed at the centre of a nationally owned social protection agenda, with a strong commitment by the GoL for its continued expansion and an understanding of its strategic relevance.

In the light of what seems to be a remarkable case of success, it is worth asking what were the drivers of the high-level policy progress achieved, and more specifically what was the role—if any—of the ambitious learning agenda that was put in place to generate evidence on the effectiveness and efficiency of the CGP.

An initial important factual observation is that the main decisions that marked the high-level consolidation of the CGP were taken at a time when the more robust results regarding the impact of the CGP were not available yet (see Figure 11.1). The decision to increase the coverage of the programme throughout Phase II, or the GoL's commitment to take over the administrative and direct costs of the programme—only to pick two—were taken at a time (September 2011 and April 2013) when there was only limited evidence available on the CGP, and the main impact evaluation results were not available yet.

In fact it appears that high-level programme consolidation was achieved as a result of a range of diverse factors. The evaluation evidence represented only one of several components of a multi-tiered influencing strategy, and possibly had more of an indirect rather than direct effect. Three elements apart from the evaluation results themselves appear to have been particularly critical for the CGP high-level consolidation: relationship building, practical showcasing, and political bargaining.

11.4.1 A Multi-Tiered Influencing Strategy

The first element was the building of strong relationships amongst institutions, and amongst key players within each institution, around a shared vision. The initial introduction of the pilot CGP happened thanks to a tri-partite institutional set-up, particularly: (i) commitment of donors such as the EU to provide financial support to pilot and test such an initiative; (ii) Commitment of UNICEF to source and provide relevant expertise and technical support; and (iii) the government's commitment to find and test an innovative approach or programme to address poverty and vulnerability which are drivers of HIV/AIDS in Lesotho. Regular dialogue at technical level, but also at ministerial level prior to the transition maintained the pressure pulse on the government's commitment. The EU Ambassador and UNICEF representative regularly raised the issue in meetings with the Minister of Social Development and with the Minister of Finance. There is no doubt that the excellent collaboration between EU, UNICEF, the MOSD, and other stakeholders and the move towards a unified assistance scheme and a more equitable social protection system have been key in the success of this programme.

Second, the policy dialogue was strongly influenced by exposure to credible pilot project implementation. The fact of having in place a professional technical assistance package since the early stages of the CGP operation, a strong investment in organizational reform and capacity building, the use of new technologies in implementation and the investment on solid information management systems were critical elements to build interest and trust amongst stakeholders regarding the reliability and scalability of the CGP. More than this, the strength of conceptual arguments was built around exposure to practical implementation (by making things happen), equally or more strongly than by generating rigorous evidence. Showcasing solid implementation systems on the ground was an effective mechanism to overcome ideological resistance to cash transfers at a number of levels (poverty targeting, use of cash, dependency). This influencing strategy triggered, for example, the organization of high-level visits on the field when payments were happening, which were found to be highly influential. Study tours to countries operating cash transfer systems at large scale (Colombia, Brazil) were also instrumental in the direction of strengthening the case for the practical applicability and political wisdom of the CGP model in Lesotho.

Third, the broader political dimension mattered, both at the international and at the domestic level. The decision for the government to commit domestic resources to the CGP came primarily through the agreement under the Extended Credit Facility with IMF for bridging funds and support to its budget.[26] As part of the agreement a benchmark on social expenditure based on current levels was agreed (M300 million).

CGP Phase I came to an end in 2011 and to abide by EDF conditionality of not falling below the benchmark, the government took the decision the take over CGP costs in the regular budget. The EU, IMF, and other development partners included a number of indicators on expansion of the CGP and its enactment into law as performance targets tied to the release of the general budget support for the period 2011–13.

Moreover, this was reinforced through a bilateral financing agreement between the GoL and the EC on the second phase of support to the CGP that required the government to commit to co-financing and gradual takeover of the cost of the programme that was agreed in 2011, and honoured subsequently, despite the change in government.

---

[26] Government needed this support to the gap due to the sudden decline of revenue from the Southern Africa Customs Union (SACU), which constituted 60 per cent of budget. An agreement of three years (2010–13) was reached to allow to Lesotho government to consolidate its fiscal position.

There was also domestic political considerations of continuing transfers for 10,000 households reached during Phase I, as well as a progressive realization amongst political and traditional leaders of the returns of the CGP in terms of political consensus at grassroots level. This in turn created increasing pressure for coverage expansion across a higher number of political constituencies. It also contributed to increasing the political cost associated with the fact of the CGP being eventually discontinued, de facto locking the government in a position to take direct responsibility for the programme in case donor support was reduced.

11.4.2 Influence of the CGP Evaluation on High-Level Policy Change

Rigorous evidence produced through the different evaluation components mentioned in Section 11.3 also had a role in influencing the progressive consolidation of CGP in the government agenda. Indeed in the early stages of the process much of the criticism from key stakeholders (e.g., MOF) was grounded on the lack of evidence that CGP was an affordable and beneficial intervention that the government could integrate into its budget. Yet, the most solid and comprehensive evaluation results regarding the CGP effectiveness and fiscal sustainability were produced in early 2014, once key government commitments had already been taken. On the contrary, the early results emerging from the original RA, the targeting analysis, and the local economy analysis were critical to build the case for the CGP, protect the pilot from attacks, and push the high-level agenda forward.

The case of Lesotho highlights the importance of timing in the provision of evidence to support political decisions. The evidence generated throughout the different stages of the evaluation was significantly more influential in relation to its availability at key moments rather than in relation to the rigour of the methods used to generate it. At any critical window of opportunity for political decision, the argument was built on the basis of whatever evidence was available, drawing either from domestic results available until then or from the international literature. As a result of this, two 'secondary' components of the evaluation agenda ended up having a very important influence on the political process.

The RA results were the only available findings on the CGP effectiveness for the whole period of its consolidation (from early 2012). They were based on a relatively small sample, mainly descriptive in nature and focused primarily on the use of transfers, rather than other more fundamental dimensions of behavioural change. The study did not have grounds to draw robust conclusions on the causal effects of the programme on most of the programme's key indicators. In fact, at the time key technical advisors to the evaluation were reluctant to recommend the rapid appraisal since its conclusions would not be statistically valid. UNICEF insisted on going forward, however, and the RA results eventually proved to be critical in early stages of the programme to respond to criticism and advocate (with EU and the GoL) for roll-out and expansion of the programme. Based on the RA, the government and its partners in the social protection sector were reassured of the potential of CGP to generate significant results and impacts in beneficiary communities. This was only later confirmed by the full impact evaluation. Timing was in this case more important than the strength of the evidence, whether it has established causality or the level of inference the study enabled.

The results about the local economy effects of the CGP were also extensively used for advocacy within government by MOSD, particularly with MOF. They became available soon after the baseline survey was completed, yet still in time to influence policy decisions in the last phase of consolidation. They provided a strategic and solid argument regarding the broader effects of the CGP on increased benefits to the wider community, which was received with interest and complemented well the findings of the RA. The strategic importance of evidence generated through the RA and local economy study is well documented by the constant referral to findings from these studies in high-level speeches throughout the period.[27]

At a broader level the World Bank safety nets review pointed out the importance of developing a clear national vision for social protection. The evaluation reports also expressed the need to elaborate a plan that articulated the role of the CGP within a package of social assistance programmes currently operating in Lesotho. This possibly contributed to creating a conducive environment to trigger the process of formulation of a national social protection strategy that culminated with the recent approval by the GoL.

Drawing from these considerations it is reasonable to conclude that the evaluation results together constituted a secondary drive of the high-level policy reform agenda, compared to the other factors mentioned earlier in this section. Instead, the evaluation helped generate important momentum with government and development partners on the ground, particularly the presentation of the preliminary results, which made for a favourable environment for next steps such as the formulation of the strategy. Furthermore, the evaluation influenced more fundamentally the fine-tuning of the operational design of the CGP on a number of levels, as documented in the next section.

---

[27] UNICEF and EU representatives in the Integrated Social Safety Net (ISSN) workshop with MOF, February 2014; UNICEF representative at advocacy meeting to bring consensus among principal secretaries to commit their respective ministers on the approval of the NSDP and NSPS, September 2014; Director of Planning from the MOSD during technical validation of the NSPS, May 2014.

The analysis of the Lesotho case study also suggests that the evaluation may have played an equally important role in a more indirect fashion, as it contributed to a 'culture' of evidence-based decision-making. The credibility of the policy reforms agenda that originated from the implementation of the CGP pilot was increased for the very fact of having a rigorous, multifaceted, and long-term learning agenda in place in two ways. On the one hand, the credible promise of production of robust evidence, even though it was provided much later, was taken as a very positive signal by key stakeholders—particularly MOF—in a context where there was a strong awareness of the need for more informed decision-making in the sector.

On the other hand, the continued monitoring of progress and emerging evidence over time including the initial findings on what the beneficiaries were likely using the money for and how it was helping them (RA), evidence on the nature and characteristics of those targeted by the programme (Baseline Report) and the fact that it was more or less giving money to the right people (Targeting Report) helped shaping up different dimensions of the CGP design at all stages of its development. The continuous generation of information and learning over time through different evaluation outputs contributed to reinforcing the internal and external credibility of MOSD as an institution commitment to constant improvement, results, and change.

Particularly, thanks to the continued technical support provided by UNICEF, progress was sought and achieved on several of the fronts that had been identified as weaknesses of the programme and the system in the early components of the evaluation. This included the implementation of a large number of recommendations made by external evaluators, as well as the establishment of an ambitious agenda of reform and testing of new solutions. Such a strong orientation towards learning provided an opportunity for internal questioning and capacity building within MOSD, improving the quality of internal technical debate and the ability to advocate for the programme externally.

11.5 EVALUATION RESULTS AND THE FINE-TUNING OF CGP DESIGN

In addition to supporting the policy dialogue process (see Section 11.4), the independent studies and evaluations that were commissioned by UNICEF and the government as part of the CGP pilot provided additional feedback to implementing partners on how the programme was being implemented on the ground, and perceived by the communities. Moreover, they provided a set of recommendations on how the programme could improve based on the evidence generated and international best practice. Over time some of these have permeated into changes in programme design and others have initiated further reviews and assessments, reflecting the likely influence of the learning agenda.

The process of turning inputs from the external evaluation agenda effectively into programme design decisions and implementation was facilitated by the existence of a set of institutional arrangements (quarterly implementation reports, the weekly management meetings) to enable continuous learning and improvement within the CGP programme itself.

11.5.1 Change in the Structure and Value of the Transfer

The programme originally used a flat per household payment model with each household, irrespective of size, receiving M360 every quarter. This modality was revised in 2013 with payments to households being linked to the number of children within them, as recommended by the RA and baseline impact evaluation report. The linking of the value of the transfer to household size has resulted in a higher transfer value per member, for large households, and thus improving the progressiveness and equity of the programme.

11.5.2 Review of the Targeting Design

The targeting analysis highlighted a number of areas for potential improvement of the targeting approach and suggested to undertake a comprehensive review of the targeting methodology as a whole, indicating avenues for a possible revision of the PMT instrument, a need for restructuring the community validation process and the importance of better articulating the two targeting methodology. A comprehensive targeting review was undertaken in the context of the elaboration of a new strategy of NISSA expansion, including the exploration of alternative targeting design, the revision of the current PMT and tightening the methodology for the community validation.

11.5.3 Establishment of Case Management Systems

The lack of systems and procedures for how to redress the complaints were highlighted as areas needing particular attention in the evaluation. The setting up of a complaints mechanism will be a priority during Phase III of the CGP. An improved community development framework, as well as more participative referral mechanisms are also part of the planned adjustments to the CGP's design.

11.5.4 Improvement of Payment Systems

The rigorous impact evaluation provided a strong indication on the importance of a functional payment system to ensure payments are made regularly and in a predictable manner. Most of the challenges faced in this respect arose from a combination of difficult logistical conditions surrounding physical distributions of cash and weak management capacities.

As the current system becomes more reliable, MOSD has decided to pilot the integration of all its transfer programme's payments, and is also currently testing the use of mobile payments modalities. These types of improvements have the potential to improve cost-effectiveness and are particularly important in the new context of full government financing.

11.5.5 Coupling CGP with Other Interventions

Recommendations made in the baseline study, ratifying the original aims of the programme, emphasized the importance of increasing the value of the CGP particularly during months of high food insecurity and combining the CGP with other complementary interventions. A number of successful experiments were run in relation to this.

Following a food security crisis in 2012, a number of development partners used the CGP targeting and payment mechanisms—namely NISSA—to quickly identify and reach the population most vulnerable to the food emergency (Niang and Ramirez, 2014). A review of the NISSA has been launched with an aim at expanding the use of a common targeting mechanism across a broader range of interventions (OVC bursaries, PA, etc.). In fact, both the Disaster Management Authority (DMA) and the UN's regional strategy for disaster risk reduction have called for NISSA to be expanded and used for other social protection programmes, not just the CGP.

The Linking Food Security to Social Protection Programme pilot (LFSSP), initiated in July 2013, also provides households eligible for CGP vegetable seeds and training on homestead gardening.[28] The idea was that the coupling of cash support with seeds and training would result in stronger impacts on the food security of beneficiary households.[29]

---

[28] The training included information on food preservation practices, and guidelines for achieving healthier diets and nutrition. The programme was rolled out in Litjotjela and Malaoneng Community Councils for a period of six months, and was intentionally provided to 780 households eligible for CGP.

[29] Initial impact estimates from an evaluation built on the back of the overall CGP experimental design study, comparing households that received the CGP and the LFSSP with households that only received the LFSSP, show positive effects of the combination of the two programmes (Dewbre et al., 2015).

11.5.6 Move towards Harmonization and Integration

Several pieces of the evaluation insisted on the importance of harmonizing the CGP with other interventions (social assistance, productive and social services), recommending to examine the possibility of the CGP exploiting some of the systems such as payments and case management and how it can contribute to strengthening of existing systems. As mentioned earlier, a Social Safety Net pilot has been set up with the aim of testing the integration of the administrative systems between the CGP, Public Assistance Programme, and the OVC school bursaries.

11.6 CONCLUSIONS

This chapter discussed the role played by the evidence produced as part of the evaluation of the CGP in Lesotho in determining the trajectory of consolidation of the programme that evolved from a relatively small-scale donor-funded pilot into a nationally owned programme centred at the core of a revised social protection policy framework. The evaluation brought together a broad-based learning agenda, comprising experimental design impact evaluation, rapid appraisals, qualitative fieldwork, general equilibrium modelling, costing review and fiscal sustainability, and other studies and reviews.

This broad-based learning agenda played an important—yet secondary, or complementary—role as an advocacy tool to influence high-level policy decision-making. Other forces were the principal drivers of observed changes in policy: relationship building, showcasing of implementation results and the realization of political gains from the programme expansion. The evidence generated by the evaluation was instrumental in making the case for CGP consolidation by and large only to the extent to which it was available at times of critical decisions. Results from components of the evaluation of weaker methodological rigour, such as the RA, proved to be more influential as they provided results in the early phases of the project, when important policy decisions were being made. The evaluation did, however, generate momentum with the government and development practitioners on the ground, making for a favourable environment for other important activities such as the formulation of the social protection strategy.

The evaluation also contributed to a 'culture' of evidence-based decision-making. In this sense, even if the timing of evaluation results was not optimal for large policy decisions, it made a larger contribution to the development of the system. The very fact of having a rigorous and continuous learning system in place indirectly increased the credibility of the policy building exercise. This not only contributed to presenting the programme externally as committed to change and continuous improvement, but also generated internal dynamism and awareness of technical challenges, increasing the programme's ability to advocate for itself, and openness to testing and experimentation.

The learning agenda influenced the design of the programme throughout the period of implementation, with operationalization of a number of recommendations from the external evaluators, including the revision of the payment value and the coupling of the CGP with an additional emergency top-up transfer. The evaluation was also successful in raising awareness of some of the operational challenges of the programme and instigating additional reviews. Important design refinements were made despite challenges in feeding back the learning agenda to a group of stakeholders with differing roles and responsibilities and a transitional financing, contracting, coordination, and leadership arrangement gradually moving away from the development partners towards the MOSD.

The rapid evolution of the social protection sector witnessed in recent years poses a number of challenges in terms of social protection policy reform and evaluation in Lesotho. Together with the World Bank sector review, the CGP evaluation contributed towards increased engagement of development partners with the government on how to move towards a more systemic approach with strengthened harmonization and integration of programmes within a clear national vision. This transition has been further consolidated with the recent approval of the NSPS, which provides a solid foundation for increasing harmonization across interventions with a view at achieving cost-effectiveness and cost-efficiency gains in the sector.

The production of evidence through rigorous monitoring and evaluation has a critical role to play in this context. On the one hand, it is increasingly important to apply a similarly rigorous and comprehensive evaluation approach adopted in the case of the CGP to other components of the social protection package that have received less attention (OAP, PA, OVC bursaries, school feeding, the newly proposed infant grant). This will permit to continue improving the operation effectiveness and impact orientation of each intervention. Moreover, uniform evidence across programmes can also guide decisions as to how to achieve further rationalization and simplification in the sector by concentrating resources on more efficient and impactful programmes. At a higher level, it is going to be critical to introduce a results framework and establish more structural monitoring and evaluation processes that look at the effectiveness of the sector as a whole, moving beyond the evaluation of pacific programmes to document the overall sector contribution to poverty reduction, redistribution, and the promotion of human development.

Annex 11.1. Main Characteristics of CGP Evaluation Components

	Approach							Reference
	Quantitative				Qualitative			
	Methods	Location and Sample	Time	Methods	Location	Time		
Rapid Assessment	Descriptive statistics concerning: a) use of the transfer by beneficiaries, and perceived contribution of the CGP on household and children well-being; b) trends of indicators of interest and change over time subjectively perceived by beneficiaries.	Three community councils (Mathula, Semonkong, and Thaba-Khubelu) of the pilot phase of the CGP (Phase I—Round 1A). Representative survey of 300 beneficiary HHs.	Data collection: March 2011 Report: April 2011	1) two FGDs in each village with CGP recipients; 2) in each village semi-structured interviews with chiefs, health workers, teachers, traders, nurses, village support groups.	Two villages in each of three community councils (Mathula, Semonkong, and Thaba-Khubelu).	Data collection: February 2011 Report: April 2011		Kardan et al. (2011)
Targeting Assessment	1) comparison of consumption expenditure levels and poverty rates between CGP eligible and non-eligible households; 2) inclusion and exclusion errors; 3) Coady-Grosh-Hoddinott index; 4) evaluation of PMT and NISSA scoring system.	All EDs within the 10 Community Councils of Phase 2 of the CGP pilot. Household survey representative of the population in EDs: 1,484 eligible HHs and 1,569 non-eligible HHs.	Data collection: June–August 2011 Report: January 2012	1) interviews with programme officials; 2) semi-structured interviews with officials from MOHSW and staff from WV and Ayala; 3) FGD with CGP eligible and non-eligible households; 4) KII with chiefs, councillors, members of the VAC.	1) and 2): Maseru 3) and 4): Two villages within two selected community councils (Tebe-Tebe and Makheka/Rapoleboea)	Data collection: June–August 2011 Report: January 2012		Pellerano et al. (2012)

(continued)

Annex 11.1. Main Characteristics of CGP Evaluation Components (continued)

	Approach						Reference
	Quantitative			Qualitative			
	Methods	Location and Sample	Time	Methods	Location	Time	
Local Economy-Wide Impact Evaluation (LEWIE)	Ex-ante simulation of impacts in the local economy with general equilibrium analysis. Estimation of nominal and real income multipliers: 1) total 2) by eligible vs. ineligible households 3) by production sectors.	See above + business enterprise survey of 228 enterprises non representative of the composition of local businesses.	*Data collection*: June–August 2011 *Report*: November 2012				Taylor et al. (2014)
Impact Evaluation	RCT design for household level impact analysis of eligible population with difference-in-difference estimation strategy	All EDs within the ten Community Councils of Phase 2 of the CGP pilot. Household survey representative of the eligible population in EDs: *Baseline*—747 HHs in treatment group, 739 HHs in control group *Follow-up*—706 HHs in treatment group, 647 HHs in control group	*Data collection*: Baseline: June–August 2011, Follow-up: June–August 2013 *Report*: April 2014	1) FGD 2) KII 3) Participatory tools for group analysis (social mapping, well-being analysis, livelihood scoring, institutional mapping).	2/3 villages (depending on number of beneficiaries) in each community councils randomly selected (Metsi-Maholo and Malakeng in Mafeteng district, Litjotjela, and Malaoaneng in Leribe)	Data collection: April–May 2013 Report: December 2013	Pellerano et al. (2014); Daidone et al. (2014)

(*continued*)

Annex 11.1. Main Characteristics of CGP Evaluation Components (continued)

	Approach						Reference
	Quantitative				Qualitative		
	Methods	Location and Sample	Time	Methods	Location	Time	
Costing and Fiscal Sustainability	1) Review of historical costs of the CGP between October 2007 and December 2012; 2) Simulation of future costs of CGP under different scenarios; 3) CGP affordability under the Government of Lesotho's Medium-Term Fiscal Framework.	N/A	*Report:* March 2014				Kardan et al. (2014)

Note: CGP—Child Grants Programme; ED—Electoral Division; FGD—Focus Group Discussion; HH—household; KII—Key Informant Interview; MOHSW—Ministry of Health and Social Welfare; NISSA—National Information System for Social Assistance; PMT—Proxy Means Test; VAC—Village Assistance Committee; WV—World Vision

REFERENCES

Ayala Consulting (2010). 'Report on the Lesotho Child Grants Programme Assessment and Recommendations for Expansion'. UNICEF-Lesotho (with EU funding and technical support from FAO).

Bulwani, G. (2012). 'Institutional and Organisational Arrangements for Integrated Social Development'. Report prepared for the Government of Lesotho. UNICEF-Lesotho (with EU funding and technical support from FAO).

Daidone, S., Davis, B., Dewbre, J., and Covarrubias, K. (2014). 'Lesotho's Child Grants Program: 24-month Impact Report on Productive Activities and Labour Allocation'. Protection to Production Project Report. Rome: FAO.

Dewbre, J., Daidone, S., Davis, B., Miguelez, B., Niang, O., and Pellerano, L. (2015). 'Lesotho Child Grant Programme and Linking Food Security to Social Protection Programme'. Protection to Production Report. Rome: FAO.

Gentilini, U., Honorati, M., and Yemtsov, R. (2014). 'The State of Social Safety Nets 2014'. The World Bank, Washington, DC.

Government of Lesotho (2013). 'Millenium Development Goals Status Report 2013'. Maseru.

Grosh, M. del Ninno, C., Tesliuc, E., and Ouerghi, A. (2008). 'For Protection and Promotion: The Design and Implementation of Effective Safety Nets'. The International Bank for Reconstruction and Development/The World Bank, Washington, DC.

Kardan, A., MacAuslan, I., Merttens, F., and Pellerano, L. (2011). 'A Rapid Assessment of the Lesotho Child Grants Programme'. Report prepared for the Government of Lesotho. Maseru: UNICEF-Lesotho (with EU funding and technical support from FAO). Prepared by Oxford Policy Management.

Kardan, A., Sindou, E., and Pellerano, L. (2014). 'Lesotho Child Grants Programme. The Historic and Future Costs of the CGP and Its Affordability'. Maseru: UNICEF-Lesotho (with EU funding and technical support from FAO). Prepared by Oxford Policy Management.

Ministry of Health and Social Welfare (2009). 'Lesotho Demographic and Health Survey'.

Ministry of Social Development (2010). 'Organizational Development Strategy'.

Niang, O. and Ramirez, B. (2014). 'Using social protection systems to implement emergency cash transfers: the case of Lesotho'. *Humanitarian Exchange Magazine*, (62). Available at: <http://odihpn.org/magazine/using-social-protection-systems-to-implement-emergency-cash-transfers-the-case-of-lesotho/> (accessed 20 November 2015).

OPM (2014). 'Qualitative Research and Analyses of the Economic Impact of Cash Transfer Programmes in sub-Saharan Africa'. Lesotho Country Case Study Report. From Protection to Production project report, FAO: Rome.

Pellerano, L., Hurrel, A., Kardan, A., Barca, V., Hove, F., and Beazley, R. (2012). 'CGP Impact Evaluation. Targeting and Baseline Evaluation Report'. Report prepared for the Government of Lesotho. Maseru: UNICEF-Lesotho (with EU funding and technical support from FAO). Prepared by Oxford Policy Management.

Pellerano, L., Moratti, M., Jakobsen, M., Bajgar, M., and Barca, V. (2014). 'The Lesotho Child Grants Programme Impact Evaluation: Follow-up Report'. Maseru: UNICEF-Lesotho (with EU funding and technical support from FAO). Prepared by Oxford Policy Management.

Samson, M., Mac Quene, K., van Niekerk I., and Kaniki, S. (2007). 'Feasibility Study for a Child Grant in Lesotho'. Government of Lesotho report commissioned by UNICEF.

Taylor, E., Thome, K., and Filipski, M. (2014). 'Evaluating Local General Equilibrium Impacts of Lesotho's Child Grants Programme'. Report prepared for the From Production to Protection project. Rome: UN Food and Agriculture Organization of the United Nations.

Thomson, A. and Kardan, A. (2012). 'Support to Lesotho HIV and AIDS Response: Empowerment of Orphans and Other Vulnerable Children. Final Evaluation'. Maseru: UNICEF-Lesotho (with EU funding). Prepared by Oxford Policy Management.

UNGASS (2005). 'Lesotho 2005 UNGASS Report: The Status of the National Response to the 2001 Declaration of Commitment on HIV and AIDS'.

UNICEF (2011a). 'Child Poverty in Lesotho'.

UNICEF (2011b). 'OVC Situational Analysis'.

UNICEF (2012). 'Support to Lesotho HIV and AIDS Response: Empowerment of Orphans and Vulnerable Children (OVC)'. End of Project Report.

World Bank (2011). 'Lesotho Public Expenditure Review'. Washington, DC.

World Bank (2013). 'Lesotho: A Safety Net to End Extreme Poverty'. Washington, DC: Human Development Department, Social Protection Unit, Africa Region.

12

The Social Cash Transfer Programme of Malawi

The Role of Evaluation from the Pilot to the Expansion

Gustavo Angeles (University of North Carolina at Chapel Hill), Sara Abdoulayi (University of North Carolina at Chapel Hill), Clare Barrington (University of North Carolina at Chapel Hill), Sudhanshu Handa (University of North Carolina at Chapel Hill and UNICEF), Esmie Kainja (Government of Malawi, Ministry of Gender, Children, Disability and Social Welfare), Peter Mvula (University of Malawi, Centre for Social Research), Harry Mwamlima (Government of Malawi, Ministry of Finance, Economic Planning and Development), Maxton Tsoka (University of Malawi, Centre for Social Research), and Tayllor Spadafora (UNICEF)

12.1 INTRODUCTION

Malawi's Social Cash Transfer Programme (SCTP) is an unconditional cash transfer programme targeted at the ultra-poor and labour-constrained households of the country. The main objectives of the programme are to alleviate poverty, hunger, and starvation in the targeted households, as well as improving health, nutrition, and education conditions of the children living in those households. The SCTP is a key component of Malawi's social protection portfolio as it enables the government to reach one of the most vulnerable and destitute groups of the population, that is the ultra-poor who are severely constrained from participating in labour activities due to age (too old or young), chronic illness, or disability, and are, therefore, unlikely to benefit from work-based social programmes. The SCTP is implemented by the Ministry of Gender, Children, Disability, and Social Welfare (MoGCDSW) with policy oversight from the Ministry of Finance,

Economic Planning and Development (MoFEPD). The programme started in 2006 and is currently undergoing continued expansion. At the time of writing this chapter, April 2015, there were over 100,000 households enrolled in the programme with a target of reaching 175,000 households by the end of the year.

From its inception, there was a demand for evidence of the effectiveness and scalability of the programme from policy makers, programme managers, and development partners. This led to the integration of operational, targeting, and impact evaluation components into various stages of the programme, including during the pilot phase. This chapter describes how the evidence produced from these evaluations has been used for programmatic improvements and for shifting the policy environment in support of the expansion of the SCTP and social protection in general. It gives the background of social protection in Malawi, explains the origins and growth of the SCTP, and outlines the evidence of impacts produced by the SCT Pilot Scheme (commonly referred to as the 'Mchinji Pilot') evaluation and more recent impact evaluations. It also explains the influence the evidence had on programme funding, political buy-in, and programme implementation.

12.2 SOCIAL PROTECTION IN MALAWI

Malawi has long been counted among the poorest countries in the world. In 2006, when the SCT Pilot Scheme was beginning, gross domestic product (GDP) per capita was estimated at US$600, placing Malawi last in the ranking of 229 countries (CIA 2007). Poverty was widespread throughout the country, as evidenced by high poverty headcount ratios and poverty gaps. About 52 per cent of the roughly thirteen million people of Malawi (Government of Malawi and World Bank 2007) were poor, with 28 per cent living on less than one dollar per day (Government of Malawi and World Bank 2007). Despite this level of poverty, the country had no effective social protection system as the large majority of households had historically relied on informal practices of mutual exchanges for providing support (Ellis, Kutengule, and Nyasulu 2003). During the early 2000s, the Government of Malawi (GoM), in collaboration with development agencies, engaged in several macroeconomic growth activities (debt cancelation, infrastructure investment, trade policies), which generally failed to benefit the poorest households (Miller, Tsoka, and Reichert 2010). At the micro level, ad hoc poverty reduction programmes implemented by the government covered only a small fraction of the poor and were largely ineffective. According to the Malawi Poverty and Vulnerability Assessment (GoM and World Bank 2007) poverty remained almost unchanged between 1998 and 2005. HIV/AIDS also has had a significant impact on families in Malawi. In the first half of 2000s, the prevalence rate among people aged 15–49 years was about 15 per cent, strongly affecting the productive capacity of the country and increasing the number of orphans (UNICEF 2006). By the mid-2000s, about 20 per cent of Malawi's children (about one million children) were orphans, and half of them had lost one or both parents to AIDS (Acquired Immune Deficiency Syndrome) (UNICEF 2006). These children were living in a wide array of mainly informal care arrangements (UNICEF 2011). As a result, many poor households were elderly- or child-headed households with several children as dependents. These circumstances increased the burden on the relatively few able-bodied adults to provide for the household, or households resorted to relying more heavily on children for labour or other negative coping mechanisms for survival. Kainja (2012) found that orphans and their caretakers heavily relied on coping strategies like *ganyu* (informal work), early sexual relationships, early marriage, harvest of premature maize, and selling of assets, which had detrimental effects on their livelihoods and increased their vulnerability as well. AIDS increased the proportion of households that had few to no individuals of working age. In addition, these labour-constrained families are less likely to benefit from other types of social support programmes that require some form of labour in exchange for cash or inputs.

12.2.1 Origins of the Social Cash Transfer Programme

It is against this backdrop that the GoM and development partners began to explore the possibility of implementing a national, government-led cash transfer (CT) programme in Malawi. The earliest social protection strategy in Malawi was put forth in the Poverty Reduction Strategy of 2002, which was presented to the World Bank and International Monetary Fund (IMF) to access HIPC (Highly Indebted Poor Countries) resources. While the HIPC proposal was not successful, this constituted the first formal proposal of cash transfers as a potential social protection intervention for Malawi. However, no progress was made during the early 2000s despite the apparent government commitment evidenced by the inclusion of social protection in the Poverty Reduction Strategy.

The next opportunity for cash transfer programmes came in the mid-2000s when three important policy development processes were underway. First, the government established Social Protection as the second theme of the 2006–11 Malawi Growth and Development Strategy (MGDS) (GoM 2006), which was the successor of the Poverty Reduction Strategy of 2002. In this document, social protection was defined as 'policies and practices that protect and promote the livelihoods and welfare of people suffering from unacceptable levels of poverty and/or are vulnerable to risks and shocks'. The MGDS was the framework of reference for social policies and development work throughout the country.

The second policy process began in 2004 when GoM, with support from UNICEF (United Nations Children's Fund), began designing the National Plan of Action for Orphans and Vulnerable Children (NPA for OVC). The first objective of the NPA was the establishment of safety nets for caregivers of OVC. The NPA received strong political support and was launched by the president of Malawi on 16 June 2005. With political support secured, GoM moved to operationalize the NPA under the framework of the MGDS. UNICEF started a round of consultations with government agencies, development partners, and researchers on the components of the safety net for OVC caregivers. At that time, cash transfer programmes were increasingly being recognized as a promising social protection tool, as the evidence on their effectiveness from impact evaluations conducted in Latin America and a few African countries was becoming available.

Establishing a government-led CT programme was one of the chief options under consideration as a safety net programme (Schubert and Huijbregts 2006). UNICEF, with the agreement of the GoM, initiated a bidding process for the design of a CT programme. Previous experience with CT programmes in Malawi was limited to a few programmes conducted by NGOs (non-government organizations) operating in small geographical areas as alternatives to humanitarian aid. An example of such a programme is the Dowa Emergency Cash Transfer implemented by Concern Worldwide with funding from the United Kingdom's Department for International Development (DFID), which responded to the poor harvest in Northern Dowa in 2006 (Samson, Van Niekerk, and Mac Quene 2010). Thus, by the mid-2000s, GoM had no experience in implementing CT programmes on a local, much less national scale. This lack of existing technical expertise in this arena would later prove to be challenging as GoM sought to support significant expansion of the programme through the pilot phase with limited staff and protocols in place.

The third landmark event that would define the CT programme in Malawi was the 'Intergovernmental Regional Conference on Social Protection' held in Livingstone, Zambia, in March 2006. Government officials attended the conference where country experiences with social transfers were presented and the evidence of their effectiveness for reducing poverty and other outcomes was discussed in depth. The conference conclusions strongly endorsed social transfers as a way to directly reduce poverty and inequality. The outcome of the conference was the issuance of the 'Livingstone Call for Action on Social Protection', calling on African countries to use social cash transfer programmes as a policy tool for vulnerable groups. The Livingstone Call for Action also asked governments to put together costed national Social Cash Transfer (SCT) plans and integrate them into National Development Plans (African Union 2006).

In addition to the conference discussions, delegates visited the site of Zambia's Pilot Social Cash Transfer Scheme in Kalomo district, where the design and experience of the programme was presented. The demonstration effect of this visit was very high and made a significant impression on the

Malawi delegates. The Kalomo experience was pivotal in influencing the design of Malawi's CT programme and the GoM ultimately adopted several of the features of the Zambia model for its own pilot programme. Specifically, the Malawi SCT Scheme (SCTS) Pilot incorporated the same eligibility criteria—targeting poor, labour-constrained households—and used the same community-based targeting process, which required strong involvement of the communities and local authorities in the selection of beneficiaries. Malawi was one of the thirteen signatory countries of the Livingstone Call for Action, committing GoM to the development of a national social cash transfer programme which would be integrated into the National Development Plans and National Budget.

The GoM's participation in the 2006 Livingstone Conference gave renewed energy to the process of developing a social protection policy and programme in Malawi. UNICEF invited the lead consultant of the group advising the Kalomo project to visit Malawi to participate in discussions with the GoM on the CT programme. By this time, the government had created a Social Protection Steering Committee (SPSC) and an associated Social Protection Technical Committee (SPTC), which were charged with designing a National Social Protection Policy and Programme and with overseeing social protection interventions in the country. An agreement was reached in the SPSC to conduct a limited operational research in Mchinji to test whether implementing a similar model in Malawi would be operationally feasible and to begin to adapt the model to the Malawian context. This trial phase ran from April to June 2006. By June, interested parties within GoM felt confident that the model could work from an operational standpoint in Malawi, and they decided to move forward with designing a full-fledged pilot. The SPSC put forth a design proposal to the Cabinet for a four-district pilot, which was approved by the Cabinet in November 2006 with the qualification that the number of districts should be increased from four to seven and be accompanied by an impact evaluation. The seven districts for the pilot were selected by the Cabinet, and intentionally ensured programme coverage in all three regions of the country: Chitipa and Likoma (from the North), Mchinji and Salima (from Central), and Mangochi, Machinga, and Phalombe (from the South).

12.3 THE MALAWI SOCIAL CASH TRANSFER SCHEME PILOT AND THE 'MCHINJI PILOT' EVALUATION: 2006–2012

The first payments for the Malawi SCTS Pilot were distributed to 400 households in September 2006 in Mchinji district. The objectives of the pilot were to: 1) reduce poverty, hunger, and starvation in households that are both ultra-poor and labour-constrained; 2) increase school enrolment and attendance of children living in target households and to improve their health and nutrition status; 3) generate information on the programme's feasibility, cost, and impact with a view to learning for scaling up the SCTS to the rest of the country (Shubert and Huijbregts 2006; UNICEF 2007b). As mentioned in Section 12.1, the families which were the focus of the SCT programme have extremely limited labour resources. Therefore target households are defined as ultra-poor households with proportionally few able-bodied members in the 19–64 age range that are fit to work (either due to absence of members in this age range, or chronic illness, or disability of those within range). The threshold for eligibility is less than one able-bodied member aged 19–64 per three dependents.

The SCTS used a community-based, multi-stage, participatory process to identify beneficiary households. The targeting of SCTS beneficiaries involved community members, community level government officials, and district officials. Four meetings, three community-level and one district-level, were required for finalizing the list of beneficiaries. In the first meeting, community members would elect local representatives to serve on the village group's Community Social Support Committee (CSSC). These community members were charged with significant responsibility for identifying potential beneficiaries, as they are requested to produce a list of the poorest households, representing up to 12 per cent of the local population of the Village Cluster (VC). These households would be surveyed for additional data and then ranked according to the information provided. The poorest 10 per cent of households in the VC would make up the beneficiary list. The community would then meet to review the list, after which the final list was sent to the District Assembly (DA) office for verification and approval. A final community meeting would be held to transparently announce the approved final list of beneficiaries.

The transfers were paid in cash to beneficiaries each month by DA accounting staff. They were accompanied by security escorts to secure pay points close to the villages, usually in common areas such as schools. The transfer amount varied based on household size and composition. Table 12.1 describes how the monthly transfer amount was calculated during the period from 2006 to 2012.

As is evident in Table 12.1, the programme gave a bonus to households with children in primary or secondary school, giving a higher transfer for children in secondary school to offset the higher educational costs. The child school bonus is designed to encourage school enrolment (the second objective of the SCTS Pilot) although there is no verification mechanism of school attendance since the programme is entirely *unconditional*.

The transfer amounts were determined by the technical committee using the gap between the ultra-poverty line at that time (MWK6,447 per month, roughly US$46 at the time for a 5.8 person household) and the average monthly expenditure of households in the lowest income quintile

Table 12.1. Transfer Amounts by Household Size and School Bonus

Household Size	Monthly Cash Transfer (MWK)		
	2006–12	2013–15	2015–Present
1 person	600	1,000	1,700
2 persons	1,000	1,500	2,200
3 persons	1,400	1,950	2,900
4+ persons	1,800	2,400	3,700
School Bonus			
Per child in Primary	200	300	500
Per child in Secondary	400	600	1,000

(MWK5,103, roughly US$37).[1] The minimum transfer amount of MWK600 was fixed taking the minimum amount received by a government pensioner (MWK700 per month) as a reference at that time. The SPTC designed the transfer amount to vary with the size of the household, and to offer additional support for school-aged children. These transfer amounts would remain in place from the start of the programme in 2006 through to 2012, eroding the real value from MWK600 to MWK501 and indeed a fall in value even in US dollar terms from 4.3 to 2.4 (Miller, Tsoka, and Reichert 2010; Reserve Bank of Malawi Website).[2] This necessitated a technical review of transfer amounts, commissioned by UNICEF and the government, which resulted in an adoption of a new payment scheme.

12.3.1 The SCTS Pilot: Roll-Out and Expansion

As has been noted in other country cases, the launch of an SCT programme was a politically sensitive issue. Detractors claimed that giving money away to poor people would only serve to create more dependency, and could not succeed in empowering families and facilitating opportunities to rise out of extreme poverty. Proponents cited solid evidence to the contrary from other country programme evaluations, but at the same time recognized the need to act strategically in order to allow the programme time to gain a foothold nationwide. These and other political factors played an influencing role in the selection of the pilot districts and the condition that impact evaluation be included as part of the pilot project. The strategic selection of the districts was necessary to build countrywide support for the SCT programme and the

---

[1] Based on Miller et al. (2010), the exchange rate was roughly MWK139.53 to a US dollar.
[2] The rural price index increased from 214.6 in 2006 to 256.8 in 2012 according to the CPI (Consumer Price Index) data on Malawi National Statistics Office Website.

impact evaluation was necessary to provide evidence that would bring both the proponents and the detractors together.

The decision to launch the pilot in Mchinji district first was taken due to a number of factors, most notably that it would facilitate more learning and demonstration opportunities, a stated objective of the pilot. Mchinji has the advantage of being located just over an hour away by car (100 kilometers) from Lilongwe, making it a convenient staging ground for policy makers and other stakeholders to closely monitor the development of the pilot and visit the site frequently. Additionally, Mchinji district was right in the middle of the poverty ranking (number fourteen of the twenty-eight districts of the country), with a poverty profile that was considered average in the country (Schubert and Huijbregts 2006). Mchinji also had a particularly motivated and capable District Commissioner (DC), supported by a strong District Assembly, and district team.

Expansion to the other six pilot districts was to begin shortly thereafter, with the goal of providing full coverage in all seven districts by 2009. However, because of insufficient implementation capacity and limited funding support, the proposed expansion did not go as planned. In fact, through 2012, the pilot was only operational at full scale in Mchinji and Likoma (a small island with few beneficiaries). From 2006 through to the end of 2008, Mchinji was well underway mostly in the impact evaluation intervention and few operational research clusters, but there was limited coverage in the other districts. By the end of 2008, Chitipa and Phalombe were just coming online for the programme, with capacity assessments and training of the District Assemblies. As a result, the external evaluation of the pilot (which ran from March 2007 to April 2008) was conducted only in Mchinji. Therefore, the evaluation of the Malawi SCTS Pilot came to be widely known as the 'Mchinji SCT Pilot Evaluation', without reference to the larger coverage area of the full pilot.

Initial funding for the start-up including the operational research was provided by UNICEF, and funding for the pilot from 2007 to 2012 was largely covered by the Global Fund for Tuberculosis, AIDS and Malaria Global Fund through the National AIDS Commission (NAC), with extensive technical support provided by UNICEF. Given that the targeting mechanism would enable identification of households with orphans, proponents advocated for the SCT programme as a poverty mitigation programme for OVC. The Mchinji experience showed that indeed the SCTS Pilot was reaching a substantial proportion of orphans—by April 2007, in its first year of operation, the pilot reached 2,442 households in which 7,480 children were living, 6,013 of whom were orphans (UNICEF 2007a). About US$9.3 million was provided to NAC by the Global Fund to support the pilot over the period of about five years.[3]

---

[3] Funding was provided through the Global Fund Round 5 OVC grant, which had a priority focus on interventions that targeted OVCs.

In mid-2008, the SPTC began drafting the National Social Support Policy (NSSP), which defined where the range of social protection programmes would be housed within the government, and outlined the programme development strategies. The NSSP was presented to the Cabinet later that year but was not discussed as it was not high on the agenda. Nevertheless, while waiting for approval of the policy, the SPTC (with support from UNICEF) continued developing the National Social Support Programme to define programme plans and align all social protection interventions outlined in the NSSP under one framework. In April 2012, a new president took office and by June 2012, two months later, the government approved the policy. The National Social Support Programme, which detailed SCT programme implementation plans, was also approved shortly thereafter by the SPSC.

Although the original plan was for fairly rapid expansion of the SCT programme (according to Schubert and Huijbregts (2006), there were to be 32,000 households by December 2008, and 143,000 households by December 2013), in practice there were only about 13,029 households in nine districts receiving cash transfers by December 2013 (Ayala communication). Funding limitations and capacity constraints at both national and district levels, as well as the lack of political support, as mentioned earlier in this section, slowed comprehensive coverage in the seven pilot districts. In sharp contrast to the slow pace of expansion of the SCT programme was the introduction and rapid expansion of the Fertilizer Input Subsidy Programme (FISP), which the government initiated in 2005 despite sharp criticism from the IMF and World Bank.[4] Targeted towards 'resource-poor' agricultural households and heavily funded through the National Budget, the programme reached 1.6 million beneficiary households in just three years, providing subsidized fertilizer and maize seed, and free legume seeds. The programme has been credited for the sharp rise in agricultural production in Malawi since 2005 and has enjoyed strong political and public support. The contrasting experiences of the FISP and the SCT programme in Malawi are representative of the tension throughout the region within governments, favouring 'productive programmes' that can lead directly to growth over cash transfers, which are viewed as 'unproductive' and potentially leading to 'dependency'.

An unintended consequence of the delays in approving the NSSP was that donors were hesitant to provide significant additional support for the SCTS Pilot. The delay to approve the NSSP from 2009 to 2012 made donors (that were otherwise willing to finance the scheme) somewhat apprehensive about GoM's commitment to advancing the cash transfer agenda, particularly since results from the Mchinji evaluation (discussed in Section 12.3.2) were very positive. Donors were interested in funding official government programmes,

---

[4] *New York Times* (2007).

and therefore had trouble justifying large amounts of funding to an initiative under a policy that had yet to be officially adopted by government.

While there was some hesitation in providing new funding, donors were not completely hands-off prior to the adoption of the NSSP. The German Government (through KfW) began discussions with GoM as early as 2009 and proceeded with negotiations even in the absence of an approved NSSP. Additionally, in 2010 when there was a gap in NAC funding, Irish Aid stepped in and funded four months of transfers until NAC picked up funding again. Other donors, such as the European Union (EU), made their funding for expansion to additional districts contingent upon GoM's approval of the NSSP.

The KfW and GoM negotiations that began in 2009 were finalized in 2011 when KfW and the GoM signed an agreement to provide funding for the SCT programme for three and a half years. In 2012, KfW funds that were originally programmed to expand the programme to full coverage in the existing seven districts were reallocated to cover the funding shortfall which was created when NAC funds dried up. Other development partners also stepped up, providing resources for programme scale-up. In 2013, Irish Aid agreed to fund one additional district (Balaka), and in 2014 KfW topped up contributions to enable full coverage in the original seven pilot districts. The EU came in with funding to expand in seven additional districts[5] (which were launched in November 2014) and the World Bank is providing resources for two additional districts, Nkhata Bay and Dedza, which started in early 2015. Noticeably absent was DFID, despite their strong support for almost identical programmes in neighbouring Zambia and Zimbabwe.

Since the SCT programme began, the GoM has contributed significant resources in the form of staffing, vehicles, and other in-kind contributions. Though formal financial commitments from the Ministry of Finance lagged behind in the early years of the programme, the situation has improved significantly. In 2009–10, GoM included the SCT programme in the National Budget. This was taken as a significant sign of commitment to the programme as part of Malawi's core social protection strategy. With increases in donor commitments came additional financial commitments from GoM. Year by year, GoM has steadily increased contributions from the National Budget. GoM first contributed funds in the 2010–11 fiscal year in the amount of MWK50 million. In 2011–12, GoM provided about MWK70 million, which increased to MWK100 million and more than quadrupled to MWK450 million in 2012–13 and 2013–14 respectively.[6] For 2014–15, the Minister of Finance made a commitment of MWK1.2 billion, bringing

---

[5] The EU-funded districts are Chikwawa, Mulanje, Mwanza, Mzimba, Neno, Nsanje, and Zomba.

[6] Only a portion of this was disbursed due to implementation challenges.

the government commitments up to about 10 per cent of the combined donor contribution from KfW, EU, Irish Aid, and UNICEF (UNICEF-Malawi, personal communication). However, of the committed funds that year, only about one quarter (MWK 320 million) were distributed due to continuing logistical challenges. To date, GoM has contributed a cumulative total of MWK1.531 billion. Additionally, in 2013, GoM showed their commitment to the programme by launching a new district (Thyolo) on its own initiative; first payments were made in Thyolo in March 2014.

An additional obstacle that stifled the expansion of the SCT programme is capacity constraints. The implementation of the SCT programme is largely decentralized, with the bulk of the programme implemented by district-level officials. However, participation at the central government level is a critical component for all types of support, including training, and operational and financial oversight. When the programme began, there was not yet a dedicated team within the ministries tasked with overseeing the programme. Technical capacity at the central level was extremely constrained, as, until recently, there were only two or three people at the national level who were supporting all of the districts. These few individuals were responsible for training district and community teams on targeting and implementation of the SCTS. Given the need to provide multiple rounds of quality training, it was not possible to move as quickly as envisioned. The end result was a slow introduction of the scheme in six of the pilot districts; by 2009, when the pilot was supposed to have completed, actual transfers had not begun to be received by households in two districts, and only a portion of the Traditional Authorities (TAs) in those districts had been targeted. There was an intense debate regarding the need to establish a management unit within the central government. Eventually, an agreement was reached on a staffing plan at the central and district levels, which was in part motivated by the conditioning of financial support from development partners on such a plan. As of April 2014, about 40 per cent of these positions had been filled. Staff funding is covered by government funds, as funding from donors such as KfW and the EU are restricted to transfers, investment in programme infrastructure, such as building a Management Information System (MIS), and purchasing equipment.

In 2012, a new wave of expansion began in earnest, which started with the retargeting of existing coverage areas, and targeting of TAs not previously covered in the existing nine districts. Targeting and retargeting took significantly longer than planned, in part due to the lengthy community-based targeting process. By December 2013, retargeting had been completed, but still fewer than 30,000 households in nine districts were receiving cash transfers. However, over the next twelve months, a major push to complete targeting in the remaining TAs in the existing nine districts, as well as in seven new EU funded districts, marked a significant and accelerated expansion which more than tripled the number of households receiving transfers. In

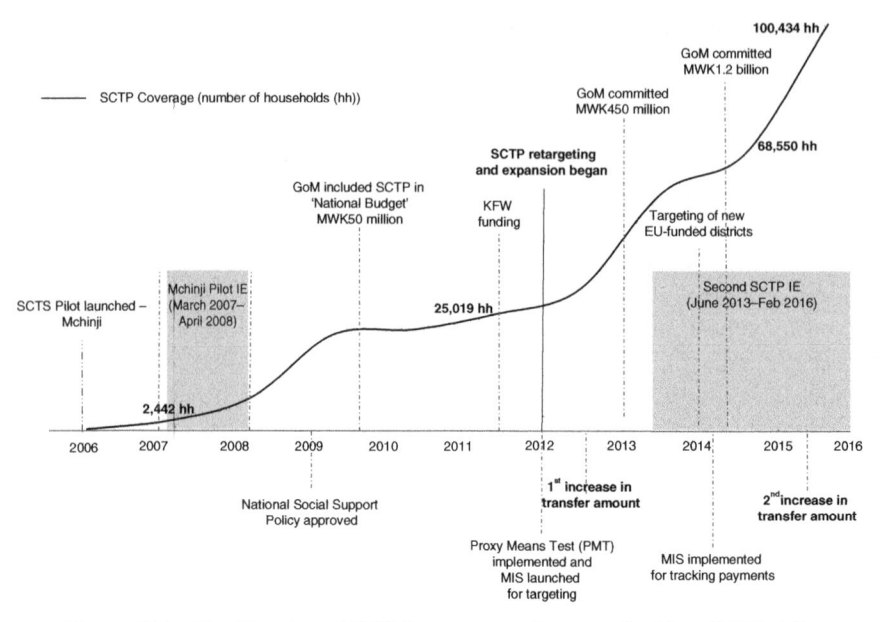

Figure 12.1. Key Events and SCT Programme Coverage by Year (2007–16)

January 2015, targeting started in two World Bank funded districts. By April 2015, beneficiaries in eighteen districts were receiving SCT payments, with GoM having achieved full coverage in ten of the districts for a total of over 100,000 households receiving programme benefits. Figure 12.1 summarizes the programme timeline and expansion.

12.3.2 The Mchinji SCTS Pilot Evaluation (2007–2008): Objectives and Results

The GoM's decision to start with a pilot programme was taken with the objective of generating information on the feasibility, costs, and benefits of a cash transfer programme as a critical component of the government's social protection portfolio (the third objective of the SCTS Pilot). To this end, the pilot design incorporated independent evaluations of operations, targeting, and impact as a mechanism for measuring to what extent the programme objectives were being met, as well as evaluating implementation effectiveness. The results and experience of the pilot were to be used for the scale-up of the programme to the national level.

The external evaluation of the SCTS Pilot was implemented from March 2007 to April 2008, and conducted by Boston University's Center for International Health and Development (CIHD) and the University of Malawi's

Centre for Social Research (CSR). The establishment of the evaluation was somewhat serendipitous, as researchers at CIHD had won a grant from the United States Agency for International Development (USAID) somewhat independently to conduct research on OVC in Malawi, and offered to evaluate the pilot by pooling those funds with additional top-up funds from UNICEF. The impact evaluation used a mix of quantitative and qualitative approaches to examine programme impact on a variety of household and individual outcomes. The quantitative analysis was based on a matched control pre- and post-evaluation design, with longitudinal household data collected at three moments in time: baseline (March 2007), four to five months later (July 2007), and at twelve months (March 2018). The SCTS Secretariat identified eight Village Development Committees (VDCs) in Mchinji of which it assigned four to treatment, and four as comparison. With about 100 households per VDC, a total of 800 households were examined in the impact evaluation.

The evaluation findings were widely distributed among the agencies involved in the SCTS Pilot and they were used by the government to make operational decisions on the next steps of the programme and to make adjustments to programme design and implementation, as well as for advocacy for public support and funding, both within GoM and externally with donors. Results were also used in the formulation of the NSSP which named the SCT programme as an integral component of the social protection strategy. In Section 12.3.3 we illustrate some of the key findings that were acted upon in the subsequent scale-up.

12.3.3 The Influence of Evidence on Programme Targeting, Operations, and Expansion: 2008-2012

Results from the Mchinji Pilot Impact Evaluation (IE) had an important influence on modifications to targeting and programme operations and management over the subsequent years. A major initiative to update the targeting process was undertaken and implemented in 2012. The 2008 Targeting Evaluation (Miller, Tsoka, and Reichert 2008b) noted that the targeting criteria needed to be more clear and additional oversight was needed to monitor the eligibility of the beneficiaries beyond the Community Social Support Committee (CSSC) and community review process. During the pilot, beneficiary selection criteria were not sufficiently well defined to be implemented uniformly by CSSC members and, without an MIS system, oversight was incredibly challenging. The targeting redesign included a more straightforward definition of ultra-poor that CSSC members could readily identify in a uniform manner.

A stronger verification system was implemented to screen the lists submitted by the community and was used to create a more objective ranking system for the households. Beneficiary selection is now done through a mixed approach combining community-based selection and Proxy Means Testing (PMT), with oversight provided by the local DC's Office and the District Social Welfare Office (DSWO). Community members are appointed to the CSSC by other community members and they are responsible for the initial identification of households that meet the eligibility criteria. These lists are to include roughly 12 per cent of the households in each Village Cluster (VC). The households are then subjected to the PMT, by which the MIS ranks them according to a set of predetermined criteria. A second community meeting is held to discuss the ranking and add any additional names to the list that were overlooked in the first round. The list is then re-ranked and the results are screened to reduce the final list of beneficiaries to the number of households needed to achieve the target coverage rate of 10 per cent of households in a VC. The District Social Support Committee uses the MIS to verify the lists and approves them accordingly. At the third community meeting, the names of the approved beneficiaries are announced to the community and programme identification cards are made. This new system has improved the monitoring and oversight to avoid issues of corruption that may have previously influenced the selection of beneficiaries; it also serves to streamline the process, reducing the time and resources needed to conduct the targeting exercise, while effectively maintaining community participation in the process. This new targeting process was employed during the targeting of new coverage areas in the pilot districts as well as the retargeting of existing coverage areas that began in late 2012. It was also implemented for targeting households in new expansion districts in 2013–15, ensuring a transparent and uniform targeting process for all programme areas. The targeting process, however, is still very time intensive, and it remains to be seen whether the community feels as much ownership of the programme since the use of the PMT means that a degree of decision-making has been taken out of their hands.

Until recently, the expansion strategy for selecting new districts for the SCTP has been a source of contention. While some development partners advocated for achieving full coverage in existing districts before targeting new districts, the government had consistently argued for using new funds to increase the number of districts included in the programme. Additionally, the selection of the districts was not based on their poverty ranking, as was envisioned in the NSSP, but was based on other, less clearly defined criteria. One reason may lie in the fact that the southern region has a greater concentration of poorer districts, and policy makers felt it was critical to include districts from all three regions of the country so as not to show favouritism, as described previously. Only in the last two years has the expansion strategy shifted to full coverage in existing districts and a more transparent, poverty ranking approach for selecting expansion districts. It should be noted, however, that these early expansion decisions may have had significant influence on garnering cross-regional, long-term policy support for the SCT programme in Malawi.

Operational issues that were revealed through the Operations Evaluation (Miller, Tsoka, and Reichert 2008a) were also addressed in the years following the evaluation and before the major expansion. As noted earlier, the lack of an electronic MIS proved highly problematic in maintaining programme accountability and made reporting from the district level a major technical challenge. Districts had few resources and limited training and capacity to provide to the central government the information that was required by donors to accurately account for programme funds. In 2010, payments were interrupted due to a sudden halt in the flow of donor funds until GoM could properly account for programme spending. The burden of these technical challenges fell heavily on the beneficiary households, as the support they were counting on was suspended indefinitely and without prior notice. Only in 2012 did payments resume, but in an erratic way. In 2013 there were no payments until the end of the year. However, all arrears accumulated throughout 2013 were paid by the end of 2013.

Some of these technical and accountability challenges have been resolved with the implementation of the electronic MIS. The MIS has been launched in two stages: the targeting portion of the MIS was brought online prior to the major expansion push in 2012, and the payment tracking portion was fully implemented as of 2014. The MIS now enables programme implementers to monitor activities, beneficiary payments, costs, and outputs. The system is able to generate regular monthly reports for the DC that are also shared and discussed with the SPTC at the national level. The MIS has also provided a mechanism for improving case management. The system has a process through which households can be dropped in the case that the household disintegrates. However, the mechanism for replacement of dropped households is still under development, as primary focus has shifted to improving the processes through which beneficiaries can file complaints.

Perhaps the most politically challenging change in the programme during this time period was the increase of the transfer amount in 2012. Inflation had been a significant problem in Malawi and the transfer amount was proving too low to help SCT households withstand the economic hard times. As a result, UNICEF commissioned a study to evaluate various approaches for recalculating the transfer level that were linked to inflation data (Mangani and White 2012). The study used data from Malawi's Second Integrated Household Survey (IHS2) as a basis for the new calculations, as results of the Third Integrated Household Survey (IHS3) were not yet available. The new transfer levels were approved and implemented in early 2013 (see Table 12.1). However, as IHS3 data became available, it was clear that the new transfer levels were still below the commonly accepted minimum threshold for critical impacts (the equivalent of 20 per cent of household consumption). While there was discussion about the need to raise the transfer level again, it was determined that, at that time, raising the transfer level would be both politically and financially untenable and so the transfer level was not changed. The transfer amounts were finally increased starting from May 2015 (see Table 12.1),[7] in good part as result of evidence from the 2013 baseline survey of the current impact evaluation which simulated expected impacts based on different transfer levels (see Section 12.4.1).

The Mchinji Impact Evaluation Report itself showed many positive impacts of the programme, ranging from food security (Miller, Tsoka, and Reichert 2008c, 2011) to health (Luseno et al. 2014) to schooling and child labour (Miller and Tsoka 2012) and even productive impacts (Covarrubias, Davis, and Winters 2012; Boone et al. 2013). These were the first results from an African cash transfer programme based on a rigorous evaluation design, and they were widely cited throughout Eastern and Southern Africa as an example of what an unconditional cash transfer could achieve. Results were also widely disseminated within Malawi and used by the SPSC to advocate for expansion of the SCTS, both to obtain additional funding from donors and to gain additional national political support. Though the programme did not expand immediately after the IE results came out in 2009, the existence of such strong positive evidence on the programme's impacts, especially on the productive impacts, was important for the eventual KfW decision to provide financial support to the programme.[8] KfW's leadership in engaging with government on support for the SCT paved the way for other donors, such as the EU and Irish Aid, to follow suit, establishing a package of support that has enabled the rapid expansion since 2012.

12.4 THE SECOND MALAWI SOCIAL CASH TRANSFER PROGRAMME IMPACT EVALUATION: 2013–2016

A second major impact evaluation of the Malawi SCTP[9] began in 2012 and will run through 2016. A key feature of the second evaluation was a local economy study which MoFEPD felt was important for increasing political

---

[7] The first transfers at the increased amounts would take place at the end of June, for the term May–June 2015.

[8] It is worth noting that the Malawi SCTP is the only cash transfer programme in the world supported by KfW. Social protection is not their usual area of investment, but the decision to fund was driven by evidence of significant impacts on several key measures.

[9] The Social Cash Transfer Scheme Pilot was rebranded as the Social Cash Transfer Programme as major expansion commenced in 2012.

support for the programme, and in turn for bringing additional financial resources from the Ministry of Finance. The IE is a three-year, mixed methods experimental-design study implemented by the University of North Carolina at Chapel Hill (UNC) and the CSR. The baseline and mid-line follow-up evaluations were funded by UNICEF, KfW, Irish Aid, and the UN FAO-Rome, while the International Initiative for Impact Evaluation (3ie) and the EU are providing funding for the endline survey. Both KfW and EU included funding for the IE as part of their package of support towards the expansion of the programme. The evaluation was conducted in Salima and Mangochi districts as they were scheduled for programme expansion in 2013. Baseline data were collected from June to November 2013. A total of 3,531 eligible households were interviewed in July–August, prior to enrolment in the programme, with qualitative interviews and focus groups carried out in the treatment group in November. Mid-line data collection was done from November 2014 to January 2015, with qualitative interviews and focus group discussions (FGDs) in February 2015. The results were still being processed at the time of completing this chapter. Endline data collection was scheduled for October–November 2015.

12.4.1 Baseline Results (2013): Targeting, Transfer Size, and Simulations

Baseline results were presented to GoM and other stakeholders at a workshop in January 2014. The picture depicted by baseline data is that SCTP households are both ultra-poor and vulnerable. Not only is overall consumption-based poverty high among eligible households, but the ultra-poverty gap and squared gap are five times higher than those among a comparable sample of households from the Malawi IHS3. Vulnerability is manifested in two ways. First, at the household level, SCTP households have higher dependency ratios and thus many fewer prime-age members to provide economic support to the household. Second, SCTP households rely on household heads who are older, in poorer health (often disabled or having chronic illnesses), and have virtually no schooling. The majority of children in these households are either fostered or orphaned and are living in homes without a biological parent.

Results from FGDs suggest that households selected by the GoM's SCTP targeting criteria (ultra-poor and labour-constrained) are the same types of households that community members felt were the poorest and most vulnerable. FGD participants estimated that between 45 and 71 per cent of community members were ultra-poor, and a further 19–28 per cent were poor; this is in agreement with baseline quantitative ultra-poverty and poverty rates (60 per cent and 85 per cent, respectively). A key characteristic that community members ascribed to ultra-poor households was the absence of household members who were old enough or able to work. Baseline quantitative data support this claim, as 26 per cent of SCTP-eligible households had no fit-to-work adult. These households live in extreme hardship, including food insecurity, poor quality housing, low enrolment levels in primary schools, and high rates of child *ganyu* (informal) labour. Therefore, the new targeting mechanisms for the SCTP appear to be reaching households that the community itself also recognizes as poor and vulnerable (Abdoulayi et al. 2014).

The quantitative targeting analysis showed that, while the programme is reaching ultra-poor labour-constrained households, the inclusion error is estimated to be as high as 55 per cent and the exclusion error is estimated at 54 per cent (Handa 2014). These figures are higher than the pilot figures, reflecting the difficulty in balancing high quality community-based targeting with realistic time and resource pressures as the programme tries to expand rapidly. However, though the errors have increased since the pilot, the figures are below or in line with other similar SCT programmes. Further analysis of the PMT indicated that the weighting of particular variables used in the calculation of the PMT may need adjustment to improve targeting and reduce errors, and as a result of this analysis, a review and update of the PMT is currently being conducted.

During the Baseline Results Workshop, the evaluation team also presented simulations of expected impacts on a selection of key indicators at current transfer levels. These simulations provided an evidence-based foundation on which to build the discussion among stakeholders on the potential benefits of increasing the transfer level. In the weeks following the workshop, UNICEF and the evaluation team worked to create an advocacy package for policy makers that could convey clearly the expected impacts at various transfer amounts. Both the simulated impacts of increasing the transfer amount and the analysis of the PMT were highly influential in the policy discussions between GoM and funders that ensued. As a result of this dialogue, the transfer size was formally increased in May 2015.

12.4.2 Results from the Mid-Line Survey (2014)

When the mid-line quantitative survey was conducted (November 2014–January 2015) the large majority of households had received six payments on a fairly regular basis but a bit less than 60 per cent thought that they were to receive payments for more than two years. So, it seems that they were in the process of perceiving the transfers as an increase in their permanent income. Mid-line impact results do not show an increase in consumption in the overall group of beneficiaries, although there was a significant shift towards specific consumptions items, namely clothing, education, and household furnishings (see Table 12.2 for the summary of key impacts). This shift is consistent with

Table 12.2. Summarized Key Impacts of the SCTP Mid-line Impact Evaluation Results

	All households	Poorest 50 per cent of households at baseline
CONSUMPTION		
Mean total annual per capita consumption expenditure (MWK—real)	5,019.13	6,592.25**
Mean annual per capita food consumption (MWK—real)	2,450.53	3,760.81**
POVERTY		
Poor (per cent)	−6.0**	
FOOD SECURITY		
Number of meals eaten per day	0.17*	0.17*
SCHOOLING		
Net enrolment ages 6–13	0.13**	0.14**
Net enrolment ages 14–17	0.15**	0.17**
HEALTH		
Chronic illness (age 10+)	−0.04**	−0.03**
Any illness last two weeks	−0.07**	−0.07**
Sought treatment at health facility	0.09**	0.12**
Sought treatment of diarrhea? (age <5)	0.09*	0.12**
Sought treatment of fever? (age <5)	0.22**	0.23**
HIV RELATED RISK		
Sexual debut (had sex, age 13–19)	−0.05**	
PRODUCTIVE		
Bought goat/sheep	0.09**	0.13**

Notes: * 5% significance; **1% significance. Baseline was conducted June–September 2013, and mid-line was conducted November 2014–January 2015.

the perceptions of beneficiaries about how they are supposed to use the transfer, with 70 per cent believing they must use the transfer to purchase school supplies and 35 per cent believing they must purchase appropriate clothing for children. The transfers had a significant impact on the poorest half of beneficiary households: There were significant increases in total consumption, as well as in food, clothing, furnishing, health, and education expenditures in the group of poorest households. For this group, the transfers represent a much larger share of their baseline consumption. Although food consumption does not show a significant increase in the overall group, short-term food security indicators do show significant improvements, with more meals eaten per day, and the poorest 50 per cent of households are 9 percentage points less likely to worry about food in the last week. As a result, there are significant programme impacts on subjective well-being measures reported by household heads, such as quality of life and expectations about future well-being (optimism about the future). School enrolment rates increased significantly for those aged 6–17. There have been lower self-reports of chronic illness and of any illness in the last two weeks; and, seeking care at a health facility has increased in all age groups and among those less than five years for treatment of diarrhoea or fever. There have been some impacts on productive activities of beneficiary households as well. A significantly higher proportion of beneficiary households now owns a sickle, and the overall expenditure on agricultural implements is higher. Production of chicken has also increased in beneficiary households. Beneficiary households were more likely to have opened an enterprise in the last twelve months, although there is no change in the profitability of enterprises. Beneficiary households were less likely to change eating patterns in response to shocks from high prices of food, and were also more likely to rely on own savings as a coping mechanism when they encountered shocks. This demonstrates how the programme is having some productive impacts even at the early stages, and is increasing the resilience of beneficiary households in the face of common shocks (Abdoulayi et al. 2015).

With regard to the local economy study commissioned by FAO, simulations indicate that the SCTP generates an income multiplier of 1.25 in nominal terms. This indicates that for each MWK1 of transfer from the SCTP generates an additional MWK0.25 of total income within the programme area (Thome et al. 2015).

These results will be important to demonstrate that the programme is working and that the government is providing the human resources and associated infrastructure necessary to support the expansion of the programme, a precondition for continued support from development partners.

12.5 THE FUTURE OF MALAWI'S SCTP: EVIDENCE, CHALLENGES, AND OPPORTUNITIES

By April 2015, the SCTP had reached more than 100,000 households across eighteen districts, with ten districts having achieved full coverage. GoM is still hopeful that they will continue expansion to reach all twenty-eight districts in the country, but at the moment there is no funding confirmed to support the last ten districts.

The GoM and development partners continue to search for solutions that would reduce implementation costs, which were shown to be high in a study conducted by an independent consulting firm (Ayala Consulting 2012). As such, GoM has committed to piloting innovations that could streamline the system, such as e-payment. It is anticipated that this mode of payment will improve the efficiency and regularity of payments and reduce the burden on district-level staff; however, e-payment is not without its challenges. At the request of GoM, with funding support provided by Irish Aid, Oxford Policy Management (OPM) and CSR are conducting an evaluation comparing three payment modalities: mobile payments through Airtel Money, delivering payment through banks by way of Opportunity International Bank of Malawi (OIBM), and traditional manual cash payments. The shift to third party payments was encouraged by multiple development partners to increase transparency, efficiency, and relieve some pressure on limited human resource capacity. Although the evaluation is ongoing, GoM has already decided to fully transition to third-party payment by the end of 2015. Thus far, the evaluation has revealed that e-payment comes with its own set of challenges. Some areas are lacking in the infrastructure required to implement e-payment. In some areas, mobile network coverage is unavailable, making Airtel Money impractical. Additionally, the number of Airtel Money agents has been declining due to low profitability, making it difficult for beneficiaries to access their funds. In some regions where OIBM is being used to make payments, there are cases where there are no ATMs available near beneficiaries for them to draw the money. This has meant that beneficiaries have encountered similar challenges with e-payment as they do during manual payments, given that they must walk long distances to queue at these super agents or behind mobile vans to get their cash. GoM plans to use evaluation results to improve the e-payment process and to make decisions on which payment modalities are most appropriate in different locations.

Although the scale-up of the programme is moving more quickly, there are some lingering obstacles that could continue to prove challenging. Key issues are capacity constraints, the need to further streamline operations to make them more efficient and sustainable, especially with regard to targeting and e-payment, and building a predictable funding stream. The SCTP requires a substantial team of skilled, committed staff from both central and district governments to operate effectively. These bodies were not in place in the pilot and expansion districts until recently. In fact, recruitment and orientation of many of the district-level officers were only done in 2014.

Based on the changes to the programme following the recommendations from the Mchinji SCTS Pilot Evaluation, and the reactions to simulated impacts and recommendations presented at the SCTP Impact Evaluation Baseline Workshop in 2014, it is likely that the results of the current evaluation will be looked at as an important source of evidence for making further improvements to the SCTP and advocating for increased support and financial backing (from both donors and GoM) to create a sustainable funding stream. While it has taken some time to implement most of the programmatic improvements to the SCTP, there is a clear signal that data and recommendations coming out of these rigorous impact evaluations is influencing policy decisions in Malawi. Information on programme costs and potential economic impacts (i.e., economic multiplier effects) are in high demand to demonstrate the programme's cost-effectiveness. These figures are likely to play a prominent role in policy discussions in the near future.

12.6 CONCLUSION

The Malawi experience holds several key lessons for policy makers and SCT programme implementers. In the Malawi case, we are offered a window into the complexities of executing evaluation recommendations, which are inevitably intertwined with political processes and funding flows. Despite implementing the first rigorous quantitative impact evaluation of a cash transfer programme in Africa, and despite those results showing across the board positive impacts in both social and productive domains, the expansion of the SCTP during 2008–12 stalled due to primarily a lack of commitment and organization within government, and fragmentation in approach among development partners. Indeed at this same time, even as the SCTP stalled, a major alternative poverty alleviation programme aimed at achieving productive impacts (FISP) expanded rapidly with heavy funding from the Treasury, although the poverty-targeting of that programme is significantly worse than the SCTP (Kilic, Whitney, and Winters 2015), and the SCTP itself demonstrated important productive impacts.

Nevertheless, the Mchinji IE results continued to be cited by UNICEF and the ministries within the country throughout the period of 2008–12, and served as an important piece of evidence to keep the dialogue open around the potential for the SCTP to alleviate poverty. This eventually attracted the attention of other development partners (Irish Aid, KfW, EU) and, along with increasing commitment from government itself, led to the second expansion phase starting in 2012, which is currently ongoing. Key drivers of the new donor support post-2012 were the approval of the National Social Protection Policy, a plan for building human resource capacity in the ministry to implement a larger programme, changes to the programme targeting and administration to improve efficiency, and the implementation of another rigorous impact evaluation, this time on a much larger scale. This new evaluation, though still ongoing, has already provoked some key changes in programme design—the refinement of the PMT and the increase in the transfer level.

While the future of the SCTP currently looks very bright, the process to get to this stage has been slow and taken nearly ten years. Continued success will require commitment from the government in terms of gradually increasing financial support, both for direct payments of cash as well as for human resources to serve an expanded programme. In this regard, the current impact evaluation, including the local economy and economic effects, can provide concrete evidence to maintain support for the programme. Indeed the Malawi experience shows that in the absence of political commitment, having evaluation results available which demonstrate strong positive impacts can help keep the discussion going and eventually bring support. There is no doubt that the existence of the Mchinji evaluation was important for bringing the programme to where it is today. There is also strong likelihood that the results of the current evaluations will provide not only further evidence for continued support but also recommendations for further programme refinements.

ACKNOWLEDGEMENTS

This chapter greatly benefitted from the information and comments on the programme provided through interviews and emails by Francisco Ayala, Ayala Consulting; Benjamin Davis, UN (United Nations) FAO (Food and Agriculture Organization of the United Nations); Chantal Elmont, Ayala Consulting; Mayke Huijbregts, UNICEF; Patience Kanjere, KfW (Kreditanstalt für Wiederaufbau (German Development Bank)); Laurent Kansinjilo, Government of Malawi, Ministry of Gender, Children, Disability and Social Welfare; Maki Kato, UNICEF; Mr. Blessings Nkhoma, Government of Malawi, Department of Finance, Planning and Development, Salima District Council; Ted Sitimawina, Government of Malawi, Ministry of Finance, Economic Planning, and Development. The authors are very grateful to all of them for their time and contributions to the chapter.

REFERENCES

Abdoulayi, S., Angeles, G., Barrington, C., Brugh, K., Handa, S., Hill, M.J., Kilburn, K., Otchere, F., Mvula, P., Tsoka, M., and Natali, L. (2014). 'Malawi Social Cash Transfer Program Baseline Evaluation Report'. The Transfer Project, University of North Carolina at Chapel Hill.

Abdoulayi, S., Angeles, G., Barrington, C., Brugh, K., Handa, S., Kilburn, K., Otchere, F., Martorano, B., Mvula, P., Peterman, A., Palermo, T., Rock, A., and Tsoka, M. (2015). 'Malawi Social Cash Transfer Program Midline Evaluation Report'. The Transfer Project, University of North Carolina at Chapel Hill.

African Union (2006). 'Social Protection—A Transformative Agenda: The Livingstone Call for Action'. African Union, Zambia.

Ayala Consulting (2012). 'Social Cash Transfer Program. Inception Report prepared for the Ministry of Gender, Children and Social Welfare'.

Boone, R., Covarrubias, K., Davis, B., and Winters, P. (2013). 'Cash transfer programs and agricultural production: the case of Malawi'. *Agricultural Economics*, 44: 365–78. doi: 10.1111/agec.12017.

Central Intelligence Agency (2007). 'The World Factbook 2007'. Washington, DC. Available online at: <https://www.cia.gov/library/publications/download/download-2007/index.html> (accessed 31 October 2015).

Covarrubias, K., Davis, B., and Winters, P. (2012). 'From protection to production: productive impacts of the Malawi Social Cash Transfer scheme'. *Journal of Development Effectiveness*, 4(1): 50–77.

Ellis, F., Kutengule, M., and Nyasulu, A. (2003). 'Livelihoods and rural poverty reduction in Malawi'. *World Development*, 31(9): 1495–510.

Government of Malawi (2006). 'Malawi Growth and Development Strategy, 2006–2011'.

Government of Malawi and World Bank (2007). 'Malawi Poverty and Vulnerability Assessment'. Full Report.

Handa, S. (2014). 'Targeting in Malawi's Social Cash Transfer Program'. Presentation given by the University of North Carolina and University of Malawi's Centre for Social Research at the Baseline Stakeholders Workshop, Lilongwe, Malawi.

Kainja, E.T. (2012). 'A study of child related policies, services and the needs of orphans in Malawi'. University of Leeds.

Kilic, T., Whitney, E., and Winters, P. (2015). 'Decentralised beneficiary targeting in large-scale development programmes: insights from the Malawi farm input subsidy programme'. *Journal of African Economies*, 24(1): 26–56.

Luseno, W., Singh, K., Handa, S., and Suchindran, C. (2014). 'A multilevel analysis of the effect of Malawi's social cash transfer pilot scheme on school-age children's health'. *Health Policy and Planning*, 29(4): 421–32.

Malawi National Statistics Office Website. <http://www.nsomalawi.mw/latest-publications/consumer-price-indices/69-consumer-price-index-rural.html> (accessed on 26 April 2015).

Mangani, R. and White, R. (2012). 'Costing and Analysis of Transfer Levels for the Malawi Social Cash Transfer Programme'.

Miller, C. and Tsoka, M. (2012). 'Cash transfers and children's education and labour among Malawi's poor'. *Development Policy Review*, 30: 499–522. doi: 10.1111/j.1467-7679.2012.00586.x.

Miller, C., Tsoka, M., and Reichert, K. (2008a). 'Operations Report. External Evaluation of the Mchinji Social Cash Transfer Pilot'. USAID, Boston University, UNICEF.

Miller, C., Tsoka, M., and Reichert, K. (2008b). 'Targeting Report. External Evaluation of the Mchinji Social Cash Transfer Pilot'. USAID, Boston University, UNICEF.

Miller, C., Tsoka, M., and Reichert, K. (2008c). 'Impact Evaluation Report. External Evaluation of the Mchinji Social Cash Transfer Pilot'. USAID, Boston University, UNICEF.

Miller, C., Tsoka, M., and Reichert, K. (2010). 'Targeting Cash to Malawi's Ultra-Poor: A Mixed Methods Evaluation'. *Development Policy Review*, 28(4): 481–502.

Miller, C., Tsoka, M., and Reichert, K. (2011). 'The impact of the Social Cash Transfer Scheme on food security in Malawi'. *Food Policy*, 36(2): 230–8.

New York Times (2007). 'Ending Famine, Simply by Ignoring the Experts', 2 December.

Reserve Bank of Malawi Website. <http://www.rbm.mw/Statistics/MajorRates> (accessed on 26 April 2015).

Samson M., Van Niekerk, I., and Mac Quene, K. (2010). 'Designing and Implementing Social Transfer Programmes'. Economic Policy Research Institute, 2nd edition.

Schubert, B. and Huijbregts, M. (2006). 'The Malawi Social Cash Transfer Pilot Scheme, Preliminary Lessons Learned'. Paper presented at the Conference on Social Protection Initiatives for Children, Women and Families: An Analysis of Recent Experiences, New York, October 2006.

Thome, K., Taylor, J. E., Tsoka, M., Mvula, P., Davis, B., and Handa, S. (2015). 'Local Economy-wide Impact Evaluation (LEWIE) of Malawi's Social Cash Transfer Programme'. FAO.

UNICEF (2006). 'Malawi's Children: The missing face of AIDS'. UNICEF, Malawi.

UNICEF (2007a). 'Project profile: Social Cash Transfer Pilot'. Malawi.

UNICEF (2007b). 'Q&A: The Malawi Social Cash Transfer Pilot'. Malawi.

UNICEF (2011). 'Vulnerability and Child Protection in the face of HIV'. United Nations Technical Review Team on programming for children affected by HIV and AIDS in Malawi, UNICEF and the Australian Agency for International Development.

13

The Impact of a Promise Realized

South Africa's Child Support Grant

Michael Samson (EPRI), Carolyn J. Heinrich (The University of Texas at Austin), John Hoddinott (Cornell University and IFPRI), George Laryea-Adjei (UNICEF), Thabani Buthelezi (DSD), Lucie Cluver (University of Oxford and University of Cape Town), Selwyn Jehoma (EPRI), Maureen Mogotsi (DSD), Thilde Stevens (DSD), Ingrid van Niekerk (EPRI), and Evelyne Nyokangi (EPRI)

13.1 INTRODUCTION

Since 1994 the Government of South Africa has recognized poverty as the number one scourge facing the country. Unemployment rose during the first decade of the nation's democracy, reducing income, worsening poverty, and increasing inequality (Samson et al. 2002).[1] The government mounted a multidimensional response—initially with the Reconstruction and Development Programme (RDP) and subsequently with a range of often fiscally constrained interventions. To tackle the particularly pernicious effects of deprivation on children, the Department of Social Development launched the Child Support Grant (CSG) in 1998. By 2015 the CSG succeeded in erasing half of South Africa's food poverty gap and represented the government's most successful instrument tackling poverty. Figure 13.1 shows that in 2013 the CSG together with other social grants erased more than two-thirds of South Africa's food poverty gap—compared with a poverty reduction from social grants of only about one-third in 1993 (Samson et al. 2013).

A number of studies have identified South Africa as being one of the most unequal countries in the world; with inequalities existing in education, health, and

---

[1] Samson et al.'s (2002) report to the Committee of Enquiry for Comprehensive Social Security reported rising poverty rates and falling employment from 1993 to 2000. The first social and economic impact assessment of South Africa's social grants corroborated these trends. Leibbrandt et al. (2005) found a substantial decline in real income from 1995 to 2000, a finding substantiated by Hoogeveen and Özler (2006).

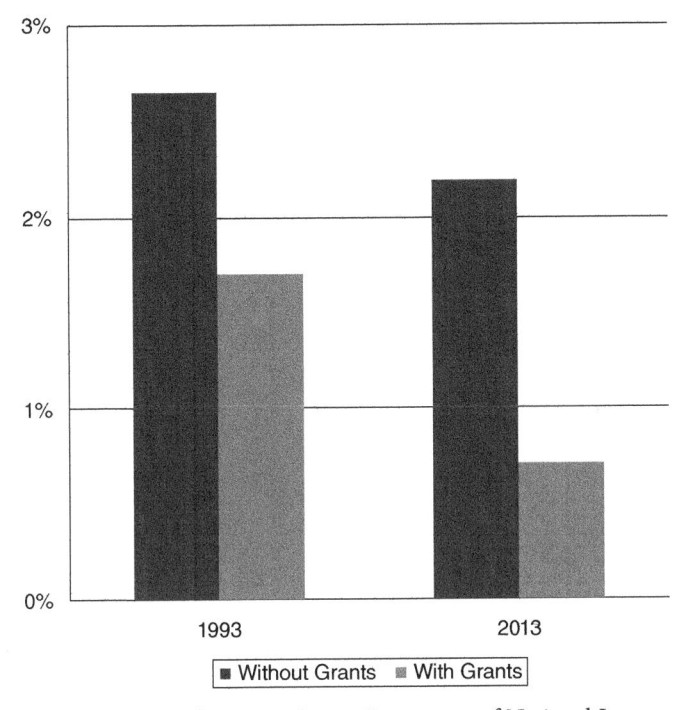

Figure 13.1. Food Poverty Gap as Percentage of National Income

basic infrastructure, as well as in access to safe water, sanitation, and housing (Hoogeveen and Özler 2006). In 2011, the Gini coefficient for aggregate household expenditure and income (included salaries, wages, and social grants) per capita stood at 0.65 and 0.69 respectively (DPME 2012). Children in South Africa grow up in a highly unequal society which entrenches poverty traps and social exclusion (Berry et al. 2013). Inequality interacts with poverty to exacerbate vulnerability and reinforce a vicious cycle of inter-generational transmission of deprivation.

The South African government's response to the problems of inequality and poverty included multidimensional efforts to strengthen the social wage. The Millennium Development Goal (MDG) Country Report 2013 noted that close to 60 per cent of government spending is allocated to the social wage (StatsSA 2013). The South African government provides social wages primarily through free primary healthcare, no-fee-paying schools, RDP housing, and social grants (particularly Old Age Pensions grant and CSG). Figure 13.2 illustrates the substantial increase in the impact of social grants on inequality from 1993 to 2013 (Samson et al. 2013).

13.1.1 South Africa's Policy Response to Child Poverty: The CSG

The CSG is one of the most significant components of South Africa's social grant system, reaching 11,703,165 poor children each month (as of March

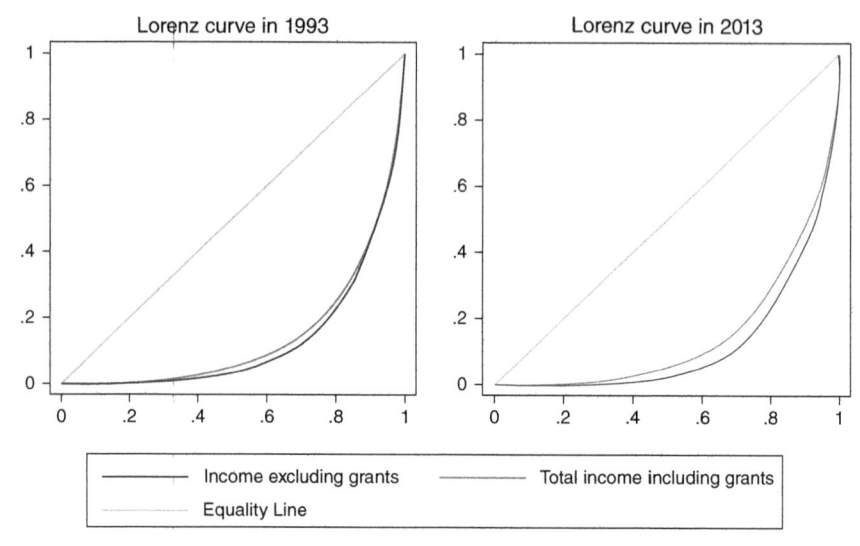

Figure 13.2. The Impact of Social Grants on Inequality

2015) (SASSA 2015). This programme has been successful in reducing household poverty, in addition to improving critical child developmental outcomes such as health, nutrition, and school attendance. The CSG is recognized as being 'the first major change in the field of social policy' in post-Apartheid South Africa, since it was aimed at improving the conditions of poor children as well as addressing inequalities stemming from discriminatory Apartheid-era policies (Case, Hosegood, and Lund 2005).

Over the past sixteen years, this cash transfer programme has evolved into one of the most effective social protection systems in the developing world. This has been primarily due to: (1) substantial increases in the CSG's coverage, as a result of extensions in the grant's maximum age eligibility threshold from 7 to 18 years; (2) reforms to the other eligibility requirements; and (3) improvements to the targeting mechanism.[2]

This chapter examines the first integrated quantitative–qualitative impact evaluation of the CSG and related research. A significant portion of the chapter is dedicated to investigating the influence of the study on the policy development process, especially as it pertains to realizing the social security rights of children in South Africa. This chapter is structured as follows. Section 13.2 provides detail of the history of the CSG. Section 13.3 discusses the origins of the impact evaluation commissioned in 2009 by the South African Department of Social Development (DSD), the South African Social

---

[2] Improving the targeting mechanism entails implementing strategies that reduce both the exclusion error (i.e., the percentage of eligible non-beneficiaries) and the inclusion error (i.e., the percentage of ineligible beneficiaries).

Security Agency (SASSA), and the United Nations Children's Fund (UNICEF) South Africa to rigorously evaluate the impact of the CSG on 'key aspects of child and adolescent welfare' (DSD, SASSA, and UNICEF 2012: 1). Section 13.4 describes the research approach used, the methodology and challenges of project management. Section 13.5 reports some of the evaluation findings, as well as results from similar studies on the impact of the CSG. The evaluation's influence on the policy development process is examined in Section 13.6, and Section 13.7 concludes.

13.2 HISTORY OF THE CSG PROGRAMME

In April 1998, the South African government introduced the CSG to replace the limited State Maintenance Grant (SMG).[3] This followed the Lund Committee recommendation that the grant recognize the realities of family life in South Africa, the most important being that many children are not cared for by their biological parents—the SMG was only payable to mothers without partners. Furthermore, the Committee proposed that the grant should have broader coverage, targeting children residing in the poorest 30 per cent of households (irrespective of race) (DSD, SASSA, and UNICEF 2012). The legislative framework for the broader CSG is enshrined in the South African Constitution, under Section 27(1)(c) of the Bill of Rights, which states that every South African citizen has a right 'to have access to [...] social security, including, if they are unable to support themselves and their dependents, appropriate social assistance' (South Africa 1996). Section 27(2) of the Constitution compels the State to ensure the progressive realization of a social security grant; whilst Section 28(1)(c) solidifies the State's commitment to provide special protection to vulnerable children, by specifically outlining a child's rights to social services (Rosa and Meintjes 2004; Dutschke 2006).

The Department of Welfare and Population Development (DWPD), renamed as the Department of Social Development (DSD) in 1998, produced the 'White Paper for Social Welfare in South Africa' which established the core principles for South Africa's social security system, including access for children. The document defines social security as '[a] wide range of public and private measures that provide cash or in-kind benefits, or both, first, in the event of an individual's earning power permanently ceasing, being interrupted, never developing, or being exercised only at unacceptable social cost and such person being unable to avoid poverty; and secondly in order to maintain

---

[3] The SMG has limited coverage with only 0.2 per cent of all African children receiving the grant, 1.5 per cent of all white children, 4 per cent of all Indian children, and 4.8 per cent of all coloured children (DSD et al. 2012: 1).

children' (DWPD 1997: 47). The document thus commits the South African government to the responsibility of offering immediate relief for basic needs, in cash or in kind, to children with the aim of reducing poverty.

The CSG is a cash transfer programme that provides monthly payments, to be paid to the child through the 'primary caregiver', defined as a person related or not related to the child, who takes primary responsibility for meeting the daily care needs of the child (e.g., biological parents, grandparents, guardians, etc.) (DSD, SASSA, and UNICEF 2012). Eligibility for the grant is determined through a means test, so that children are eligible if their caregiver's income falls below a set threshold.[4] When the CSG was formalized in 1998, a grant of R100 per child was provided to caregivers with eligible children (from birth to the child's seventh birthday) in order to meet the basic needs of the age cohort that is most vulnerable to poverty and underdevelopment (Hall 2007). However, in line with the recommendations of the Taylor Committee, the DSD progressively included older children into the benefit programme (Taylor Report 2002).[5]

In February 2003, Thabo Mbeki (the former President of the Republic of South Africa) announced that the CSG would be extended to include qualifying children under the age of fourteen. This extension was to be phased in over three years and mandated through modifications to the Social Assistance Act (No. 59 of 1992) (Meintjes et al. 2003). The extensions occurred in the following way: as of 1 April 2003, children under the age of nine qualified. As of 1 April 2004, children under the age of eleven qualified. Finally, as of 1 April 2005, children under fourteen years qualified for the CSG. The age eligibility was raised again to children under fifteen years (in 2009) and children under sixteen years (in 2010). Subsequent policy reforms extended the CSG to include sixteen-year-olds in 2011 and finally seventeen-year-olds in 2012, brought to fruition many years of lobbying by advocacy groups to extend the grant to all children (McEwen and Woolard 2012). Figure 13.3 illustrates these extensions in the CSG's eligibility criteria related to age. The key events related to the CSG are also illustrated in Figure 13.3 to provide a holistic picture of the CSG's evolution.

The grant amount has similarly increased from a monthly payment of R100 (in 1998) to R320 per child (as of October 2014), representing a nominal 220 per cent increase in the grant amount (Hall 2014). According to data from Statistics South Africa (StatsSA), the increase in the value of the CSG represents a real increase in purchasing power since the nominal growth in the value of the CSG outpaced the growth rate of the consumer price index (CPI).

---

[4] From 1998 to 2008, the threshold remained unchanged at a household income of R800 per month (in urban areas) and R1100 per month (in rural areas or in an informal dwelling), regardless of the primary caregiver's marital status. As of October 2014, the CSG threshold is R3200 per month for single caregivers, andR6400 per month (joint income) for caregivers with a partner (Samson et al. 2001).

[5] The South African Constitution defines any person under the age of 18 years as a child.

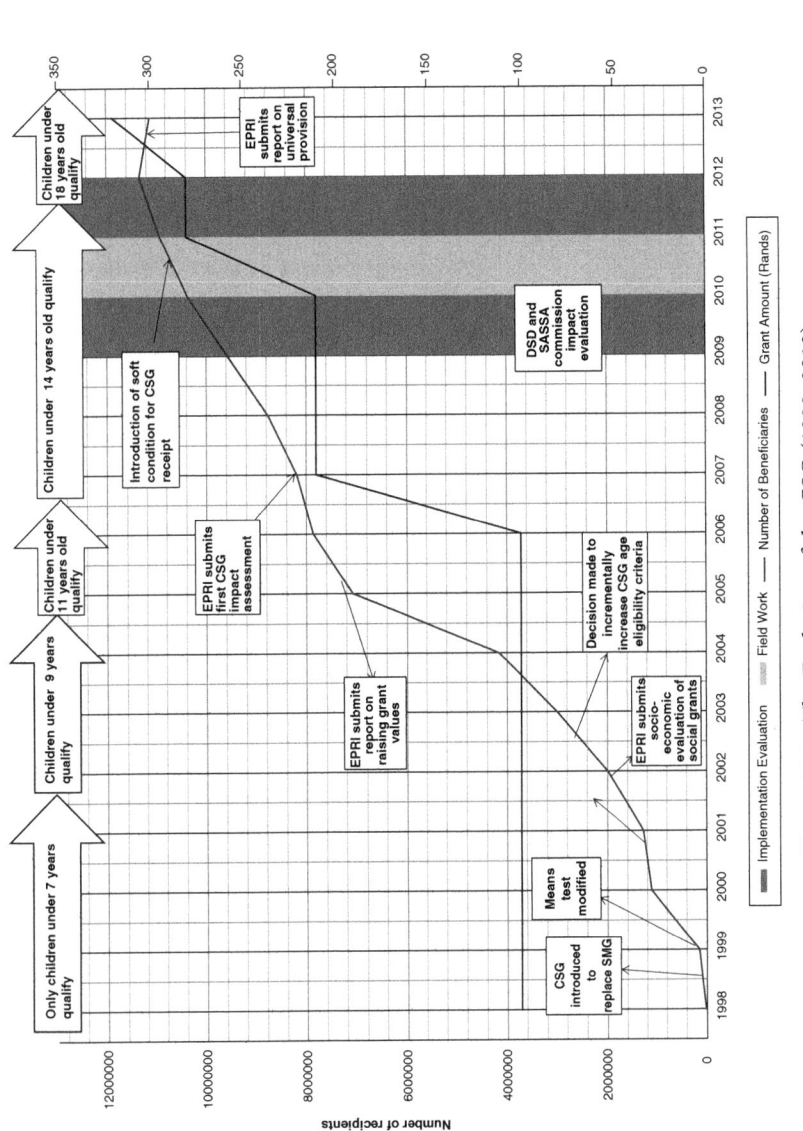

Figure 13.3. The Evolution of the CSG (1998–2012)

Source: SASSA (2008, 2012, 2014)

Finally, as from January 2010, Section 6(1)(h) was amended to include a developmental condition of school attendance (Hall 2011). It is important to note that beneficiaries remain eligible to receive payment in cases where this condition is not met, although poor awareness of the rights-based nature of the condition has led to interrupted benefits in some cases (UNICEF 2013; Heinrich and Brill 2015).

13.3 ORIGINS OF THE IMPACT EVALUATION

South Africa's DSD and SASSA are charged with jointly monitoring and evaluating the implementation of social programmes, with the CSG being the largest of these programmes—in terms of coverage. The Monitoring and Evaluation (M&E) that is undertaken aims to provide evidence that supports the policy, strategy, and planning processes, in addition to contributing to the development of an effective performance management system. From 2001 to 2007, a number of non-experimental studies informed ongoing reforms and expansions of the CSG, but no comprehensive integrated qualitative–quantitative evaluation assessed the impact of the CSG on beneficiaries. In November 2007, UNICEF and DSD jointly organized a workshop with national and international evaluation experts to discuss how to design an ongoing multi-year M&E framework for the CSG, as well as specific design options for an impact evaluation of the CSG. This workshop played a key role in DSD and SASSA understanding the benefits of such a framework and institutionalizing such a framework into the department's activities. A key outcome of the workshop was a commitment by DSD and SASSA to a rigorous assessment of the CSG both for public accountability and to potentially provide the basis for a large resource allocation to this programme, as well as to identify any shortcomings in design or implementation. The latter was considered to be one of the most important benefits to be derived from an impact evaluation, since it is these shortcomings that undermine the ability of the CSG to reach a large number of children living in severe poverty and in food-insecure households (du Toit 2011).[6]

Prior to the commission of the evaluation, most of the work assessing the CSG's impact had been carried out by academics using secondary data. In the cases where the DSD had conducted studies, none focused exclusively on the CSG or utilized a methodology that could rigorously measure the impact of the CSG on its beneficiaries (with the exception of Samson et al.'s (2011) quasi-experimental assessment, published as a chapter in *Social Protection for Africa's Children*). Instead, most analyses tended to be descriptive

---

[6] Approximately 20 per cent of households had inadequate or severely inadequate access to food at the time (du Toit 2011).

studies that used nationally representative household surveys or administrative data from the grant administration system, that is the Social Pension System (SOCPEN). Thus, the CSG impact evaluation presented an opportunity for the government to invest in collecting primary data that could address its specific interests and concerns.

The impact evaluation was then designed to address the following questions:

(1) How does early versus late enrolment affect the well-being of children and their families? Some of the dimensions of well-being considered include health, schooling, and nutrition (as measured by anthropometric indicators).
(2) How does early versus late enrolment affect access to and use of preventative health care and nutrition services?
(3) How has the extension of the CSG to adolescents enhanced their well-being? Four of the domains considered included adolescent exposure to risky behaviour (e.g., sexual activity, alcohol and drug use, pregnancy, criminal activity, and gang membership), schooling outcomes, time allocation, and labour supply decisions.
(4) What factors influence the ability of children to access the CSG? This involved an exploration of barriers to initial application; in addition to factors that determine the duration and continuity of receipt, and current receipt of the grant.

13.4 THE RESEARCH APPROACH

13.4.1 Research Design, Questionnaires, and Data

The sampling process for the study took place in two stages. First, a random sample of locations, defined as the catchment areas for specific pay points, was drawn from SASSA's administrative database (SOCPEN). These locations were sampled from each of the five selected provinces: Eastern Cape, Gauteng, KwaZulu-Natal, Limpopo, and Western Cape. Second, children were randomly selected from the known pay points and allocated to one of two groups—ten-year olds who enrolled in the CSG programme shortly after birth or those who enrolled at age four or more. In addition, adolescents were selected around the age cut-off for eligibility in 2010, including those receiving and not receiving the CSG. Three questionnaires were designed to gather information on children, adolescents, and their households. Households with participating adolescents were given the CSG Adolescent Questionnaire and the CSG Household Questionnaire, while homes with participating young children were given the CSG Young Child Questionnaire and the CSG Household Questionnaire. During the data analysis phase, the research team compared the results of the survey to other national household surveys, including the 2008 National Income Dynamics Survey (NIDS) and the 2010 General Household Survey (GHS), and found the sample largely representative of the national population.

13.4.2 Impact Evaluation Methodology

The qualitative and quantitative evaluation teams developed an integrated and comprehensive theory of change for the CSG that included: (1) a hypothesis of mechanisms through which the CSG produces impacts; (2) a common set of evaluation questions to be addressed jointly in the qualitative and quantitative studies; and (3) the key indicators of impact and also unintended outcomes. This framework provided the foundation for a preparatory qualitative project, with the findings used to refine the quantitative evaluation strategy and questionnaire design.

At its inception, the impact evaluation was largely a quantitative study with a qualitative assessment set for the final stages. However, the benefits of integrating a qualitative component in the overall evaluation strategy became increasingly apparent to the researchers and evaluation stakeholders. An integrated evaluation would facilitate a greater understanding of programme impacts and provide clarity on the mechanisms which produce them. A primary objective of undertaking the impact evaluation was to improve SASSA's and the DSD's knowledge of how beneficiaries use the CSG; the pathways through which the CSG improves child development, health, education, and other aspects of well-being; and the individual, household, and community or administrative factors that prevent eligible children accessing the CSG. The impact evaluation therefore included both quantitative and qualitative investigations of programme effects, including an exploration of programme implementation and its relationship to programme impacts.

The Economic Policy Research Institute (EPRI) employed a preparatory qualitative (field) research evaluation, prior to finalizing the quantitative research design and methodology. EPRI in partnership with the Institute of Development Studies (IDS) and the International Food Policy Research Institute (IFPRI) conducted the qualitative research in four provinces (Eastern Cape, Gauteng, Kwazulu-Natal, and Limpopo), stratifying the sample using a range of observable characteristics (age, race, gender, settlement type, access to the CSG, exclusion from the CSG, and the age of their children when the grant was first received) to reflect the profile of CSG beneficiaries and non-beneficiaries living in South Africa's rural, urban, and peri-urban settlements.

This research component focused on the decisions and processes surrounding CSG applications; the experiences around receipt of the grant at pay points (e.g., accessibility and service delivery standards); use of the grant and service access; the circumstances and issues concerning adolescents; and access to services (e.g., child protection, early childhood development, and social welfare programmes). The team employed two research methods as part of the qualitative evaluation strategy. First, the researchers conducted seven focus group discussions in each of the selected provinces.[7] Second, they conducted four key informant interviews with SASSA staff, education workers, health workers, and community leaders in each of these localities. This qualitative component greatly enhanced the impact evaluation's capacity to identify and characterize issues of importance to the population being studied, its need for the intervention, attributes of the intervention and its implementation, and the (potential) anticipated and unanticipated programme effects. This evaluation approach also enabled researchers to identify issues that needed to be investigated further with the subsequent quantitative research methods.

At the same time, quantitative data involving a larger sample of the population was collected. The sampling strategy, employing the programme's administrative data, improved the precision and consistency of measures, which allowed for more accurate and nationally representative empirical analyses of the scope, incidence, patterns, and other associations among CSG intervention variables and outcomes. The quantitative methodology utilized by the CSG evaluation aimed to measure causal programme impacts as the difference between observed outcomes for the beneficiaries and their counterfactual, that is, a proxy for what outcomes would have been for this group had they not received the CSG. This study necessarily employed non-experimental methods to identify an appropriate counterfactual. A randomized experiment was impossible because there is no practical or legal scope for randomly allocating grants in South Africa.

The non-experimental approach selected takes advantage of variations in the "dosages" (length of time receiving the CSG) by matching children on their *propensity* to receive a given "dosage" of the CSG. The outcomes of children with higher actual dosage (longer receipt of the CSG and from early childhood) are then compared with those with lower dosage (shorter receipt of the CSG and only after the early childhood period) to estimate the impact of early versus late enrolment on important outcomes. For example, one analysis carried out as part of the impact evaluation matched children receiving the CSG in the first two years of life, to a comparable group of children with

---

[7] The individuals selected into the focus group fell into one of the following categories: female early recipients, female late recipients, female non-beneficiaries, adolescent girls, adolescent boys, the male partners of CSG recipients, and a separate group for female recipients with adolescent children.

similar observable characteristics that influence their probability of applying for, or receiving the CSG but who only first received the CSG when they were older.[8] The impact of the programme on a range of outcomes (e.g., preventative health and nutrition care, immunization status, anthropometry, attendance at pre-schools, school attendance, sexual risk, etc.) was then estimated as the average difference in the outcomes for each treatment household from a weighted average of outcomes in each similar comparison group household from the matched sample.

13.5 LESSONS OF REACH AND IMPACT

13.5.1 Access to the CSG

The take-up rate for the CSG, which refers to the percentage of children within the eligible group who actually receive the grant, varies over different age groups. Evidence shows that take-up rates peak for children aged 7–10 years, while infants and adolescents have relatively low take-up rates. The impact evaluation also reported some of the reasons cited by caregivers for why eligible children are currently not receiving the grant. These include: (1) misinformation about the eligibility criteria (e.g., means test threshold, age, and nationality); (2) lacking the required paperwork (e.g., parents ID documents, child's birth certificate and clinic card, marriage certificate, and proof of address);[9] (3) prohibitive transportation costs, especially for rural applicants who have to travel long distances to reach application office or pay-out points; (4) avoiding the stigmatization associated with receiving welfare; and (5) the application process being time consuming or difficult (DSD, SASSA, and UNICEF 2012). However, the study did find that the likelihood of the child being enrolled before they were two years old increased by 13 percentage points if the mother was given a CSG enrolment form when the child was born.

---

[8] The matching was done on the basis of observable child (age, sex, relationship to household head, race, place at birth), caregiver (age, schooling), and paternal (age) characteristics as well as characteristics of the household at time of birth (housing quality, exposure to shocks, access to a SASSA office, receipt of the Old Age Grant or CSG for other household members).

[9] Section 11(1) of the 2008 Regulations of the Social Assistance Act (of 2004) states that SASSA can process CSG applications without original documentation, if alternative proof is provided. This proof can be in the form of a sworn statement (an affidavit) or paperwork from the Department of Home Affairs showing that the applicant has applied for formal documents. However, a lack of awareness of this regulation has led to eligible applicants not applying for the grant and in some cases being turned away by SASSA officials.

13.5.2 Impact of the CSG

13.5.2.1 Cash Transfers Impact a Child's Early Life Outcomes

The qualitative research found that Early Childhood Development (ECD) services—crèches, pre-schools, and day-care centres—are highly valued by parents and caregivers in South Africa. ECD services are seen as important for several reasons: pre-school learning gives children a head start when they start at primary school; children need to interact with others to acquire social skills; crèches and day-care centres provide a secure environment for children; and ECD services provide child care during the day, which is especially important for working mothers. Many respondents reported that the CSG is used to pay for ECD services, that the CSG is specifically intended to contribute to these costs, and that without the CSG they might struggle to send their children to pre-school.

Table 13.1 shows that receipt of the CSG in the first two years of life increases the likelihood of a child's growth being monitored through clinic visits by 7.7 percentage points, and that the difference is significant at the 10 per cent level. Children whose mothers have less than eight grades of schooling have, on average, lower HAZ (Height-for-Age Z-Score) scores. However, early receipt has a positive and significant impact on the height-for-age Z-score of children whose mothers have more than eight grades of schooling. This is an important finding given that early life nutritional status has long-term effects on physical and cognitive development. The CSG interacts with mothers' education to improve nutritional outcomes, demonstrating an important developmental synergy.

13.5.2.2 Cash Transfers Improve Child Health

The qualitative research found an important reciprocal relationship between the CSG and health care services: health services facilitate access to the CSG, and CSG cash is used to access health care. CSG cash is spent on many basic needs, including health care. Since children are prone to childhood illnesses and injuries, the CSG plays an important role in protecting the health of poor children.

The quantitative analysis found that early enrolment reduces the likelihood of a child experiencing illness in the fifteen-day period prior to the administration of the survey (see Table 13.1). This effect is statistically significant for boys. The results show that boys with delayed enrolment into the CSG programme had a 9.1 percentage point (significant at the 10 per cent level) higher predicted likelihood of being ill, compared with boys enrolled at birth. Children enrolled at birth and whose mothers have eight or more grades of schooling have a predicted likelihood of being ill of 19.6 per cent, which is 8.5 percentage points

318   *Michael Samson et al.*

Table 13.1. Dose-Response Estimates of CSGs' Impact on Child Outcomes

	All children	Girls	Boys	Mother has <8 grades schooling	Mother has 8+ grades schooling
Early life outcomes					
Growth monitored	0.077*	0.080	0.010	0.120	0.060
	(1.69)	(0.79)	(0.18)	(0.64)	(0.70)
Height-for-age Z-score	0.072	0.194*	−0.026	−0.071	0.184**
	(1.11)	(1.84)	(−0.28)	(−0.48)	(2.56)
Proportion of children receiving all immunizations					
Polio	0.003	−	−	−	−
	(0.06)				
Diphtheria, pertussis, and tetanus	−0.012	−	−	−	−
	(−0.31)				
Hepatitis	0.006	−	−	−	−
	(0.14)				
Measles	−0.007	−	−	−	−
	(−0.20)				
Attended crèche or nursery school	−0.042	−0.029	−0.056	0.062	−0.069*
	(−1.36)	(−0.51)	(−0.99)	(0.73)	(−1.84)
Schooling and learning					
Grade attainment	−0.14**	−0.251**	−0.047	−0.376	−0.032
	(−2.33)	(−2.56)	(−)	(−3.16)	(−)
Delayed enrolment	0.036	0.125**	−0.046	0.148**	−0.015
	(0.90)	(2.19)	(0.49)	(1.85)	(−)
Grade repetition	0.009	0.077	−0.036	0.080	−0.029
	(−)	(1.54)	(−0.64)	(1.10)	(−)
Arithmetic test score	−0.44*	−0.72**	0.12	−0.41	−0.46*
	(−1.76)	(−2.00)	(0.40)	(−1.00)	(−1.64)
Reading score	−0.026	−0.123**	0.070	−0.067	−0.017
	(−0.605)	(−2.05)	(−)	(−0.88)	(−)
Health					
Illness in last fifteen days	0.045	0.006	0.091*	−0.031	0.085**
	(−)	(0.12)	(1.52)	(−0.41)	(2.18)

Notes:
(1) Significance: *, significant at the 10 per cent level; **, significant at the 5 per cent level; ***, significant at the 1 per cent level.
(2) Robust t-statistics

lower than comparable children enrolled at age six. The study found no evidence of health impacts on children whose mothers have less than eight grades of schooling. This finding suggests that having an educated mother (eight or more years of education) complements the CSG in its improvement of child health outcomes, providing another example of developmental synergy.

13.5.2.3 Cash Transfers Allow Households to Invest in Schooling and Learning

The qualitative research found that children miss days of school, or drop out altogether, due to many economic and social drivers. The main reasons are economic: money for school fees, uniforms, shoes, transportation, the need to work for income, or lack of food at home so they cannot concentrate, and lack of food to bring to school.

The quantitative analysis reported in Table 13.1 shows that children enrolled in the CSG at birth completed more grades of schooling than children enrolled at age six and have significantly higher arithmetic test scores. Early CSG enrolment improves girls' grade attainment by one quarter grade compared with enrolment in the CSG at age six. This is a large impact given that most children in the sample had only completed four grades of schooling. The primary pathways through which this occurs are: reductions in delayed entry and reductions in grade repetition. Furthermore, the study found that early receipt of the CSG reduces delayed school entry of girls and children whose mothers have less than eight grades of schooling by 12.5 and 14.8 percentage points respectively. It was also found that girls who enrolled early obtain higher marks on tests of mathematical ability and reading.

For children whose mothers have less than eight grades of schooling, early enrolment in the CSG raises grade attainment by 0.38 grades (or 10.2 per cent). The CSG has no impact on grade attainment on children whose mothers have eight or more grades of schooling. These results suggest that the CSG is playing a compensatory role in narrowing the gap between children whose mothers have not completed primary school and children whose mothers have at least some secondary education.

Table 13.2 shows that adolescents residing in households that receive the CSG have lower absentee rates (compared with adolescents in households with no CSG recipient) even when the adolescents themselves do not receive the CSG. Adolescent males particularly benefit from residing in a CSG recipient household. Adolescent males in households currently receiving the CSG are absent approximately seven days fewer than males in households not receiving the CSG. The study also found that early receipt of the CSG (in the first seven years of life) reduced the likelihood that a child will grow up into an adolescent who will work outside the home. Additionally, there appears to be a particularly important impact in terms of reduced work outside of the home for females who received the grant in early childhood. This is an important finding given the substantial literature on the negative correlation between children's work and schooling outcomes.

Table 13.2. Dose-Response Estimates of CSGs' Impact on Adolescents' Outcomes

	All Adolescents	Females	Males
Average days absent from school			
Group 3 vs Group 0	−2.22	0.03	−3.85
	(−2.11)	(0.04)	(−1.63)
Groups 1, 2, and 3 vs Group 0 and 4	−2.26	−0.82	−7.05
	(−1.60)	(−1.08)	(−2.10)

Notes:
(1) Significance: *, significant at the 10 per cent level; **, significant at the 5 per cent level; ***, significant at the 1 per cent level.
(2) Robust t-statistics.
(3) Group 0 (no current CSG in household and household never received CSG for adolescent), Group 1 (currently receiving CSG for adolescent), Group 2 (household has received CSG in the past for adolescent and currently receives CSG for another household member), Group 3 (household never received CSG for adolescent but currently receives CSG for another household member), and Group 4 (households that received CSG for adolescent in the past).

13.5.2.4 Cash Transfers Reduce Risky Behaviour Amongst Adolescents

An analysis of adolescent risky behaviours provides evidence of the CSG's ability to reduce six main risky behaviours—early sexual debut and the number of sexual partners, pregnancy, alcohol use, drug use, criminal activity, and gang membership.

The study documents significant positive associations between current receipt of the CSG and the likelihood that an adolescent female will abstain from sexual activity (by 11 percentage points), particularly in cases where the female received the grant in early childhood. Receipt of the CSG reduced the number of sexual partners for both adolescent males and females, with the number of sexual partners declining steadily as the duration of receipt increases. The evidence suggests that child-focused grants such as the CSG can have positive protective impacts on adolescents. This result documents a particularly important return on the CSG investment given that the number of AIDS-related deaths amongst adolescents increased by 50 per cent between 2005 and 2012, with prevalence rates amongst 15–19-year-old girls being eight times higher than that of boys (UNAIDS 2012; UNICEF 2013).

The study also found a statistically significant association between receipt of the CSG and lower rates of pregnancy. These positive effects are stronger when the grant had been received since early childhood. Receipt of the CSG also reduces alcohol and drug use, particularly for females, and again with the effect strengthened by early childhood receipt of the CSG. The study also found a statistically small relationship between receipt of the grant and adolescents not engaging in criminal or gang activities.

13.6 IMPACT ON POLICY DEVELOPMENT

The DSD's (2010) Strategic Plan 2010–15 states that the department is committed to institutionalizing evidence-based policy making in the DSD and the social development sector, with the expectation that it would result in 'efficient, effective and development-oriented public service, and an empowered, fair and inclusive citizenship' (DSD 2010:15). This section draws from interviews with relevant stakeholders and provides details on the six different ways in which the CSG impact evaluation influenced policy development in South Africa. The sub-sections involve aspects relating to: institutional and operational arrangements within SASSA; universalization of the CSG; income support to pregnant women and infants; CSG eligibility expansion to twenty-one years of age; popular participation in governance; and strengthening political will.

13.6.1 Institutional and Operational Arrangements Within SASSA

The impact evaluation demonstrated that accessing the CSG early improves the developmental outcomes of beneficiary children. Receipt of the CSG (from birth) yields powerful impacts that strengthen the human capabilities of children, enabling them to better break the intergenerational transmission of poverty. These findings contributed to the creation of high-level awareness of the importance of ECD interventions for strengthening the developmental impacts of the CSG. The drafting of the ECD Policy, which places emphasis on the first 1000 days of a child's life (from conception to two years of age), demonstrates this increased awareness. The 2011 National Development Plan also references this effect, due to its proposal of introducing nutritional interventions for pregnant women and young children, in addition to further extensions of ECD services to children under the age of five years (NPC 2011).

However, the evaluation revealed that large numbers of eligible children are unable to access the CSG for a variety of reasons. This led SASSA, in collaboration with the DSD and UNICEF, to undertake a study on 'Preventing Exclusion from the CSG'—exploring the extent to which eligible infants and youth aged 12–17 years are excluded, and evaluating existing information and outreach programmes.[10] Drawing from the evidence collected, SASSA

---

[10] This study was carried out using data from the GHS (General Household Survey) 2011, the NIDS (National Income Dynamics Survey) wave 2, and SOCPEN (Social Pension System). UNICEF and SASSA have recently commissioned EPRI to carry out a follow-up study to review exclusion from the CSG. The evidence of developmental impact motivates this focus on reducing exclusion.

instituted a number of information and outreach programmes to reach potential beneficiaries, particularly those residing in remote areas. SASSA's Strategic Plan for 2011–12 to 2013–14 included the implementation of a series of Integrated Community Registration Outreach Programmes (ICROP) (PMG 2011). In the period following the impact evaluation, SASSA also allocated additional resources towards monitoring the exclusion error and better identifying eligible non-beneficiaries.

The impact evaluation also raised SASSA's awareness of the importance of ensuring eligible children have continuous access to the CSG all the way into adolescence, as it reinforces the positive impacts of the grant. In an effort to improve access to the CSG (and other social grants), SASSA has made the payment system more efficient and reduced the cost of paying grants by close to 50 per cent (Buthelezi 2014, personal communication).[11] This was accomplished primarily through two activities. Firstly, the Special Investigating Unit (SIU) was tasked by the then Minister of Social Development to investigate fraud in the social grant system.[12] This resulted in a number of public servants being prosecuted. The government also declared a period of indemnity enabling people who had been receiving grants unlawfully to avoid prosecution if they cancelled their grants. SASSA also undertook a re-registration process from April 2012, with the introduction of the new payment system. This process required that all beneficiaries, children, and procurators had to biometrically register, in order to continue receiving their grant. An amount of R2 billion in misappropriated funds was returned following this exercise and a number of 'ghost' beneficiaries were prosecuted for fraud.

Finally, the DSD's M&E Unit's involvement in the impact evaluation meant that policy makers were able to immediately draw on what was being learnt to inform policy. This has led the DSD to more proactively engage in the evaluation process. Rather than simply utilizing impact evaluation findings once the final evaluation report is validated, the DSD now engages with evaluations at a policy level. Continued engagement in the evaluation process from an assessment's inception aims to encourage the policy unit to inform policy development more immediately and more comprehensively.

13.6.2 Universalization of the CSG

The impact evaluation clearly showed that there are a number of eligible children not accessing the grant because of supply side challenges, that is

---

[11] The costs of providing social security payment dropped from R3.5 billion (in 2011) to under R2 billion (in 2013) per annum (Buthelezi 2014, personal communication).

[12] The SIU is an independent statutory body that is accountable to parliament and the president of South Africa. It conducts investigations upon request, and reports on the outcomes.

structural, institutional, and administrative issues. The impact evaluation prompted the consideration of various strategies to address the issue of exclusion, including universal provision of the grant. Universal provision is expected to promote early enrolment and reduce exclusion errors, because the means test creates significant barriers for the poor. The public good argument can also be used to support universal provision, since the impact evaluation found that the CSG generates impacts that are valued by society (e.g., improved education and health outcomes, reduced sexual risk, etc.). In general, the government wants every child in South Africa to experience these impacts from an early age, given the CSG's cumulative effect. Furthermore, universal provision is expected to improve the welfare of children who are ineligible because their caregiver's income falls just above the means test threshold, despite their living in similar resource-constrained conditions and facing similar human capability deprivations as those that qualify for the grant. Evidence from the CSG impact evaluation provided the impetus for further discussions on the benefits of universal provision.

Following the impact evaluation, the DSD commissioned EPRI to assess the feasibility of eliminating the means test and providing the grant to all children—the feasibility of universal provision of the CSG (Samson et al. 2012). The study found that universal provision is economically feasible and will contribute to economic growth, and that it will reduce the administrative burden of providing the grant. A further justification is that universal provision builds solidarity and social support that strengthens the sustainability of the programme. Proponents of universal provision also argue that every child should have access to basic support from the state irrespective of their family income.

While the proposal for universalizing the CSG predates the impact evaluation, the results from the study strengthened the DSD's support for the position. SASSA officials have responded to the report by declaring universal provision to be a medium-term objective of government. Findings from the impact evaluation were also considered during high level brainstorming meetings on the potential for further reforms to the CSG. The impact evaluation therefore created a political space for further engagement on issues ranging from additional income support for more 'vulnerable' groups to strategies for reducing exclusion errors.

13.6.3 Pregnant Women

Evidence from the impact evaluation showed the benefits of early receipt of the CSG, especially for improved human-capital outcomes (see Section 13.5). Income support to poor pregnant women is expected to lead to in-utero gains in nutrition if the grant money is used to purchase food and other goods (or services) that facilitate a healthier pregnancy. Thus, the impact evaluation has become part of a larger pool of evidence that supports interventions for improved maternal and child nutrition (NPC 2011).

Income support to pregnant women can also help address the high rates of exclusion found amongst eligible infants (aged 0–1), as a result of parents not applying for the grant during the child's infancy. This provision will create opportunities for SASSA to go into local communities to inform eligible women about their unborn child's eligibility for the CSG, and to assist these women to prepare the documentation needed to register their child for the programme. Providing income support to pregnant women will also allow SASSA to compile a registry that can be used to ease these women's transition from one programme to another, that is from receiving the income support to receiving the CSG once the child is born or to link these women to other complementary programmes.

There is a belief amongst policy makers that registering children from birth will have the biggest effect on reducing the exclusion rate amongst eligible infants, as well as ensure greater impacts from the grant. At the operational level the process of enrolling eligible children in the CSG when the infant's birth certificate is issued would require SASSA to work closely with the DSD, the Department of Home Affairs, hospitals, and clinics, which may be difficult given the coordination challenges that inter-sectoral collaborations often face.[13] In addition, there are many remote areas in South Africa where pregnant women do not have access to hospitals or clinics. These areas already represent a serious challenge to those concerned about the exclusion of eligible children, because eligible children born in these areas (or at home) tend to be excluded from the CSG for a longer period of time. Concrete strategies are required to specifically target these areas.

13.6.4 Infants

The evaluation assisted policy makers to recognize that additional income support to eligible infants can enhance the CSG's immediate impact on nutrition and cognitive outcomes, and SASSA has specifically focused on infant exclusion in their past two studies of grant take-up. The evaluation has also contributed to proposals for an inclusive and holistic ECD package of services outlined in the government's Draft ECD Policy and strengthened the government's policy position on other forms of ECD services (e.g., pre-schools, crèches, and day-care facilities).

---

[13] It might be more challenging to coordinate with clinics than hospitals, due to their large number.

13.6.5 Expansion to Twenty-One Years of Age

The impact evaluation showed that extensions to the CSG's age eligibility criteria had significant positive benefits for the newly included cohorts, so similar effects can be expected for eligible 18- to 21-year-olds. This expansion would also align the CSG with the FCG, which a child can receive up until the age of twenty-one (if they are in education). It has been clear for a long time that young people need support beyond the age of eighteen. There is a high level of poverty amongst the youth, and once poor children turn eighteen they lose a crucial source of support (in the form of the CSG grant) at a time when they need to make the transition from childhood to adulthood, and from high school into further education and training or work. This extension would also acknowledge the fact that many young adults in South Africa do not complete schooling by the age of eighteen, due to late enrolment and the high rate of grade repetition (Branson, Hofmeyr, and Lam 2014). The CSG impact evaluation provided evidence that demonstrates the potential value of offering income support to this age cohort, especially through its positive impact on schooling outcomes and consequently likelihood of gaining employment. There is now a policy proposal within the DSD advocating for this extension in the near future. Given the financial implications of this type of expansion, any further steps concerning implementing this extension in age eligibility will require support from the Cabinet and approval from the Treasury.

13.6.6 Popular Participation in Governance

The results from the CSG impact evaluation addressed many of the issues raised by those critical of the CSG programme. The impact evaluation improved SASSA's communications drive, with representatives engaging with the media, community-based organizations, non-governmental organizations, religious organizations, and traditional leaders in a bid to disseminate the results of the study. The media became very involved in disseminating the information to the public and encouraging discussions around the results.[14] In particular, the finding that adolescents receiving the grant are less likely to become pregnant has refuted pernicious myths that preoccupy both policymakers and the public. Civil society organizations such as Black Sash and the Alliance for Children's Entitlement to Social Security (ACESS) have used evidence from this and other studies to challenge South Africa to do more for children living in poor households, through the development of a more

---

[14] The evidence coming out of the impact evaluation made the front pages. George Laryea-Adjei (Former Deputy Head of UNICEF South Africa) wrote an op-ed in the *Mail & Guardian* (Laryea-Adjei 2012).

comprehensive social security system. For example, in the light of the importance of early receipt of the CSG the Black Sash and ACESS continue to demonstrate how challenges facing the Department of Home Affairs (in providing official documents) result in persistent rates of exclusion. They also assist families who are having difficulty in accessing the grant, and strongly advocate for broader coverage by means of the removal of the income eligibility criteria.

Furthermore, the impact evaluation showed that SASSA has more work to do in terms of communication and outreach strategies in order to raise awareness of the programme, by revealing that some eligible beneficiaries could not access the CSG because they did not understand the eligibility criteria. Before introducing biometrics SASSA went out into communities to engage with the relevant stakeholders. This enhanced the consultative process strengthening the arm of civil society. SASSA now engages closely with community and civil society stakeholders on issues concerning the specific vulnerabilities of children, particularly orphans and/or child-headed households. The DSD is now considering further expansions to the CSG in order to deepen its impact on children facing greater vulnerabilities. The findings were also shared broadly within SASSA, which improved SASSA officials' awareness of the obstacles caregivers face in accessing the CSG, as well as the potential benefits to children that are foregone when CSG transfers are interrupted or stopped (Heinrich and Brill 2015). This has helped SASSA officials, especially those working at the front desk interacting with clients on a daily basis, in tackling these bottlenecks.

13.6.7 Strengthening Political Will

In South Africa, despite opposing views there has been considerable political support for grants supporting the poor. This has been demonstrated by the pace at which the state has extended the coverage of the CSG. In addition, the 2007–8 African National Congress (ANC) manifesto contained proposals for further pro-poor interventions. The impact evaluation has strengthened the argument for providing the CSG to children living in resource-poor households, primarily because the evidence is positive and convincing. The Democratic Alliance (South Africa's official opposition party) drew from the impact evaluation their 2013 policy statement on social protection (Democratic Alliance 2013), in which they outline their support for a social protection system targeted at the most vulnerable sections of the population. The impact evaluation has therefore contributed to the evidence base that proponents of the CSG can use to advocate for further expansions to the programme to those within government who question the value of providing social assistance.

As South Africa transitions from a middle-income to a high-income country, decision making has become more sophisticated and evidence-based. At all levels evidence forms the basis for policy proposals and can be used to drive further interventions or policy changes. The CSG impact assessment strengthened broad support for institutionalizing the rigorous evaluation of programmes across all departments. There are currently a number of government departments carrying out impact evaluation that aim to demonstrate a programme value to society. This linking of impact evaluations to the policy process helps reduce the adverse politicization of programmes.

13.7 CONCLUSIONS

South Africa's CSG represents the government's most effective instrument in tackling poverty and inequality. In addition, the impact assessment documents the vital role of the CSG in promoting nutritional, educational, and health outcomes. Early receipt significantly strengthens a number of these important impacts, providing an investment in human capital that reduces multiple dimension indicators of poverty, promotes better gender outcomes, and reduces inequality. The study also demonstrates that adolescents receiving the CSG benefit from more positive educational outcomes and are somewhat less likely to engage in child labour. In the context of high adolescent HIV (Human Immunodeficiency Virus) prevalence, the impact in reducing adolescent risky behaviours—including sexual activity, alcohol use, and drug abuse—demonstrates a particularly high return to this vital social investment. These impacts are stronger when adolescents have received the grant from early childhood.

The impact evaluation has significantly influenced the policy development process; especially the provision of social security for poor and vulnerable children in South Africa. Firstly, the CSG impact evaluation strengthened government support for rigorous approaches to monitoring and evaluating the impact of current programmes on the target population. This is critical in a country like South Africa, where a significant portion of the population is living in poverty and the state has limited resources to allocate to addressing this issue, since information from impact evaluations can be used to assess the effectiveness of the programmes, identify entry points for strengthening the programmes, and motivate for expansions to the evaluated programmes. In the case of the CSG impact evaluation, results from the study have been used to advocate universal provision, providing additional income support to poor pregnant women and infants, as well as further expansion of the age eligibility criterion to twenty-one years.

The impact assessment also highlighted challenges with administrative systems (including the management information system) and targeting processes, leading to reforms and particularly an ongoing commitment to reach every eligible child. In particular, the DSD and SASSA have addressed barriers to enrolment such as identification document challenges. They have also committed to new initiatives to reduce exclusion error, including promoting better communications and awareness-building for those eligible for the grant.

13.7.1 Moving Forward

The CSG remains South Africa's most promising instrument for breaking the intergenerational transmission of poverty and for promoting child development—strengthening the country's human resource base which in the twenty-first century represents the foundation of the wealth of nations. The Government of South Africa has committed to universal provision of the CSG, which represents the most effective approach to tackling exclusion of poor children while eliminating arbitrary distinctions and building a more socially cohesive society. Universal provision will also pave the way to in-hospital registration of children for the grant, which will smash the main barrier limiting the take-up of the grant by infants. The DSD recently accepted a study on 'vertical expansion' of the CSG (Samson et al. 2015), which recommends options to expand benefits for particularly vulnerable children and offers opportunities to expand developmental linkages such as early childhood development initiatives and youth development programmes. The impact assessment firmly established the CSG as the bedrock of South Africa's developmental social policy.

REFERENCES

Berry, L., Biersteker, L., Dawes, A., Lake, L., and Smith, C. (eds) (2013). *South African Child Gauge 2013*. Cape Town: Children's Institute, University of Cape Town.

Branson, N., Hofmeyr, C., and Lam, D. (2014). 'Progress through school and the determinants of school dropout in South Africa'. *Development Southern Africa*, 31(1): 106–26.

Buthelezi, T. (Manager, DSD) (2014, Personal communication). 'Review of the CSG Impact Evaluation'. Email to the authors, 18 December.

Case, A., Hosegood, V., and Lund, F. (2005). 'The reach and impact of child support grants: evidence from KwaZulu-Natal'. *Development Southern Africa*, 22(4): 467–82.

Democratic Alliance (DA) (2013). 'DA Policy on Social Protection'. Cape Town: DA.

DPME (Department of Performance Monitoring and Evaluation) (2012). 'Development Indicators 2012'. Pretoria: DPME. Available online at: <http://www.thepresidency.gov.za/MediaLib/Downloads/Home/Publications/DPMEIndicators2013/DPME%20Indicators%202013.pdf> (Accessed 3 March 2015).

DSD (2010). 'Strategic Plan 2010–2015'. Pretoria: DSD. Available online at: <http://www.gov.za/sites/www.gov.za/files/DSD%20Strategic%20Plan%202010%20-%202015_0.pdf> (accessed 3 March 2015).

DSD, SASSA, and UNICEF (2012). 'The South African Child Support Grant Impact Assessment: Evidence from a Survey of Adolescents and Their Households'. Pretoria: UNICEF.

du Toit, D. (2011). 'Food Security'. Department of Agriculture, Forestry and Fisheries. Pretoria: Directorate of Economic Services.

Dutschke, M. (2006). 'Defining Children's Constitutional Right to Social Services'. A Project 28 Working Paper. Cape Town: Children's Institute, University of Cape Town. Available online at: <http://www.ci.org.za/depts/ci/pubs/pdf/rights/workpap/Right_to_social_services.pdf> (accessed 4 March 2015).

DWPD (Department of Welfare and Population Development) (1997). 'White Paper for Social Welfare in South Africa'. Pretoria: Department of Welfare and Population Development. Available online at: <http://www.gov.za/sites/www.gov.za/files/White_Paper_on_Social_Welfare_0.pdf> (accessed 4 March 2015).

Hall, K. (2007). 'Where to Draw the Line? Targeting and Leakage in the Child Support Grant'. Paper presented at the First annual Charlotte Manye Maxeke Conference on the Economics of Social Protection, hosted by the National Department of Social Development and the Department of Economics, University of Pretoria, 12–15 June. Cape Town: Children's Institute, University of Cape Town.

Hall, K. (2011). 'The Child Support Grant: Are Conditions Appropriate?' Children Count Brief. Cape Town: Children's Institute, University of Cape Town.

Hall, K. (2014). 'Income and Social Grants—Child Support Grants'. Available online at: <http://www.childrencount.ci.org.za/indicator.php?id=2&indicator=10> (accessed 3 February 2015).

Heinrich, C. J. and Brill, R. (2015). 'Stopped in the Name of the Law: Administrative Burden and its Implications for Cash Transfer Program Effectiveness.' World Development, 72: 277–95.

Hoogeveen, J. and Özler, B. (2006). 'Poverty and inequality in post-apartheid South Africa: 1995–2000', in Bhorat R. and Kanbur H. (eds), *Poverty and Policy in Post-Apartheid South Africa*. Cape Town: Human Sciences Research Council, 59–94.

Laryea-Adjei, G. (2012). 'Child Grant Is SA's Best Investment'. *Mail & Guardian*, 20 June. Available online at: <http://mg.co.za/article/2012-06-28-child-grant-is-sas-best-investment/> (accessed 3 February 2015).

Leibbrandt, M., Levinsohn, J. A., and McCrary, J. (2005). 'Incomes in South Africa since the Fall of Apartheid'. National Bureau of Economic Research (NBER) Working Paper 11384.

McEwen, H. and Woolard, I. (2012). 'The fiscal cost of child grants in the context of high adult mortality in South Africa: a simulation to 2015'. *Development Southern Africa*, 29(1): 141–56.

Meintjes, H., Budlender, D., Giese, S., and Johnson, L. (2003). 'Children "in need of care" or in need of cash'. Questioning Social Security Provisions for Orphans in the Context of the South African AIDS pandemic. Cape Town: Children's Institute, and the Centre for Actuarial Research, University of Cape Town.

NPC (National Planning Commission) (2011). 'National Development Plan: Vision for 2030'. Pretoria: The Presidency. Available online at: <http://beta2.statssa.gov.za/

wp-content/uploads/2013/07/NDP-2030-Our-future-make-it-work.pdf> (accessed 3 March 2015).

PMG (Parliamentary Monitoring Group) (2011). 'South African Social Security Agency (SASSA) Strategic Plan 2011'. Available online at: <https://pmg.org.za/committee-meeting/13178/> (accessed 31 March 2015).

Rosa, S. and Meintjes, H. (2004). 'Extending the Child Support Grant to Children under 18 years'. Cape Town: Alliance for Children's Entitlement to Social Security. Available online at: <http://www.ci.org.za/depts/ci/pubs/pdf/rights/facts/csgextto18fs.pdf> (accessed 4 March 2015).

Samson, M., Babson, O., Haarmannn, C., Haarmann, D., Khathi, G., Mac Quene, K., and van Niekerk, I. (2001). 'Social Security Take-Up and Means Test in South Africa'. Cape Town: Economic Policy Research Institute. Available online at: <http://www.epri.org.za/wp-content/uploads/2011/03/rp24.pdf> (accessed 4 March 2015).

Samson, M., Babson, O., Haarmann, C., Haarmann, D., Khathi, G., Mac Quene, K., and van Niekerk, I. (2002). 'Research Review on Social Security Reform and the Basic Income Grant for South Africa'. Report commissioned by the ILO. Cape Town: Economic Policy Research Institute. Available online at: <http://epri.org.za/wp-content/uploads/2011/03/rp31.pdf> (accessed 25 May 2015).

Samson, M., Heinrich, C., Kaniki, S., Regalia, F., Mac Quene, K., Muzondo, T., van Niekerk, I., and Williams, M. (2011). 'Impacts of South Africa's Child Support Grant', in S. Handa, S. Devereux, and D. Webb (eds), *Social Protection for Africa's Children*. London: Routledge, chapter 7.

Samson, M., Jehoma, S., Khadka, A., Meintjes, C., Ndoro, R., Brouwers, A., Brown, B., Dang, L., Fajth, V., Green, S., Mbabu, D., Mintzer, E., Karlsson, S., Kuruc, K., Pendurthi, N., Scher, J., Shapiro, R., Solovy, A. J., Sul, J.-Y., and Wichert, O. (2013). 'Twenty Year Review of Social Protection Programmes in South Africa'. Background document to the report submitted on the 13 September 2013. Report commissioned by the Presidency Department of Performance Monitoring and Evaluation. Cape Town: Economic Policy Research Institute.

Samson, M., Nyokangi, E., Yang, M., and Kenny, K. (2015). 'A Study to Explore the Options and Make Recommendations for the Vertical Expansion of the Child Support Grant'. Report commissioned by the DSD. Cape Town: Economic Policy Research Institute.

Samson, M., Renaud, B., Miller, E., de Neubourg, E., Deonauth, T., Mac Quene, K., and Van Niekerk, I. (2012). Feasibility study on the universal provision of the Child Support Grant in South Africa. Economic Policy Research Institute, UNICEF.

SASSA (2008). 'Annual Report 2007/2008'. Pretoria: South African Social Security Agency.

SASSA (2012). 'Annual Report 2011/2012'. Pretoria: South African Social Security Agency.

SASSA (2015). 'Statistical Report 3 of 2015'. Pretoria: South African Social Security Agency.

South Africa (1996). 'Constitution of the Republic of South Africa'. Pretoria: The Presidency. Available online at: <http://www.thehda.co.za/uploads/images/unpan005172.pdf> (accessed 3 March 2015).

StatsSA (2013). 'Millennium Development Goals'. Country Report 2013. Pretoria: Statistics South Africa.

Taylor Report (2002). 'Transforming the Present—Protecting the Future, 2002'. Report of the Committee of Inquiry for Comprehensive Social Security for South Africa. Pretoria: Government of the Republic of South Africa.

UNAIDS (Joint United Nations Programme on HIV and AIDS) (2012). 'Report on the Global AIDS Epidemic 2012'. Geneva: UNAIDS.

UNICEF (2013). 'Towards an AIDS-Free Generation—Children and AIDS: Sixth Stocktaking Report'. New York: UNICEF.

Part III

Synthesis of Results

14

Conclusions and Policy Implications for Cash Transfer Programmes

Benjamin Davis (FAO), Sudhanshu Handa (University of North Carolina at Chapel Hill and UNICEF), Nicola Hypher (Save the Children), Natalia Winder Rossi (UNICEF), Paul Winters (IFAD and American University), and Jennifer Yablonski (UNICEF)

14.1 OVERVIEW

Given the importance of cash transfer programmes in social protection strategies in sub-Saharan Africa (SSA), it is critical to understand not only the programme impacts but also the processes that facilitate the continued improvement of programmes. This book has provided evidence on the impact of cash transfer programmes in eight SSA countries that were supported by the Transfer Project: Ethiopia, Ghana, Kenya, Lesotho, Malawi, South Africa, Zambia, and Zimbabwe. The objective of this concluding chapter is to draw lessons from the accumulated evidence on the impact of cash transfer programmes in SSA and understand the role and influence of evaluative research in the policy process.

Section 14.2 provides a summary of the evidence of the impacts from the eight countries. Perhaps the most interesting and policy-relevant conclusion is that unconditional cash transfers lead to significant social *and* productive impacts on beneficiary households, even though they are not tied to any specific behaviour. The evidence provides a strong case for unconditional transfers in Africa, as compared to conditional cash transfers, in terms of: (i) broad range of impacts across sectors, (ii) flexibility for households to manage their expenditures, and (iii) similar (and in some cases higher) impacts, with lower operational costs.

Unconditional transfers effectively allow households to invest money according to their own specific needs, and the evidence presented in this book show positive impacts across a wide spectrum of domains. Moreover, the social impacts, particularly those around secondary school enrolment, are similar in magnitude to those found in conditional programmes such as Path (Jamaica), Progresa (Mexico), and Familias en Accion (Colombia). In addition to showing a broad range of impacts across sectors, the evidence also clearly counteracts concerns around cash transfers creating dependency or their 'misuse', which is a common preoccupation amongst policy makers. This raises questions about the need to place conditions on cash transfer to obtain desirable outcomes, which is a key consideration in SSA given the costs and administrative burden of enforcing conditions and the fact that they may distort incentives, as well as the logistical and institutional challenges they present. Indeed, conditioning cash on behaviour tied to social sectors might actually mitigate their ability to support sustainable livelihoods strengthening in the short and medium term, which the book recognizes as important pathways out poverty for poor households.

Lessons on the political economy of evaluations from the eight SSA countries are presented in Section 14.3. The results suggest that for impact evaluations to be effective in influencing decision-making processes, they need to be embedded in the process of policy and programme design and implementation. Much of the policy impact is in the credibility evaluations create in the programme design and implementation process and their contribution to a learning environment where issues that arise are addressed. This produces a situation where programmes can be promoted and directed in a manner in which evidence is brought to bear as needed in decision making, both in terms of political commitment and decisions to scale-up a programme as well as in modifying aspects of design and implementation to improve impact. This suggests that the standard practice of having external, and often geographically distant, independent evaluators being the primary drivers of the evaluation process is not ideal if the objective is to guide policy and improve the programme. External evaluations may determine if a programme achieves its objectives, but they are unlikely to play a role in engaging in broader government policy decisions and the implementation of the programme. This trade-off is critical for the Transfer Project, recognizing the role of evaluations and learning agendas not only to 'assess' programme results, but to progressively strengthen the design and implementation to enhance impacts.

Finally, Section 14.4 provides some suggestions for moving forward. When numerous evaluations are done on a specific intervention such as cash transfer programmes, questions are legitimately raised on the value of continuing to pursue additional costly evaluations—given the evidence that cash transfers are effective in achieving development objectives is compelling, the value of cash transfers have been clearly demonstrated over and over again. Yet, a key conclusion of this book is that the learning environment itself is critical for moving beyond the 'case for cash transfers' and addressing design and implementation issues that can enhance impacts. Further, there are always additional and country-specific policy and programme implementation issues to carefully consider. Beyond a research agenda, there are also issues of the best institutional structures for advancing an agenda including the mix of different stakeholders and the approaches to evaluation.

14.2 EVIDENCE ON THE EFFECTIVENESS OF CASH TRANSFER PROGRAMMES

Drawing on the evidence provided in the chapters, as well as on the full range of studies from the impact evaluations, in this section we bring together the evidence on the effectiveness of cash transfer programmes forming part of the Transfer Project.[1]

14.2.1 Poverty and Well-Being

Cash transfers make people happier and give beneficiaries hope, a precondition for families to want to invest in the future. This sentiment echoed through both the qualitative and quantitative analysis. In Ghana the programme increased happiness by 16 percentage points (pp); in Kenya recipients showed a 6 percentage points increase in the quality of life index; in Malawi the share of households who believed that life would be better both two and three years in the future increased by 17 percentage points; and in Zambia the share of households who feel that they are now better off increased by 45 percentage points. In Zimbabwe, the programme increased the Satisfaction with Life Scale by 12 per cent. And in Ghana, recipients spoke about the important effect on 'self-esteem' and 'hope' that the programme had brought about.

There were notable improvements in consumption and poverty, such as the ability of households to smooth their consumption within seasons and between years. The Zambia Multiple Categorical Targeting Grant (MCTG) model increased total per capita consumption and reduced the moderate and severe poverty headcount, poverty gap, and severe poverty gap. In Kenya, the Cash Transfer for Orphans and Vulnerable Children (CT-OVC) programme increased consumption in beneficiary households, which led to a 13 percentage points reduction in the proportion of households living below a $1-per-day poverty line. The Malawi Social Cash Transfer Programme (SCTP) increased per capita consumption among the ultra-poor, reducing the headcount, the poverty gap, and the severity of poverty gap. Similarly, the

---

[1] For Zambia we include the twenty-four-month follow-up results for both the CG and MCTG models of the SCT programme. For Malawi, we include the results from both the SCTP expansion as well as the Mchinji pilot.

Zimbabwe Harmonized Social Cash Transfer (HSCT) programme reduced the food poverty headcount among smaller households.

14.2.2 Cash Transfers Improve Education and Health Outcomes

Cash transfer programmes have had a strong and consistent impact across countries on school enrolment, most clearly among secondary age children (usually aged 12–17), who face the largest financial barriers to schooling. These impacts on secondary level enrolment range from 5 to 15 percentage points in Ethiopia, Ghana, Kenya, Lesotho, Malawi, South Africa, and Zambia, and were a common refrain in qualitative fieldwork across countries. These effect sizes compare favourably to those from conditional cash transfer programmes around the world. Most programmes report equal impacts for boys and girls. Only one of these programmes, the Lesotho Child Grant Programme (CGP), reports lower impacts for girls relative to boys (4 versus 8 percentage points), while for the Zambia MCTG model the programme only had positive and significant impacts for girls (19 percentage points). Evidence on other education indicators suggests that cash transfers also reduce repetition (Ghana, Kenya) and increase school attendance (Ghana, Malawi, Lesotho). In one case (Kenya), impacts are significantly greater for families that face larger out-of-pocket costs for schooling. In South Africa, early receipt of the Child Support Grant (CSG) was associated with improved grade completion and attainment, especially for girls and for children whose mothers have less than eight grades of schooling. Early receipt also reduced the likelihood that the child will work outside the home as an adolescent. In Malawi, the SCTP led to a positive impact on education expenditures—over 100 per cent increase in the case of the ultra-poor beneficiaries. Finally, the Zambia, Zimbabwe, and Lesotho programmes led to large effects on children's access to shoes and clothing, a key factor in school attendance.

Cash transfer programmes have had a consistently significant impact in reducing morbidity, with somewhat less consistency in the impact on use of health care. Programmes in Zambia (Child Grant (CG) model), Kenya, Malawi, Lesotho, and South Africa all reduced morbidity in children, measured as diarrhoea (for young children) or illness, with impacts ranging from 15 percentage points in Lesotho to 5 percentage points in Zambia (CG model) and South Africa. In both Kenya and Ghana the programmes led to increased use of preventative care. In Kenya, for example, there was a 12 percentage points increase in well-baby clinic attendance, a 15 percentage points increase in full immunization, and a 16 percentage points increase in health card ownership among pre-schoolers. These impacts emerged only after four years suggesting that health impacts may take longer to manifest themselves than those for schooling which appear almost immediately. In Ghana, the Livelihood Empowerment Against Poverty (LEAP) programme was explicitly linked to the National Health Insurance Scheme, leading to a 20 percentage points increase in access to health insurance. In four countries—Zambia, Zimbabwe, Kenya, and Malawi—the programme led to increase in health expenditures. Finally, both the Kenya and Lesotho programmes led to significant increase in access to birth certificates and/or registration.

14.2.3 Cash Transfers Increase Food Security and Nutrition Outcomes

Cash transfers had a clear and consistent impact on improving food security and nutrition security across all countries, based on both objective and self-reported measures, and from both the quantitative and qualitative fieldwork. Food security was measured in different ways across Zambia, Zimbabwe, Malawi, Ethiopia, Ghana, and Lesotho—the share of households eating more than one meal a day, the number of months with extreme food security, a variety of food security indices, the share of children going hungry or with few meals—but in each country household food security status improved. For example, in Zambia (CG model) there was an 8 percentage points increase in households having more than one meal per day, while in Lesotho the programme led to an 11 percentage points reduction in the proportion of children who had to eat fewer meals because of food shortage.

Participation in a cash transfer programme led to an increase in food expenditure between 10 to 30 per cent in Zambia, Zimbabwe, Kenya, and Malawi-Mchinji, a part of which was spent on significantly larger amounts of animal-based foods, particularly meat and dairy, contributing to increased dietary diversity among beneficiaries. The Ethiopia SCTP had a positive impact on both caloric availability as well as dietary diversity. The Malawi SCTP led to an approximately 20 per cent increase in food expenditure for ultra-poor households. No impact on food expenditure or dietary diversity was found in Ghana or Lesotho, a result in part related to the unpredictability or timing of delivery of cash to beneficiaries, though qualitative fieldwork in these countries reported increased purchases around payment dates.

The impact of cash transfer programmes on child anthropometric measures has been less clear. The Zambia CG model led to an improvement in Infant and Young Child Feeding, as well as an improvement in early childhood development indicators, although this is yet to translate into significant improvements in more long-term anthropometric scores. The CG model in Zambia and the CSG in South Africa did show evidence of significantly reduced stunting among better-educated mothers while in Malawi the programme significantly reduced under-nutrition. No impacts were found with the Kenya CT-OVC, the Ethiopia SCTP, or the Zimbabwe HSCT. Yet, there are consistent impacts on intermediate nutrition indicators—dietary diversity, meal frequency, food consumption as well as participation in health and nutrition activities which are expected to contribute to nutrition outcomes in the longer term. The lack of consistent impacts on anthropometric outcomes is likely due to the complex multiple underlying determinants of nutritional status and the short time-frame of most evaluations. Economic determinants are one among a number of factors that determine nutrition outcomes such as stunting. Moreover, with the exception of the Zambia CG model and South Africa, the relatively small number of young children among the labour-constrained populations targeted by the programmes covered in this book made it difficult to obtain sufficiently powered samples for anthropometric outcomes.

14.2.4 Cash Transfers Increase Adolescent Well-Being and Facilitate the Safe Transition to Adulthood

As noted earlier in the book, an important innovation of the Transfer Project has been to gather information on adolescents through dedicated modules administered directly to adolescents. This has been motivated in part by the fact that there is a generalized HIV (Human-Immunodeficiency Virus) prevalence in many southern African countries, that the labour-constrained model attempts to reach HIV-affected households, and that the incidence of new HIV infections is highest among young people. The evidence to date suggests that cash transfers can in fact also contribute to facilitating a safe transition for adolescents and youths to adulthood. The safe transition has a number of dimensions, including age at first sex (sexual debut), condom use and age disparate sex, forced and transactional sex, and multiple concurrent partners, which have implications for HIV risk. Other dimensions typically measured in these modules include adolescent mental health, hope, aspirations, and perceptions of the future.

These dimensions represent new and cutting-edge research into understanding psychosocial impacts of participating in CT programmes, with possible links to changes in multiple areas, including HIV risk, economic outcomes, and intergenerational effects. The Kenya CT-OVC, for example, led to an 8 percentage points reduction in sexual debut, a 6 percentage points reduction in pregnancy, and a 5 percentage points reduction in the probability of showing depressive symptoms among young people. The CSG in South Africa led to a 16 percentage points reduction in sexual debut, and those receiving the grant at earlier ages had reduced number of sexual partners for adolescents, reduced pregnancy as well as reduced likelihood of alcohol and drug use in teenage years. In Zimbabwe, the HSCT postponed sexual debut by 13 percentage points among youth aged 13–20 at baseline and increased the likelihood of condom use at first sex. There is evidence of heterogeneous impacts within countries; for example, there appear to be larger impacts on males in Kenya and larger impacts among female-headed households in Zimbabwe. This emerging evidence from Kenya, Zimbabwe, and South Africa (and forthcoming in other countries) thus shows that social cash transfers can play a critical role in addressing the underlying social and economic drivers of the HIV epidemic: inequality, education, food insecurity, and poverty.

14.2.5 Cash Transfers Positively Impact Beneficiary Livelihoods

An additional important innovation of the Transfer Project has been the focus on the economic impacts of cash transfers on beneficiary households and the communities in which they live. Cash transfer programmes have had a variety of impacts on household livelihood strategies, particularly with regard to agricultural activities. Zambia's CG model led to a 34 per cent increase in the area of worked land as well as an increase in the use of agricultural inputs, including seeds, fertilizers, and hired labour as well as increased investment in non-farm enterprises. The growth in input use led to an approximately 50 per cent increase in the value of overall production, which was primarily sold rather than consumed on farm. By improving livelihoods the cash transfer produced an income multiplier at the household level: the increase in per capita consumption induced by the programme was 25 per cent greater than the transfer itself.

Lesotho's CGP increased crop input use and expenditures, including an 8 percentage points boost in the share of households using pesticides (from a base of 12 per cent). As in Zambia, the increase in input use led to an increase in maize production and, for labour-constrained households, in sorghum production, as well as in the frequency of garden plot harvest. In Zimbabwe, the HSCT led to an increase in expenditure on fertilizers and in the share of households producing groundnuts, while in Malawi the SCTP led to an increase in both maize and groundnut output. The cash transfer programme led to an increase in seeds expenditure in Ghana, and to a decrease in Kenya, though in neither case did the transfers lead to growth in agricultural production. In both Kenya and Malawi-Mchinji, however, the cash transfer did increase the share of family food consumption obtained from home production. The qualitative studies told a consistent story that households with even a little bit more in labour and physical assets were better able to take advantage of the cash for productive purposes.

In almost all programmes in which it was measured, cash transfers increased the ownership of livestock. This ranged from all types of animals, large and small, in Zambia and Malawi, to small animals in Kenya, Lesotho, Ethiopia, and Zimbabwe. No impact on livestock ownership was found in Ghana. Similarly, the programmes in Zambia, Zimbabwe, Ethiopia, and Malawi led to growth in the purchase of agricultural tools, with no impact in

Kenya, Lesotho, and Ghana. Finally, the Zambia CG model led to a 16 percentage points increase in the share of households operating non-agricultural business enterprises, while the Zimbabwe and Malawi programmes led to an increase in the formation of these businesses. The Kenya CT-OVC led to a similar increase among female-headed households, and a decrease among male-headed households. While the Zambia MCTG model did not increase the share of households with non-agricultural business enterprises, it did lead to a significant increase in total revenue and profit.

14.2.6 Cash Transfers Lead to Increased Flexibility in Household Labour Allocation

Along with the growth in agricultural activities, the programmes have led to increased flexibility in labour allocation and time use. In most of the countries included in this book, in the context of severe liquidity constraints, casual agricultural wage labour is an activity of last resort. The shift from agricultural wage labour of last resort to on-farm activities was consistently reported by beneficiaries in Kenya, Ghana, Lesotho, Malawi, and Zimbabwe. As one elderly beneficiary said, 'I used to be a slave to ganyu but now I am a bit free.' In Zambia, the CG model led family members to reduce their participation in, and the intensity of, agricultural wage labour. The impact was particularly strong for women, amounting to a 17 percentage points reduction in participation and twelve fewer days a year. Both men and women increased the time they spent on family agricultural and non-agricultural businesses. In Kenya and Lesotho, this shift varied by age and gender, while in Ghana, the LEAP programme also increased on-farm activities.

The cash transfers had mixed results on child labour, which may be a result of the conflicting incentives caused by the programmes—while each had an emphasis on school attendance, this may conflict with the increase in livelihood activities, which often involves child labour. A reduction in child on-farm labour was found in Kenya and Lesotho, and for girls in Zimbabwe. The Malawi-Mchinji found a switch from off-farm wage labour to on-farm activities for children, while the later Malawi evaluation found a reduction in off-farm wage labour and no increase in on-farm activities. The Zimbabwe HSCT led to a reduction in casual wage labour (maricho) for children among smaller households. No clear impacts were found in Zambia or Ghana.

14.2.7 Cash Transfers Lead to an Improved Ability to Manage Risk

Cash transfers have allowed beneficiary households to better manage risk in almost all countries. Qualitative studies in Kenya, Ghana, Lesotho, Zimbabwe,

Ethiopia, and Malawi found that the programmes increased social capital and allowed beneficiaries to 're-enter' existing social networks and/or to strengthen informal social protection systems and risk-sharing arrangements, results corroborated by econometric analysis in Zambia, Ghana, and Lesotho. Receiving the transfer allowed beneficiaries to support other households or community institutions, such as the church.

A reduction in negative risk coping strategies, such as begging or changing eating patterns, was seen in Malawi, Ethiopia, and Lesotho, while beneficiary households in almost all countries were less likely to take their children out of school. The cash transfer programmes led to increased savings in Zambia, Kenya, and Ghana. Moreover, the cash transfer programmes allowed households to be seen as more financially trustworthy, to reduce their debt levels and increase their creditworthiness, for example in Zambia and Zimbabwe. In many cases, however, households expressed continued aversion to risk and reluctance to take advantage of their greater access to credit.

14.2.8 Multiplier Effects in the Local Economy

When beneficiaries receive cash they spend it and the impacts of the transfer are then transmitted to others inside and outside the local economy, often to households that are not eligible for cash transfers, who tend to own most of the local businesses. These income multipliers were estimated using an innovative village economy model, called the LEWIE (Local Economy-Wide Impact Evaluation) model. LEWIE models constructed for the cash transfer programmes in Kenya, Lesotho, Ghana, Malawi, Zambia, Zimbabwe, and Ethiopia simulated income multipliers ranging from 2.52 in Hintalo-Wajirat in Ethiopia to 1.34 in Nyanza, Kenya. That is, for every Birr transferred by the Ethiopian SCTP programme in Hintalo-Wajirat, up to 2.52 Birr in income can be generated for the local economy under model assumptions.

When credit, capital, and other market constraints limit the ability of local producers to increase production, the increase in demand brought about by the cash transfer programme may lead to higher prices and consequently a lower 'real' income multiplier. Simulations incorporating such constraints find that the real income multiplier, taking into account inflation, is lower than the nominal income multiplier, although remaining significantly greater than one in all seven countries. While evidence on prices from the quantitative evaluations has not shown any inflationary effects of the cash transfers, given the existence of poorly functioning markets in much of rural SSA, some constraints on local production and the supply of goods are likely. The key insight from the LEWIE model is that non-beneficiaries and the local economy also benefit from cash transfer programmes through trade and productive linkages. Maximizing the income multiplier may require complementary interventions that target both beneficiary and non-beneficiary families to resolve these constraints.

14.2.9 What Explains the Differences in Results Across Countries?

While a broadly consistent story has emerged from across the eight countries regarding the social and economic impacts, the story is nuanced with important differences across the countries. A number of factors are behind these differences, which are important to delineate for analytical and programmatic purposes.

First, regularity of the transfers is important in considering programme results. Regular and predictable transfers facilitate planning, consumption smoothing, moderate risk taking, and investment, in anticipation of future payments. Households that receive lumpy and unpredictable transfers are likely to spend the money differently. At the time of the evaluations in each country, the operational performance of paying transfers varied widely. The transfers were delivered regularly throughout the evaluation period in Zambia and Ethiopia, while in Ghana payments were meant to be bimonthly, but were made very irregularly. The Lesotho CGP was the only programme with a quarterly payment, and it was also affected by significant delays. This has likely undermined impacts on household consumption, poverty, and dietary diversity; qualitative research in Lesotho, for example, found that effects on food consumption and dietary diversity were concentrated around pay dates.

Second, the amount of the transfer given to a beneficiary household also matters. Some countries used a flat transfer while others varied the transfers by household size. None of the programmes, with the exception of South Africa, had mechanisms to regularly adjust the transfer amount for inflation, which meant that the real value of the transfers eroded over time. As a result of these factors, the value of the transfers as a share of beneficiary household per capita consumption varies across countries. The size of the transfer as a share of per capita consumption of beneficiary households ranged from 7 per cent in Ghana to almost 30 per cent in Zambia, at the time of their respective impact evaluations. For those countries utilizing a flat rate, the per capita value varies by household size: in Kenya the transfer represented 14 per cent of per capita consumption for average size households, and ranged from 10 per cent to 22 per cent for large and small households, respectively.[2]

Third, the demographic profile of beneficiary households also matters. Most of the cash transfer programmes supported by the Transfer Project by design

---

[2] See Davis and Handa (2015) for a discussion of transfer sizes.

have a large proportion of missing generation, labour-constrained households, with older, often elderly household heads, and with older children (such as the CT-OVC in Kenya, SCTP in Malawi, LEAP in Ghana, CGP in Lesotho, HSCT in Zimbabwe, SCTP in Ethiopia, and the MCTG model in Zambia). The CG model in Zambia, with a target population of young families with small children, and the CSG in South Africa, which eventually targeted all children aged eighteen and younger in poor families, were the exceptions. Differential availability of adult labour may explain a large part of the differences in the productive impacts that are observed across programmes. This is illustrated in Zambia, where the CG model had stronger livelihood-related impacts, while the MCTG had larger impacts on schooling. Although labour-constrained households may hire labour, as well as carry out economic activities themselves, households with available adult labour are in a stronger position to take advantage of the availability of cash for livelihood activities, in both the short and the long run.

Targeting effectiveness and access are also critical in explaining outcomes and were, in many countries, assessed through separate targeting assessments, often based on baseline analysis. To cite two examples, in Lesotho, targeting was found to be fairly effective at identifying poor households but there were substantial exclusion errors due to financial constraints. The targeting process was found to be fair and transparent, albeit with potential for improvement in households' understanding of the selection process. In South Africa, the evaluation provided information on differential access to the CSG, especially for infants and adolescents, and identified the factors associated with low take-up, including misinformation on eligibility criteria, lack of required registration documents, prohibitive transport costs, stigma, and the application process being time-consuming or difficult. The evaluation found that the likelihood of a child being reached by the programme before they reached the age of two increased by 13 percentage points if the mother was given a form when the child was born.

Finally, differential access to assets besides labour, the nature of local markets, the effectiveness of local committees in implementing a given programme, the availability and quality of public services, and the nature of programme messaging, all play a role in influencing the impacts of the programme. For example, qualitative studies found that households with a bit more in assets were better able to take advantage of the cash transfer for productive investment. Qualitative studies also found that dynamic local markets provided more opportunities for productive investment as well. Strong messaging about caring for children in the Lesotho programme coincided with large impacts on children's clothing and shoes despite small overall consumption impacts.

The extent to which programmes have created linkages with social services and facilitated access is also critical to impact, especially on health, education, and nutrition outcomes for children. Conditioning cash payments on school enrolment or health clinic visits has not been implemented in the SSA context on a wide scale for a variety of reasons, including supply-side constraints which effectively discriminate against the most isolated and socially excluded, capacity issues with monitoring conditions, and programmes having objectives that go well beyond single sector objectives. This flexible approach which allows households to invest the money where they see fit is consistent with the larger range of impacts (consumption, social, productive, and adolescents) that characterize the SSA experience and which contrasts sharply with the Latin American evidence, where most evidence is limited to the sectors conditioned by the programmes. Nevertheless, there remain opportunities to leverage cash transfers to enhance impacts on schooling, health, and other objectives, without constraining households through conditions, for example by providing complementary services or peer-support networks that are linked to schooling and health, and that support families to invest in human capital. In Zambia, health and education effects seemed to be constrained by supply-side effects as schools and health facilities are not easily accessible in most study communities. In Lesotho, as mentioned earlier, the messaging of the programme—that the transfer should be used in the interest of children—was strictly followed by beneficiaries. Although birth registration was not required to enrol in the Zambia CG model, mechanisms were put in place to provide incentives, leading to an increase in birth registration.

14.3 LESSONS ON THE POLITICAL ECONOMY OF EVALUATIONS

The country chapters (Chapters 5–13) provide the individual stories regarding the role of the evaluation in the policy process, and the political economy chapter (Chapter 2) highlights the evolution of the Transfer Project, the role of evaluative research in influencing social protection policy and design, and examines factors that shape the extent and nature of this influence. This section summarizes the key emerging lessons.

As a starting point, we examine why a number of African governments engaged in evaluation of cash transfer programmes in the first place. While much of the initial motivation for conducting impact evaluations was donor driven, there was a conscious effort by development partners to involve government counterparts from the start and, in most cases, governments embraced this approach, often for their own reasons. This was both to ensure the programme was seen as beneficial in the light of potential criticisms as well as to answer specific questions, such as those linked to conditionality. In

Kenya, there was a pre-pilot to prove the concept and a pilot with a rigorous evaluation to assess impact. Similarly, evaluations in South Africa were designed to improve understanding of impact, to consider certain issues such as programme access and to provide the evidence base to advocate for further expansions, especially to those more sceptical of social assistance. In Zambia, an impact evaluation was seen as valuable to build the case for cash transfers, and in particular for the categorical targeting approach, and to gather sufficient support for a potential scale-up. Given the challenging relationship between donors and the government in Zimbabwe, the evaluation was embraced by all parties as a means to ensure a data-driven approach determined the success of the programme. Ethiopia's interest in the evaluation was less on its impact and more on proving the idea and that a given implementation structure and particular institutional arrangements would work. In Lesotho, the learning agenda overall aimed to provide rigorous evidence on a new approach in the context of fairly extensive existing social protection, to improve programme effectiveness and efficiency and to address concerns, especially from the Ministry of Finance over dependency and value for money, related to the lack of evidence that the programme would be affordable and beneficial. So while in most cases initially donor driven, the SSA governments generally embraced the evaluations and saw value for their own domestic purposes.

The country chapters document significant policy and programme developments in recent years, with the impact evaluation playing a role in shaping these developments to a greater or lesser extent in the different countries. Many of the countries experienced a shift in the narrative of social protection accompanied with increases in funding and coverage. In Zambia, the government-approved budget allocation to the SCT represented a tripling in the size of the programme and an eightfold increase in government budget to the programme. Although this was in the context of a conducive policy environment, the impact evaluation, through providing rigorous, timely, and accessible evidence played an important role in changing the narrative around social protection and influencing scale-up. The Ghana chapter similarly notes that the evaluation helped to change the narrative around social protection and brought high level interest in the programme by government. A similar story emerges in Kenya where the evaluation played a role in demonstrating cash transfers as viable and affordable in creating a beneficial impact in broader political developments. This contributed to greater investment in social protection by donors and government as well as buy-in from other sectors and the inclusion of social protection as part of Kenya's national HIV prevention and response strategy.

In Lesotho, the CGP evolved in a short spell of time from a relatively small-scale donor-funded pilot into a nationally owned programme, with an expansion of coverage, greater institutional capacity, and increased domestic funding, which is at the core of the social protection policy framework. This was achieved through a combination of relationship building, demonstration of credible programme implementation (to which results of the evaluation contributed directly), and the favourable political environment, with the evaluation playing an important role. In South Africa, the strong findings on the positive outcomes of early receipt of the CSG contributed to increased political support for universalization and expansion to include pregnant women, in part to address exclusion, as well as renewed policy focus on early childhood development, additional income support for more vulnerable groups and other ages. This is partially because the clear evidence of effectiveness de-politicized the programme. In Ethiopia, the impact evaluation demonstrated the effectiveness of alternative institutional arrangements, with the Ministry of Labour and Social Affairs taking a leading role in implementing social protection, allowing for policy discussions around the replication of the approach in other regions.

> While there is considerable diversity across the case study countries, an analysis of the process across the countries suggests that evidence produced by the national evaluations and related research contributed to:
> - Building the overall credibility of an emerging social protection sector;
> - Strengthening the case for social protection as an investment, not a cost, and addressing public perceptions and misconceptions;
> - Supporting learning around programme design and implementation to inform programme improvements in key areas such as targeting, access, transfer size, and the role of complementary activities; and
> - Shaping policy discussions beyond the national context and informing regional social protection agendas.

Across the country narratives, a key value of the evaluation was that it created credibility for the cash transfer programmes and, by extension, to an emerging social protection sector. It seems that it was not simply the impacts that were valued but the mere fact that a systematic approach to analysing the programmes was being pursued generated confidence among policy makers about the programme. This created a sense that the programme was serious at being effective, especially in ensuring confidence in the programme and its impacts for a broader audience. In Zambia, previous evaluations had experienced difficulties in attributing changes to the programme itself and therefore had limited influence on policy. In contrast, the fact that the impact evaluation of the SCT programme in 2010–15 was rigorous and provided attributable impacts significantly contributed to the enhancement of the reputation and credibility of the intervention among key audiences. In Lesotho, although the attributable programme impacts were not yet available when the critical decisions were being made, the evidence of potential impacts and promise that these would be confirmed through the impact evaluation as well as indirect effects from the increased credibility of the policy building exercise were important in informing policy decisions. In addition, the continuous generation of information and learning contributed to reinforcing the internal and external credibility of Ministry of Social Development as an institution committed to constant improvement, results, and change and a solid platform of learning by doing. A key message coming out of the chapters is then that more than the impact evaluation results themselves, the mere existence of rigorous evaluations facilitates programme credibility. However, while evaluation findings were found to be effective in promoting perceptions of impact and affordability and building political momentum for social protection generally, the evidence they provided was not in most cases perceived as the major driver of government decisions to scale up or increase financing, although they may in some instances have been major political *enablers* of such a scale-up, as in the case of Zambia.

The impact evaluation results and accompanying costing analyses were also influential in changing perceptions of social protection from simply a cost, to an affordable and worthwhile investment. The broad scope of the impact evaluations, particularly the focus on productive impacts and local economy effects, was important in influencing audiences beyond the social welfare sector. This evidence helped frame social protection within ongoing policy discourses and priorities, for example as a contribution to inclusive growth, and thereby gain political support. In Zambia, the evaluation challenged perceptions that cash transfers were handouts and created dependency by demonstrating human capital and productive impacts—thus allowing the ministry to cite the programme as 'an engine for inclusive growth'—which fit within the policy agenda of the new government. The existence of a poverty impact was often key in driving interest and discussion of a broad audience. For example, in Zambia, the poverty-related findings and multiplier effects calculated by the LEWIE model caught the attention of different audiences in government, the Cabinet Office, and Ministry of Finance in particular. Although the objectives of cash transfers are often focused on health and education indicators, it was the 13 per cent reduction in poverty that captured the interest of the Kenyan government. In Ghana, the productive impacts gained a great deal of interest and the multiplier effects coming out of the LEWIE model were even cited by the president of Ghana in a speech. Similarly, in Lesotho, the results about the local economy effects were used extensively for advocacy by the Ministry of Social Development, particularly with the Ministry of Finance, and provided a solid argument regarding the broader effects of CGP on the wider community.

The evaluations, as part of broader learning agendas, had important impacts on programme design and implementation. Specific design and operational changes were made to programmes in Kenya, South Africa,

Lesotho, and Ghana following presentation of the evaluation findings. In Zambia, a targeting study assessed the effectiveness and acceptability of targeting approaches and, in doing so, led to a review of the role of the Community Welfare Assistance Committees (CWACs) and of poverty targeting. In Lesotho, the evaluations, including initial baseline analysis, informed improvements in programme operations and further reviews, such as the revision of the payment value to vary according to number of children, and the linkage with emergency response. Early baseline analysis in Ghana showed that the transfer size was too small to be effective, which led directly to an initiative to increase the amount. In South Africa, the review of exclusion and effective reach provided evidence that led to improved information and outreach especially in remote areas, strengthened monitoring to avoid exclusion error, improved payment system efficiency, and reduced the cost of paying grants in order to address barriers to accessing grants. However, findings were not always automatically translated to design changes, in many instances due to competing priorities. For example, despite evaluation recommendations indicating the need to increase transfer values in order to enhance programme impact in Kenya and Malawi, resources were used to extend coverage rather than increase or index transfer values.

There are also indications that the body of evidence in aggregate has contributed to shape regional processes and sectoral debates. For instance, the Government of South Africa and the African Union Commission, in collaboration with UNICEF (United Nations Children's Fund), led the *African Union Expert Consultation on Children and Social protection Systems*, which took place in Cape Town in April 2014. Evidence on impacts as well as lessons learned from programme implementation and financing were presented by and discussed among government delegates, including representatives from social development and welfare ministries, as well as finance, planning, and other related ministries. The evidence influenced the final recommendations approved by the High Level Forum and included in the 2014 Malabo Declaration. The results from the From Protection to Production (PtoP) project as well as the broader outcomes were presented on numerous occasions to the World Bank—UNICEF Community of Practice on cash transfer programmes in SSA, which brings together the implementers of government-run cash transfer programmes from fifteen countries in the region. The PtoP results in particular touched a nerve in terms of the urgency of supporting the livelihoods of cash transfer beneficiaries, and have facilitated discussion on how to improve implementation of cash transfer programmes so as to foster productive inclusion, as well as on the design of potential complementary interventions. New evidence from the impact evaluations of the CSG in South Africa and the Kenya CT-OVC programme on delayed sexual debut, pregnancy, inter-generational sex, and other related risky behaviours has strengthened evidence around impacts on HIV prevention and thus contributed to enhance the case for social protection as a critical component of an integrated HIV/AIDS response.

14.3.1 Key Factors Shaping the Role of Evaluation in Influencing Policy and Programmes

Given the discussion in Section 14.3 on the role that evaluative research and associated products have played in influencing social protection policy and programmes, the Transfer Project experience offers interesting lessons on the key factors which shaped this role. A number of factors were identified as having a positive effect on the influence of the evidence: (i) evaluations being embedded in national policy processes; (ii) relationship-building and multi-disciplinary research teams; (iii) messaging and packaging of evidence; (iv) the relationship between demand and supply of evidence; and (v) the creation of a regional learning agenda, including the establishment of a regional community of practice.

The impact evaluations were embedded in national policy processes, involving international experts and researchers, government counterparts, and national research institutions to ensure policy-relevant evaluation design and promote the use of results to inform policy and programme development. In this way close interaction between different stakeholders promoted the development of strong trust relationships and, most importantly, national ownership of the process and end results. The fact that the evaluations create a learning environment with a broader learning agenda beyond just impact—as opposed to a single stand-alone impact evaluation—has meant that the evaluations have been more useful at providing more comprehensive and critical input.

Some elements of the process are implicit and not always formally reported in evaluation reports, including trust and relationship-building between the researchers and government counterparts. Embedding the learning and research agenda into national processes, as well as including both international and national members in the composition of the research teams, contributed to developing a strong sense of trust. The evaluation team typically played the role of independent technical experts, while the Transfer Project served as the honest broker between the interests of the researchers, development partners, and the government. The existence of research teams which included national and international quantitative and qualitative researchers from different disciplines alongside more operational and policy-oriented researchers in ongoing dialogue with national stakeholders meant that as the research agenda evolved, the teams could produce policy-relevant research and analysis on context-specific issues. In some cases, these were stand-alone pieces, but often they drew upon each other's ongoing research, making use of quantitative and qualitative data.

Of course, there is a need for clarity of the roles between evaluator and policy makers and among evaluation partners, but this experience does raise questions about the independence of evaluations. Independent evaluations are often valued to ensure that the evaluation is done in a scientific manner and that results are not influenced by the closeness of programme managers and evaluators. This is reasonable if the primary motivation of an evaluation is solely accountability. Yet, if the objective is to influence government policy and policy debates the evidence presented in this book clearly shows that proximity and interdependence of the evaluators, government programme team, and partner agencies is more likely to be effective.

The accessibility, packaging, and messaging of findings and accompanying presentations contributed to the extent to which evaluation evidence influenced policy and design. Because the evaluation process generally engaged local stakeholders, the messages that came out of the evaluations were often used at critical junctures. In Zambia, the timing of the release of findings was critical in influencing key decisions—through the production of briefs, including a specific policy brief on poverty, and strategic presentations that seized the policy momentum. In Ghana, effective advocacy was undertaken though nationwide events and media engagement, which translated evidence into clear and digestible messages, and allowed the use of messages by a variety of stakeholders. Further, at different stages of the evaluation process key evidence was used to adjust the Kenyan programme. Even beyond governments, civil society used certain results at key moments to argue for social protection. In South Africa, SASSA (South African Social Security Agency) engaged with the media, community-based, and non-governmental organizations to disseminate the results and the media became very involved in disseminating the information to the public and encouraging discussions around the results. Nonetheless, the relevance and influence of evaluation findings is to a large extent determined by the point in the policy cycle at which they are delivered. This can be hard to predict and accommodate within the timeframe of evaluation activities. Use of modelling approaches and analysis of baseline studies prior to the completion of the formal evaluation enabled some flexibility to produce timely inputs, as in the case of the Ghana process.

Even where the main impact evaluation results were not available at critical moments, the fact that key information was made available and individuals within the country were very familiar with that information allowed the results of the evaluations to be most profitably used, all along the duration of the evaluations. For Zimbabwe, though impacts were measured in the short term (only after one year) the results, even if viewed as preliminary by the evaluation team, were seen in a positive light by government and provided timely inputs into improving a key component of the programme (harmonization).

In Lesotho, the multifaceted evidence from studies, reviews, and analysis formed part of a collaborative advocacy strategy to build the case for CGP and influence high level decision making. In particular, early analyses from the rapid appraisal and the LEWIE model were made available at a critical decision making time and therefore were critical in influencing the government decision to take on the programme. Although these analyses did not have grounds to draw robust conclusions on causal effects, it did demonstrate the potential impacts at key moments.

Along with timely messages, the fact that the evaluations create a learning environment with a broader learning agenda—as opposed to a single stand-alone impact evaluation—has meant that the evaluations have been more useful at providing more comprehensive and critical input. This can be most clearly observed in Lesotho, where a broad-based learning agenda consisted of a rapid appraisal, baseline data analysis, a targeting assessment, local economy effects assessment as well as other social protection sector reviews. Targeting analysis was also done in Kenya, Ghana, Zambia, Zimbabwe, and Malawi and played some role in the consideration of targeting. As noted, in Ghana analysis of transfer size from the baseline study led to immediate changes in amounts provided and a similar analysis opened up the discussion of transfer size, eventually leading to an increase in benefit levels in early 2015.

There was an important regional learning effect in the evolution of programmes and the central role of rigorous impact evaluations, in part facilitated by the Transfer Project. UNICEF, FAO keep, the University of North Carolina at Chapel Hill), and Save the Children were common actors in almost all of the national processes described in this book, and this commonality contributed to the development of a regional learning culture, together with informal and formal mechanisms that promoted information exchange. Annual Transfer-Project-supported workshops, where the design and findings of impact evaluations (and other related research) were discussed among a range of researchers and policy makers, provided the space for information and experience exchange as well as opportunities to raise awareness among policy makers and donors of the role of social protection in relation to a broad range of impacts and benefits.

In Zambia, the increasing availability of evidence on the impact of cash transfers in Africa and the fact that it was an emerging priority for donors influenced the design of the SCT programme in 2010. These factors combined with the conducive policy environment contributed to the decision to scale up the programme. The close involvement, and leadership, of government in the evaluations meant that policy makers were able to immediately draw on what was being learnt to inform policy. The Ministry of Community Development in Zambia provided leadership and extensive involvement from the early stages as the evaluations were considered as Government-of-Zambia-commissioned evaluations (even though procured through UNICEF). The narratives presented in the country chapters suggest that it was then critical that the evaluation team was available to contribute to policy discussions and influence the social protection agenda. Equally important is that both the programme and the evaluation are embedded within government structures and that there is a high level of government ownership of both processes. Leadership within the key ministry in implementing randomization and in communication of the approach—that is, extensive involvement of ministry in early stages and constructive relationships—lays a solid foundation for using and communicating findings in the future.

Overall, the country narratives suggest that the evaluation process has played a critical role in programme quality and effectiveness within countries in which they were implemented. Evaluations played a role in effective implementation and demonstrated the credibility of the programmes. There is also some evidence that there were positive externalities in the evaluations across the region. Policy makers being exposed to regional evidence seemed to influence policy making. On the other hand, discussions on the evidence by government delegates at regional fora such as the African Union, and others, also raised the profile of this evidence, and contributed to increased credibility of the sector, as well as to emerging discussion on the role of cash transfers in achieving sector outcomes such as agriculture, HIV, health, and others.

Of course, even with this evidence on the way in which cash transfer evaluative research contributed to policy and programme changes, other factors can affect the role of evaluation. The relationship between the evidence and policy/programme change was not found to be linear, and there were a number of critical external factors which determined changes. A number of factors external to the evaluation process also play a strong role in influencing policy and programmatic change or condition the role that evidence plays in policy discussions. These included trade-offs between evaluation recommendations and policy agendas, particularly in relation to programme design or scale-up choices, the influence of external actors, and financial or other capacity constraints. The role of evaluations then depends on the general context in the country as well as whether other sources of information are being brought to bear.

14.4 MOVING FORWARD: RESEARCH AGENDA AND INSTITUTIONAL CONSIDERATIONS

Given the evidence presented here and elsewhere, it is clear that cash transfers programmes are effective in achieving key development outcomes. This does not mean that new evaluations and new research should not be conducted, but does point to the need to be clear about the purpose of further research. In this section, some possible directions for future research are considered and some reflections on how and why we conduct evaluations are offered, based on the experience of the Transfer Project.

Cash transfers are a core part of social protection policies and of effective overall developments strategies, but clearly other policy actions are needed. While the evidence suggests a broad range of impacts of transfers, these vary by location and recipient and it may be possible for impacts to be enhanced through complementary and coordinated interventions. For example, cash transfers have shown to be beneficial to households with children affected by HIV, but additional actions such as improvements in health care access and care practices, among others, are also merited. Similarly, cash transfers have been shown to have productive impacts for some but not all beneficiaries. The productive benefits of cash transfers might be enhanced if accompanied by agricultural or other productive interventions that facilitate, and/or increase the impact of, productive investment, such as technical assistance. Of course, these and similar 'cash-plus' interventions hypothesize that complementary interventions have a greater return when combined with transfers and correspondingly the impact of transfer will be greater if complementary interventions are provided.

However, governments are often reluctant to provide more than one programme to a given household with the idea that if a household is already receiving government support, they should not receive assistance from another programme. This is a legitimate concern, often shared by rural communities, where coverage of the poor and vulnerable is incomplete and resources are limited. However, it potentially limits the impact of government investment if cash-plus provides a greater return than a transfer programme and another programme would independently. There are also practical administrative reasons for attempting to create complementarity. Most cash transfer programmes create a data collection system that identifies vulnerable households within the country. If this is adequately created, there is little value to creating alternative systems for other programmes. Instead, this can be used as the basis for identifying candidates for potentially complementary interventions. While using interventions to complement cash transfers seems to be a reasonable approach, these cash-plus interventions should be assessed using rigorously designed impact evaluations to determine if they are effective. Evaluating cash-plus programmes is one suggested area of future research.

The inclusion of the LEWIE model as part of the mixed method approach to evaluate cash transfer programmes in SSA has opened up new areas of research. LEWIE models can be used to explore potential longer-term impacts and compare the costs and benefits of cash transfer programmes. Governments and donors have repeatedly made it clear that they want to know from an investment perspective whether and to what extent the benefits of cash transfers, many of which (like children's schooling) are long-term, exceed the costs. LEWIE models can also be used to examine which productive or market interventions can alter or enhance the local-economy impacts of cash transfer programmes. In certain situations, complementary interventions aimed at raising productivity, by stimulating supply, may be able to avoid inflation and thus close the gap between the real and nominal income gains from social programmes. At the same time, income transfers can loosen cash constraints on local production activities, making local supply more responsive and bolstering income multipliers. Moreover, most of the cash transfer programmes discussed here target households with few or no assets, including able-bodied labour. If these programmes expanded to include other households, what would be the impacts? How should complementary (e.g., productive) interventions be targeted in order to maximize their impacts on employment, income, and welfare?

Even within the cash transfer programmes there is a need to better understand the pathways through which impact occurs. For example, impacts on nutritional outcomes are found in some studies yet the pathway through which these nutritional effects occur are complex. It might be that households use cash directly to purchase nutritious foods or it might be that beneficiaries use the funds for home production, which leads to greater agricultural output and better nutrition. Similarly, the reason why cash leads to increased school enrolment could be explored further. It might be that child labour is needed less or it might be that cash provides the liquidity necessary to pay the costs of schooling (e.g., uniforms as found in Zambia). There are a host of other pathways to explore which if better understood could help to design complementary policies and possibly improve design of existing programmes, ultimately resulting in greater impacts. A second area of potential research is in understanding the pathways of impact.

Of course, cash transfers are only one part of social protection systems. While they have been widely evaluated, other types of instruments have not. These include in-kind transfers, public works, health insurance, removal of user fees for access to health services, birth registration, and so on. Some of these instruments may be more challenging to evaluate than cash transfer programmes due to issues of self-selection and the fact that some (health insurance) protect against shocks that are dramatic but infrequent. But rigorous approaches to evaluating these types of programmes are available. As social protection moves beyond cash transfers, these new programmes should be evaluated. A third suggested area of future research is of programmes that form part of the broader social protection agenda.

Conclusions and Policy Implications   357

There are still other issues to explore with regard to the impact of cash transfers that have not yet been considered. While transfers appear to re-allocate labour from off-farm to on-farm, the general impact on time use of household members and, more broadly, the implication of transfer receipt on intrahousehold allocation of resources, has been less explored. Collecting data on time use and more gender-specific information would provide insight into intrahousehold dynamics. Relatedly, there is little information on whether transfers have an impact on addressing the economic drivers of domestic violence although there is some initial analysis in Zimbabwe and data from Zambia has just been processed. More broadly, there remain questions on whether transfers help address issue of social exclusion among marginalized groups and facilitate participation in social networks. Initial results suggest they do, but more information is required. A fourth area of future research is in expanding the breadth of indicators of impact.

A final issue that is often raised by governments relates to the cost and associated benefits of cash transfer programmes. While there are often questions about the cost-effectiveness of transfer programmes, conducting such an analysis is not appropriate. Cost-effectiveness analysis relies on comparing the costs per unit of benefit of a particular indicator. The key is in identifying a single clear indicator, or finite set of indicators, to analyse and identify the per-unit cost of increasing that indicator. Of course, as seen in this book, the impacts of cash transfers are widespread and across numerous indicators rendering a cost-effectiveness approach inadequate. There are, of course, a whole host of issues with cost–benefit analysis that are beyond the scope of this book. But what is clear is that governments are concerned about the costs of cash transfer programmes and a final area of research relates to careful consideration of the costs of the programmes which also then consider the full range of potential programme benefits across all domains.

Beyond the research agenda, the discussion in this book highlights the importance of creating a learning environment where evaluations feed into the policy process. This is only possible with an institutional structure that creates such an environment. Through expanding the interaction between evaluation specialists, donors, and governments, the Transfer Project has initiated this process for the evaluation of cash transfer programmes. But ultimately this represents a small fraction of programmes and stakeholders involved in a country's development. Even with its strength, there is insufficient participation by local universities and think tanks in the evaluations and subsequent policy discussions. This is partly an issue of training in that the approaches to rigorous evaluation have only emerged recently. But it is also that a culture of evaluation has yet to emerge and, until it does, a learning environment cannot be effectively created. If it can emerge, it is more likely that effective and uniform data collection systems will be created and that national surveys will include programme-related question on standardized questionnaires. Clearly, there needs to be a broader push to address regional institutional gaps to create an effective learning agenda.

REFERENCE

Davis, B. and Handa, S. (2015). 'How Much Do Programmes Pay? Transfer Size in Selected National Cash Transfer Programmes in Africa'. The Transfer Project Research Brief 2015–09. Chapel Hill, NC: Carolina Population Center, UNC-Chapel Hill.

Index

Tables, figures, and boxes are indicated by an italic *t*, *f*, and *b* following the page number.

Adato, M 3
adolescent development 62–3 *t*, 64, 340–1
  HIV/AIDS 31
  Kenya, Cash Transfer Programme for Orphans and Vulnerable Children 133, 140
  South Africa, Child Support Grant 319–20 *t*
  Zimbabwe, Harmonized Social Cash Transfer Programme 243–4
Africa Community of Practice on cash transfer programmes 32
African National Congress (ANC) 326
African Union (AU) 354
  Social Policy Framework 30, 170
  social protection 30–1
African Union Commission 30, 350
African Union Expert Consultation on Children and Social Protection Systems (2014) 30, 350
African Union Ministers of Social Development 30
Airtel Money 301
Akomea, Nana 148 n2–149 n2
Alliance for Children's Entitlement to Social Security (ACESS, South Africa) 325, 326
American Institutes for Research (AIR) 78, 79, 80, 235
attrition 55–6
  Tigray pilot social cash transfer programme 179

Beazley, R 219
behavioural psychology 64–5
Black Sash (South Africa) 325, 326
Brazil 148, 164
business enterprise survey (BES) 104, 108–9

Carraro, L 219
Cash Transfer Programme for Orphans and Vulnerable Children (CT-OVC) (Kenya) 50
  adolescent behaviour 133, 140
  behavioural change 132, 135
  capacity building strategy 120, 138
  child labour reduction 132–3
  children's education 129–31
  components of evaluations 122–3, 124
  concerns over misuse of cash 134–5
  conditionality 135–6, 141
  consumption levels 129, 337
  decision to conduct impact evaluation 123
  demonstration of practicality of cash transfers 126, 137, 139
  design of impact evaluation 124–5
  development impacts of programme 128–9, 130–1 *t*, 132–4
  dissemination of evaluation findings 140–1
  effective use of cash 135
  evaluations of 122
  expansion phase (2009–14) 121
  external support for 138–40
  health impacts of 131–2
  HIV/AIDS risk 133, 140
  household size and impact of 132, 141
  indirect effects of evaluation 138
  influence of evaluation on programme expansion and policy 137–41
  issues and results from impact evaluation 125–36
  labour participation impacts of 133
  lessons from evaluation of 142–3
  Local Economy-Wide Impact Evaluation 123, 134
  long-term value of evaluation evidence 142–3
  management information system 120
  number of enrolled households 121
  number of orphans 117
  objective of 117
  objectives of evaluation 124
  Operations Manual 120, 138
  origin and growth of 117–18
  OVC Secretariat 120
  pilot phase (2007–9) 120–1
  poverty reduction 129, 139
  pre-pilot phase (2004–6) 119–20
  production impact of 133
  proxy means testing 127, 137
  qualitative study of impacts of 133–4, 138
  role of evaluation 118, 142
  sexual debut 133
  social capital increase 134
  success of 142
  targeting of the programme 126–8, 137–8
  value of transfer 134, 138, 141

cash transfer programmes
  complementary interventions 355, 356
  costs of 357
  coverage of 146
  cross-country differences in impacts of 344–6
  demographic profile of recipient households 6, 343–4
  effectiveness of 1, 2, 17, 337–46, 354
  expansion in sub-Saharan Africa 17
  future research 355–7
  impact of 335
  impact on local economies 95
  impacts of 74
  (ir)regularity of payment 344
  labour allocation 342
  objectives of 4, 6, 94
  poverty reduction 337–8
  production impacts 94
  programmes in Transfer Project 5 t
  risk management 342–3
  social protection strategies 6
  spillover effects 95, 112–13
  targeting process 6–7
  unconditional 6, 335–6
  well-being 337
  see also adolescent development; educational impacts; food security; health impacts; household livelihoods and productivity; policy influence of impact evaluations; value of cash transfers
Center for International Health and Development (CIHD, Boston University) 292–3
Centre for Social Research at the University of Malawi 78, 292–3, 297, 301
child development 339–40
Child Grants Programme (CGP) (Lesotho) 49, 248
  baseline evaluation survey 258–9
  birth registration and child health 261–2 t
  case management systems 272
  community networks 263, 265 t
  components of evaluation 256–7, 276–8
  concerns over cash transfer programme 266
  consolidation of 248, 256, 267
  costing review and fiscal sustainability 265–6, 278
  coupling with other interventions 273
  drivers of policy change 266–71
  educational impacts 260–1 t
  enhanced resilience 263, 265 t
  evolution and development of 249–50 f, 251–6
  expansion of 255
  experimental design of impact evaluation 49, 249
  food security 258–9, 262, 263 t
  government absorption of costs 254–5
  government takeover of (2012–14) 252–5
  harmonizing and integration with other interventions 274
  health impacts 261–2 t
  household livelihoods 262–3, 264 t
  influence of evaluation on consolidation of 267, 269–71, 274–5
  influence of evaluation on programme improvement 271–4, 275
  influence of practical demonstration of 268
  Local Economy-Wide Impact Evaluation 259–60, 270, 277
  management information system 251
  Ministry of Social Development 253
  National Information System for Social Assistance 251, 251 b, 273
  objective of 248
  objectives of evaluation 256
  origins of (2005–9) 249–51
  payment system 273
  political influences on consolidation of 268–9
  rapid assessment of early phase of 257–8, 269–70, 276
  relationship building 267–8
  systems building (2010–11) 251–2 b
  targeting assessment 259, 276–7
  targeting process 251, 272
  value of transfer 248, 272
child labour, impact of cash transfer programmes 342
  Ghana 159
  Kenya 132–3
  Tigray 183
Colombia 121, 164
community targeting 6–7
comparative cross-country studies 73–4, 87–90
  conceptual framework 74–5
  critical analysis of 76–7
  daily debriefings 76
  data analysis 76
  feedback sessions 76
  flexibility of 77
  focus group discussions 75
  integration with qualitative findings 77
  methods, timing and sequencing 75–6
  reporting 76

Index

sampling 75
strength of approach 76-7
Concern Worldwide 284
conditional cash transfer programmes (CCTs) 3
consumption levels, and cash transfer programmes
  impact of 337
  Kenya 129, 337
  Malawi 298-9, 337
  questionnaire design 58-9
  Zambia 207, 210 t
  Zimbabwe 241, 242 t

Davis, B 3
Deloitte Advisory Service 227
Democratic Alliance (South Africa) 326
Department for International Development (DFID, UK) 23, 120, 123
  Malawi 284
  Zambia 201, 204
  Zimbabwe 236
dependency, concerns about 336
  challenging 26, 36
  Ghana 162
  Kenya 134-5
  Lesotho 266, 347
  Malawi 287
  Zambia 204, 217, 349
Determined, Resilient, AIDS-free, Mentored and Safe (DREAMS) initiative 31
Devereaux, S 3
difference-in-differences (DD) approach 45, 67-8, 207
dissemination of evaluation findings 25
  Ghana 162, 164, 165
  Kenya 140-1
Dowa Emergency Cash Transfer 284

Economic Policy Research Institute (EPRI) 314, 323
educational impacts of cash transfer programmes 338
  Ghana 158-9
  Kenya 129-31
  Lesotho 260-1 t
  Malawi 300
  South Africa 319
  Tigray 186
  Zambia 209
  Zimbabwe 241-2
Endowment Fund for the Rehabilitation of Tigray (EFFORT) 176, 193
e-payment 301
Ethiopia
  community care coalitions 54, 170

direct support beneficiaries 169-70
drought 169
food security strategy 169
national social protection policy 170, 191
non-experimental design of impact evaluation 54-5
Productive Safety Net Programme 169
Social Cash Transfer Programme 54
thematic focus study 83-4, 85, 86
see also Tigray; Tigray pilot social cash transfer programme
European Union (EU)
  Lesotho 249, 253, 254, 255, 267
  Malawi 290, 291, 296, 297
evaluation of cash transfer programmes, *see* impact evaluations
evidence-based policy making 19
external validity 43, 65

Filipski, M 95
Fizbein, A 3
focus group discussions (FGDs) 72, 75
Food and Agriculture Organization (FAO) 4, 23, 155, 180, 297, 353
food security, and cash transfer programmes 339
  Ghana 156
  Lesotho 258-9, 262, 263 t
  Malawi 299-300
  Tigray 182-4
  Zambia 210 t
framing, and policy influence of research 20
From Protection to Production (PtoP) 125
  key feature of 43
  key motivation behind 59
  methodology 9-10
  objective of 4
  productive activity questions 59, 60-1 t
  research innovation 59-61
  social protection and agriculture 31-2
fuel subsidies 154-5

Gadeberg, M 19
Garcia, M 3
General Algebraic Modelling System (GAMS) 103n2
general equilibrium (GE) effects 94
German Agency for Technical Cooperation (GTZ) 202
German Development Bank (KfW) 290, 291, 296, 297
Ghana 147
  external development partners 148
  fuel subsidies 154-5
  future of social protection 165-6
  Ghana Living Standard Survey 149, 150

Ghana (cont.)
    improvements in social protection 150
    Ministry of Gender, Children and Social Protection 150
    multiplicity of social protection schemes 149
    national champions of social protection 147–8
    National Social Protection Policy 150
    National Social Protection Strategy 146, 147, 150
    political influences on social protection 148–9, 166
    Poverty Reduction Strategy (2002–5) 147
    social protection in 147–50
    weaknesses in social protection system 149
    see also Livelihood Empowerment Against Poverty Programme (LEAP) (Ghana)
Global Fund for HIV, TB and Malaria 119, 288

Handa, S 3, 128
happiness, and cash transfer programmes 337
    Ghana 160
health impacts of cash transfer programmes 338–9
    Ghana 156–8
    Kenya 131–2
    Lesotho 261–2 t
    Malawi 300
    South Africa 317–18
    Tigray 186
Helpage International 172
HIV/AIDS 6, 22, 117
    adolescent development 11, 31, 340–1
    Kenya 133, 140
    Lesotho 247, 249–50, 267
    Malawi 282, 283
    negative impact of 17
    policy influence of impact evaluations 350–1
    prevalence of 62
    Tigray 169, 172
    Zambia 198–9, 202
    Zimbabwe 230
Hoddinott, J 3
household livelihoods and productivity 341–2
    Ghana 159
    Kenya 133
    Lesotho 262–3, 264 t
    Malawi 300
    Tigray 185
    Zambia 212

impact evaluations
    attrition 55–6
    conceptual framework for questionnaire design 56–7 f
    control groups 44
    counterfactual problem 44, 66–7
    cross-country differences in results 344–6
    defining characteristic of 65
    design of 24, 43
    dissemination of findings 25
    estimation features 55 t, 56
    expanding application of 356
    expanding indicators of impact 357
    flexibility in design of 66
    future research 355–7
    implementation 24–5
    literature on 2–3
    motivations for 346–7
    myth of independent evaluation 65–6
    objective of 44
    political and operational constraints 43
    political economy of 336, 346–51
    questionnaire design 57–8 t, 59
    research methodology 7–8 t, 9–11
    understanding pathways of impact 356
    see also methodology; policy influence of impact evaluations; qualitative methods in impact evaluations; quantitative methods in impact evaluations
Institute for Statistical, Social and Economic Studies (ISSER, University of Ghana) 52, 155
Institute of Development Studies (IDS) 180, 314
Intergovernmental Regional Conference on Social Protection (Livingstone, 2006) 148, 284, 285
internal validity 43, 45, 52, 53, 65
international development institutions (IDIs) 38–9
International Food Policy Research Institute (IFPRI) 54, 314
International Initiative for Impact Evaluation (3ie) 52, 297
International Labour Organization (ILO) 39
International Monetary Fund (IMF) 28, 39, 254, 268, 289
Irish Aid 172, 290, 291, 296, 297, 301

Keck, M E 20
Kenya
    acceptance of social assistance 118
    establishment of national social protection system 121

expansion of cash transfer programmes 139, 140, 142
experimental design of impact evaluation 49, 50
National Safety Net Programme 121, 139
National Social Protection Policy 118
number of orphans 117
OVC Plan of Action 117
taxation reform 140
Vision 2030 development roadmap 139
see also Cash Transfer Programme for Orphans and Vulnerable Children (CT-OVC) (Kenya)
Kenya Integrated Household Budget Survey (KIHBS) 128
Kenya Postal Corporation (PCK) 120
Kenya Social Protection Conference Week (2015) 141, 143

labour allocation, impact of cash transfer programmes 342
Latin America, and conditional cash transfer programmes (CCTs) 3
Lesotho
 harmonization and integration of social protection programmes 255–6
 National Social Development Policy 248
 National Social Protection Strategy 248, 255–6
 National Strategic Development Plan (2012–17) 248
 poverty and vulnerability in 247
 spending on social protection 248
 see also Child Grants Programme (CGP) (Lesotho)
Livelihood Empowerment Against Poverty Programme (LEAP) (Ghana) 52
 beneficiaries' lack of information 163
 conditionality 151
 coverage of 150, 153
 dissemination of evaluation findings 162, 164, 165
 educational impacts 158–9
 evidence-based narrative of effectiveness of 161–4
 as evolving programme 162
 expansion of 153–4 f
 food security 156
 fuel subsidy reform 154–5
 funding of 150, 155
 health impacts 156–8
 household productive activity 159
 impact on households' well-being 155–6
 impacts of 157 t
 inconsistent implementation 151–2
 integration with complementary services 153
 irregular payments 152, 153, 156, 162–3
 local economic impact 161
 Local Economy-Wide Impact Evaluation 113, 155, 161
 management information system 152
 non-experimental design of impact evaluation 52–3
 objectives of 151
 political influences on 148–9, 166
 programme improvements 163–4
 proxy means testing 152–3
 qualitative impact evaluation 155
 quantitative impact evaluation 155
 regularization of payments 164
 social inclusion and happiness impacts 160
 south-south cooperation 164
 targeting process 152–3
 targets of 150–1
 value of transfer 153, 163, 164
living standards measurement surveys (LSMS) 103
Livingstone Call for Action on Social Protection 284, 285
Livingstone Conference (2006) 148, 284, 285
Local Economy-Wide Impact Evaluation (LEWIE) 9, 10, 28, 60, 112–13, 343–4
 activity and factor accounts 99, 100 t
 business enterprise survey 104, 108–9
 combining multiple data sources 105–7
 data sources and timing 105 t
 design of 98–102
 estimating models 103–9
 future research 355–6
 Ghana 113, 155, 161
 household and business surveys 103
 household groups 98–9
 impact of cash transfers in local market 96–7 f
 income multipliers 111–12 f, 343–4
 Kenya 123, 134
 Lesotho 259–60, 270, 277
 LEWIE multipliers 109–10
 location and trading partner questions 108
 Malawi 300
 market closure assumptions 101, 102 t
 model assumptions 101–2
 modification of surveys 103–4
 population sizes 107–8
 prices 95
 reasons for 95
 robustness tests and experiments 111 t
 selection of businesses 108–9
 theory and methodology 95–8
 Tigray 180–1, 185

Local Economy-Wide Impact Evaluation
    (LEWIE) (cont.)
  timing of data collection 104-5
  validation of results 110-12
  Zambia 207, 212
  Zimbabwe 237-8, 245
  zone of influence 99-101 t
longitudinal studies, and qualitative approach
    to impact evaluations 78, 90
  analysis and reporting 80-1
  cohorts 78
  conceptual framework and research
    questions 78-9
  critical analysis of 81-2
  labour-intensive nature of 82
  loss of participants 82
  methods, timing and sequencing 79-80
  pitfalls 81
  sampling 78
  strength of approach 81
  time-consuming nature of 82
Lund Committee (South Africa) 309

Mahama, John Dramani 113
Malabo Declaration (2014) 32n8, 350
Malawi, Social Cash Transfer Programme
    (SCTP) 48, 281-2
  accelerated expansion of pilot 291-2
  accountability issues 295
  baseline results from second impact
    evaluation (2013) 297-8
  capacity constraints 291, 295
  case management 295
  child school bonus 286
  choice of Mchinji district for pilot 287-8
  Community Social Support
    Committee 286
  consumption levels 298-9, 337
  context of 282-3
  contrasted with Fertilizer Input Subsidy
    Programme 289, 302
  coverage of 300
  educational impacts 300
  eligibility 286
  evaluation of pilot programme 292-3
  expansion strategy for pilot
    programme 294-5
  experimental design of impact
    evaluation 48-9
  food security 299-300
  funding of 288, 289-91, 296
  future of 303
  government commitment to 290-1
  health impacts 300
  household productive activity 300
  impacts of 299 t

influence of evaluation on programme
    expansion and policy 293-5, 301-2, 303
influence of Zambia's programme 284-5
key events 292 f
limited expansion of pilot programme 288,
    289, 291
Local Economy-Wide Impact
    Evaluation 300
longitudinal study 78-81
Malawi Growth and Development
    Strategy 283
management information system 295
mid-line survey results (2014) 298-9
National Plan of Action for Orphans and
    Vulnerable Children 284
National Social Protection Policy 289, 302
objectives of 281, 285-6
obstacles to expansion 301
origins of 283-5
payment system 287, 301
pilot programme 285
political concerns over 287
positive impacts of 296
poverty in Malawi 282
Poverty Reduction Strategy (2002) 283
second impact evaluation (2013-16)
    296-7
Social Protection Steering Committee 285
Social Protection Technical
    Committee 285, 289
target households 286, 297-8
targeting process 286, 293-4
value of transfer 286-7 t, 295-6, 297
Malawi Poverty and Vulnerability
    Assessment 282
Mbeki, Thabo 310
mental health, impact of cash transfers on 64
methodology 7-8 t, 9-11
  challenges of 10
  Local Economy-Wide Impact
    Evaluation 9, 10
  mixed methods approach 7, 10
  From Protection to Production
    project 9-10
  village economy general equilibrium
    modelling 7, 9
  see also Local Economy-Wide Impact
    Evaluation; qualitative methods in
    impact evaluations;
  quantitative methods in impact evaluations
Moore, C 3

National Institutes for Health (NIH) 125
Norwegian National Committee for
    UNICEF 119
nutritional impacts 339-40

Index

Opportunity International Bank of Malawi (OIBM) 301
orphans and vulnerable children (OVC) 6
Oxfam 203
Oxford Policy Management (OPM) 74, 77, 124, 155, 180, 257, 301

Pan-African Conference on Inequalities (2014) 113, 164
parallel trends assumption 45-6, 52
Patriotic Front (PF, Zambia) 215
payment system of cash transfer programmes
 (ir)regularity of payment 344
 Lesotho 273
 Malawi 285, 301
 South Africa 322
 Tigray 174-5, 188
policy influence of impact evaluations 1, 18, 19, 25-6, 40-1
 building credibility of social protection sector 26-8
 capacity and resource constraints 39-40
 contribution to regional agendas 30-2
 credibility created by 336, 348-9
 embeddedness in national policy processes 32-4, 351, 354
 external factors 37-40
 factors shaping 351-4
 influence of development partners 38-9
 information exchange 37
 institutional structure 357-8
 messaging and packaging of evidence 35-6, 352
 national political considerations 38
 political economy context 336, 346-51
 programme design and implementation 29-30, 349-50
 promoting perceptions of affordability 28
 regional learning effect 37, 350, 353-4
 relationship between evidence supply and demand 36-7, 352-3
 relationship building 34-5, 351-2
 strengthening case for social protection as investment 28, 349
 timing 35, 36, 269
policy influence of research 19-22
 areas of influence 20-1
 barriers to 21
 engagement with policy makers 21
 factors conditioning 21-2 *t*
 framing of findings 20
 medium of communication 20
 political economy context 21
 requirements for success in 21
policy windows 35

poverty reduction, and cash transfer programmes
 impact of 337-8
 Kenya 129, 139
 Zambia 209, 217-18
pregnancy, impact of cash transfers on 31, 64, 243, 320, 340
President's Emergency Plan for AIDS Relief (PEPFAR, USA) 31
propensity score matching (PSM)
 methods 45
proxy means testing 6-7, 29
 Ghana 152-3
 Kenya 127, 137
PtoP, *see* From Protection to Production (PtoP)

qualitative methods in impact evaluations
 characteristics of 72
 common methods 72
 comparative cross-country studies 73-7
 comparison of design approaches 87, 88-9 *t*, 90
 as complement to quantitative approaches 71
 focus group discussions 72
 ideal design 90-1
 individual interviews 72
 longitudinal approach 78-82, 90
 overview of Transfer Project impact evaluations 73 *t*
 purposive sampling 72
 thematic focus studies 82-7, 90
 varied use of 71
quantitative methods in impact evaluations 7-9
 attrition 55-6
 comparative cross-country studies 87-90
 conceptual framework for questionnaire design 56-7 *f*
 consumption levels 58-9
 control groups 44, 46, 47, 48, 49, 50, 51-2
 core evaluation designs 46 *t*
 counterfactual problem 44, 66-7
 deductive/inductive approaches 71-2
 difference-in-differences (DD) approach 45, 67-8, 207
 estimation features 55 *t*, 56
 experimental designs 44, 45, 47-50, 65
 external validity 43, 65
 internal validity 43, 45, 52, 53, 65
 non-experimental designs 44-5, 50-5, 65
 parallel trends assumption 45-6, 52
 productive activity questions 59, 60-1 *t*
 propensity score matching (PSM)
  methods 45

quantitative methods in impact evaluations (*cont.*)
  questionnaire design 57-8 *t*, 59
  Regression Discontinuity Design 54
  transition to adulthood 62-3 *t*, 64
questionnaire design 57-8 *t*, 59
  adolescent development 62-3 *t*, 64
  conceptual framework 56-7 *f*
  productive activity questions 59, 60-1 *t*

Regression Discontinuity Design (RDD) 54
research, influence on social policy 19-22 *f*
  see also policy influence of impact evaluations
resilience 59
risk management/preferences, and impact of cash transfers 64-5, 342-3

Save the Children UK 4, 23, 353
Schady, N 3
Sikkink, K 20
social inclusion, and cash transfer programmes
  Ghana 160
  Lesotho 263, 265 *t*
  Tigray 185, 188
  Zambia 212
social policy, influence of research on 19-22 *f*
  see also policy influence of impact evaluations
social protection programmes
  agriculture 31-2
  building credibility of social protection sector 26-8
  effectiveness of 17
  expansion in sub-Saharan Africa 17
  HIV/AIDS 31
  as investment not cost 28
  promoting perceptions of affordability 28
  regional agendas 30-2
South Africa, Child Support Grant (CSG) 53
  additional support to eligible infants 324
  adolescent development 319-20 *t*
  birth registration 324
  coverage of 307-8
  data collection and analysis 313-14
  dissemination of evaluation findings 325
  early child development impact 317, 321
  educational impacts 319
  effectiveness of 308
  eligibility 310
  extending eligibility to twenty-one years of age 325
  fraud 322
  future of 328
  health impacts 317-18
  history of programme 309-11 *f*, 312
  impact of social grants on inequality 307, 308 *f*
  impact on child outcomes 318 *t*
  impact on food poverty gap 306, 307 *f*
  influence of evaluation on policy development 321-8
  institutional and operational arrangements 321-2
  Integrated Community Registration Outreach Programmes 322
  methodology of impact evaluation 314-16
  Monitoring and Evaluation 312
  non-experimental design of impact evaluation 53, 315-16
  origins of impact evaluation 312-13
  payment system 322
  political support for 326
  popular participation in governance 325-6
  poverty and inequality in South Africa 307-8
  pregnant women 323-4
  preventing exclusion from 321-2
  questions to be answered by evaluation 313
  raising awareness of programme 326
  sampling process in evaluation 313
  take-up rate 316
  thematic focus study 83, 84, 85-6
  universal provision 322-3
  value of transfer 310
South African Department of Social Development (DSD) 308, 309, 312, 321
South African Social Security Administration (SASSA) 53, 308-9, 312, 321-2
spillover effects 95, 112-13
  see also Local Economy-Wide Impact Evaluation (LEWIE)
Strengthening Coherence Between Agriculture and Social Protection 31-2
Swedish International Development Agency (SIDA) 119, 120

targeting process of programmes 6-7, 344
  Ghana 152-3
  Kenya 126-8, 137-8
  Lesotho 251, 259, 272
  Malawi 285, 293
  Tigray 173-4, 187
  Zambia 202-4, 212-13 *f*, 219-20, 223
  Zimbabwe 227, 233-4, 235-6
Taylor, J E 95
Taylor Committee (South Africa) 310
Terms of Reference (TORs) 24
thematic focus studies, and qualitative approach to impact evaluations 82-3, 90
  analysis and reporting 85-6

conceptual framework and research
    questions 83–4
  critical analysis of 86–7
  methods, timing and sequencing 84–5
Tigray
  community care coalitions 54, 170,
    173–4, 193
  demographic and economic characteristics
    of 168–9
  direct support beneficiaries 169–70
  drought 169
  Productive Safety Net Programme 169, 192
  scaling up cash transfer programme 192–3
  see also Tigray pilot social cash transfer
    programme
Tigray People's Liberation Front
  (TPLF) 170, 176
Tigray pilot social cash transfer programme
  adapting to changes in beneficiary
    households 175
  anthropometric measures 186–7
  assessment of evaluation 189–91
  asset accumulation 185
  attrition 179
  champions of evaluation 177
  community-based targeting 173–4
  community care coalitions 187, 190
  cost of evaluation 194
  development outcomes of 183 *t*
  educational impacts 186
  end of pilot 191
  evaluation implementation problems 190
  evaluation methods 178–81
  evaluation's impact on social protection
    policy 190–1, 194
  evolution of 170–1 *f*
  food security 182–4
  funding of 172, 176
  geographical areas covered by 172–3
  health impacts 186
  household income impact 184–5
  households targeted by 173
  impact on trust and social cohesion 188
  inspiration for other regional pilot
    schemes 193
  knowledge gains from evaluation 189–90
  Local Economy-Wide Impact
    Evaluation 180–1, 185
  maternal health 186
  monitoring of 175
  multiplier effects 185
  objectives of 171–2
  origins of evaluation 175–6
  payment system 174–5, 188
  purpose of evaluation 176–7
  qualitative impact evaluation 180

quantitative impact evaluation 178–80
  questions to be answered by
    evaluation 177
  regional social protection committee 190
  role of social workers 189
  sample sizes in evaluation 179 *t*
  scaling up 192–3
  social inclusion 185
  survey timing by round 179 *t*
  targeting process 173–4, 187
  value of transfer 174, 182, 192
time preferences, impact of cash
  transfers 64–5
Transfer Project 4, 353
  design of impact evaluations 24, 43
  dissemination of findings 25
  implementation of impact
    evaluations 24–5
  information exchange 37
  key feature of 43
  objectives of 23
  origins and approach of 22–4
  pillars of 23
  programmes in project 5 *t*
  research innovations 3–4, 11
  research methodology 7–8 *t*, 9–11
  scope of 4
  see also From Protection to Production (PtoP)
transition to adulthood 62–3 *t*

unconditional cash transfer programmes 6, 59
  impacts of 335–6
United Nations Children Fund
  (UNICEF) 4, 23, 24, 32, 353
  Kenya 117, 119, 123, 138
  Lesotho 248, 250, 251, 253, 255, 257, 267,
    270, 271
  Malawi 282, 283, 284, 288, 291, 295,
    297, 302
  South Africa 309, 312
  Tigray 171, 172, 175, 191
  Zambia 204
  Zimbabwe 227, 229, 230–1
United States Agency for International
  Development (USAID) 293
University of North Carolina at Chapel Hill
  (UNC) 4, 23, 52, 78, 125, 155, 235,
    297, 353

value of cash transfers
  Ghana 153, 163, 164
  Kenya 134, 138, 141
  Lesotho 248, 272
  Malawi 285–7 *t*, 295–6, 297
  South Africa 310
  Tigray 174, 182, 192

value of cash transfers (cont.)
  variations in 344
  Zambia 207
  Zimbabwe 228
Victor, M 19
vulnerability, as targeting criteria 6

well-being, impact of cash transfer
    programmes 337
World Bank 32, 39
  Kenya 123, 125, 138, 139–40
  Lesotho 255, 257, 270
  Malawi 289, 290
  Zambia 216
World Food Programme (WFP) 257
World Vision 170

Yale University 52

Zambia
  agricultural subsidies 198, 199–200
  Community Welfare Assistance
    Committees 199, 220–1
  Farmer Input Support
    Programme 199–200, 223
  National Social Protection Policy 200, 216
  National Social Protection Strategy 199
  policy response to poverty and
    vulnerability 198–200
  poverty and inequality in 198
  Poverty Reduction Strategy Paper 199
  Public Welfare Assistance
    Scheme 198–9, 202
Zambia's cash transfer programme 47–8, 197, 221–2
  assessment of evaluations 221–2
  child development 210, 211 t
  Child Grant Programme 47, 205, 206, 208 b, 212–13 f
  Child Grant Programme
    evaluation 217–18
  community-wide social impacts 212
  conceptual framework of evaluation 206
  concerns over targeting 223
  consumption levels 209–10 t, 337
  consumption smoothing 209
  educational impacts 211
  enhanced resilience 212
  evaluation design 206
  evolution of (up to 2010) 200–2
  evolution of (2010–13) 204–7
  experimental design of impact
    evaluation 47–8
  factors influencing design of 204
  factors influencing scale-up
    decision 214–15 f, 216–17

food security 210 t
freeze in spending on 223
harmonized targeting model 219–20
household productive activity 211
impacts of different targeting
  processes 213 f
influence of evaluation on programme
  expansion and policy 214, 217–18, 222
influence of targeting assessment on
  programme design 220–1
key features of (2010–13) 206
Local Economy-Wide Impact
  Evaluation 207, 212
main findings of impact evaluation 209–14
methodologies of impact evaluation 207, 208 b
Multiple Categorical Targeting
  Grant 47–8, 205, 206, 208 b, 213 f, 337
objectives of 205, 206
pilot schemes 202–3
policy and evaluation milestones 201 f
poverty reduction 210 t, 217–18
programme design 204–5
purpose of impact evaluation 206
recent developments 222–4
scaling up of programme 214
targeting assessment (2013) 218–20
targeting process 202–3, 213–14 f, 219–20, 223
thematic focus study 83, 84–5, 86
value of transfer 209
Zimbabwe, Harmonized Social Cash Transfer
    Programme (HSCT) 51
  adolescent development 243–4
  areas for improvement 239–40
  baseline survey for impact
    evaluation 236–8
  Child Protection Fund 229
  consumption levels 241, 242 t
  district selection for phased roll-out 232
  economic and political context 226–7, 229–30
  educational impacts 241–3
  enhanced resilience 243
  evolution and development of 228, 229 f
  funding of 229, 238
  grievance handling procedures 240
  history of 229–32
  households targeted by 228, 234, 237 f
  impact evaluation 241–4
  impact evaluation design 234–5
  impact on Basic Education Assistance
    Module receipt 241–3
  implementation 238–9
  influence of evaluation on programme and
    policy 244–5

key impacts of 241 *t*
Local Economy-Wide Impact Evaluation 237–8, 245
longitudinal study 79, 80, 81, 235
management information system 227, 231–2, 233–4
Ministry of Public Service, Labour and Social Welfare 227, 228, 230, 239
mixed methods impact evaluation 227, 234–5
monitoring and evaluation framework 227, 233
non-experimental design of impact evaluation 51–2, 235
objectives of 228
Operations Manual 232, 234, 240
process evaluation 238–40
programme design 232
stakeholders' use of evidence 227
targeting analysis 227, 235–6
targeting process 233–4
test run of 232
trust and accountability among stakeholders 245
value of transfer 228
violence among young people 244
weak harmonization with other programmes 239–40
Zimbabwe Agenda for Sustainable Socio-Economic Transformation (ZIMASSET) 229
Zimbabwe Violence Against Children survey 244